Lecture Notes in Computer Science 13140

More information about this subseries at https://link.springer.com/bookseries/7410

Joaquin Garcia-Alfaro · Jose Luis Muñoz-Tapia ·
Guillermo Navarro-Arribas ·
Miguel Soriano (Eds.)

Data Privacy Management, Cryptocurrencies and Blockchain Technology

ESORICS 2021 International Workshops, DPM 2021 and CBT 2021
Darmstadt, Germany, October 8, 2021
Revised Selected Papers

 Springer

Editors
Joaquin Garcia-Alfaro (iD)
Institut Polytechnique de Paris
Palaiseau, France

Jose Luis Muñoz-Tapia (iD)
Universitat Politècnica de Catalunya
Barcelona, Spain

Guillermo Navarro-Arribas (iD)
Universitat Autonoma de Barcelona
Bellaterra, Spain

Miguel Soriano (iD)
Universitat Politècnica de Catalunya
Barcelona, Spain

ISSN 0302-9743   ISSN 1611-3349 (electronic)
Lecture Notes in Computer Science
ISBN 978-3-030-93943-4   ISBN 978-3-030-93944-1 (eBook)
https://doi.org/10.1007/978-3-030-93944-1

LNCS Sublibrary: SL4 – Security and Cryptology

This Springer imprint is published by the registered company Springer Nature Switzerland AG
The registered company address is: Gewerbestrasse 11, 6330 Cham, Switzerland

Foreword from the DPM 2021 Program Chairs

This volume contains the post-proceedings of the 16th Data Privacy Management International Workshop (DPM 2021), which was organized within the 26th European Symposium on Research in Computer Security (ESORICS 2021). The DPM series started in 2005 when the first workshop took place in Tokyo (Japan). Since then, the event has been held in different venues: Atlanta, USA (2006); Istanbul, Turkey (2007); Saint Malo, France (2009); Athens, Greece (2010); Leuven, Belgium (2011); Pisa, Italy (2012); Egham, UK (2013); Wroclaw, Poland (2014); Vienna, Austria (2015); Crete, Greece (2016); Oslo, Norway (2017); Barcelona, Spain (2018); Luxembourg (2019); and (held virtually) Guildford, UK (2020).

This 2021 edition was intended to be held in Darmstadt, Germany, but was finally held virtually, due to the COVID-19 pandemic, together with the ESORICS main conference and all its workshops.

In response to the call for papers, we received 26 submissions. Each submission was evaluated on the basis of significance, novelty, and technical quality. The Program Committee performed a thorough review process and selected seven full papers, complemented by one position paper and three short papers. The result was a technical program covering topics such as cyber-incident risks involving privacy violations, privacy-preserving location techniques, use of learning approaches to handle privacy management issues, data minimization, policies, and regulation.

We would like to thank everyone who helped at organizing the event, including all the members of the organizing committee of both ESORICS and DPM 2021. Our gratitude goes to Michael Waidner, the general chair of ESORICS 2021. During the event, we had the valued assistance and help of Martina Creutzfeldt. Thanks go as well to all the DPM 2021 Program Committee members, additional reviewers, all the authors who submitted papers, and to all the workshop attendees.

Finally, we want to acknowledge the support received from the sponsoring institutions: Institut Mines-Télécom, Institut Polytechnique de Paris (Telecom SudParis and Samovar Confiance Numérique), Universitat Autònoma de Barcelona (UAB), Universitat Politécnica de Catalunya, the UNESCO Chair in Data Privacy, and Cybercat. We also acknowledge support from the following projects and grants from the Spanish Government: TIN2017-87211-R, SECURITAS RED2018-102321-T, and Beatriz Galindo BG20/00217.

November 2021

Miguel Soriano
Guillermo Navarro-Arribas
Joaquin Garcia-Alfaro

Foreword from the DPM 2021 Program Chairs

DPM 2021 Organization

Program Chairs

Joaquin Garcia-Alfaro   Institut Polytechnique de Paris, France
Guillermo Navarro-Arribas   Universitat Autònoma de Barcelona, Spain
Miguel Soriano   Universitat Politecnica de Catalunya, Spain

Program Committee

Esma Aïmeur   University of Montreal, Canada
Ken Barker   University of Calgary, Canada
Elisa Bertino   Purdue University, USA
Jordi Casas-Roma   Universitat Oberta de Catalunya, Spain
Mauro Conti   University of Padua, Italy
Frédéric Cuppens   Polytechnique Montreal, Canada
Nora Cuppens-Boulahia   Polytechnique Montreal, Canada
Nicolas E. Diaz Ferreyra   University of Duisburg-Essen, Germany
Sabrina De Capitani di   Università degli Studi di Milano, Italy
  Vimercati
Josep Domingo-Ferrer   Universitat Rovira i Virgili, Spain
Sara Foresti   Università degli Studi di Milano, Italy
Jose Maria de Fuentes   Universidad Carlos III de Madrid, Spain
Sebastien Gambs   Université du Québec à Montréal, Canada
Javier Herranz   Universitat Politècnica de Catalunya, Spain
Marc Juarez   University of Southern California, USA
Christos Kalloniatis   University of the Aegean, Greece
Florian Kammueller   Middlesex University London and TU Berlin, Germany
Sokratis Katsikas   Open University of Cyprus, Cyprus
Hiroaki Kikuchi   Meiji University, Japan
Evangelos Kranakis   Carleton University, Canada
Alptekin Küpçü   Koç University, Turkey
Costas Lambrinoudakis   University of Piraeus, Greece
Maryline Laurent   Institut Mines-Télécom, France
Giovanni Livraga   University of Milan, Italy
Brad Malin   Vanderbilt University, USA
Chris Mitchell   Royal Holloway, University of London, UK
Martín Ochoa   AppGate Inc., Colombia
Melek Önen   EURECOM, France
Gerardo Pelosi   Politecnico di Milano, Italy
Silvio Ranise   Fondazione Bruno Kessler, Italy
Kai Rannenberg   Goethe University Frankfurt, Germany
Ruben Rios   University of Malaga, Spain

Pierangela Samarati   Università degli Studi di Milano, Italy
Vicenç Torra   Umeå University, Sweden
Yasuyuki Tsukada   Kanto Gakuin University, Japan
Alexandre Viejo   Universitat Rovira i Virgili, Spain
Isabel Wagner   De Montfort University, UK
Jens Weber   University of Victoria, Canada
Lena Wiese   University of Göttingen, Germany
Nicola Zannone   Eindhoven University of Technology, The Netherlands

Steering Committee

Joaquin Garcia-Alfaro   Institut Polytechnique de Paris, France
Guillermo Navarro-Arribas   Universitat Autònoma de Barcelona, Spain
Josep Domingo-Ferrer   Universitat Rovira i Virgili, Spain
Vicenç Torra   Umeå University, Sweden

Additional Reviewers

Alessandro Brighente   Riccardo Longo
David Harborth   Utku Tefek
Stefano Berlato   Osman Biçer
Fred Tronnier   Ehsan Nowroozi
Ziqi Zhang

Foreword from the CBT 2021 Program Chairs

The 5th International Workshop on Cryptocurrencies and Blockchain Technology (CBT 2021) was held in collaboration with the 26th European Symposium on Research in Computer Security (ESORICS 2021) and the 16th International Workshop on Data Privacy Management (DPM 2021). Due to the COVID-19 outbreak, the event was held virtually.

We wish to thank all of the authors who submitted their work. This year, CBT received 31 submissions. The review process was conducted virtually, using the EasyChair platform, by the Program Chairs and all the members of the Program Committee, with the help of some external reviewers. Based on the reviews and the discussion, six papers were accepted for presentation at the workshop as full papers, complemented by six short papers.

We would like to thank all of the people involved in CBT 2021. We are grateful to the Program Committee members and the external reviewers for their help in providing detailed and timely reviews of the submissions. We also thank all the members of the ESORICS 2021 local organization team for all their help and support. Thanks go as well to Springer for their support throughout the entire process. Last but by no means least, we thank all the authors who submitted papers and all the workshop attendees.

Finally, we want to acknowledge the support received from the sponsoring institutions: Universitat Politécnica de Catalunya, Institut Polytechnique de Paris (Telecom SudParis and Samovar Confiance Numérique), Universitat Autònoma de Barcelona (UAB), BART (Inria, IRT SYSTEMX, Institut Mines-Télécom), Cybercat, and Bandit. We acknowledge support as well from the Beatriz Galindo grant BG20/00217.

November 2021

Jose Luis Muñoz-Tapia
Guillermo Navarro-Arribas
Joaquin Garcia-Alfaro

CBT 2021 Organization

Program Chairs

Joaquin Garcia-Alfaro   Institut Polytechnique de Paris, France
Guillermo Navarro   Universitat Autònoma de Barcelona, Spain
Jose Luis Muñoz-Tapia   Universitat Politècnica de Catalunya, Spain

Program Committee

Shashank Agrawal   Western Digital Research, USA
Daniel Augot   Inria Saclay, France
Georgia Avarikioti   ETH Zurich, Switzerland
Spiridon Bakiras   Hamad Bin Khalifa University, Qatar
Iddo Bentov   Cornell Tech, USA
Alex Biryukov   University of Luxembourg, Luxembourg
George Bissias   University of Massachusetts at Amherst, USA
Joseph Bonneau   New York University, USA
Karima Boudaoud   University of Nice, France
Jeremy Clark   Concordia University, Canada
Mauro Conti   University of Padua, Italy
Sanchari Das   University of Denver, USA
Vanesa Daza   Universitat Pompeu Fabra, Spain
Matteo Dell'Amico   EURECOM, France
Sven Dietrich   City University of New York, USA
Kaoutar Elkhiyaoui   EURECOM, France
Esha Ghosh   Microsoft Research, USA
Hannes Hartenstein   Karlsruhe Institute of Technology, Germany
Ethan Heilman   Boston University, USA
Ryan Henry   University of Calgary, Canada
Antonio Faonio   EURECOM, France
Jordi Herrera-Joancomarti   Universitat Autonoma de Barcelona, Spain
Ghassan Karame   NEC Research, Germany
Jiasun Li   George Mason University, USA
Daniel Xiapu Luo   Hong Kong Polytechnic University, Hong Kong
Giorgia Marson   University of Bern, Switzerland
Shin'ichiro Matsuo   Georgetown University, USA
Pedro Moreno-Sanchez   IMDEA, Spain
Cristina Pérez-Solà   Universitat Oberta de Catalunya, Spain
Simon Oya   University of Waterloo, Canada
Elizabeth Quaglia   Royal Holloway, University of London, UK

Alfredo Rial	University of Luxembourg, Luxembourg
Alessandra Scafuro	North Carolina State University, USA
Edgar Weippl	SBA Research, Austria

Steering Committee

Rainer Böhme	Universität Innsbruck, Austria
Joaquin Garcia-Alfaro	Institut Polytechnique de Paris, France
Hannes Hartenstein	Karlsruher Institut für Technologie, Germany
Jordi Herrera-Joancomart	Universitat Autònoma de Barcelona, Spain

Additional Reviewers

Alessandro Brighente	Maryam Ehsanpour
Héctor Masip Ardevol	Rahul Saha
Giuseppe Vitto	Abhimanyu Rawat
Saskia Bayreuther	Lukas Aumayr
Oliver Stengele	Marc Leinweber
Maja Schwarz	Aljosha Judmayer

Contents

DPM Workshop: Risks and Privacy Preservation

Best Security Measures to Reduce Cyber-Incident and Data Breach Risks

Hiroaki Kikuchi[1,3]($\boxtimes$), Michihiro Yamada[2], Kazuki Ikegami[2], and Koji Inui[1]

[1] School of Interdisciplinary Mathematical Sciences, Meiji University, Tokyo, Japan
kikn@meiji.ac.jp
[2] Graduate School of Advanced Mathematical Sciences, Meiji University,
4-21-1 Nakano, Chiyoda, Tokyo 164-8525, Japan
[3] RIKEN Center for Advanced Intelligence Project (AIP), Tokyo, Japan

Abstract. Corporations plan to adopt appropriate combinations of data privacy managements to mitigate the risk of data breach. Examples of such well-established measures include the certification of an information security management system, a periodic security auditing, and dedicated positions such as a Chief Information Officer (CIO). However, the effectiveness of introducing each of these measures to reduce the risk of data breach is unclear. To assess the effective risk reduction, this work combines the big data of cyber incidents with the attributes of corporations and computes the relative risk with respect to these security measures. Our analysis of five-year data from about 6,000 corporations reveals a negative effect for most measures. The results must be biased by industry characteristics associated with the risk of cyber incidents such as business style and company scale, which are known confounding factors. After investigating company attributes individually, we identify the significant confounding factors that represent obstacles to risk analysis. Using hypothesis testing and multiple logistic regression analysis, we adjust odds ratios for 17 security measures, social responsibilities, environmental conditions, and employment arrangements. The results confirm that an environmental auditing reduces the risk by one-third at a statistically significant level.

1 Introduction

Data breaches are one of the most critical threats for many industries. Data breaches, cyber-incidents, and privacy violations have become very common. According to one report [4], the personal information or personally identifiable information (PII) for a total of 5.61 million individuals were compromised in 443 cyber incidents in 2018 alone. This resulted in damage estimated at 2.5 billion USD, increasing by annually.

To mitigate the risk of cyber-incidents, corporations have to take some appropriate security measures. These include a certification of an information security management system (ISMS), a financial records are audited periodically by a trusted agency, and a creation of dedicated positions such as a Chief Information Officer (CIO). The US National Institute of Standards and Technology

J. Garcia-Alfaro et al. (Eds.): DPM 2021/CBT 2021, LNCS 13140, pp. 3–19, 2022.
https://doi.org/10.1007/978-3-030-93944-1_1

(NIST) has developed a cybersecurity framework [2] that acts as an authoritative source for information security and helps executives in IT companies and policy makers to invest in the protection of their customer databases. However, security is not free and adopting a security framework is voluntary. Companies need to choose the minimal but the most effective subset of available security measures to reduce the risk of possible attacks. Nevertheless, it is still not clear exactly *by how much the risk can be reduced if these security countermeasures are introduced.*

To address the model of cyber-incidents and data breaches, many studies have been made. Edwards et al. modeled the trends in cyber-incidents within the US by analyzing the 2,234 separate incidents occurring from 2005 to 2015 in the public dataset of the Privacy Rights Clearinghouse [8]. Their model aims to predict the total number of cyber-incidents based on history of events. Although the nation-wide trends in incidents are modeled, incident risks for each company are still unknown. Romanosky [14] examined the breach and litigation rate, by industry, and identify the industries that incur the greatest costs from cyber events. She analyses a dataset of cyber incidents in US collected by Advisen for the purpose to sell the commercial insurance industry. Hence, its aim is to clarify the corporate loss such as revenue reduction, lawsuit, and employment measures. Her model of cyber-incident cost per company predicts the total cost of incident via a function of independent variables, the number of records, a type of event (e.g., data breach, security incident, and privacy violation), a firm type (e.g., governmental, private), an industry sector (e.g., financial, healthcare, and retail trade), and year of event. Unfortunately, neither of Edwards or Romanosky's study consider security measures that corporation take for cyber risk. We should note that cyber-incident risk depends significantly on what security measures and management system are established in a target company.

In this paper, we aim to quantify the effectiveness of security measures in reducing data breaches and cybersecurity risks. To assess the effective reduction of risk, we combine the big data of cyber-incidents with the big data of corporation attributes related for security measures, e.g., a certification of management system (e.g., ISMS, EMS, RM and OHSMS), a dedicate position of CIO and CSIO, privacy and security policies, types of security auditing (e.g., internal, or external), and types of protection for whistle-blowers. We investigate more than 200 security measures, during a five-year period by 1,413 Japanese companies. Using these data, we seek to examine reductions in cyber incidents and identify whether there is a significant correlation between sets of measures and cybersecurity threats. We show the comparison between our work and the related works in Table 1.

However, the assessment of security measures is not trivial. The set of measures varies with companies and hence it is hard to compare risks of several companies with different conditions. The data breach risk may be skewed by industries. For instance, industries of the business-to-customer (B2C) suffer from data breach more frequently than the business-to-business industries. The ISO management systems are mostly certified in large corporations because the process of

Table 1. Cyber-incidents and data breaches analysis

Items	Edwards [8]	Romanosky [14]	This work
Incident Data	US PRC	US Advisen	JP JNSA data, Security Next
Security measure	–	–	TK CSR Survey
# companies	2,234	4,571	1,413
Objective variable	Breach counts and size	Incident costs (frequency)	Incident frequency
Variables	Frequency, size, year, type	Revenue, lawsuit, records, industry, repeat, year	*Scurity-measures*, records, industry, year

PDCA (Plan-Do-Check-Action) cycle is costly for small companies. Therefore, a naïve analysis of incidents conjunction with ISMS certification resolves a false consequence that *the certification of ISMS increases cyber-incident risk.* (We will show this in Sect. 4.5.) Such characteristics that skew the outcome of security measures are known as confounding factors or *confounders.* In risk assessments evaluating the magnitude of risk, it is important to control for confounding to isolate the effect of a particular hazard.

To discard the false effect by confounder, we perform Mantel-Haenszel test, a statistical hypothesis testing. After investigating corporate attributes individually, we identify the significant confounding factors that form major obstacles to risk analysis. Using multiple logistic regression analysis, we adjust the odds ratios (ORs) taking into account the stratifications for 17 security measures, social responsibilities, environmental factors, and employment measures. It aims to provide useful knowledge to the executives to make decision what security measures to be deployed required for their company.

Our contributions in this work are as follows.

1. We propose a methodology for clarifying the degree to which cyber incident risks are reduced with security measures. Our method combines two data resources and performs a statistical analysis to calculate the effectiveness of the measures.
2. We have conducted a large-scale analysis that gives useful and reliable empirical results for a list of security measures that are confirmed as reducing the risk at a statistically significant level. The effects are quantified via adjusted odd ratios. Our analysis reveals that data breaches are the most common cyber-incidents over years and suggests that the most effective security measure significantly reduces data breach risks.
3. We identified some potential confounding factors that represent obstacles to the accuracy of cyber incident analyses; they should be discarded before the assessment of security risks.

2 Related Works

Edwards et al. modeled the trends in cyber incidents within the US by analyzing the 2,234 separate incidents occurring from 2005 to 2015 in the public
dataset of the Privacy Rights Clearinghouse [8]. They employed Bayesian generalized linear models to model the number of victims in an incident and the
frequency of data compromises. Ravi et al. [11] applied the opportunity theory
of crime, institutional anomie theory, and institutional theory to identify the
factors affecting data breaches. They found that investment IT security correlates with a high risk of data breach. Martin et al. [12] used multidimensional
scaling and goodness-of-fit tests to analyze the distribution of data breaches and
linked their model with the current discussion on the goodness of fit, pricing,
and risk measurement in the actuarial domain. Maochao et al. [13] investigated
cyber-hacking breach-incident interarrival times and breach sizes, proposing a
stochastic procedure for predicting both the interarrival time and the breach
size.

Romanosky et al. [14] examined the extent to which identity theft decreased
following the introduction of data breach notification laws, using panel data from
the US Federal Trade Commission from 2002 to 2009. The analysis finds that
the Information, Manufacturing and Retail industries suffer the greatest losses
from cyber incidents, which implies these industries suffers cyber incidents more
frequently than other industries. Yamada et al. [10] investigated 15,000 data
breaches occurred in 12 years and estimated the mean total loss caused by the
data breach. The proposed model estimates the total loss suffered by data breach
more accurately than some of the existing mathematical models.

Hatamian et al. [18] propose a framework aimed at supporting enterprises to
protect their data against adversaries and unauthorized accesses. They develop
two components, vulnerability checker and malware checker to discriminate privacy and security misbehaviors. Dupont et al. [17] studies the current status
of healthcare delivery organization against security concerns. Based on a literature study and observation of network traffic, they explore how cyber attack
could impact patient health. Sakuma and Inomata studied the effectiveness cyber
insurance in [7]. Kokaji et al. report trends of risk management in financial industries [9].

3 Data

For our analysis, we used two datasets, each comprising cyber incident records.
Table 2 shows the main statistics. Both datasets cover major public incidents
notified via official websites in Japan, although their coverage differs slightly.
We, therefore, used the union of the datasets as a comprehensive resource for
describing cyber incidents.

Table 3 shows the numbers of corporations in the CSR dataset, and the number of cyber incident events in JNSA and Security Next. It shows the intersection
of both incidents datasets are not so large and the aggregation improves the coverage of incidents. We examine the union of them for our analysis.

Table 2. Specification of incident datasets

Dataset	Duration	# Records	# Companies
JNSA	2005–2017	15,569	8,853
Security next	2013–2018	174	121

Table 3. Number of corporations compromised with cyber incidents

	2013	2014	2015	2016	2017	Total
CSR	1,210	1,305	1,325	1,408	1,413	6,661
JNSA	12	19	21	25	12	89
Security next	13	17	22	29	24	105
Duplication	6	9	16	24	12	67
# targets	19	27	27	30	24	127

3.1 The JNSA and the Security Next

The Japan Network Security Association (JNSA) is a nonprofit organization aiming to promote standardization related to network security and enhance public welfare through awareness, education, research, and information-dissemination activities related to network security. In 2019, more than 200 security-related companies belonged to JNSA.

Since 2002, the JNSA Security Damage Investigation Working Group has collected information about cyber incidents reported in newspapers, Internet news, and documents related to incidents published by individual organizations. The JNSA dataset contains incident attributes that include date, information management and holding officer, industry type, social contribution degree, number of victims, classified leakage information, incident cause, leakage route, incident handling quality, and kinds of information leaked (name, address, phone number, or date of birth) [3].

Security Next[1] is a commercial website that publishes a comprehensive list of cyber incidents in Japanese industries. Because the JNSA dataset is limited to publicly available data sources, we augmented it by incorporating the cyber incidents published via the Security Next website for the period 2013 through 2017. Security Next employs a dedicated team of analysts who collect data from news websites, newsfeeds, and news vendors and publish event notices daily. We believe that our combined dataset provides the comprehensive of available cyber-incident datasets.

The JNSA dataset is available on request to the JNSA working group. The statistics of cyber-incidents are annually reported from JNSA web page [4]. The data of Security Next is acquired via crawling official website.

---

[1] https://www.security-next.com/.

Table 4. Statistics for the CSR dataset

Year	# Companies	(Listed)	Mean # employee	# Questions	# Security questions
2013	1210	(1157)	2672	753	185
2014	1305	(1259)	2582	764	186
2015	1325	(1284)	2646	811	193
2016	1408	(1364)	2579	832	197
2017	1413	(1370)	2627	840	207

3.2 Toyo-Keizai Corporate Social Responsibility (CSR) Survey

The Toyo Keizai Corporate Social Responsibility (CSR) survey contains the CSR status of the more than 1,305 corporations that responded to questionnaires sent to all 3,580 listed companies [6]. The annual survey has been conducted since 2005 by Toyo Keizai Inc., a major publisher specializing in economics and business. Each CSR dataset record contains values for the following nine fields: Basic corporate data, CSR & financial valuation and ratings, CSR overall, Governance, legal compliance, and internal controls, Workforce and HR utilization, For consumers and business partners, Corporate citizenship, Relationship between companies and politics, and Environment. For example, CSR data includes the number of employees, the fraction of female managers, the officer dedicated to environmental management, and the volume of greenhouse gas emissions.

In our study, we focused on the security-related queries such as whether the CIO is named, whether the ISMS (ISO/IEC 27001) is certified, and whether the financial records are audited by a trusted agency. We chose 17 basic security-related questions from among the total of 800 questions in the CSR dataset, as listed in Table 5. Various styles of answer are allowed in the survey, depending on the type of queres; (labeled Cxxx), two environmental questions (Exxx), and one employment question (Kxxx). Table 4 shows the statistics for the companies in the CSR dataset. The number of companies is increasing year by year and the latest dataset covers most major companies in Japan.

The Toyo Keizai CSR data is available from commercial online service[2]. We match records of CSR data with the incidents specified in the JNSA and Security Next by means of name of corporation and year of incident.

4 Analysis of Cyber Incidents

4.1 Types of Cyber Incidents

Advisen distinguishes between 11 separate categories of cyber incidents and the JNSA dataset has 12 incident categories, which are too many when aiming to understand the fundamental characteristics. Therefore, we aggregated some of the categories, reorganizing the data into the following five incident categories, matching Romanosky's approach [1].

---

[2] http://www.toyokeizai.net/csr/english/.

Table 5. List of security-related questions in the CSR dataset

ID	Variable	Description
C122	Whistle	Has a protection of anonymous whistle-blowers
C139	Internal-Cntl	Has committee for internal control
C147	CIO	Has a CIO (Chief Information Officer)
C150	CFO	Has a CFO (Chief Financial Officer)
C161	PP	Defines a privacy policy
C153	SP	Has information security policy
C155	Audit-Int	Is tested by an internal security auditor
C157	Audit-Third	Is tested by a third-party security auditor
C207	Audit-Ind	Is tested by a security auditor independent of the stakeholders
C159	ISMS	Certified information security management system
C120	Whistle-Int	Has a point of contact for internal whistle-blowers
C202	Whistle-Ext	Has a point of contact for external whistle-blowers
C227	RM/CM	Has an established risks-and-crisis management scheme
C229	RM/CMP	Has basic policies for risks-and-crisis management
E082	Audit-env	Conducts an environmental audits
E087	EMS	Certified environmental management system
K136	Labor-M	Occupational health and safety management system

Data Breach. Unintentional disclosures of PII such as customer records, tax notifications, medical data, and financial data are classified as data breaches. This category does not include the theft of laptop computers or smartphones containing PII. Inappropriate data delivery by a careless employee is also in this category. Data breaches are usually caused by human actions.

Security Incident. Many of the data disclosures are caused by malicious hackers, who exploit vulnerabilities in software or operating systems to compromise a company's website and databases. Infection by malware and ransomware can lead to the theft of intellectual property or disruption of business services. Denial-of-service attacks and brute-force attempts to log in are also in this category. These incidents are caused deliberately by malicious third parties.

Malicious Insider. Unauthorized access to personal data or confidential documents does not always come from outside, usually via the Internet. Internal threats caused by malicious employees also represent a major cause of cyber incidents. This type of threat can be prevented by proper security management rather than by security technology. Therefore, we distinguish these attacks from external attacks.

Misconfiguration. Many cyber incidents are caused by improper configurations of a company's system. This category includes not fixing known vulnerabilities, using obsolete versions of data, and leaving default passwords unchanged.

Table 6. Contingency between security measure M and cyber incidents

Measure M	Incidents $=$ Yes	No	Total
Yes	a	b	$m_1 = a + b$
No	c	d	$m_2 = c + d$
Total	$n_1 = a + c$	$n_2 = b + d$	N

Stealing. A stolen laptop computer or storage device that contains PII is classified into this category.

4.2 Relative Risk and Hypothesis Testing

The *relative risk* (RR) is the chance that a company (or group) that adopts a measure M will suffer from a cyber-incident relative to the chance that a company without M will suffer from the same incident. Given the 2×2 contingency table given in Table 6, the relative risk of M can be defined as $\mathrm{RR}(M) = \frac{Pr(\text{incident}|M)}{Pr(\text{incident}|\overline{M})} = \frac{a/m_1}{c/m_2}$ If $RR \leq 1$, the implication is that measure M has a strong effect of reducing incidents. That is, a company that adopts M is less likely to be compromised by an incident.

To determine whether the effect is an important difference, we conduct hypothesis testing. We test the null hypothesis

H_0: the proportion of companies suffering cyber incidents among the group of companies that adopt measure M is equal to the proportion of companies suffering incidents that do not use M.

H_1: The proportion of companies suffering from cyber incidents among the group of companies that adopt measure M is not identical for both groups.

The *chi-square test* compares the observed frequencies for each group in the contingency table with the expected frequencies, assuming that the null hypothesis is true. For a 2×2 table, the test statistic χ^2 is computed as $\chi^2 = \frac{N(|ad - bc| - N/2)}{n_1 n_2 m_1 m_2}$, which is distributed as a chi-square (χ^2) distribution with 1 degree of freedom.

4.3 Mantel-Haenszel Test

In analysis, a model is often skewed because of potential *confounding factor* that influences both dependent and independent variables [16]. For example, factors such as age, gender, and educational levels often affect health status and so should be controlled in risk assessment. To control confounding factor, Mantel-Haenszel test allows to test the association between a binary predictor and a binary outcome such as incident occurrence while taking into account the stratification.

Suppose a binary outcome (e.g., cyber incident) and a binary measure (e.g., ISMS). We want to test if the effect of security measure is independent from k-types confounding variable (e.g., industries). A stratified data is summarized in a series of 2×2 contingency tables. Under the null hypothesis that there is no association between the outcome and the measure, the test statistics $\chi^2 = \frac{(\sum_k n_i - \mu_i)^2}{\sum_k \sigma(n_i)}$, follows χ^2 distribution with 1 degree of freedom. Where, n_i, μ_i and $\sigma(n_i)$ are the number of outcome with i-th value, the mean, and the variance, respectively.

4.4 Multiple Logistic Regression

Multiple logistic regression allows one to take into account stratification and matching [15]. When using multiple logistic regression, a coefficient of the logistic model provides the adjusted OR for a particular good measure, which is free from potential confounding factors.

Let p_{iy} be the probability that company i suffers from an incident in year y expressed as $p_{iy} = \frac{1}{1+e^{-z_i}}$, where z_i is m-variable polynomial

$$z_i = \alpha + \beta_1 x_1 + \cdots + \beta_m x_m + \beta_{b_i} b_i + \beta_y c_y + \beta_d d_i \qquad (1)$$

and b_i, c_y, and d_i are dummy variables designating the industrial category for company i, the social economics for year y, and the size of company i, respectively. Boolean variables $x_1, \ldots, x_m$ are set to 1 if the corresponding security measure is adopted by company i.

The *odds ratio* (OR) is an alternative measure to RR. Recalling Table 6, the probability of an incident given measure M is $p = a/(a+b)$ and the odds of suffering an incident are $p/(1 \quad p)$ to 1. The *adjusted OR* of suffering an incident when explanatory variable $x_1 = 1$ is given by

$$\widehat{OR} = \frac{Pr(\text{incident}|x_1 = 1)/(1 - Pr(\text{incident}|x_1 = 1))}{Pr(\text{incident}|x_1 = 0)/(1 - Pr(\text{incident}|x_1 = 0))} = \frac{e^{\alpha + \beta_1 + \beta_2 x_2 + \cdots}}{e^{\alpha + 0 + \beta_2 x_2 + \cdots}} = e^{\beta_1}.$$

If $a \ll b$, we can assume $a + b \approx b$ and, therefore, OR will be a close approximation to RR. That is,

$$RR = \frac{a/(a+b)}{c/(c+d)} \approx \frac{a/b}{c/d} = OR. \qquad (2)$$

It is generally preferable to work with OR rather than RR because the former has better statistical properties.

In this analysis, we investigate the model defined in Eq. (1) for each company i in the TK CSR dataset. There are $m = 119$ security measures, b_i is a 14-dimensional dummy variable specifying membership of the corresponding industrial categories, and d_i is the logarithm of the number of employees. To conduct the multiple logistic regression analysis, we used a generalized linear model $\mathtt{glm()}$ function in R.

4.5 Results of Analysis

We first constructed an RR table (see Table 7), which contained the results from the answers given by compromised corporations to 17 questions about their security measures (Table 5). The results for the N corporations associated with each question were obtained for the five-year period 2013–2017 and the total number of corporations affected was 6,661. For example, 4,975 corporations had a rule for protecting whistle-blowers (C122 (whistle)), with 106 incidents occurring during this period, resulting in a positive RR of 1.118. That is, by protecting employees acting as whistle-blowers, the risk of recording a security incident increased by 11.8% above cases where such a guideline did not exist.

We were then able to identify statistically significant factors (security measures) at the 0.05 and 0.01 levels for the chi-square test, marked with ∗∗ and ∗∗∗, respectively, in Table 7. Surprisingly, most security measures had negative effects ($RR > 1$), based on this analysis. In particular, the number of incidents increases for some measures, namely C161 (PP), C227 (RM/CM), C229 (RM/CMP), and K136 (Labor-M) exceeded the 0.01 level of significance. Even ISMS, well known as a "cure-all" countermeasure, was assessed as having $RR = 1.313$, implying a 31%-higher risk of cyber incidents occurring. Although the results are for a five-year period, results for any single year were very similar, confirming that most measures appeared to have negative effects.

Remark 1. Negative effects are confirmed by relative-risk analysis over five years for the security measures whistle, CIO, CFO, PP, SP, auditing, ISMS, RM, and Labor-M.

However, the RR values for security measures may sometimes differ substantially with respect to important characteristics such as the type of business and the scale of a corporation. Such characteristics are known as *confounding factors*.

4.6   Confounding Factors

We show the result of Mantel-Haenszel test for some confounding factors in Table 8. With statistical significant level (∗∗∗ for 0.01, ∗∗ for 0.05), we find that the industrial *sector* that company belongs, the *scale* of company and the *year* often have confounding effect on cyber incidents.

Industrial Sectors. B2C corporations may be more likely to suffer data breaches than B2B corporations. That is, *the style of business* must be a confounder for incident risk. Therefore, we explore the underlying proportions of compromised companies with respect to their industrial sector, as defined by the Securities Identification Code Committee.

Table 9 gives the numbers of cyber-incident-affected corporations for the various industrial sectors, as specified by TOPIX-17 [5]. The number of corporations varies across sectors, with 1,227 corporations being classified as "IT & Services, others". Note that the number of compromised corporations (labeled as "hacked") for the sector "Electric power & gas" was 11 out of 56 corporations. The rate of compromise for companies in this sector is significantly high at 18.6%, which is about 10 times higher than the average rate of 1.9%.

This is understandable, in that "Electric power & gas" corporations provide infrastructure services to many customers and need to deal with a large quantity

Table 7. Relative risks for various security measures (skewed by confounders!)

Table 8. Mantel-Haenszel test (p-value)

Measure	N	Hacked	RR	p-value	Sector	Scale	Year
C122 Whistle	4,975	106	1.118	0.028 **	0.030 **	0.770	0.019 **
C139 Internal-cntl	2997	50	0.875	0.232	0.986	0.023 **	0.182
C147 CIO	1,901	38	1.048	0.803	0.695	0.109	0.745
C150 CFO	2,248	56	1.307	0.017 **	0.003 ***	0.707	0.012 **
C161 PP	4,424	106	1.257	0.000 ***	0.000 ***	0.041 **	0.000 ***
C153 SP	4,934	104	1.106	0.054	0.053	0.908	0.042 **
C155 audit-int	4,346	93	1.122	0.070	0.083	0.973	0.057
C157 audit-ext	3,238	68	1.101	0.302	0.286	0.889	0.376
C159 ISMS	999	25	1.313	0.171	0.417	0.756	0.248
C120 Whistle-int	5,086	108	1.114	0.026 **	0.026 **	0.647	0.019 **
C202 Whistle-ext	3,543	76	1.125	0.154	0.256	0.306	0.174
C207 Audit-ind	4,687	102	1.141	0.017 **	0.022 **	0.800	0.016 **
C227 RM/CM	3,920	101	1.351	0.000 ***	0.000 ***	0.021 **	0.000 ***
C229 RM/CMP	3,650	97	1.394	0.000 ***	0.000 ***	0.019 **	0.000 ***
E082 Audit-env	3,541	70	1.037	0.721	0.206	0.003 ***	0.727
E087 EMS	3,722	71	1.001	0.933	0.342	0.000 ***	0.984
K136 Labor-M	2,656	66	1.303	0.007 ***	0.000 ***	0.982	0.005 ***

of PII data, such as monthly invoices and payment receipts. This leads to a particularly high risk of incidents and may act as a confounder in our analysis.

Company Scale. Large-scale corporations are at higher risk of targeted attacks, with *company scale* being considered as a confounder in cyber-incident risk assessment.

To show the relationship between company scale and the risk of cyber incidents, we show scatterplots of the logarithm of the number of employees (X-axis) against the number of security measures deployed (Y-axis in Fig. 1) and against the number of victims (customers) (Y-axis in Fig. 2). In both plots, we highlight the corporations that have ever been compromised in red. Note that the dots are denser in the right-hand side of the graph and that most compromised corporations are large-scale corporations. Obliviously, there is a positive correlation between the number of employees and the number of security measures (management programs). This implies that many types of security measures have delayed effects in large-scale corporations, which may therefore present as fake effects of increasing cyber-incident risk.

We adopt a company-scale criterion that the number of employees in "Small and medium" corporations is <300, is <1,500 for "Large 1" corporations, and is ≥1,500 for "Large 2" corporations. Table 10 gives results for compromised

Table 9. Number of compromised corporations with respect to the TOPIX-17 industrial series (partial)

TOPIX-17 series	2013		2014		2015		2016		2017		Total		
	N	Hacked	N	Hacked	N	Hacked	N	Hacked	N	Hacked	N	Hacked	[%]
IT & services, others	215	4	233	6	237	4	269	6	273	6	1227	26	2.1
Banks	31	4	37	2	37	4	42	2	42	4	189	16	8.5
Retail trade	102	1	106	3	106	4	108	5	119	2	541	15	2.8
Electric appliances	127	3	129	4	129	2	140	0	136	3	661	12	1.8
Electric power & gas	12	0	12	2	11	2	12	3	12	4	**59**	**11**	**18.6**
Construction & materials	97	3	105	2	107	2	114	2	115	0	538	9	1.7
Textiles & chemicals	119	2	131	1	139	0	136	3	141	2	666	8	1.2
Transportation & logistics	40	0	44	2	44	2	42	1	45	2	215	7	3.3
Commercial & wholesale trade	121	0	129	2	131	3	142	1	134	0	657	6	0.9
Financials (ex. Banks)	28	0	36	2	36	3	41	0	39	0	180	5	2.8
Foods	52	0	54	0	59	1	64	2	59	0	288	3	1.0
Auto & transportation equip	60	1	66	0	68	0	66	0	66	0	326	3	0.9
Machinery	65	0	77	0	77	0	88	3	86	0	393	3	0.8
Steel & nonferrous metals	31	0	33	0	32	0	30	0	30	0	156	1	0.6
Energy resources	5	0	6	0	6	0	6	0	6	0	29	0	0.0
Pharmaceutical	24	0	26	0	30	0	32	0	33	0	145	0	0.0
Real estate	28	0	32	0	33	0	31	0	32	0	156	0	0.0
Others	53	1	49	1	43	0	45	0	45	0	235	2	0.9
Total	1210	19	1305	27	1325	27	1408	30	1413	24	6661	127	1.9

Table 10. Number of compromised corporations for three company scales

Scale	2013		2014		2015		2016		2017		Total	
	N	Hacked	N	Hacked	N	Hacked	N	Hacked	N	Hacked	N	Hacked
Small and medium	320	1	359	2	366	0	400	3	380	3	1825	9
Large 1	478	9	516	7	523	9	561	8	571	9	2649	42
Large 2	407	9	426	18	435	18	447	19	461	12	2176	76
Total	1210	19	1305	27	1325	27	1408	30	1413	24	6661	127

corporations in these three categories over the five years 2013–2017. Note that the number of compromised corporations increases as their scale increases, confirming the trend seen in the scatterplots. We conducted a chi-square test to confirm that the company scale is statistically significant, enabling rejection of the null hypothesis that incident occurrence is independent of the scale of corporations. Figure 2 shows that ISMS-certified corporations (highlighted in red) are distributed more frequently as the number of employees increases. The corporations located at the bottom of the plot are incident-free.

Type of Event. The type of cyber incident may also be associated with the frequencies of events. For example, the most frequent incident type is the Data Breach, which occurs frequently in B2C services. This points to the type of incident being a confounder.

We show the annual statistics for cyber incidents for the period 2014–2018 with respect to the five main incident causes and the 17 industrial sectors in

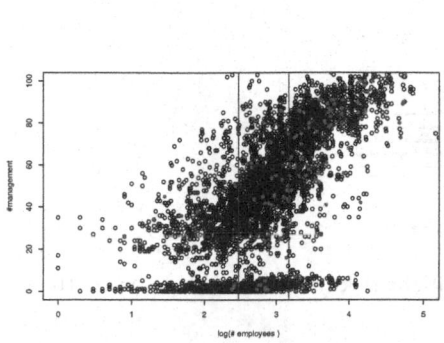

Fig. 1. Corporations plotted by number of employees (X-axis) and number of types of security management (Y-axis)

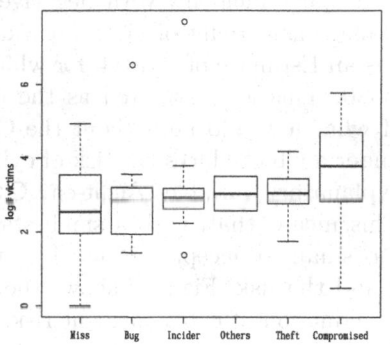

Fig. 2. ISMS-certified corporations plotted by number of employees (X-axis) and number of victims (customers) (Y-axis)

Table 11. Counts of cyber incidents

	2013	2014	2015	2016	2017	Total
Data breach	8	18	12	12	16	66
Security incident	6	7	5	8	5	31
Malicious insider	1	1	2	2	2	8
Misconfiguration	2	2	4	4	2	14
Stealing	1	0	4	5	1	11
Others	1	0	0	0	0	1
Unknown	0	0	1	0	1	2
Total	19	28	28	31	27	133

Fig. 3. Boxplot of cyber incidents

Tables 11. Note that the trend is stable across the five years. For the relationship between the quantity of PII and the incident type, Fig. 3 displays a boxplot of the number of victims (the number of PII records disclosed or lost because of the incident). It shows the largest diversity for compromising events that include malware and target attacks.

4.7 Multiple Logistic Regression

To mitigate the side effects of confounders, we perform a multiple logistic regression for the explanatory variables associated with the risk of incidents. Table 12 shows the results of the logistic regression, where the explanatory variables are classified into five categories, namely a (constant), b (industrial sector), c (analysis year), d (company scale), and e (security measures). For each of the

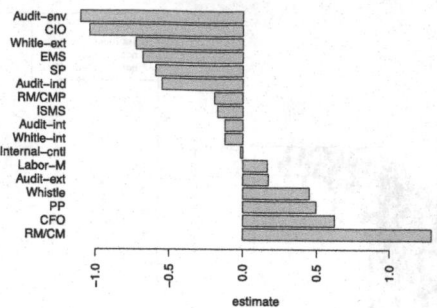

Fig. 4. Best security measures to reduce incident risk (smaller estimate are better)

explanatory variables, a coefficient (Estimate), the standard error (S.E.), p-value $(Pr(> |z|))$ and OR are provided.

The estimated coefficient indicates the positive or negative effect on the odds of a cyber incident, with negative coefficients being better from the security management point of view. For example, the coefficient of variable C147 (CIO) has an Estimate of -1.044, for which the adjusted OR is computed as $e^{-1.044} = 0.330$. This is interpreted as the odds of cyber incidents with a CIO is 0.33 of what it would be without the CIO position. In other words, a management under a CIO reduces the risk of cyber incidents by two-thirds. In particular, the explanatory variables Audit-env CIO, and Whistle-ext are flagged with * or **. This means that, with a small standard error, the corresponding p-values are too small to accept the null hypothesis that there is no relationship between p and the risk. Figure 4 shows the best security measures ranked by the order of reduction of cyber-incident risk. Measures with estimate less than 0 indicate good ones that performs well in reducing risks. Overall, note that 11 of the 17 security measures (64%) are confirmed as effective in reducing cybersecurity risks.

Remark 2. The security measure to conduct an environmental auditing (Audit-env) reduces the odds of cyber-incident to 0.330 of that without such auditing as statistically significant level. The additional measures establishment of a CIO, and having an external point of contact for whistle-blowers (Whistle-ext) are also confirmed as effective with OR of 0.352, and 0.484, respectively.

4.8   Discussion

Based on the adjusted odds ratio via multiple logistic regression, we can identify significant confounders that have estimated values at significant levels. Within the category of industrial sectors (*b*), the "Electric power & gas" sector is the only one confirmed as significant. Its adjusted OR is 11.291, which is 11 times higher than that for "Foods" sector, which is designated as the reference sector (with the odds of 1.0). The explanatory variable for the logarithm of the number

Table 12. Logistic regression results

	Variable	Estimate	S.E.	$Pr(>|z|)$	OR
a	(Intercept)	−7.570	1.018	0.000 ***	–
b sector	Electric power & gas	2.424	0.943	0.010*	11.291
	Banks	1.569	0.825	0.057	4.802
	Retail trade	1.054	0.742	0.156	2.869
	Transportation & logistics	0.981	0.837	0.241	2.666
	IT & Services	0.603	0.725	0.406	1.827
	Construction & Materials	0.384	0.786	0.625	1.469
	Electric appliances	0.160	0.791	0.840	1.173
	Commercial & wholesale trade	0.125	0.841	0.882	1.133
	Textiles & chemicals	−0.002	0.767	0.998	0.998
	Financial (ex. banks)	−0.056	0.920	0.952	0.946
	Auto	−0.165	0.955	0.863	0.848
	Machinery	−0.184	0.910	0.840	0.832
	Steel	−0.675	1.305	0.605	0.509
c year	2014	0.219	0.324	0.500	1.244
	2015	0.242	0.333	0.468	1.274
	2016	0.156	0.342	0.649	1.168
	2017	−0.257	0.367	0.483	0.773
d scale	log # employees	0.276	0.100	0.006 **	1.317
x measures	E082 Audit-env	−1.109	0.515	0.031 *	0.330
	C147 CIO	−1.044	0.329	0.001 **	0.352
	C202 Whitle-ext	−0.726	0.289	0.012 *	0.484
	E087 EMS	−0.681	0.439	0.121	0.506
	C153 SP	−0.593	0.592	0.317	0.553
	C207 Audit-ind	−0.550	0.475	0.247	0.577
	C229 RM/CMP	−0.193	0.607	0.751	0.824
	C159 ISMS	−0.171	0.318	0.591	0.843
	C155 Audit-int	−0.122	0.370	0.741	0.885
	C120 Whitle-int	−0.121	0.751	0.872	0.886
	C139 Internal-cntl	−0.015	0.255	0.952	0.985
	K136 Labor-M	0.162	0.288	0.575	1.175
	C157 Audit-ext	0.169	0.273	0.537	1.184
	C122 whistle	0.451	0.684	0.509	1.570
	C161 PP	0.496	0.563	0.379	1.642
	C150 CFO	0.622	0.319	0.051	1.863
	C227 RM/CM	1.292	0.682	0.058	3.640

of employees is also verified, with an adjusted OR of 1.317 in category d. There is no significant variable in category e (year), implying that frequency of cyber-incidents is stable in five years.

Remark 3. The significant confounders in an analysis of cyber-incident risk are the industrial sector involved and the company scale.

The estimated ORs in Table 12 are inconsistent with the RRs in Table 7. We need to explain this discrepancy. First, the existence of significant confounders skews the risk, including particular sectors such as Electric power & gas and the company scale. We have verified that RR approaches OR when the number of corporations per sector and the company scales are adjusted. Therefore, we should carefully discard these known confounding factors before performing the analysis.

5 Conclusion

In this paper, we report on cyber incident risks, using big-data analysis to identify those security measures that are effective in reducing such risks. By combining the big data of cyber incidents with the big data of company attributes, we compute the RR factor with respect to the various security measures. We noted that the statistics of cyber incidents are often skewed by confounding variables often associated with company characteristics. Based on the analysis of five years of data about 6,000 corporations and 17 security measures, we found that those corporations classified as belonging to the "Electric power & gas" sector had a significantly large probability of being compromised. Using multiple logistic regression analysis, we found that the adjusted ORs of 11 security measures were effective in reducing the risk of cyber incidents, at a statistically significant level. In particular, our analysis demonstrated that conducting environmental auditing, establishing a CIO position, and having an external point of contact for whistle-blowers are effective, with relative ORs of 0.330, 0.352, and 0.484, respectively.

Acknowledgments. We thank the Japan Network Security Association for the cybersecurity incident dataset. This work was supported by SPS KAKENHI, Grant Numbers JP16K03755 and JP18H04099.

References

1. Romanosky, S.: Examining the costs and causes of cyber incidents. J. Cybersecur. **2**(2), 121–135 (2016)
2. Framework for Improving Critical Infrastructure Cybersecurity version 1.1. NIST (2018)
3. JNSA Dataset. Information Security Incident Survey Report (2017)
4. JNSA Working group: Report on Information Security Incidents in 2018. https://www.jnsa.org/result/incident/2018.html. Accessed February 2018
5. TOPIX Sector Indices/TOPIX-17 Series. Tokyo Stock Exchange Inc. http://www.jpx.co.jp/markets/indices/line-up/files/fac_13_sector.pdf. Accessed June 2018
6. TOYO KEIZAI Japan CSR Data 2018. QUICK. Corp. (2018)
7. Sakuma, J., Inomata, A.: Proposal for improvement of penetration on investigation and analysis of cyber insurance. Internet Oper. Technol., 1–8 (2019). IPSJ

8. Edwards, B., Hofmeyr, S., Forrest, S.: Hype and heavy tails: a closer look at data breaches. J. Cybersecur. **2**, 3–14 (2016)
9. Kokaji, A., Harada, Y., Goto, A.: A consideration of assessment on cybersecurity in financial institutions. Electron. Intellect. Property, 1–5 (2019). IPSJ
10. Yamada, M., Kikuchi, H., Matsuyama, N., Inui, K.: Mathematical model to estimate loss by cyber incident in Japan. In: Proceedings of 5th International Systems Security and Privacy (ICISSP 2019), RP-49, pp. 1–8 (2019)
11. Sen, R., Borle, S.: Estimating the contextual risk of data breach: an empirical approach. J. Manag. Inf. Syst. **32**(2), 314–341 (2015)
12. Eling, M., Loperfido, N.: Data breaches: goodness of fit, pricing, and risk measurement. Insur.: Math. Econ. **75**, 126–136 (2017)
13. Xu, M., Schweitzer, K., Bateman, R., Xu, S.: Modeling and predicting cyber hacking breaches. IEEE Trans. Inf. Forensics Secur. **13**, 2856–2871 (2018)
14. Romanosky, S., Telang, R., Acquisti, A.: Do data breach disclosure laws reduce identity theft? J. Policy Anal. Manage. **30**(2), 256–286 (2011)
15. Pagano, M., Gauvreau, K.: Logistic regression. In: Principles of Biostatistics, pp. 470–487. Chapman and Hall/CRC (2018)
16. Mantel, N., Haenszel, W.: Statistical aspects of the analysis of data from retrospective studies of disease. J. Natl. Cancer Inst. **22**, 719–748 (1959)
17. Dupont, G., dos Santos, D.R., Costante, E., den Hartog, J., Etalle, S.: A matter of life and death: analyzing the security of healthcare networks. In: Hölbl, M., Rannenberg, K., Welzer, T. (eds.) SEC 2020. IAICT, vol. 580, pp. 355–369. Springer, Cham (2020). https://doi.org/10.1007/978-3-030-58201-2_24
18. Hatamian, M., Pape, S., Rannenberg, K.: ESARA: a framework for enterprise smartphone apps risk assessment. In: Dhillon, G., Karlsson, F., Hedström, K., Zúquete, A. (eds.) SEC 2019. IAICT, vol. 562, pp. 165–179. Springer, Cham (2019). https://doi.org/10.1007/978-3-030-22312-0_12

Synthesizing Privacy-Preserving Location Traces Including Co-locations

Jun Narita[1]([✉]), Yayoi Suganuma[1], Masakatsu Nishigaki[1], Takao Murakami[2], and Tetsushi Ohki[1]

[1] Shizuoka University, Hamamatsu, Shizuoka, Japan
{narita,suganuma}@sec.inf.shizuoka.ac.jp,
{nisigaki,ohki}@inf.shizuoka.ac.jp
[2] AIST, Koto-ku, Tokyo, Japan
takao-murakami@aist.go.jp

Abstract. Location traces are useful for various types of geo-data analysis tasks, and synthesizing location traces is a promising approach to geo-data analysis while protecting user privacy. However, existing location synthesizers do not consider friendship information of users. In particular, a co-location between friends is an important factor for synthesizing more realistic location traces.

In this paper, we propose a novel location synthesizer that generates synthetic traces including co-locations between friends. Our synthesizer models the information about the co-locations by two parameters: friendship probability and co-location count matrix. The friendship probability represents a probability that two users will be a friend, whereas the co-location count matrix comprises a co-location count for each time instant and each location. Our synthesizer also provides DP (Differential Privacy) for training data. We evaluate our synthesizer using the Foursquare dataset. Our experimental results show that our synthesizer preserves the information about co-locations and other statistical information (e.g., population distribution, transition matrix) while providing DP with a reasonable privacy budget (e.g., smaller than 1).

Keywords: Synthetic trace · Co-location · Differential privacy · Laplace mechanism · Wavelet transform · Viterbi algorithm

1 Introduction

With the widespread use of mobile phones, LBS (Location-Based Services), which utilize a user's location information for some services (e.g., predicting traffic congestion, user-tailored route suggestion), are becoming increasingly popular. LBS providers can also provide a large amount of location traces (time-series location trails) to a third party (data analyst) to perform various geo-data analyses such as finding popular POIs (Point-of-Interests) in the surrounding area [1] and modeling human mobility patterns [2]. However, the disclosure of location

J. Garcia-Alfaro et al. (Eds.): DPM 2021/CBT 2021, LNCS 13140, pp. 20–36, 2022.
https://doi.org/10.1007/978-3-030-93944-1_2

traces raises serious privacy concerns. For example, location traces may include sensitive locations such as frequently visited hospitals and users' home.

To address the privacy issue, privacy-preserving location synthesizers (e.g., [3–5]) have been widely studied. The location synthesizer trains a generative model from real trace data, and then generates synthetic traces based on the trained generative model. Ideal synthetic traces should preserve various statistical features (e.g., population distribution [1], transition matrix [6]) of real trace data while being able to protect user privacy. Synthetic traces can also be used as a synthetic dataset for research purposes [7] and competitions [8].

However, the existing location synthesizers do not take into account friendship information between users. In particular, friends tend to be in the same place at the same time [9], which is also known as a *co-location* [10,11]. Thus, a co-location between friends is an important factor for synthesizing more realistic location traces. For example, a synthetic trace dataset including co-locations between friends may be useful for studying the effect of friend recommendation [9].

In this paper, we propose a novel location synthesizer that generates synthetic traces including co-locations between friends. To preserve co-locations information, our proposed method trains two parameters from real trace data: *friendship probability* and *co-location count matrix*. The friendship probability models a probability that two users will become friends. The co-location count matrix comprises a co-location count for each time instant and each location, and models a location that is likely to be visited by friends at a certain time period (e.g., bars at night). Both the friendship probability and the co-location count matrix provide strong privacy guarantee: *DP (Differential Privacy)* [12], a gold standard for data privacy. Our contributions are as follows:

- We propose a novel location synthesizer that generates location traces including co-locations between friends. Our proposed method models the information about co-locations between friends by two parameters: *friendship probability* and *co-location count matrix*. Both the friendship probability and the co-location count matrix provide DP for training data.
- We show that synthetic traces generated by the proposed method provide high utility and privacy using the Foursquare dataset [9]. Specifically, we show that our synthetic traces preserve the information about co-locations and other statistical features (e.g., population distribution, transition matrix) while providing DP with a reasonable privacy budget ε (e.g., $\varepsilon \leq 1$).

2   Related Work

2.1   Co-locations

In this paper, we define a co-location as an *event that two users are in the same place at the same time*. In particular, we focus on a co-location between friends and use it to generate synthetic traces. Olteanu et al. [10,11] showed that co-location information improves the accuracy of location estimation attacks. They also studied the users' benefits of sharing co-locations and the impact of co-locations on location privacy [13]. Yang et al. [9] showed a correlation between co-location information and friendships on Twitter.

However, no studies have utilized co-location information for generating synthetic traces, to the best of our knowledge.

2.2   Location Synthesizers

Location synthesizers have been widely studied for over a decade (see [3,5] for detailed surveys). Bindschaeder and Shokri [3] proposed generating synthetic traces by a synthetic location generation model that considers semantic features of locations (e.g., most people stay a night at their home locations, which are geographically different but semantically the same). He et al. [4] proposed generating synthetic traces that satisfy small ε-differential privacy by training a transition probability matrix common to all users. Murakami et al. [14] proposed generating synthetic traces with high utility by clustering a transition matrix for each user using tensor factorization.

However, there are no studies in which a co-location between friends is considered for generating synthetic traces, to our knowledge. As shown in [9], there is a positive correlation between co-locations and friendships; i.e., friends tend to be in the same place at the same time. Therefore, location synthesizers considering such co-location information are important to synthesize more realistic traces. To our knowledge, we are the first to address this issue.

3   Problem Formalization

3.1   Notations

Let $\mathbb{N}$, $\mathbb{Z}_{\geq 0}$, $\mathbb{R}$, and $\mathbb{R}_{\geq 0}$ be the set of natural numbers, non-negative integers, real numbers, and non-negative real numbers, respectively. For a finite set $\mathcal{Z}$, let $\mathcal{Z}^*$ be the set of all finite sequences of elements of $\mathcal{Z}$.

Let $\mathcal{U}$ be a finite set of users in training data, and $n \in \mathbb{N}$ be the number of users; i.e., $n = |\mathcal{U}|$. Let $u_i \in \mathcal{U}$ be the i-th user. We discretize locations by dividing an area of interest into some regions or extracting some POIs. Let $\mathcal{X}$ be a finite set of locations, and x_i be the i-th location. We also discretize time by, for example, rounding down minutes to a multiple of 30. Let $\mathcal{T}$ be a finite set of time instants, and $t_i \in \mathcal{T}$ be the i-th time instant.

We also show the basic notations used in this paper in Table 1.

3.2   Friendship Data

In this paper, we use *friendship data* and *real trace data* as training data to generate synthetic location traces including co-locations.

The friendship data contains friendship information between any pair of two users, and therefore can be represented as an adjacency matrix of size $n \times n$. If two users are friends, then the corresponding element will be assigned value

Table 1. Basic notations in this paper.

Symbol	Description
$\mathcal{U}$	Finite set of users
n	Number of users ($n = |\mathcal{U}|$)
$\mathcal{X}$	Finite set of locations
$\mathcal{T}$	Finite set of time instants
$\mathcal{E}$	Finite set of events ($\mathcal{E} = \mathcal{X} \times \mathcal{T}$)
$\mathcal{S}$	Finite set of training traces ($\mathcal{S} \subseteq \mathcal{U} \times \mathcal{E}^*$)
u_i	i-th user ($u_i \in \mathcal{U}$)
x_i	i-th location ($x_i \in \mathcal{X}$)
t_i	i-th time instant ($t_i \in \mathcal{T}$)
$\mathbf{A}$	Adjacency matrix ($\mathbf{A} \in \{0,1\}^{n \times n}$)
$\mathbf{a}_i$	i-th row of the adjacency matrix $\mathbf{A}$ ($\mathbf{a}_i \in \{0,1\}^n$)
s_i	i-th training trace ($s_i \in \mathcal{S}$)

	u_1	u_2	u_3	u_4	u_5
u_1	0	0	1	0	1
u_2	0	0	1	0	0
u_3	1	1	0	0	0
u_4	0	0	0	0	1
u_5	1	0	0	1	0

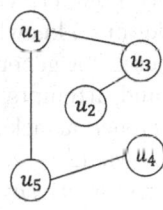

Fig. 1. An example of friendship data ($n = 5$).

"1"; Otherwise, "0". The diagonal elements are "0" because there is no friend relationship between the user and him/herself. Figure 1 shows an example of the friendship data. In this example, user u_1 is a friend with u_3 and u_5. u_2 is a friend with u_3.

Let $\mathbf{A} \in \{0,1\}^{n \times n}$ be an adjacency matrix, and $\mathbf{a}_i \in \{0,1\}^n$ be the i-th row of $\mathbf{A}$. In Fig. 1, $\mathbf{a}_1 = (0,0,1,0,1)$, $\mathbf{a}_2 = (0,0,1,0,0)$, $\cdots$, $\mathbf{a}_5 = (1,0,0,1,0)$. The friendship data can also be represented as a graph (as shown in Fig. 1), where a node represents a user and an edge represents a friendship between two users.

3.3   Trace Data

We define an event by a pair of a location and time instant, as in [5]. The trace data contains a location trace for each user, and a location trace contains events. Figure 2 shows an example of the trace data. Co-location events are marked in red. In this example, users u_2 and u_3 have a co-location event at location x_1 and time instant t_1. u_1 and u_2 have a co-location event at x_2 and t_2.

Let $\mathcal{E} = \mathcal{X} \times \mathcal{T}$ be a finite set of events. Let $\mathcal{S} \subseteq \mathcal{U} \times \mathcal{E}^*$ be a finite set of training traces, and $s_i \in \mathcal{S}$ be the i-th training trace. Figure 2 can be rewritten

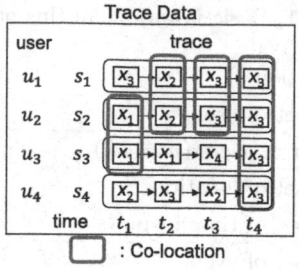

: Co-location

Fig. 2. An example of trace data ($n = 4$). (Color figure online)

as $\mathcal{S} = \{s_1, s_2, s_3, s_4\}$ and $s_1 = (u_1, (x_3, t_1), (x_2, t_2), (x_3, t_3), (x_3, t_4)), \cdots, s_4 = (u_4, (x_2, t_1), (x_3, t_2), (x_2, t_3), (x_3, t_4))$.

3.4 Threat Model and Differential Privacy

Threat Model. In this paper, we consider privacy preservation against an attacker with any background knowledge other than the training data (friendship data and trace data) used for generating synthetic traces. The attacker obtains the synthetic traces, and attempts to violate user privacy in the training data (e.g., membership inference attacks [15,16]) based on the synthetic traces and his/her background knowledge.

To strongly protect user privacy in the training data from the attacker with any background knowledge, we use *differential privacy (DP)* [12,17] as a privacy metric. DP provides user privacy against attackers with any background knowledge and is known as a gold standard for data privacy. Below we explain DP for friendship data and trace data in detail.

DP for Friendship Data. In graphs, there are two types of DP: *edge DP* and *node DP* [18]. Edge DP hides the existence of one edge (friendship). In contrast, node DP hides the existence of one node (user) and all edges connected to the node, and hence guarantees much stronger privacy than edge DP. Therefore, we use node DP to protect user privacy in the friendship data.

Formally, node DP considers two *neighboring* adjacency matrices $\mathbf{A}$ and $\mathbf{A}'$ that differ in one user and his/her all friendship information. For example, consider a graph obtained by removing u_3 and all edges connected to u_3 in Fig. 1. Let $\mathbf{A}' \in \{0, 1\}^{4 \times 4}$ be its adjacency matrix. In this case, $\mathbf{a}'_1 = (0, 0, 0, 1)$, $\mathbf{a}'_2 = (0, 0, 0, 0)$, $\mathbf{a}'_3 = (0, 0, 0, 1)$, and $\mathbf{a}'_4 = (1, 0, 1, 0)$. $\mathbf{A} \in \{0, 1\}^{5 \times 5}$ in Fig. 1 and $\mathbf{A}'$ in this example are neighboring adjacency matrices.

Then node DP [18] is defined as follows.

Definition 1 (ε_1-node DP). *Let $\varepsilon_1 \in \mathbb{R}_{\geq 0}$. A randomized algorithm $\mathcal{M}_1$ provides ε_1-node DP if for any two neighboring adjacency matrices $\mathbf{A}$ and $\mathbf{A}'$*

that differ in one node and its adjacent edges and any $Z \subseteq \mathrm{Range}(\mathcal{M}_1)$,

$$\Pr[\mathcal{M}_1(\mathbf{A}) \in Z] \leq e^{\varepsilon_1} \Pr[\mathcal{M}_1(\mathbf{A}') \in Z]. \tag{1}$$

Intuitively, node DP guarantees that an adversary who obtains the output of $\mathcal{M}_1$ cannot determine whether a particular node is included or not with a certain degree of confidence. This property is independent of the adversary's background knowledge. ε_1 is called the *privacy budget*. When the privacy budget ε_1 is small (e.g., $\varepsilon_1 \leq 1$ [19]), privacy of each node (user) is strongly protected.

DP for Trace Data. We can also consider two types of DP for trace data: *event-level DP* and *user-level DP* [20]. Event-level DP protects one event in a trace, whereas user-level DP protects the entire history (i.e., whole trace) of one user. Thus, user-level DP guarantees much stronger privacy than event-level DP. We use user-level DP to protect user privacy in the trace data.

Formally, we consider two *neighboring* sets S and S' of training traces such that S' is obtained by adding or removing a training trace of one user in S. For example, consider a set S' of training traces obtained by removing s_3 in Fig. 2; i.e., $S' = \{s_1, s_2, s_4\}$. S in Fig. 2 and S' in this example are neighboring.

Then user-level DP can be defined as follows.

Definition 2 (ε_2-user-level DP). *Let* $\varepsilon_2 \in \mathbb{R}_{\geq 0}$. *A randomized algorithm* $\mathcal{M}_2$ *provides* ε_2-*user-level DP if for any two neighboring sets* S *and* S' *of training traces that differ in one trace and any* $Z \subseteq \mathrm{Range}(\mathcal{M}_2)$,

$$\Pr[\mathcal{M}_2(S) \in Z] \leq e^{\varepsilon_2} \Pr[\mathcal{M}_2(S') \in Z]. \tag{2}$$

User-level DP guarantees that an adversary who obtains the output of $\mathcal{M}_2$ cannot determine whether a particular user is included or not in trace data. Again, privacy of each user is strongly protected when the privacy budget ε_2 is small (e.g., $\varepsilon_2 \leq 1$). In addition, the privacy budget for each user in the training data can be calculated as the sum of ε_1 and ε_1 by the composition theorem [21]. Therefore, user privacy in the training data is strongly protected by using ε_1-node DP with small ε_1 for friendship data and ε_2-user-level DP with small ε_2 for trace data.

4 Proposed Method

4.1 Overview

Figure 3 shows the overview of generating synthetic traces using our proposed method. The proposed method uses a location dataset that includes both trace data and friendship data (e.g., Foursquare dataset in [9]) as training data. To distinguish between trace data in the training data and synthetic trace data, we refer to the former trace data as *real trace data*.

In a nutshell, the proposed method generates co-locations between friends using two parameters: *friendship probability* $p' \in [0, 1]$ and *co-location count*

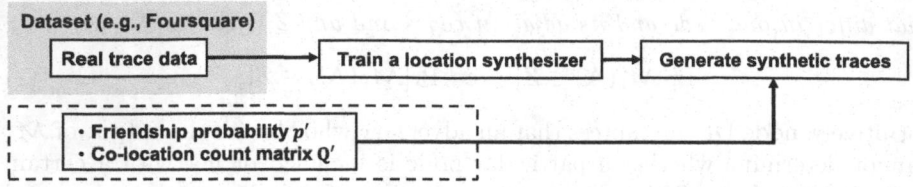

Fig. 3. Overview of generating synthetic traces using the proposed method. p' and $\mathbf{Q}'$ in the dotted box are parameters in the proposed method to generate co-locations.

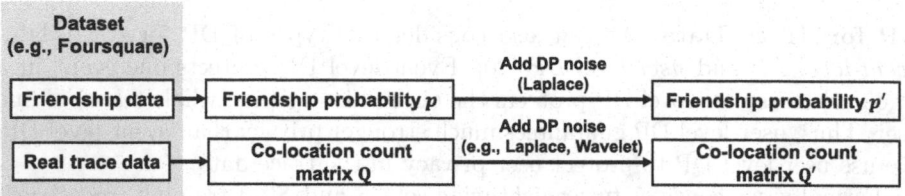

Fig. 4. Overview of training parameters p' and $\mathbf{Q}'$ in the proposed method. p' and $\mathbf{Q}'$ provide node DP and user-level DP, respectively.

matrix $\mathbf{Q}' \in \mathbb{Z}_{\geq 0}^{|\mathcal{T}| \times |\mathcal{X}|}$. The friendship probability p' represents the probability that two users are friends. The co-location count matrix $\mathbf{Q}'$ includes a co-location count for each time instant and each location. For example, if friends tend to meet at a bar from 6PM to 8PM, then the corresponding elements in $\mathbf{Q}'$ have large co-location counts.

The proposed method randomly generates friendship information in synthetic traces using p'. Then it generates co-locations between friends at a specific location and time instant using $\mathbf{Q}'$. The generated co-locations preserve the information about $\mathbf{Q}'$; e.g., friends tend to meet at a bar from 6PM to 8PM. After generating co-locations, the proposed method generates the remaining events in synthetic traces using existing location synthesizers that model human movement patterns as a *transition matrix*. Such location synthesizers include the location synthesizers in [3–5,22]. In our experiments, we use the synthetic data generator in [22] because it is easy to implement and provides user-level DP with a small privacy budget. We train the existing location synthesizer using real trace data.

Figure 4 shows the overview of training p' and $\mathbf{Q}'$ in the proposed method. From friendship data, we calculate the friendship probability $p \in [0, 1]$. Then we generate p' by adding the Laplace noise [12] to p. The noisy friendship probability p' provides *node DP*.

From real trace data, we calculate the co-location count matrix $\mathbf{Q}$ by simply counting co-locations between friends. Then we generate a co-location count matrix $\mathbf{Q}'$ that provides *user-level DP* by adding noise to $\mathbf{Q}$. The simplest way to provide DP for $\mathbf{Q}'$ is to add the Laplace noise to each element in $\mathbf{Q}$. However, the total amount of the Laplace noise can be very large because the number of elements in $\mathbf{Q}$ is large ($|\mathcal{T}||\mathcal{X}|$ elements in total). Therefore, we use a DP mechanism based on the Wavelet transform called *Privelet* [23]. Privelet (for one-dimensional nominal data) applies a nominal Wavelet transform to a one-dimensional frequency matrix, and adds independent Laplace noise to each wavelet coefficient (each node in a tree structure). Privelet can add noise effectively when a category or tree structure of locations is known. For example, the Foursquare dataset [9] has a category (e.g., "travel & transport", "shop & service") and sub-category (e.g., "train station", "subway", "electronics store", "hobby shop") of POIs [24], and each POI is associated with a category and sub-category. In this case, Privelet can be used to provide DP for $\mathbf{Q}'$ with a much smaller amount of noise for each POI category and each time instant (e.g., "travel & transport" from 7AM to 9AM). In our experiments, we compare Privelet with the Laplace mechanism, and show that the former significantly reduces the noise.

Features. The main feature of our proposed method is that it can generate synthetic traces including *co-locations*. The synthetic traces preserve the information about p' (i.e., how likely two users will be a friend) and $\mathbf{Q}'$ (i.e., how likely a co-location event will happen at a certain location for each time instant), both of which are trained from training data. In addition, the synthetic traces strongly protect user privacy: node DP for friendship data and user-level DP for real trace data. The privacy budgets are also reasonable (e.g., smaller than 1), as shown in our experiments.

4.2   Friendship Probability p'

Calculation of p'. Below we explain how to calculate the friendship probability $p' \in [0, 1]$ in our method.

First, we calculate the friendship probability p by simply calculating the proportion of edges in friendship data; i.e., the proportion of "1"s in the non-diagonal elements of adjacency matrix $\mathbf{A}$. In the example of Fig. 1, we can calculate p as $p = 8/(5 \times 4) = 0.4$. For $b \in \mathbb{R}_{\geq 0}$, let $\mathrm{Lap}(b)$ be a random variable that represents the Laplace noise with mean 0 and scale b. Then we calculate p' by adding the Laplace noise $\mathrm{Lap}(\frac{2}{n\varepsilon_1})$; i.e., $p' = p + \mathrm{Lap}(\frac{2}{n\varepsilon_1})$.

DP of p'. Let $\mathcal{M}_1^{\mathrm{Lap}}$ be a randomized algorithm that takes an adjacency matrix $\mathbf{A}$ as input and outputs p'. Then we have the following privacy guarantee.

Proposition 1. $\mathcal{M}_1^{Lap}$ *provides ε_1-node DP.*

Proof. Let $f : \{0,1\}^{n \times n} \to [0,1]$ be a function that takes $\mathbf{A}$ as input and outputs p. Let Δf be the global sensitivity [12] of f given by:

$$\Delta f = \max_{\mathbf{A} \sim \mathbf{A}'} |f(\mathbf{A}) - f(\mathbf{A}')|, \tag{3}$$

where $\mathbf{A} \sim \mathbf{A}'$ represents that $\mathbf{A}$ and $\mathbf{A}'$ are neighboring. Let $d \in \mathbb{Z}_{\geq 0}$ be the number of "1"s in $\mathbf{A}$. Assume that $\mathbf{A}'$ is obtained by removing one node in $\mathbf{A}$.

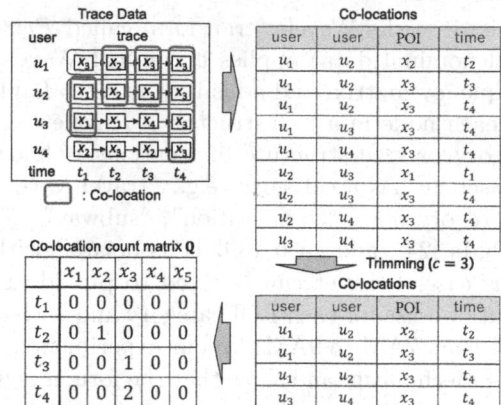

Fig. 5. Overview of calculating the co-location count matrix **Q**.

In this case, Δf takes the maximum value when the removed node has edges with all the other nodes. Thus, when $n \geq 3$, we have:

$$|f(\mathbf{A}) - f(\mathbf{A}')| \leq \frac{d}{n(n-1)} - \frac{d-2(n-1)}{(n-1)(n-2)} < \frac{d}{n(n-1)} - \frac{d-2(n-1)}{n(n-1)} = \frac{2}{n}. \quad (4)$$

Note that $f(\mathbf{A}) \leq 1$ when $n = 2$ and $f(\mathbf{A}) = 0$ when $n \leq 1$. Thus, (4) also holds when $n < 3$. When $\mathbf{A}'$ is obtained by adding one node in $\mathbf{A}$, the right-hand side of (4) becomes $\frac{2}{n+1} < \frac{2}{n}$. Therefore, $\Delta f \leq \frac{2}{n}$.

Since adding the Laplace noise $\text{Lap}(\Delta f/\varepsilon_1)$ to p provides ε_1-DP [12] and $\Delta f \leq \frac{2}{n}$, $\mathcal{M}_1^{\text{Lap}}$ that adds $\text{Lap}(\frac{2}{n\varepsilon_1})$ to p provides ε_1-node DP. □

4.3   Co-location Count Matrix Q'

Calculation of Q'. Next we explain how to calculate the co-location count matrix $\mathbf{Q}' \in \mathbb{Z}_{\geq 0}^{|\mathcal{T}| \times |\mathcal{X}|}$ in the proposed method.

From the real trace data, we calculate the co-location count matrix $\mathbf{Q} \in [0, 1]^{|\mathcal{T}| \times |\mathcal{X}|}$, which includes the number of co-locations for each time instant and each location. Here we introduce an upper limit $c \in \mathbb{Z}_{\geq 0}$ on the number of co-locations per user – when the number of co-locations reaches c, the user's co-locations are not read anymore. This is called *trimming* [25] and is used to upper-bound the global sensitivity in DP. Figure 5 shows an overview of calculating $\mathbf{Q}$ when $c = 3$. In this example, user u_1's co-locations are not read after reading three co-locations of u_1.

Then we calculate $\mathbf{Q}'$ by adding noise to $\mathbf{Q}$. In this paper, we use the Laplace mechanism or Privelet (for nominal data) [23] to add noise. The Laplace mechanism simply adds $\text{Lap}(c/\varepsilon_2)$ to each element of $\mathbf{Q}$. Privelet applies the Wavelet transform to a tree structure of locations, and adds the Laplace noise to a wavelet coefficient for each node in the tree. See [23] for more details.

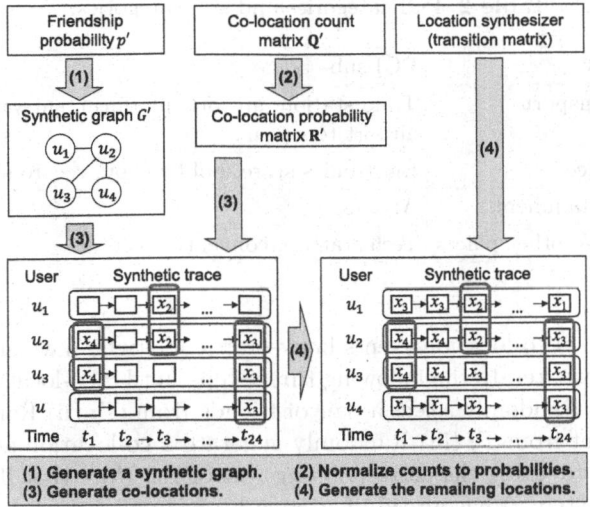

Fig. 6. Overview of generating synthetic traces in our proposed method.

DP of $\mathbf{Q}'$. Let $\mathcal{M}_2^{\text{Lap}}$ be a randomized algorithm that takes a set $\mathcal{S}$ of training traces as input and outputs $\mathbf{Q}'$ by adding $\text{Lap}(c/\varepsilon_2)$ to each element of $\mathbf{Q}$. Then we have the following privacy guarantee.

Proposition 2. $\mathcal{M}_2^{Lap}$ provides ε_2-user-level DP.

Proof. Since we read at most c co-locations per user from $\mathcal{S}$, adding or removing a training trace of one user in $\mathcal{S}$ changes each element of $\mathbf{Q}$ by at most c. Thus, the global sensitivity of each element of $\mathbf{Q}$ is at most c. Since $\mathcal{M}_2^{\text{Lap}}$ adds $\text{Lap}(c/\varepsilon_2)$ to each element of $\mathbf{Q}$, it provides ε_2-user-level DP. □

Let $\mathcal{M}_2^{\text{Wavelet}}$ be Privelet. Then $\mathcal{M}_2^{\text{Wavelet}}$ with the Laplace noise based on the global sensitivity c also provides ε_2-user-level DP. See [23] for the proof.

4.4 Generating Synthetic Traces

We generate a synthetic trace using the friendship probability p', co-location count matrix $\mathbf{Q}'$, and a location synthesizer that trains a transition matrix from real trace data (e.g., [3–5,22]).

Figure 6 shows the overview of generating synthetic traces in our proposed method. Specifically, we generate a synthetic trace for each of n users as follows.

1. Generate a synthetic graph G' with n nodes based on the Erdös-Rényi model, which randomly generates each edge with probability p'.
2. Calculate the category co-location probability matrix $\mathbf{R}' \in [0,1]^{|\mathcal{T}| \times |\mathcal{X}|}$ by normalizing each row of the co-location count matrix $\mathbf{Q}'$ so that the sum of the rows is 1. Note that an element in $\mathbf{Q}'$ may have a negative value. Thus, we calculate each row of $\mathbf{R}'$ by adding the absolute value of the minimum value to all elements and dividing them by their sum.

Table 2. POI categories and sub-categories.

POI category	POI sub-category
Travel & transport	Train station, airport, platform, subway, airport terminal
Shop & service	Electronics store, hobby shop, record shop, mall
Arts & entertainment	Arcade
Professional & other places	Tech startup, convention center

3. Generate $\theta \in \mathbb{N}$ co-location events between friends (who have an edge in G'). Specifically, we iterate the following three steps until θ co-location events are obtained: (i) Randomly select a pair of friends from G'; (ii) Randomly select a time instant from $\mathcal{T}$; (iii) Randomly generate a co-location at the selected time instant by using the corresponding row of $\mathbf{R}'$. Note that if either of the two users in step (i) has already had a co-location at a time instant selected in step (ii), we use it as a co-location in step (iii) for consistency with the previously generated co-location.
4. Generate the remaining locations in n synthetic traces using the transition matrix of a location synthesizer (e.g., [3–5, 22]). Specifically, we use the Viterbi algorithm to complement the remaining locations.

Note that the number θ of co-location events is a parameter in our proposed method. We set θ to various values in our experiments. It is also possible to calculate the frequency of co-location events (with DP noise) from real trace data, and set θ based on the co-location frequency.

Although we use the Erdös-Rényi model to generate a graph G' for simplicity, there exist more complicated and realistic graph models (e.g., Barabási-Albert model [26]) that have power-law degree distributions. An interesting avenue of future work is to incorporate such models into our proposed method.

5 Experimental Evaluation

5.1 Datasets

In our experiments, we used the Foursquare dataset in [9]. This dataset contains 22,809,624 check-ins from 114,324 users and 3,820,891 POIs. The dataset also includes the users' friendship data on SNS and a category and sub-category of POIs [24]. We used the check-in data in Tokyo (916,136 check-ins, 8,357 checked-in users, and 83,647 POIs). We set the length of a time instant to be one hour, and extracted two temporally-continuous location events from the dataset ($|\mathcal{T}| = 24$).

Since the number of check-ins for each POI is highly biased, the matrix $\mathbf{Q}$ becomes extremely sparse when we use all POIs. Therefore, we used check-in data for 100 POIs whose numbers of check-ins are the largest ($n = 8357$, $|\mathcal{X}| = 100$). The number m of POI categories was $m = 4$. The number of POI sub-categories was 12. Table 2 shows the POI categories and sub-categories.

5.2   Utility Metrics

Co-locations. To quantitatively show how our proposed method preserves the information about co-locations, we evaluated the utility of the friendship probability p' and the co-location count matrix $\mathbf{Q}'$.

Specifically, we evaluated the absolute error $|p - p'|$ between p and p' as a utility metric for p'. For utility of $\mathbf{Q}'$, co-location counts for each POI category and each time instant (e.g., "travel & transport" from 7AM to 9AM) are especially important. Thus, we did the following. Let $\mathbf{Q}^* \in \mathbb{Z}_{\geq 0}^{|\mathcal{T}| \times |\mathcal{X}|}$ be a co-location count matrix before adding noise when we do not perform trimming. $\mathbf{Q}^*$ is identical to $\mathbf{Q}$ when $c = \infty$. We calculated a *per-category* co-location count matrix $\overline{\mathbf{Q}}^* \in \mathbb{Z}_{\geq 0}^{|\mathcal{T}| \times m}$ ($|\mathcal{T}| = 24$, $m = 4$), which comprises of counts for each time instant and each POI category, by summing up counts in $\mathbf{Q}^*$ for each POI category. Similarly, we calculated a per-category co-location count matrix $\overline{\mathbf{Q}}' \in \mathbb{Z}_{\geq 0}^{|\mathcal{T}| \times m}$ by summing up counts in $\mathbf{Q}'$ for each POI category. Then we evaluated the MAE (Mean Absolute Error) and MSE (Mean Square Error) between $\overline{\mathbf{Q}}^*$ and $\overline{\mathbf{Q}}'$. The MAE is given by: $\frac{1}{|\mathcal{T}|m} \sum_{i=1}^{|\mathcal{T}|} \sum_{j=1}^{m} |\overline{\mathbf{Q}}_{ij}^* - \overline{\mathbf{Q}}_{ij}'|$, where $\overline{\mathbf{Q}}_{ij}^*$ and $\overline{\mathbf{Q}}_{ij}'$ are the (i,j)-th elements of $\overline{\mathbf{Q}}^*$ and $\overline{\mathbf{Q}}'$, respectively. The MSE is given by: $\frac{1}{|\mathcal{T}|m} \sum_{i=1}^{|\mathcal{T}|} \sum_{j=1}^{m} (\overline{\mathbf{Q}}_{ij}^* - \overline{\mathbf{Q}}_{ij}')^2$. Note that the difference between $\overline{\mathbf{Q}}^*$ and $\overline{\mathbf{Q}}'$ can be caused by two factors: trimming and adding DP noise.

Our proposed method randomly generates co-locations in synthetic traces based on p' and $\mathbf{Q}'$. Thus, when the absolute error of p' is small, our synthetic traces preserve the information about how likely two users will be a friend. When the MAE and MSE of $\overline{\mathbf{Q}}'$ are small, our synthetic traces preserve the information about how likely a co-location event between friends will happen at a certain POI category for each time instant (e.g., "travel & transport" from 7 to 9AM).

Other Statistical Features. We also evaluated how our synthetic traces preserve statistical features (other than co-locations) about real trace data. Specifically, we calculated two basic statistical features for geo-data analysis: *population distribution* and *transition probability matrix*. The population distribution ($|\mathcal{X}|$-dimensional probability vector) is a key feature to find popular POIs [1], whereas the transition probability matrix ($|\mathcal{X}| \times |\mathcal{X}|$ matrix) is a key feature to model user movement patterns [6]. For both of them, we evaluated the MAE and MSE between real trace data and synthetic traces.

5.3   Location Synthesizers

We evaluated three location synthesizers for comparison. The first synthesizer is a simple one that independently and randomly generates a location at each time instant from the uniform distribution. We denote this method by Uniform.

The second synthesizer is the synthetic data generator in [3]. This synthesizer can be applied to any kind of data, and it was applied to location traces in [5]. This synthesizer can be applied to location traces as follows. First, we train

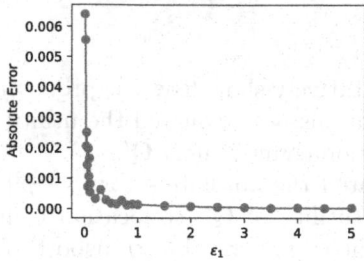

Fig. 7. Absolute error of p' versus ε_1.

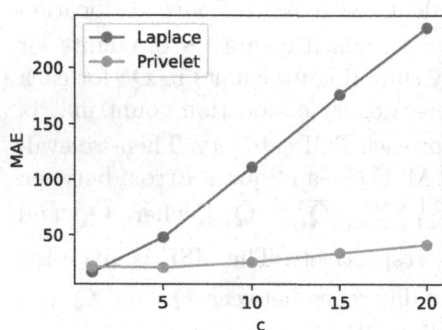

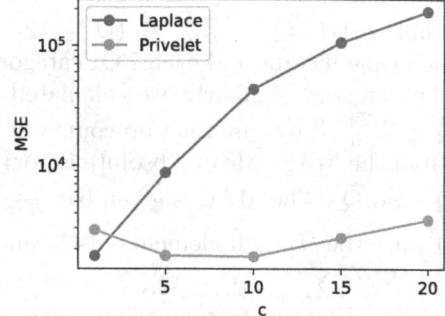

Fig. 8. MAE of $\overline{\mathbf{Q}}'$ versus c ($\varepsilon_2 = 1$).   **Fig. 9.** MSE of $\overline{\mathbf{Q}}'$ versus c ($\varepsilon_2 = 1$).

a transition probability matrix ($|\mathcal{X}| \times |\mathcal{X}|$ martrix) common to all users from real trace data, and add the Laplace noise $\mathrm{Lap}(c/\varepsilon_2)$ to each element to provide ε_2-user-level DP. Then we randomly generate the first location based on a stationary distribution calculated from the transition matrix, and then generate the remaining locations using the transition matrix. Since this method is based on the transition probability matrix, we denote this method by TPM.

The third synthesizer is our proposed method. We denote it by Proposal. In Proposal, we trained p' from friendship data by adding the Laplace noise, and $\mathbf{Q}'$ from real trace data using the Laplace mechanism or Privelet. Then we generated θ co-locations using p' and $\mathbf{Q}'$. Finally, we generated the remaining locations using TPM.

In each location synthesizer, we set the length of a time instant to be one hour, and generated a trace with the length of one day for each of n users. For each synthesizer, we generated synthetic traces five times, and averaged the utility metrics over the five runs to stabilize the performance.

5.4   Experimental Results

Friendship Probability p'. Figure 7 shows the absolute error of p' when we changed the privacy budget ε_1 from 0.01 to 5.

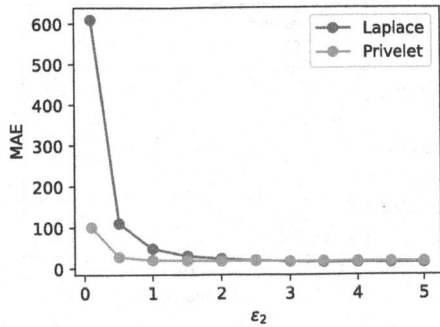

Fig. 10. MAE of $\overline{\mathbf{Q}}'$ versus ε_2 ($c = 5$).

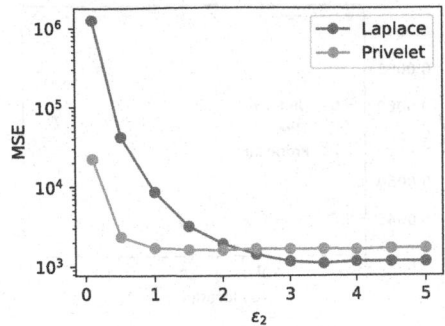

Fig. 11. MSE of $\overline{\mathbf{Q}}'$ versus ε_2 ($c = 5$).

Figure 7 shows that the absolute error rapidly decreases as ε_1 increases from 0.01 to 0.5. It also shows that the absolute error is very small and almost unchanged after $\varepsilon_1 = 0.5$, which means that we can accurately estimate the friendship probability p' with a small privacy budget $\varepsilon_1 = 0.5$ in node DP for friendship data.

Per-Category Co-location Count Matrix $\overline{\mathbf{Q}}'$. Figure 8 and Fig. 9 show the MAE/MSE of $\overline{\mathbf{Q}}'$. Here we set the privacy budget ε_2 in user-level DP for real trace data to $\varepsilon_2 = 1$, and the upper limit c on the number of locations per user in trimming to $c = 1$, 5, 10, 15, or 20.

Figure 8 and Fig. 9 show that Privelet achieves much smaller MAE and MSE than the Laplace mechanism, which means that Privelet significantly reduces the amount of noise for each POI category and each time instant (e.g., bars at night). These figures also show that when $c = 5$ and 10, Privelet achieves the smallest MAE and MSE, respectively. This indicates that there is a trade-off between the effect of trimming (which is large when c is small) and the Laplace noise (which is large when c is large).

Figure 10 and Fig. 11 show the relationship between ε_2 and MAE/MSE, where $c = 5$. We observe that the MAE and MSE rapidly decreases as ε_2 increases from 0.1 to 1, and that they remain almost unchanged after $\varepsilon_2 = 1$.

In Fig. 11, when ε_2 is 2.5 or more, the MSE of Privelet is larger than that of Laplace. One reason for this is that Privelet algorithm adds noise to each node of a tree structure and the number of targets for noise addition (i.e., the number of nodes) in Privelet is larger than the number of elements in $\mathbf{Q}$.

Other Statistical Features. Finally, we evaluated the relationship between the number θ of generated co-location events and the MAE/MSE of the population distribution and the transition matrix. Figure 12 and Fig. 13 show the MAE/MSE of the population distribution. Figure 14 and Fig. 15 show the MAE/MSE of the transition matrix. Here we set θ to $\theta = 1$, 5, 10, 50, 100, 500, 1000, or 5000.

Figure 12, Fig. 13, Fig. 14, and Fig. 15 show that when the number θ of generated co-location events is smaller than 1000, the proposed method (Proposal)

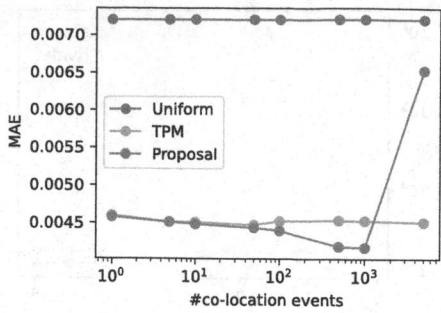

Fig. 12. MAE of the population distribution versus the number of co-location events ($\varepsilon_1 = \varepsilon_2 = 1$, $c = 5$).

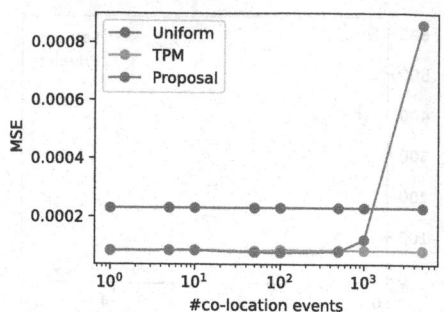

Fig. 13. MSE of the population distribution versus the number of co-location events ($\varepsilon_1 = \varepsilon_2 = 1$, $c = 5$).

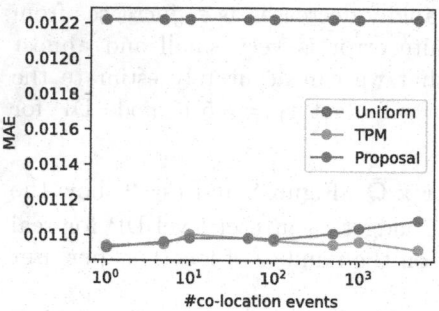

Fig. 14. MAE of the transition matrix versus the number of co-location events ($\varepsilon_1 = \varepsilon_2 = 1$, $c = 5$).

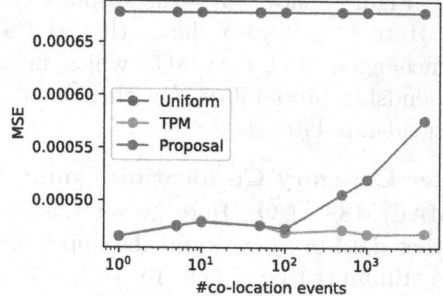

Fig. 15. MSE of the transition matrix versus the number of co-location events ($\varepsilon_1 = \varepsilon_2 = 1$, $c = 5$).

achieves much smaller MAE and MSE than the uniform synthesizer (Uniform), and almost the same MAE and MSE as the synthetic data generator in [22] (TPM). Note that TPM does not generate co-location events between friends, unlike Proposal. In other words, Proposal can generate co-location events between friends based on p' and $\mathbf{Q}'$ while keeping high utility in terms of other statistical features such as the population distribution and transition matrix.

However, when the number θ of co-location events increases from 1000, the MAE and MSE in Proposal become larger. This is because there are too many co-locations in the synthetic traces and the population distribution and transition matrix are not preserved well even if we complement the remaining locations using the Viterbi algorithm. Therefore, we should determine an appropriate value of θ in advance, either manually or automatically. One way to automatically set θ is to calculate the frequency of co-location events from real trace data while providing DP for the real trace data, and then set θ based on the co-location frequency. Exploring such automatic setting of θ is left for future work.

6 Conclusion

In this paper, we proposed a location synthesizer for synthesizing location traces including co-location events, which are important for synthetic traces to be more useful and realistic. Our proposed method generates synthetic traces using the friendship probability and the co-location count matrix, while providing node DP for friendship data and user-level DP for real trace data. We showed that our location synthesizer can generate synthetic traces that preserve the information about the friendship probability and co-location count matrix, as well as other statistical features such as the population distribution and transition matrix. We also showed that our location synthesizer provides node DP and user-level DP with reasonable privacy budgets (e.g., smaller than 1).

For future work, we plan to evaluate the utility of various location synthesizers [3–5] when they are used to complement locations other than co-locations using the Viterbi algorithm in our proposed method. Another line of future work is to automatically determine an appropriate value of θ (number of generated co-location events) while providing DP for the real trace data. It would also be interesting to incorporate the friendship level (numerical value rather than 0/1) between users into our algorithm, and to assess the accuracy of privacy attacks such as membership inference as a function of ε.

References

1. Zheng, Y., Zhang, L., Xie, X., et al.: Mining interesting locations and travel sequences from GPS trajectories. In: WWW 2009, pp. 791–800 (2009)
2. Lichman, M., Smyth, P.: Modeling human location data with mixtures of kernel densities. In: KDD 2014, pp. 35–44 (2014)
3. Bindschaedler, V., Shokri, R.: Synthesizing plausible privacy-preserving location traces. In: IEEE S&P 2016, pp. 546–563. IEEE (2016)
4. He, X., Cormode, G., Machanavajjhala, A., et al.: DPT: differentially private trajectory synthesis using hierarchical reference systems. PVLDB 8(11), 1154–1165 (2015)
5. Murakami, T., Hamada, K., Kawamoto, Y., et al.: Privacy-preserving multiple tensor factorization for synthesizing large-scale location traces. PoPETs **2021**(2), 5–26 (2021)
6. Song, L., Kotz, D., Jain, R., et al.: Evaluating next-cell predictors with extensive Wi-Fi mobility data. IEEE T-MC **5**(12), 1633–1649 (2006)
7. Iwata, T., Shimizu, H.: Neural collective graphical models for estimating spatio-temporal population flow from aggregated data. In: AAAI 2019, vol. 33, pp. 3935–3942 (2019)
8. PWS Cup 2019 (2019). https://www.iwsec.org/pws/2019/cup19_e.html
9. Yang, D., Qu, B., Yang, J., et al.: Revisiting user mobility and social relationships in LBSNs: a hypergraph embedding approach. In: WWW 2019, pp. 2147–2157 (2019)
10. Olteanu, A.M., Huguenin, K., Shokri, R., et al.: Quantifying interdependent privacy risks with location data. IEEE T-MC **16**(3), 829–842 (2016)

11. Olteanu, A.-M., Huguenin, K., Shokri, R., Hubaux, J.-P.: Quantifying the effect of co-location information on location privacy. In: De Cristofaro, E., Murdoch, S.J. (eds.) PETS 2014. LNCS, vol. 8555, pp. 184–203. Springer, Cham (2014). https://doi.org/10.1007/978-3-319-08506-7_10
12. Dwork, C., Roth, A.: The Algorithmic Foundations of Differential Privacy. Now Publishers (2014)
13. Olteanu, A.M., Humbert, M., Huguenin, K., et al.: The (co-)location sharing game. PoPETs **2019**(2), 5–25 (2019)
14. Murakami, T., Watanabe, H.: Localization attacks using matrix and tensor factorization. IEEE T-IFS **11**(8), 1647–1660 (2016)
15. Shokri, R., Stronati, M., Song, C., et al.: Membership inference attacks against machine learning models. In: S&P 2017, pp. 3–18 (2017)
16. Pyrgelis, A., Troncoso, C., De Cristofaro, E.: Knock knock, who's there? Membership inference on aggregate location data. In: NDSS (2018)
17. Dwork, C., McSherry, F., Nissim, K., Smith, A.: Calibrating noise to sensitivity in private data analysis. In: Halevi, S., Rabin, T. (eds.) TCC 2006. LNCS, vol. 3876, pp. 265–284. Springer, Heidelberg (2006). https://doi.org/10.1007/11681878_14
18. Sofya, R., Adam, S.: Differentially private analysis of graphs, pp. 543–547. Springer, Heidelberg (2016)
19. Ninghui, L., Min, L., Dong, S.: Differential Privacy: From Theory to Practice. Morgan & Claypool Publishers (2016)
20. Dwork, C., Naor, M., Pitassi, T., et al.: Differential privacy under continual observation. In: STOC 2010, pp. 715–724 (2010)
21. Fang, B.C.M., Wang, K., Chen, R., et al.: Privacy-preserving data publishing: a survey of recent developments. ACM Comput. Surv. (Csur) **42**(4), 1–53 (2010)
22. Bindschaedler, V., Shokri, R., Gunter, C.A.: Plausible deniability for privacy-preserving data synthesis. VLDB Endow. **10**(5) (2017)
23. Xiao, X., Wang, G., Gehrke, J.: Differential privacy via wavelet transforms. IEEE T-KDE **23**(8), 1200–1214 (2010)
24. FOURSQUARE DEVELOPERS. Venue categories—build with foursquare (2020). https://developer.foursquare.com/docs/build-with-foursquare/categories/. Accessed 25 Oct 2020
25. Liu, Z., Wang, Y.X., Smola, A.: Fast differentially private matrix factorization. In: RecSys 2015, pp. 171–178 (2015)
26. Barabási, A.L.: Network Science. Cambridge University Press, Cambridge (2016)

DPM Workshop: Policies and Regulation

Quantitative Rubric for Privacy Policy Analysis

Paul O'Donnell, Joe Harrison$^{(\boxtimes)}$, Joshua Lyons, Lauren Anderson,
Lauren Maunder, Sarah Ramboyong, and Alan J. Michaels[ID]

Hume Center for National Security and Technology, Virginia Polytechnic
Institute and State University, Blacksburg, USA
{paulod15,joeh24,josh13,land070,lmaunder,sarahrambo,ajm}@vt.edu

Abstract. Privacy Policies are hard to read and even harder to understand - this is a widely accepted fact that tends to discourage review by the average consumer. In this paper, we created and applied a quantitative privacy evaluation rubric to evaluate 10 distinct categories from the combined privacy policies (PP) and terms of service (ToS) from 188 companies in order to test whether those documents actually give an indication to the consumer as to their planned use and protections of personal information. This analysis was performed as part of a larger experiment aimed at tracing personal information propagation across the Internet, which has led to an independently collected baseline of personal information use and abuse, measured via email, text, and phone activity generated from one-time Internet transactions. We did not see any correlation between any metrics generated from either our privacy policy analysis or by the results from our fake identities. In our analysis of 177 company documents, as 11 companies did not have any policies, we confirm the length and difficulty in reading in reading policies and find that companies adhere to jurisdiction-based regulations in addition to finding weak industry-based trends in our scoring outputs. This paper uses quantitative privacy policy metrics as a start towards helping consumers know how their data will be used.

Keywords: Personal Identifiable Information (PII) · Privacy policy · Third party · Terms of service · Quantification · Flesch reading ease score

1 Introduction

Based on the sheer amount of spam that we receive, we are curious to see how our personal information, such as email, name, and/or other identifying information, ends up in the hands of spammers, scammers, and other third parties. In order to truly test this question, we created 300 fake identities, with identities provided to distinct popular companies via one-time online transactions to see if this information is shared and how it is used in general [24]. This personal information included ways for companies to reach us via email, text, and phone, offering

© Springer Nature Switzerland AG 2022
J. Garcia-Alfaro et al. (Eds.): DPM 2021/CBT 2021, LNCS 13140, pp. 39–54, 2022.
https://doi.org/10.1007/978-3-030-93944-1_3

them many ways to exploit our identities. We believed that by creating a virtual personally identifiable information (PII) honeypot, we would allow organizations to disperse of our information and share/sell this data to third-parties that ultimately increase traffic flow to our inboxes. This dataset comprises approximately 9 months of data collection to yield a real-world observation of personal information usage. Rather than exploring the specific collection mechanisms or raw use of the data, which is covered in [24], this paper seeks to detail the contents of PP and ToS utilizing a novel policy metric to judge company practices. In conjunction with this policy metric, we also analyzed the readability strength of the studied PPs (through a variety of metrics, though primarily through the Flesch score) to identify further relationships with the observed data. We also explored trends by company category to observe if certain categories of companies posed a stronger threat to our information security.

2   Background and Approach

Privacy is a complicated subject. There are many variables at play, from contract-based affiliates, to risk management, to liability. The impact on consumers is of particular interest to us, with a broad interest in the proper use and inproper abuse of our personal information. In terms of *abuse*, we include both sharing and excessive use. This goal leads to two specific questions: (1) how do we become informed of a company's stated and actual approach to using personal information? and (2) can we set our expectations of how the company will *actually* use our information on the published privacy policies?

As consumers, we are notified what happens with our data through a company's privacy policy. Unfortunately, privacy policies in the modern era are impractical for most consumers to read. Several studies found that consumers need around 15 years of education to comprehend the average privacy policy, (where the average reading level of the population is at the eighth grade level) [7,21], but even then, 96% of the people still missed blatant red flags in privacy policies, such as the selling of their "first born child" [26]. Another study showed that the net loss of time, if users read all their affiliated privacy policies, would cost a nation 781 billion dollars [22]. Further studies showed that even experts on legal policy law may have difficulty deciphering these privacy policies [11,20]. One of the more notable attempts to fix this problem was the creation of P3P (the Platform for Privacy Preferences [2]). This was a browser addon intended to analyze privacy policies through the parsing of natural language to inform the user of pertinent information. However, P3P disbanded in 2003, due to insufficient browser capabilities. More recently, Kelley et al. proposed the idea that companies should summarize their privacy policies in a standardized nutritional table [17]. While a useful idea, this has not been broadly adopted. In this paper, we attempt to create a similar evaluation of privacy policies, measuring 10 distinct dimensions of information sharing.

Then in 2013, Wilson created a corpus of privacy policies with annotations from experts [35]. This dataset allowed for models to be created and then reviewed internally by the software. From this dataset, several external studies have used this model to train different sets of artifical intelligence algorithms. Some notable examples include Zimmeck's work on analyzing policies of apps on the app store [37], and *Polisis*, a neural network that attempts to answer questions about PPs [15]. Specifically, Zimmeck's paper [37] looks at one million software applications. There is no systematic enforcement on the app store, and, as such, applications have differing degrees of compliance with encouragement to publish their data sharing behaviors. Notably, 50% of apps do not offer a PP, and of those that do, 10% have overt policies enabling access to user location when not contributing to the core goal of the application. The tool developed by Harkous, *Polisis* [15], uses an implementation in a chat-bot called "Pribot," which can be queried to answer questions about PPs. Their tool, then, hypothetically provides answers to specific questions that a user may have. *Polisis* was not used in our analysis of PPs, as it did not offer the functionality that we were seeking. Both *Polisis* and Zimmeck's work [37] each provide different categories with which a PP should be concerned. Other works include *PrivOnto* [28], a framework for answering questions about PPs; Sathyendra [32], which looks at choices in PPs; and *Terms of Service Didn't read* [4], which is a crowd-sourced effort to highlight and evaluate sections in privacy policies. *PrivOnto* does a very similar task to *Polisis*, with differences as to implementation. Sathyendara [32] attempts to automatically identify choices within PPs. They also use distinct expert-defined categories to help train their algorithm and refine its output, by focusing on specific important issues. Our work is similar, as well, to Cranor [11], which analyzes the PPs of 75 online tracking companies and compares them against regulatory guidelines.

On the quantitative side, there also has been a fair amount of analysis. Notable studies include works from Anton [5], Fabian [13], and from Massey [21]. Anton examined 40 financial PPs, and found that some college-level education was required to understand an average PP. Anton separated each document (e.g., ToS and PP), ran the Flesch score on each one individually, and then averaged the scores of the documents without accounting for the word count in each of the documents. Our analysis combines the ToS and PP together to account for the entire agreement. Fabian ran a quantitative analysis on 50,000 PPs, affirming the difficulty of reading and drew comparisons across different metrics, including Flesch reading ease score, Flesch-Kincaid reading ease score, Simple Measure of Goobledygook (SMoG) [23], as well as seven other metrics. Massey analyzed over 2000 policy documents, gathered from Google's top-1000 websites, from the Fortune-500 companies, and from medical companies. They found small variation based upon which group they evaluated, though they confirmed that these documents are difficult to read.

In addition to the various readability studies, there have been studies on word count, as well as on keywords. McDonald and Crannor [22] calculated a median word count of 2,514 words per PP, based upon AOL's 75 most visited websites. Common Sense Education found an average 4,225 words for 1,700 Edtech companies for both ToS and PPs [10]. Milne evaluated 483 privacy policies from a list of the most frequently visited websites, and compared their results from their prior analysis in 2001 and 2003. They found that the grade level of the policies had risen from an average Flesch grade level of 11.2 to 12.1 [25]. Kaur reviewed 2000 policy documents, collected by Massey [21], and performed a large keyword analysis [16]. They found differences by country and company, as well as a list of the most common ambiguous words and keywords.

This paper attempts to define an initial quantitative metric to rate personal information sharing behaviors based upon published PPs and ToS. We also evaluate the quantitative results from those same documents. Note that we did not consider the technical aspects of privacy for each company. In addition, there are multiple perspectives on how to judge and quantify privacy, as seen in works by Wagner [33,34], so our outputs represent only one perspecive on a company's approach to privacy.

3   Privacy Policy Model and Experimental Design

Privacy policies consist of a multitude of sections and features. Basic structure for many policies consists of sections declaring what information they collect, how they collect or protect this information, what you can do to change or request this information, and finally some choices in contact method if any issues should arise. An extensive amount of similarities are found in policies of different company categories [29]. For example, every policy category in Reddit is similarly shared in the policy of Apple and Bed Bath and Beyond [6,9,31]. This is mostly due to legal requirements to mention and inform the consumer about the stated legal rights of every individual, with templates assumed to be provided by the host organization. Examples of these sections include what information they collect, how they distribute that information to 3rd parties, and how they intend to retain this information [37].

Selecting companies for our analysis was performed loosely on a popularity basis. Companies that had the most web traffic were selected for multiple accounts to test if they selectively used information by demographics. Additionally, both political and international accounts were chosen based on popularity and relevance to current political climate, specifically aiming to measure behaviors associated with the 2020 U.S. presidential election. It is also worthwhile to note that companies were selected in tandem with our online information tracking engine, with restrictions in place to prevent collection of explicit content or undertake any type of potentially illegal action (e.g., banking or anonymous political donations) or violation to campus policies (e.g., use of dark web resources) during our one-time interactions; these restrictions led to a relatively conservative grouping of organizations that were anticipated to follow laws, cultural norms, and published policies. Once selected, we began by dividing the 188 companies chosen for our research across four people, with two people independently scoring each company's PP and ToS. Further, certain companies included a separate web browsing cookie policy, which was also included in this analysis if located.

Score	Changing Terms	Holding Service Harmless	Ignores Do Not Track (DNT) Devices	Personal Identifiable Information (PII) used for Ads	Release of information to third parties
1	Change privacy policy with changes applicable retroactively	User must defend the service against any claims/costs/liabilities if any lawsuit arises	Does not acknowledge or mention DNT signals	The service internally collects any available information of the user to sell and/or create targeted ads.	The service consistently sells/distributes PII to associated third parties for any purpose, including undefined "business purposes."
2	Change privacy policy without notification, but changes are forward-looking.	User is responsible for defending the service in cases where the user violated the company's privacy policy.	Complete recognition of these signals and denies the user the right to the website and/or continues to track the user without notification.	Collects a significant amount of PII (i.e., address, contacts, and site browsing activity). Does not collect all available PII but more than as specified in Category 3	The service collects and sends PII to third parties for them to sell advertisements or for defined "business purposes."
3	Claims to give notice but provides vague distribution details	User is responsible for defending the service in cases where the user violated others' rights/broke the law, not from policy violation	Acknowledges DNT signals and continues to track only due to lack of infrastructure to support these settings/lack of standard	Collects a 'normal' amount of PII, including name, email address, log data, general location data ascertained from IP address, etc.	The service only releases information to third parties if the user requests a service/ more information from the initial website
4	Clear notification of changes in the privacy policy	User is responsible for defending the service in cases where the user violated others; however, the service could remain accountable if they played any role in the digression	Acknowledges DNT signals and complies; however, the service does not allow full access to all of the present features	Service provides a menu to disable all but necessary cookies and collects a normal/less than normal amount of PII as defined above	The service releases PII only with previous consent from the user to show the user more relevant content
5	User permitted to opt-out of privacy policy changes/ allows for extensive copies of previous policies to ensure changes.	Service assumes the risk and takes liability away from the user if a lawsuit arises.	Service complies with DNT signals and allows the user access to the full features of the service.	Minimal to no PII is collected or used for internal targeted products or services. The user still has access to the full features of the product.	The service releases little to no information to third parties regardless of user consent and maintains internal consistency with the user's PII.

Score	Signing away moral rights	Retention of Personal Data	Deletion of PII upon request	Information being sold due to Bankruptcy	Puts sole risk on users for liabilities
1	A complete dismissal of these rights and liability of suit when the user agrees to a particular privacy policy	Full retention of all data indefinitely after a user deactivates their account	The service does not offer such a feature or continues to retain information despite a request from the user	The company/service will sell and contribute all stored customer data as the result of being bought out or merging with another company	Puts total risk on the user for any liabilities, and the service as mentioned above is not held accountable
2	The user obtains some say over their content; however, the particular service maintains most of the control	Service holds information for as long as they deem necessary/after a predefined extended period of time longer than a year	User is unable to request or delete any information; however, the service will allow less information to be collected	User is notified of acquisition; however, no action can be taken by the user to limit data being transferred	User maintains soles risk on every aspect of the site; however, service can be held liable to distribute cash compensation up to twenty dollars or in extreme cases
3	Rights are waived; however, the privacy policy places some liability on the company, and users maintain almost equal control	Service temporarily holds a reduced quantity of information or retains PII in case of potential reactivation	A user is able to request their information; however, they are unable to delete any information or request to delete is not honored	In merger or asset sales, data is sent to receiving company under the pretense of equivalent or improved privacy standards	The user and the service are mutually responsible. The service uses good faith to ensure data security and information accuracy. Will not claim responsibility for negligence
4	Waiving moral rights is optional; however, the service still has the final say over user content on the service	Information is stored after deletion of account only to comply with applicable regulations. A scheduled deletion is still in place with no intention of prolonged storage	A user is able to request to delete all their information; however, they may not be able to delete most of their information only some	User is notified that their data is forfeit due to bankruptcy/merger; however, they may only be able to delete certain aspects of their PII. Some will be transferred over to the acquisition company	Data breaches caused by the user are not protected; however, if the service experiences a breach in their databases or any other circumstance, the user is not held liable. User is protected on service negligence

Fig. 1. Quantitative privacy policy evaluation rubric

To score a company's PP and ToS, each reviewer manually sifted through those documents for the phrases and words corresponding to each of the categories in the quantitative privacy rubric. Specific keywords and phrases indicated the company in question's policy regarding each section of the rubric. By reading through documents in this manner, we ranked companies according to ten distinct categories on a 5-point scale. To analyze all 188 companies' records in a manner that accounted for natural variance in scoring between reviewers, permuted pairwise combinations of the four reviewers was employed to normalize review practices. All policies were scored by each assigned reviewer in parallel; then, at a later date, the two reviewers compared scores, and any score pairs that differed between reviewers were discussed and resolved into a single finalized score for each category (Fig. 1).

When scoring the policies, the reviewers linked an offline copy of the most current PP and ToS for each company; this allowed for a consistent, referenceable document that can be checked in the future as updates occur. This became even more important with the addition of our quantitative metrics such as word count, reading score, a measure of vagueness, and other assessments [1]. If a company had both their PP and ToS in one document, they were marked as having both.

3.1   General Assumptions

In our manual process of reviewing PPs and ToS, we worked diligently to find the pertinent information. However, because of the complicated nature of these documents, a few assumptions were made to simplify, which required some subjective intervention discussed in this section. We note, however, that it is possible that this was a human-driven process, so some chance exists for missed sections errors. The core assumptions to our methodology included:

- For foreign policies, we assumed that Google Chrome's translate function preserved enough language to proceed with the standard analysis.
- Reviewers also searched for synonymous documents at each company, such as "User Agreements" and "Legal Notice", to fill in any missing data
- The rubric's focus is weighted towards the protections explicitly afforded to the user. Thus, if debating between two scores, with doubt existing in the company's stance, the reviewers typically chose the lower score.
- Although PPs change over time, we analyzed the data collected over the past year (email, phone, text) and compared to a May 2021 snapshot.
- In rare cases, the rubric did not fit specific edge cases, such as when a company notified the consumer only on their website, so we chose a score that was of the same perceived effect,
- Privacy scores were based according to the user's interaction with the site through a standard computer, ignoring clauses pertaining to mobile apps.
- Policy addendums for only a specific state or country (e.g., CA) were ignored, as these did not apply to a vast majority of site users.
- Each of the 10 dimensions in the policy scoring rubric were equally weighted; i.e., the policy scored is derived from a 0–10 weight of each of 10 categories, leading to an aggregate score from 0–100.

3.2   Section-Specific Assumptions

In our rating of the policies, we focused on ten different distinct categories; some categories had unusual trends that were not originally accounted for in the planned process. Subjective intervention was required to seemlessly navigate the diverse nature of these policies. Collectively, our research team agreed on specific assumptions for each category and compiled this information for further review. The following bulleted list has been added for transparency and increased insight into the qualititave analysis procedures.

- Changing Terms
  - Notification on the website through a banner or pop-up was merited a score of 2 as being insufficient to catch the attention of most users.
- Holding Service Harmless
  - The phrase "Indemnify... based on the use of these services" was as far-reaching as possible, as it covers all user activity on the site.
  - If a company did not use the phrase "indemnify" on their policy, the ToS document was reviewed to attempt locating its liability clause.
- Ignores Do Not Track (DNT)
  - If a company did not mention DNT signals, it was assumed that the company does not honor them.
  - If a company mentioned *Do Not Track* and stated that "since there is no unified standard, we do not change our operations," this was rated more highly than if they said they do not comply.
- PII Used for Ads
  - Precise geolocation data was generally taken to imply that the company collects "any and all information for advertisements".
  - A policy was rated higher if the site had an option (for their specific website, not for a user's web browser) to gather only necessary cookies.
  - Websites that provided a popup or menu to disable unnecessary cookies were rated higher than those that relied on browser settings.
- Release of Information to Third Parties
  - Transfer of PII for "necessary business purposes" could refer to the sale of user data for profit. Thus, companies could foreseeably release users' PII to third parties if that clause was in place unless otherwise defined.
- Signing Away Moral Rights
  - Clauses such as: "by uploading, distributing, transmitting or otherwise using Your Content with the Service, you grant to us a perpetual, nonexclusive, transferable, royalty-free, sublicensable, and worldwide license to use, host, reproduce, modify, adapt, publish, translate, create derivative works from, distribute, perform, and display Your Content in connection with operating and providing the Service", [12], was deemed equivalent to signing away moral rights.
  - Moral rights are a subset of Intellectual Property (IP), so a company can state that the customer retains their IP, yet waive moral rights [19].
- Retention of Personal Data
  - Clauses such as "as long as necessary for the use according to this policy" were not specific enough for a high score in this category, yet were scored more highly than the absence of any explicit retention statements.
- Deletion of PII Upon Request
  - Clauses such as "the right to request to delete" was up to the company to follow through upon, and may or may not be honored. Therefore, this clause has been scored lower if absent explanation or specification for how the company would allow a user to delete information.

– Information Sold due to Bankruptcy
  • Guidance provided for business mergers, transfers, and acquisitions were equivalent to bankruptcy, even if *bankruptcy* was not explicitly mentioned.
– Puts Sole Risk on Users for Breach of PII
  • If a limitation of liability was present within the liability section of company's ToS, we extrapolated these statements to PII breaches.

3.3   Example Implementation of the Rubric

To provide a concrete example of our application of the quantitative privacy rubric, we share an exemplary analysis for Facebook [14] in Table 1. This analysis breaks down each category with a detailed explanation on why Facebook received its score and highlights the general process. Extending that analysis further to other companies, we cast each category onto a 0 through 10 scale in a linear fashion, such that rubric evaluations from categories $\{1, 2, 3, 4, 5\}$ mapped to scores of $\{0, 2.5, 5, 7.5, 10\}$. As such, each of the ten categories yielded a *score* from 0 to 10, leading to an aggregat policy score from 0 to 100. In Facebook's case, the scores of $\{3, 4, 0, 1, 1, 1, 2, 1, 1, 1\}$, map to scores of $\{5, 7.5, X, 0, 0, 0, 2.5, 0, 0, 0\}$. In addition to this affine transformation, we also tried custom weightings, as some of the distances between levels felt larger than others (e.g. the distance between level 1 and level 2 in the category "Changing Terms" feels much more severe than between level 1 and level 2 in the category "Deletion of PII upon request"), however, these custom fits did not lend significantly better fits.

4   Analysis

In our analysis of the company documents, we carefully considered both qualitative and quantitative perspectives. Our analysis included numerous evaluation metrics to highlight any significant privacy concerns for the consumer.

4.1   Qualitative Results

After grading the policies for 177/188 companies, as there were 11 companies that did not have a PPs or ToS, we found that the distribution was approximately normal, with a mean of 39.8. This distribution of aggregate privacy scores are shown in Fig. 2.

These scores were weighted by category in order to best fit our rubric to the observed data. The company with the highest score, as per our rubric, was PesaPal with a score of 68, while at the bottom end of our spectrum, Green Peace received a score of 16.

Table 1. Example implementaion of privacy policy rubric leading to an aggregate privacy score

Category	Score	Reasoning
Changing terms	3	Facebook received a score of 3, because their policy states, "We'll notify you before we make changes to this policy and give you the opportunity to review the revised policy" This statement provides the consumer with notice
Holding service harmless	4	Facebook received a score of 4, because even after the deletion or disabling of the users account, the liability terms of are heavily in favor of Facebook, "Accordingly, our liability shall be limited to the fullest extent permitted by applicable law, and under no circumstance will we be liable to you for any lost profits, ... or incidental damages arising out of or related to these Terms"
Ignores DNT	0	Assigned a score of 0, as it did not even acknowledge *Do Not Track* signals.
PII used for ads	1	Facebook received a score of 1, because they collect any and all information about the customer for use in advertisement
Release of PII	1	Facebook received a score of 1, because it distributes a significant amount of PII to third parties, including advertisers. "Information is shared with the following third parties: Partners who use our analytics services, Advertisers, Measurement partners, Partners offering goods and services in our Products, vendors and service providers, Researchers and academics"
Moral rights	1	Facebook received a score of 1, because they state "you grant us a non-exclusive, transferable, sub-licensable, royalty-free, and worldwide license to host, use, distribute, modify, run, copy, publicly perform or display, translate, and create derivative works of your content"
Retention of PII	2	A score of 2, because it stores user data for a period justified by Facebook.
Deletion of PII	1	A score of 1; while they do offer the ability to delete information, they state "content you delete may continue to appear if you have shared it with others and they have not deleted it"
Bankruptcy	1	Facebook received a score of 1, because PII is sold during business transfer. "If the ownership or control of all or part of our Products or their assets changes, we may transfer your information to the new owner"
Breach of PII	1	A score of 1, because a majority of the liability is placed on the consumer; however, Facebook can be taken to court in California if law provisions provide. "For any claim ... that arises out of or relates to these Terms or the Facebook Products ("claim"), you agree that it will be resolved exclusively in the U.S. District Court for the Northern District of California ......Our Products, however, are provided "as is", and we make no guarantees that they always will be safe, secure, or error-free"

Policy Correlation with Company Results. While almost every company had a privacy policy, we found very little evidence of traceable sharing outside the companies themselves. Of the 188 companies that we signed up to, we only received third party emails from 9 of the companies. This result makes it difficult to determine any trends in policies between companies that did share information versus those that we cannot detect/did not share our information. Of the 9

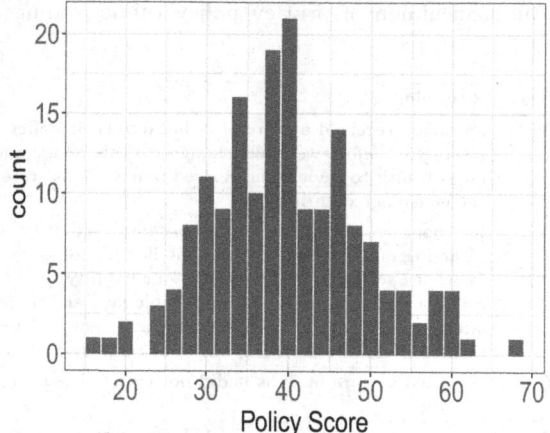

Fig. 2. Aggregate scores of policy distribution

companies that did share our information, 2 of them did not have documents, namely FreeMovies and Communist Party USA. Of the remaining 7 companies that did have documents, we recorded a score of 38.6, which is only slightly lower than the average score of 40, especially given a standard deviation of 9.36. Of the 7 companies that shared information and had privacy documents, we also observed no trends via category in the rubric.

Score by Industry. We sorted companies by their respective industries, attempting to match stock market index categories. Companies were placed into 11 categories, including cyclical, defensive, industrials, and technology companies. Political organizations and politically-aligned special interest groups were separated into their own group. Once all the companies were sorted and scored, averages were taken by industry from the re-weighted scores compared across all industries. As seen in Fig. 3, the average of the scores for the political organizations (32.4) was markedly lower than the general policy average (39.8). Only 3/16 political sites were above the overall average.

4.2 Evaluation of Our Metric

After review of 177 PPs and ToS, we found that our metric worked well in some areas, but did not segregate evenly in other areas. Both the categories "PII used for Ads", and "Release of Information to Third Parties" had a roughly uniform distribution, which would be indicative of an ideal separation. Other categories displayed in Fig. 4 had less obvious separations. In "Deletion of PII", we found that many companies stated that they held the information only for "as long as necessary for the purposes described", which according to our rubric was sufficient to garner a 4. Another trend of note is that both "Information Sold due to Bankruptcy" and "Signing Away Moral Rights" had substantially

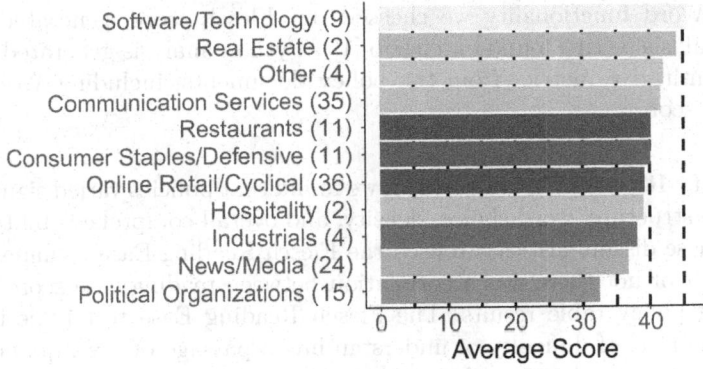

Fig. 3. Policy score by industry

less variation; this is because most companies' documents explicitly stated that (1) user PII could be sold in the event of a merger or acquisition and (2) that the company in question has the right to use, modify, adapt, publish, and sell user-generated content (i.e., posts or reviews). Interestingly, the "Ignores DNT Devices" section was conspicuous, not because of the scores companies earned in that category, but because of the large number of policies that did not mention DNT devices at all.

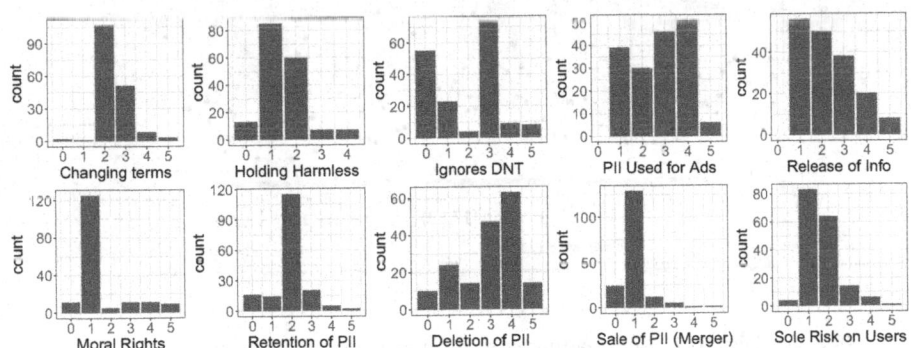

Fig. 4. Distribution of policy score

4.3   Quantitative Results

In addition to our qualitative metric, we also used a combination of Python analysis and Word analysis to generate quantitative results. Using Word, specifically through additional functionality in the check grammer options, we generated counts of vagueness, passive voice, and wordiness. Additionally, utilizing the same Word functionality we checked our Flesch score, generated by our Python analysis (script found on github [1]). Python analysis generated the rest of the quantitative metrics from the policy documents, including Word count and Flesch score.

Readability Results. In our research we found that policies varied significantly in sentence structure, word choice, density, and overall comprehensibility [8]. To quantify these dissimilarities, we used the Flesch Reading Ease formulas [18] to test whether or not there was a correlation between reading ease score and the quantifying policy table results. The Flesch Reading Ease test is designed to measure the level of difficulty of understanding a passage of text, quantified by a score between 1 and 100, with 100 being the highest reading score (easiest to read and comprehend). These are displayed in Fig. 5.

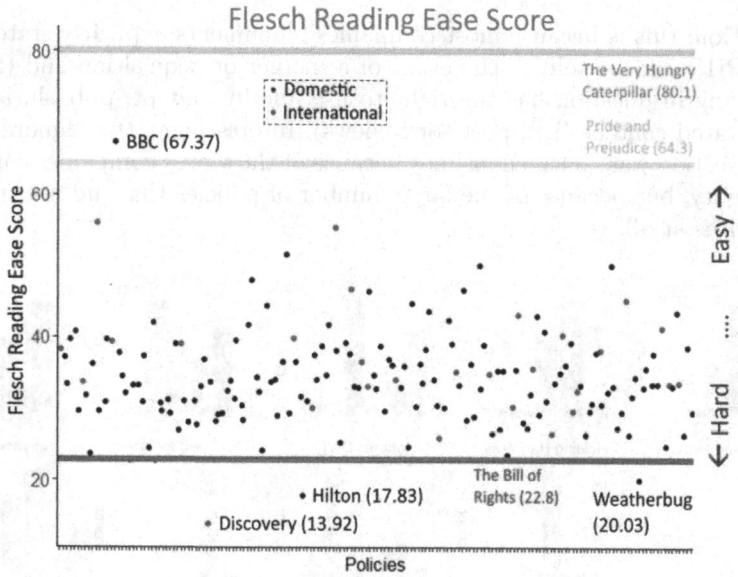

Fig. 5. Flesch reading ease for 177 companies' policies

All of the PPs analyzed scored within an average range of 35, with the highest score being 67.37 from the BBC[1] and the lowest being 13.92 from Discovery. The average reading-ease score of all of the policies that we analyzed was 30.57. For reference, the children's book *The Very Hungry Caterpillar* has a reading-ease score of 80.1, and the most challenging novel in the Harry Potter series has a score of 64.3; the United States Bill of Rights has a reading ease score of 22.8.

---

[1] We recorded a subjective score on how easy each privacy policy was to read, and BBC was in the bottom five policies to read, due to the sheer number of links that made it difficult to find information.

A score between 30 to 50 is deemed challenging to read, but understood by college graduates. In contrast, a score between 0 to 30 is considered very difficult to read, and best understandable by university graduates. Seeing that the average reading-ease score was 30.57, which translates to a Flesch-Kincaid grade level [18] of 16, we quantitatively re-affirm that PPs are difficult to read. Based on 5-years of data collected annually, the U.S. Census Bureau estimates that 32.1% of persons above age 25 have obtained a Bachelor's degree or higher [3]. This means that just under a third of the population, ages 25 years and up, is expected to truly understand these policies (Fig. 6).

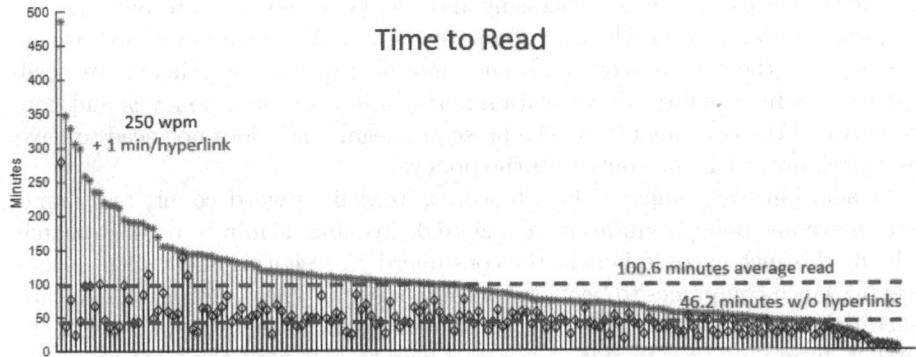

Fig. 6. Estimated time to read an average PP and ToS

Time to Read Policies. We found that the average policy took 46.2 min to read, presuming a reading speed of 250 words per minute, though including an estimated extra minute per hyperlink (many are internal pointers, though others link to external materials) brings that closer to 100 min. We found an average word length of 11,555 per company, which is substantially higher than the 4,225 words for education companies [10], or the 2,514 for the privacy policy given by McDonald [22]. There was a clear outlier to read Indeed's, however, this is because they list terms for all of their different programs in the same document. Many companies have terms and conditions for specific programs, such as a loyalty program, which were not included in our analysis. G2A, for example, has a 3,753-word PP, and a 32,953-word ToS. Our estimate of time to read these documents is likely not reflective of what the consumer must read in order to start using the services; it is also possible that policies have grown in length in an attempt to minimize lawsuits.

Ultimately, we found virtually no correlation between our policy score and either the Flesch Reading Ease Score or word count. This suggests that reading-ease scores are a greater reflection of the author rather than the contents of the policy itself. Furthermore, the writing style, verbiage, and density of the policies do not positively or negatively affect the quantifying policy table rubric. Proctor also noted no correlation between word count and Flesch-Kincaid score [30].

5   Conclusion

Our data is being used. Data breaches happen numerous times a year, as shown by recent compromises [27, 36]. More nefarious, however, is the constant leakage of our data that we compulsively "agree" to in a company's PP. In an attempt to correlate privacy policy and data sharing from the company, we analyzed 177 companies' policies. To do this, we developed a quantitative privacy policy rubric that clarifies the privacy concerns present in these policies. While there were limited correlations, we hope this rubric could help prompt standardized comparisons between different PP quantifications. Other studies in this field use methods of natural language processing and there does not seem to be generally accepted standards from which to compare results. While we found no correlation between the Flesch score and our quantification of the policies, we posit that there is in actuality no correlation between how dense a policy is and how protective of the consumer it is. The prose of a legal team does not need to have any correlation with the content of the policy.

In addition, we compared Flesch scores, as well as word count, and found that an average policy requires an associate degree and 46 min to read. Research utilizing this metric could benefit the consumer by presenting them with a score to know which companies to be most concerned about. These metrics were established to be a referenced baseline for which future policy research can build upon. Further, future analysis in this sector may help to enlighten the legal grey area that remains concerning consumer privacy. We are working to further validate our metric, and to build a more comprehensive approach. A larger-scale experiment aimed at evaluating thousands of organizations is ongoing with efforts to partially automate the manual policy evaluation process described in this paper.

References

1. https://www.github.com/humeESL/Use-and-Abuse-PII/
2. Platform for privacy preferences (P3P) project. https://www.w3.org/P3P/
3. U.S. Census Bureau QuickFacts. https://www.census.gov/quickfacts/
4. Terms of Service; Didn't Read (2020). https://tosdr.org/
5. Anton, A., Earp, J., He, Q., Stufflebeam, W., Bolchini, D., Jensen, C.: Financial privacy policies and the need for standardization. IEEE Secur. Priv. 2(2), 36–45 (2004). https://doi.org/10.1109/MSECP.2004.1281243
6. Apple: Privacy policy (2019). https://www.apple.com/legal/privacy/en-ww/
7. Banerjee, M., Karimi Adl, R., Wu, L., Barker, K.: Quantifying privacy violations. In: Jonker, W., Petković, M. (eds.) SDM 2011. LNCS, vol. 6933, pp. 1–17. Springer, Heidelberg (2011). https://doi.org/10.1007/978-3-642-23556-6_1
8. BBC: BBC news (2018). https://www.bbc.com/news
9. Bed Bath and Beyond: Privacy policy (2021). https://www.bedbathandbeyond.com/store/static/PrivacyPolicy
10. Commonsense.org: It's not you, privacy policies are difficult to read (2020). https://www.commonsense.org/education/articles/its-not-you-privacy-policies-are-difficult-to-read

11. Cranor, L.F., Hoke, C., Leon, P., Au, A.: Are they worth reading? An in-depth analysis of online advertising companiess privacy policies. SSRN Electron. J. (2014). https://doi.org/10.2139/ssrn.2418590
12. Discord: Terms of Service (2018). https://discord.com/terms
13. Fabian, B., Ermakova, T., Lentz, T.: Large-scale readability analysis of privacy policies. In: Proceedings of the International Conference on Web Intelligence, WI 2017, pp. 18–25. ACM (2017)
14. Facebook: Facebook data policy. https://www.facebook.com/about/privacy
15. Harkous, H. et al.: Polisis: automated analysis and presentation of privacy policies using deep learning. In: 27th {USENIX} Security Symposium, pp. 531–548 (2018)
16. Kaur, J., Dara, R.A., Obimbo, C., Song, F., Menard, K.: A comprehensive keyword analysis of online privacy policies. Inf. Secur. J.: Glob. Perspect. $\mathbf{27}$(5–6), 260–275 (2018)
17. Kelley, P.G., Cesca, L., Bresee, J., Cranor, L.F.: Standardizing privacy notices: An online study of the nutrition label approach. In: Proceedings of the SIGCHI Conference on Human Factors in Computing Systems, CHI 2010, pp. 1573–1582. Association for Computing Machinery, New York (2010). https://doi.org/10.1145/1753326.1753561
18. Kincaid, J.P., Fishburne Jr, R.P., Rogers, R.L., Chissom, B.S.: Derivation of new readability formulas for Navy enlisted personnel. Technical report (1975)
19. Lee, B.A.: Making sense of moral rights in intellectual property. Temp. L. Rev. $\mathbf{84}$, 71 (2011)
20. Litmannavarro, K.: We read 150 privacy policies. They were an incomprehensible disaster (2006). https://www.nytimes.com/interactive/2019/06/12/opinion/facebook-google-privacy-policies.html. Accessed June 2019
21. Massey, A.K., Eisenstein, J., Anton, A.I., Swire, P.P.: Automated text mining for requirements analysis of policy documents. In: 2013 21st IEEE International Requirements Engineering Conference (2013)
22. McDonald, A.M., Cranor, L.F.: The cost of reading privacy policies. Isjlp $\mathbf{4}$, 543 (2008)
23. Mclaughlin, G.: Smog grading - a new readability formula. J. Read. $\mathbf{12}$, 639–646 (1969)
24. Michaels, A., George, K.: Use & abuse of personal information. Blackhat, USA (2021)
25. Milne, G.R., Culnan, M.J., Greene, H.: A longitudinal assessment of online privacy notice readability. J. Public Policy Mark. $\mathbf{25}$(2), 238–249 (2006)
26. Obar, J.A., Oeldorf-Hirsch, A.: The biggest lie on the internet: ignoring the privacy policies and terms of service policies of social networking services. Inf. Commun. Soc. $\mathbf{23}$(1), 128–147 (2020)
27. OFlaherty, K.: Facebook data breach: here's what to do now (2021)
28. Oltramari, A., et al.: PrivOnto: a semantic framework for the analysis of privacy policies. Semant. Web $\mathbf{9}$(2), 185–203 (2018)
29. Pollach, I.: What's wrong with online privacy policies? Commun. ACM $\mathbf{50}$(9), 103–108 (2007)
30. Proctor, R., Ali, A., Vu, K.P.: Examining usability of web privacy policies. Int. J. Hum. Comput. Interact. $\mathbf{24}$, 307–328 (2008). https://doi.org/10.1080/10447310801937999
31. Reddit: Reddit user agreement (2021). https://www.redditinc.com/policies/user-agreement
32. Sathyendra, K., et al.: Identifying the provision of choices in privacy policy text. In: Proceedings of the 2017 Conference on Empirical Methods in NLP (2017)

33. Wagner, I., Boiten, E.: Privacy risk assessment: from art to science, by metrics. In: Garcia-Alfaro, J., Herrera-Joancomartí, J., Livraga, G., Rios, R. (eds.) DPM/CBT -2018. LNCS, vol. 11025, pp. 225–241. Springer, Cham (2018). https://doi.org/10. 1007/978-3-030-00305-0_17

34. Wagner, I., Eckhoff, D.: Technical privacy metrics. ACM Comput. Surv. **51**(3), 1–38 (2018). https://doi.org/10.1145/3168389

35. Wilson, S. et al.: The creation and analysis of a website privacy policy corpus. In: Proceedings of the 54th Annual Meeting of the Association for Computational Linguistics (Volume 1: Long Papers), pp. 1330–1340 (2016)

36. Winder, D.: Microsoft security shocker as 250 million customer records exposed online (2020)

37. Zimmeck, S., et al.: MAPS: scaling privacy compliance analysis to a million apps. Proc. Priv. Enhanc. Technol. **2019**(3), 66–86 (2019)

Rethinking the Limits of Mobile Operating System Permissions

Brian Krupp[✉]

Baldwin Wallace University, Berea, OH 44286, USA
bkrupp@bw.edu
https://mops.bw.edu/~bkrupp

Abstract. Since the introduction of the iPhone in 2007, smartphones continue to have a more disruptive role in our society. The average person spends over five hours per day using their device and research has shown intentional addictive design elements in popular applications to maximize user interaction time. While smartphones have provided new capabilities that did not exist previously, it has also allowed the limitless collection of personal data that is both sensed, inferred, and stored on the device. With millions of applications available in both the App Store and Google Play, research has shown mobile applications frequently abuse granted permissions and are not truthful in permission requests. Given a coarse-grained permission model, applications can retrieve and transmit data as frequent as possible without limit, and send data to any service without the user being aware. Only recently did mobile operating system producers start to introduce more fine grained controls. In this paper, we examine the evolution of these controls since the widespread adoption of smartphones and examine the current trends. We describe research that has provided both an improved awareness of privacy and supplemental controls for users. We also describe the shortcomings of these solutions and provide suggestions to the current permission model to limit the amount of data that can be accessed and transmitted from the device. Given the data that is available from mobile devices, it is imperative that users have more transparency in how mobile applications use their data, and that users are able to place limits on this use.

Keywords: Mobile · Privacy · Security

1 Introduction

Google and Apple dominate the smartphone market with 84.8% and 15.2% of the market share respectively [20]. These two companies determine the permissions that are available to protect personal data and limit tracking. However, these permissions have proven to be ineffective where location data is misused at large scale [8], data is shared with social networks without a user's consent [3], and practices established by these companies are violated [4]. With users spending on average more than five hours a day on their devices [9], applications are able

© Springer Nature Switzerland AG 2022
J. Garcia-Alfaro et al. (Eds.): DPM 2021/CBT 2021, LNCS 13140, pp. 55–69, 2022.
https://doi.org/10.1007/978-3-030-93944-1_4

to constantly gather and share data. Additionally, the design of applications
have been intentionally created to maximize user engagement by implementing
addictive design elements to maximize the profit to be gained.

Within the major mobile operating systems, users have the ability to set
coarse-grained permissions where they can generally permit or deny access to
personal data. However, these type of permissions do not allow the user to limit
how data is shared or restrict specific elements or attributes of data. While mobile
permission models have been trending towards more fine-grained controls to limit
the data that can be collected, the speed of implementation has not been as fast
as new methods to access additional data from the user.

In this paper, we provide a background from where mobile permissions
started and their current trends. We then examine research that provides the
user with additional control of their data. We examine three main mechanisms:
modification of the operating system, modification of applications, and capture
and inspection of data. We discuss the main approaches in each of these categories and show the advantages and disadvantages of these approaches. We also
explore research that has focused on enhancing user awareness in mobile privacy
issues. From the shortcomings of these approaches, we propose a system that
can be implemented given proven methods from previous research and native
operating system controls that currently exist, so that users can be provided
sufficient controls to protect their data. We also describe how this proposed system can improve transparency to the user, so they become more aware in how
their data is accessed and used by applications.

2   Background

While the current permission models for both iOS and Android lack sufficient
controls, it has improved from the initial controls in earlier versions of both operating systems. We describe the evolution of these early controls and how they
have shifted slightly towards providing more fine-grained controls. We also look
at examples of personal data use and how design elements affect user engagement.

2.1   Coarse-Grained Controls

In the early releases of iOS and Android, permission controls were very coarse.
We define a coarse-grained permission as one that provides general access to a
personal data resource such as location or photos. With this type of permission,
a user is unable to determine what attributes or elements in a set are restricted
nor are they able to control how the data is shared. For example, with a coarse-
grained permission on photos, a user is unable to restrict certain photos or
attributes of a photo such as the location or time that the photo was taken.
Instead, they are only able to specify access to the entire set of photos and all
attributes of those photos.

In both iOS and Android, these controls have evolved to allow more fine-
grained control. However, prior to iOS 6, applications were not required to

request access to a resource and prior to iOS 10, applications did not have to provide a usage description. Even with an improvement of providing a description, these descriptions are not verified and can be incomplete. For example, if a weather application requests access to location data to provide an accurate forecast, it may not provide details in how it shares the data.

Previously with Android, users had to accept all permissions in order to use the application. This changed with Android Marshmallow, where users could permit or deny specific requests. However, developers delayed adopting the latest APIs so they could harvest more personal data [5]. Even when applications did upgrade, they did not always follow the established policies [4].

2.2 Personal Data Use

Limiting the user to coarse-grained controls has allowed applications to harvest and share data with whomever they desire. There has been significant reporting of how personal data can be misused, from tracking individual users using their location [8] and reporting on specific categories such as weather applications [6].

From prior research, we have found significant misuse of data by applications [28]. In the example below, we include a sample from a request sent by the "WeatherBug" iOS application. In this request, not only does it include precise location information that is shared with advertisement servers, but it also includes specific information of the device including model, CPU, version, orientation, and screen sizes, which can be used to profile and track users:

"geoloc": "41.374207, -81.850240, 65.000000, 60", "ua": "Mozilla/5.0 (
    iPad; CPU OS 12_4_1 like Mac OS X) AppleWebKit/605.1.15 ...", "dinfo
    ": { "orientation": "landscape", "connectionType": "Wifi", "osVersion
    ": "12.4.1", "model": "iPad4,7", "screenSize": "1024x768"

Misuse of location data is often found in applications that can present a legitimate use case, such as weather applications. However, we also found contact information being misused with social networking applications which can also present a legitimate use case. In the example below, we include a sample request sent from the "LinkedIn" iOS application. The permission request asks for access to the user's contacts to help them discover other connections on the network. Once access is granted, all contacts and all attributes of the contacts, including emails, phone numbers, birth date, and addresses, are uploaded to the servers:

"rawContacts": [{ "emails": [{ "emailAddress": "bwempaware@gmail.com"}
    ], "bornOn": { "day": 1, "month": 7, "year": 2012}, "firstName": "
    Yellow", "middleName": "", "fullName": "Yellow Jacket",
    "addresses": [{ "address1": "275 Eastland Rd.", "city": "Berea", "
    postalCode": "44017", "state": "Ohio" ...

Does this service need all this information to discover contacts? More importantly, is a user aware that this information is being shared with the application? From these samples and other findings, it is clear that users do not have sufficient controls to limit how applications use their personal data, nor do they have the transparency to discover how applications use their data.

2.3 Towards Fine-Grained Controls

In more recent releases of iOS and Android, there are more fine-grained controls provided to the user. Both Android and iOS now allow users to limit if applications can track location in the background. Additionally, applications can be permitted to access the location once. These limits on location data have shown to be effective [30]. Additional controls in iOS 14 include the ability to provide locations that are not precise and to only allow access to certain photos. These are improvements to these controls but are still incomplete. The same ability to restrict photos can be applied to other personal data such as contacts, as well as attributes of personal data, such as the location data in photos.

Controls that deny tracking are also improving. Previously, users were able to reset advertising identifiers. With iOS 14.5, they can now deny an application's ability to track them. Facebook launched an advertising campaign attacking the change in defense of personalized advertisements [17] while Apple has been active in promoting privacy as a key differentiator of its products [7].

2.4 Addictive Design

It is worth noting that the design of applications have been intentional to maximize user engagement and use addictive design elements. Social media, news, and other applications use a swipe down gesture to check for updates, which closely emulates designs used in slot machines [2]. Social media apps like Facebook and Twitter use quantitative measures such as likes, retweets, and friend or follower counts, which have been show to release dopamine as these increase in count [24]. This addictive design is driven by a profitable advertising industry. In 2019, internet advertising revenue was $124.6 billion, which grew by 15% from year before where mobile was a majority of this revenue at $86.7 billion [19].

3 Complementary Systems

To address the limitless collection of data, researchers have investigated complementary systems or modifications to operating systems. We look at some of these approaches and both their advantages and disadvantages. In investigating complementary controls, we take a ground up approach. We first took at what has been done from the operating system to the applications that exist on the operating system, and then in capturing data that leaves the device.

3.1 OS Modification

Modifying the operating system to provide more fine-grained controls is the most effective solution in preventing application access to personal data. However, in modifying the operating system, there are several challenges that researchers face. In providing more controls, performance and user experience can be affected. One of the most well known studies, TaintDroid, modified the Android operating system and used a dynamic taint analysis approach to track the flow of data as applications [15]. Using this methodology, a low overhead was incurred and the solution was able to successfully detect personal data misuse. Another popular approach allowed the user to specify if no data, anonymous data, or fake data should be returned [37]. A decade later from this study, iOS introduced similar controls in anonymizing location.

While most research in this space has focused on Android, there has been work on iOS. ProtectMyPrivacy, proposed a system that also incorporated a crowdsourced model [10] where recommendations are provided for the most popular applications. The study found applications significantly using location, contacts, and identifiers. Other approaches to iOS have included a partial update to the operating system. One approach, PSiOS, used this approach to provide fine-grained controls for users [35]. While this approach is only a partial update, it does still require a jailbreak of the device.

It is worth noting that modifying the operating system, either for Android or iOS, does require a jailbreak of the device. In requiring a jailbreak or custom operating system, these solutions demand even a higher level of technical expertise. If these approaches are unsuccessful, the user can void their warranty and potentially "brick" their device. It is also worth noting that by customizing the operating system, you will also require the user to continually install a custom version of the operating system, which is not a scalable approach. Given that iOS is not an open source operating system, a custom version of the operating system cannot be easily developed. Even though Android is an open source operating system, different flavors are produced by phone manufacturers and also wireless carriers where the operating system running on a smartphone can be tightly coupled to the hardware, not allowing all users to utilize the custom operating system that was developed. Along with issues in scalability, there also needs to be an incentive for researchers to maintain the alternative operating system.

3.2 Application Modification

While modifying the operating system provides additional controls to users, this is not always available due to custom images of the operating system for each device and carrier, or due to the operating system not being open source. Another approach is to modify the application behavior so that fine-grained controls can be enforced. One approach looked at providing the developer with a framework where each personal data request would check against an enhanced fine-grained policy [26]. In each request, the developer would specify an intent in how they would use the data. This intent can be verified and if it failed, the request would be denied. Both iOS and Android incorporate a purpose string where the application is required to describe how a permission will be used, but this often only describes part of how the data is used and they are not verified. Some approaches have focused on verifying these strings either through library use or static analysis [14, 34].

If a developer is unwilling to adopt an additional framework to provide users with more fine-grained control, another option is to modify the application directly. Using this approach, a new layer can be introduced that captures personal data requests and allow the user to implement a fine-grained policy [12]. Other approaches looked at having a service running on the device that data requests could be sent to for authorization [21].

The challenges with these approaches are similar to the operating system. With adding a framework, there has to be an incentive for the developer to adopt the framework. Unless users demand adoption, the incentive does not exist and using a framework can limit the monetary gain from the user's personal data. Similar to modifying an operating system, there are also challenges in modifying the application. With each update to the application, a new modified version has to be created. Additionally, changes need to be made to the operating system as the code signature may no longer be valid if the application has been modified.

3.3   Data Capture

Modifying the operating system or application pose challenges in both scalability and sustainability. They also both require a certain level of technical expertise. A different approach is capturing data through a proxy or VPN and enforcing fine-grained controls. One study created a VPN called PrivacyGuard [33] that utilized a locally running VPN to capture and filter personal data. Another VPN based approach utilized machine learning and natural language processing to analyze URLs to determine application behavior [23]. This approach showed promise as they demonstrated a 84% precision of successfully predicting application behavior. Other approaches used proxy servers to provide fine-grained controls. One approach created an application that allowed the user to specify fine-grained controls such as anonymizing location, limiting certain photos or contacts, as well as limiting certain attributes [25]. Another proxy approach automated analysis of over 88k Android applications for use of physical addresses (MAC) and how applications colluded by using separately granted permissions [32].

While these solutions require less technical expertise, they do require a general understanding of how the solutions work and what benefit they provide. It is also important to note that some of these solutions use a man-in-the-middle (MITM) approach. Using this approach, a root certificate must be trusted that is used to issue and sign certificates on behalf of the destination. Using this approach, SSL/TLS traffic can be intercepted. However, if a mobile application utilizes certificate pinning, as popular mobile applications such as Facebook and Twitter do, this approach is ineffective.

3.4   Feasibility of Complementary Systems

While these alternative solutions have provided the ability to protect personal data, they are not without their own challenges. All of the solutions either require a technical level of expertise, are not scalable or sustainable over time. Additionally, these systems can be gamed or applications can work together to avoid these controls [29,32]. With challenges in providing and implementing complementary systems, research has focused on providing the user with more awareness. In providing more awareness to users, demand for more control of their data can push mobile operating system producers to offer more fine-grained controls.

4   Enhancing Awareness

4.1   User Concerns

If users do not have complementary systems readily available that they can easily install to improve the controls on their personal data, could an increased awareness motivate them to take steps to protect their personal data? Or, do users care enough in how applications use their data? One study examined user attitudes in protecting data and while they found that users shared concerns about privacy, they did little to protect themselves [11]. Another study examined attitudes on privacy where they surveyed participants on where they would perform privacy sensitive and financial tasks where users shared concerns of performing these tasks on their smartphones [13]. While privacy focused applications can increase a user's confidence in protecting their data, a study examined usability goals of these applications and found that users lack understanding of the applications [11]. What research has consistently shown is that while users do share some privacy concerns on smartphones, their actions may not align with their concerns.

4.2   Permission Awareness

While users can grant applications permissions to access personal data, it is important to know how permissions are understood. One study looked at how users perceived and comprehended permission models with an in-person survey where participants installed and played a tic-tac-toe game. In this study, users were found to be well informed on a permission's meaning, but they found that age did play a factor in the understanding of the permission [31]. On the contrary, other studies found that users do not pay much attention to the permissions where only 17% of users were attentive to requested permissions [16]. Other studies focused on the usability of privacy preserving applications and found that users generally do not pay attention to permission request from applications and just blindly accept permission requests [36].

The responsibility in understanding permissions has also been an area of focus. Where does the responsibility of understanding permissions exist? Is it with the developer or the user? One study examined this question in user awareness of permission models and found that making the decision as an end user can be problematic as they do not have the knowledge required to measure the risks associated with their choices [22]. To increase awareness of permissions,

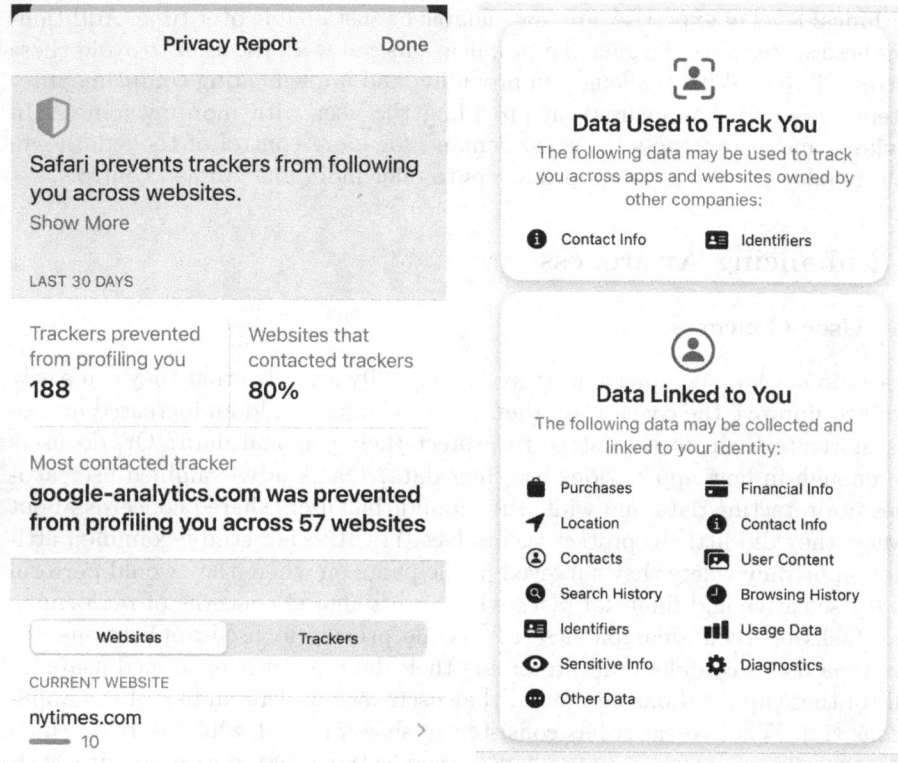

Fig. 1. Privacy Report feature (left) and Privacy Labels (right) available in both iOS and macOS

other work has focused on methods that show what an application can do with a given permission. In one study, an application was created to show how it could use data if it was given permission to personal data. From this study, they found permission decisions were quickly made and users are more likely to install applications that make less permission requests [18].

4.3   Data Transparency

While complementary systems have provided mechanisms for users to become more aware in how applications use data, other research has focused on attempting to provide more transparency. One study provided a web portal for users to see how application data was being used in real time and examined changes in user perceptions on privacy [28]. From this study, users became more aware in how mobile applications use their data and privacy concerns increased.

Within native operating systems, more transparency has been provided. Within the Safari web browser, users are able to view a "Privacy Report" that shows what trackers are being used by websites (Fig. 1). Additionally, both iOS and macOS have included "Privacy Labels" within the App Store (Fig. 1). These labels allow users to become more aware in how applications use data. However, these do rely on developers to be truthful in how data is used to track users and what data is linked or not linked to a user. Reporting has also shown that the labels can be inaccurate [1].

5   Recommendations

Complementary systems have been created and studied to provide additional controls for users. However, these approaches are not scalable, sustainable, or accessible for every user. Additionally, these solutions can require a high degree of technical expertise. While providing more transparency can improve how users perceive privacy issues on smartphones, they target a subset of the population and are not broadly available. They also only inform the user, they do not provide the fine-grained controls that are needed. While OS producers have introduced more controls in limiting access to personal data as well as additional features that improve transparency, these controls and transparency reporting is still incomplete.

A system that is accessible to everyone and that is both scalable and sustainable needs to exist within the native operating system. This is the approach we propose here in two main parts: 1) providing additional fine-grained controls and 2) providing transparency to the user. In this proposal, we focus on three personal data elements: location, contacts, and photos, to describe how sensed and stored data can be protected. We show examples in applying these to iOS, however, these same policies can be applied to Android.

5.1   Fine-Grained Controls

Permissions in both iOS and Android are coarse-grained permissions. Often, the permission grants complete access to a set of data and all the attributes in the set. It also allows the application to send the data from the device to any destination without restriction.

Set and Attribute Controls. Models have been developed to protect attributes and elements within a set of personal data [27]. It is critical to provide users with additional control given that if an application requests access to data such as a user's contacts, they have permission to access *all* contacts and *all* attributes of those contacts. This data can include emails, phone numbers, street addresses, birth dates, and much more. Users should be able to permit the individual attributes when the request is made by an application. When permission requests are made by an application, after a user selects "OK", they can then be forwarded to another screen that allows them to specify the attributes of that data they permit. This interaction is depicted in Fig. 2.

Recently, with iOS 14, users now have the ability to share only specific photos with applications instead of all photos. However, photos also contain metadata

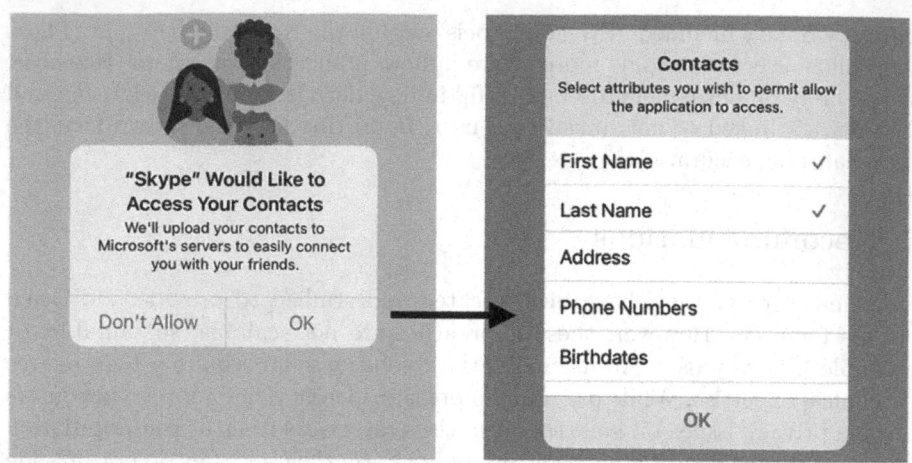

Fig. 2. Specify individual attributes of a specific permission such a contacts.

such as the time and location of the photo. Users should be able to limit access to these attributes. If the user does not grant permission to specific attributes, the data in these attributes can be removed by the operating system before the application receives it. This approach has been proven in previous research [26]. While these permissions are provided at runtime, modifications can be made to the Settings application to allow the user to later modify these permissions. Similar to photos, users should also be able to restrict or allow only specific contacts.

Destination Controls. While providing the ability to specify attributes and elements in a set of data, the user has no knowledge of where the data is received. Users should be able to control what domains applications communicate with where a list of domains with a justification for their use can be supplied when submitting the application or through static analysis. With this information, users can have a similar report to the "Privacy Report" feature (see Fig. 1) that is available in Safari for each application. This data can also provide more accurate "Privacy Labels".

Anonymous Data Controls. Recently, iOS provided the ability to anonymize a location which is suitable for applications such as weather applications, where often a precise location is not required for an accurate forecast. While the proposed controls allow a user to restrict certain contact attributes, application functionality may be affected by restricting access to data. Ideally, applications will be designed to handle rejection of permissions as they are already required to handle with coarse-grained permissions. However, if an application absolutely requires certain attributes of personal data to perform a task, the user should have the same controls as anonymizing the location where it can be applied to

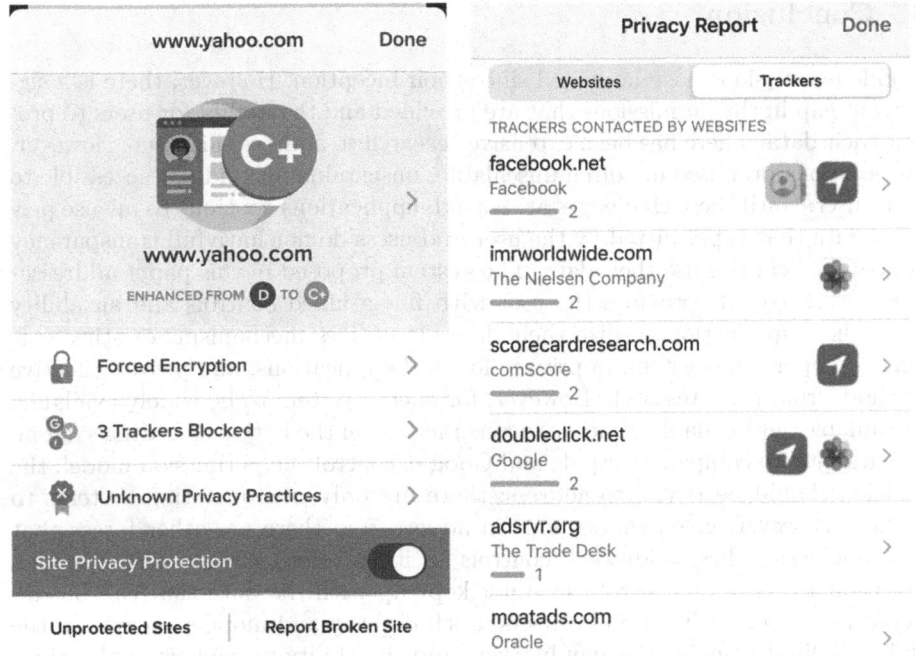

Fig. 3. Grade feature for a specific website in DuckDuckGo application (left) and prototype of how icons can be used to indicate data sent to specific domains (right).

other attributes such as phone numbers or street addresses. This can also be applied to metadata within photos such as the location and time.

5.2 Transparency

To provide more transparency to the user, a "Privacy Report" as mentioned previously can be provided to the user with a breakdown of each domain the application communicates with. In this report, the user can be provided visual clues of the data that is sent to each domain as depicted in Fig. 3. As an example, a user that provides their location can see if other domains are receiving the location using the same icon as the location permission. With each application, a grade can be applied similar to the grade "DuckDuckGo" provides for websites (Fig. 3). The grade can use tracking characteristics of domains the application communicates with and the data it shares.

The additional transparency provided to the user should be within the operating system. This allows the reporting to scale where it is accessible to every user, where other studies have only made these features available to a subset of users. With all users having more transparency, they can hold companies and application producers accountable as they will have a better understanding of what data applications access and how the data is shared.

6 Conclusion

Mobile permissions have improved since their inception. However, there is a significant gap in the permissions that are provided and the ability for users to protect their data. There has been extensive research to address this issue. However, the solutions proposed are often unscalable, unsustainable, and not accessible to every user. Until these challenges are solved, applications continue to misuse personal data that is permitted by the user and users do not have full transparency in how applications use their data. The system proposed in this paper addresses these challenges. It provides the user with fine-grained controls and an ability to see how applications utilize their data. It utilizes mechanisms existing currently in operating system, in privacy focused applications, and proven effective methods from prior research. However, for such a system to be widely available, sustainable, and scalable, it needs to become part of the native operating system. Given that two companies, Apple and Google, control the permission model, the solution should be trivial to address: there are only two operating systems to update. However, given the revenue in advertising, there are other forces that may not desire these additional controls as it can affect their business model. Additionally, privacy controls have not kept up with the data that can be collected from users. With web browsers, both desktop and mobile, users have the ability to limit tracking through blockers and the ability to see how applications use their data through reporting features. This capability along with fine-grained privacy controls should become available for all users so they can limit the use of personal data on their smartphones.

References

1. iPhone app privacy labels are a great idea, except when apple lets them deceive - the Washington post. https://www.washingtonpost.com/technology/2021/01/29/apple-privacy-nutrition-label/
2. Your Phone Is Designed Like a Slot Machine to Keep You Addicted. * Geek Insider. https://geekinsider.com/your-phone-is-designed-like-a-slot-machine-to-keep-you-addicted/
3. Several popular apps share data with Facebook without user consent, December 2018. https://www.ft.com/content/62f74704-0abf-11e9-9fe8-acdb36967cfc
4. 18,000 Android apps track users by violating advertising ID policies, February 2019. https://www.bleepingcomputer.com/news/security/18-000-android-apps-track-users-by-violating-advertising-id-policies/
5. Permission-greedy apps delayed android 6 upgrade so they could harvest more user data, July 2019. https://zd.net/2Lp3ygE
6. Popular weather app collects too much user data, security experts say, January 2019. https://on.wsj.com/2XgNDnf
7. 'Privacy matters' in apple's latest iPhone ad, March 2019. https://www.theverge.com/2019/3/14/18266276/apple-iphone-ad-privacy-facetime-bug
8. Twelve million phones, one dataset, zero privacy, December 2019. https://www.nytimes.com/interactive/2019/12/19/opinion/location-tracking-cell-phone.html?action=click&module=Opinion&pgtype=Homepage

9. How much time do Americans spend on their phones in 2020?, April 2020. https://techjury.net/blog/how-much-time-does-the-average-american-spend-on-their-phone/

10. Agarwal, Y., Hall, M.: ProtectMyPrivacy: detecting and mitigating privacy leaks on iOS devices using crowdsourcing. In: Proceeding of the 11th Annual International Conference on Mobile Systems, Applications, and Services, MobiSys 2013, pp. 97–110. ACM, New York (2013). https://doi.org/10.1145/2462456.2464460. http://doi.acm.org/10.1145/2462456.2464460

11. Assal, H., Hurtado, S., Imran, A., Chiasson, S.: What's the deal with privacy apps? A comprehensive exploration of user perception and usability. In: Proceedings of the 14th International Conference on Mobile and Ubiquitous Multimedia, MUM 2015, pp. 25–36. Association for Computing Machinery, New York (2015). https://doi.org/10.1145/2836041.2836044

12. Backes, M., Gerling, S., Hammer, C., Maffei, M., von Styp-Rekowsky, P.: App-Guard – enforcing user requirements on android apps. In: Piterman, N., Smolka, S.A. (eds.) TACAS 2013. LNCS, vol. 7795, pp. 543–548. Springer, Heidelberg (2013). https://doi.org/10.1007/978-3-642-36742-7_39

13. Chin, E., Felt, A.P., Sekar, V., Wagner, D.: Measuring user confidence in smartphone security and privacy. In: Proceedings of the Eighth Symposium on Usable Privacy and Security, SOUPS 2012. Association for Computing Machinery, New York (2012). https://doi.org/10.1145/2335356.2335358

14. Chitkara, S., Gothoskar, N., Harish, S., Hong, J.I., Agarwal, Y.: Does this app really need my location?: context-aware privacy management for smartphones. Proc. ACM Interact. Mob. Wearable Ubiquitous Technol. 1(3), 42:1–42:22 (2017). https://doi.org/10.1145/3132029. http://doi.acm.org/10.1145/3132029

15. Enck, W., et al.: TaintDroid: an information-flow tracking system for realtime privacy monitoring on smartphones. In: Proceedings of the 9th USENIX Conference on Operating Systems Design and Implementation, OSDI 2010, Berkeley, CA, USA, pp. 393–407. USENIX Association (2010)

16. Felt, A.P., Ha, E., Egelman, S., Haney, A., Chin, E., Wagner, D.: Android permissions: user attention, comprehension, and behavior. In: Proceedings of the Eighth Symposium on Usable Privacy and Security, SOUPS 2012. Association for Computing Machinery, New York (2012). https://doi.org/10.1145/2335356.2335360

17. Graham, M.: Facebook launches ad campaign to defend personalized advertising ahead of Apple privacy change, February 2021. https://www.cnbc.com/2021/02/25/facebook-ad-campaign-counters-apple-idfa-privacy-change.html

18. Harbach, M., Hettig, M., Weber, S., Smith, M.: Using personal examples to improve risk communication for security and privacy decisions. In: Proceedings of the SIGCHI Conference on Human Factors in Computing Systems, CHI 2014, pp. 2647–2656. Association for Computing Machinery, New York (2014). https://doi.org/10.1145/2556288.2556978

19. IAB: Internet advertising revenue report. https://www.iab.com/wp-content/uploads/2020/05/FY19-IAB-Internet-Ad-Revenue-Report_Final.pdf

20. IDC: Smartphone market share. https://www.idc.com/promo/smartphone-market-share

21. Jeon, J., et al.: Dr. Android and Mr. Hide: fine-grained permissions in Android applications. In: Proceedings of the Second ACM Workshop on Security and Privacy in Smartphones and Mobile Devices, SPSM 2012, pp. 3–14. Association for Computing Machinery, New York (2012). https://doi.org/10.1145/2381934.2381938

22. Jha, A.K., Lee, S., Lee, W.J.: Permission-based security in Android application: from policy expert to end user. In: Proceedings of the 2015 Conference on Research in Adaptive and Convergent Systems, RACS, pp. 319–320. ACM, New York (2015). https://doi.org/10.1145/2811411.2811493. http://doi.acm.org/10.1145/2811411.2811493

23. Jin, H., et al.: Why are they collecting my data? Inferring the purposes of network traffic in mobile apps. Proc. ACM Interact. Mob. Wearable Ubiquitous Technol. **2**(4) (2018). https://doi.org/10.1145/3287051

24. Krach, S., Paulus, F.M., Bodden, M., Kircher, T.: The rewarding nature of social interactions. Front. Behav. Neurosci. **4** (2010). https://doi.org/10.3389/fnbeh.2010.00022. https://www.ncbi.nlm.nih.gov/pmc/articles/PMC2889690/

25. Krupp, B., Jesensky, D., Szampias, A.: SPEProxy: enforcing fine grained security and privacy controls on unmodified mobile devices. In: 2017 IEEE 8th Annual Ubiquitous Computing, Electronics and Mobile Communication Conference (UEMCON), pp. 520–526, October 2017. https://doi.org/10.1109/UEMCON.2017.8248985

26. Krupp, B., Sridhar, N., Zhao, W.: SPE: security and privacy enhancement framework for mobile devices. IEEE Trans. Dependable Secure Comput. **14**(4), 433–446 (2017). https://doi.org/10.1109/TDSC.2015.2465965

27. Krupp, B., Sridhar, N., Zhao, W.: An ontology for enforcing security and privacy policies on mobile devices. In: KEOD (2014)

28. Krupp, B., Timko, E., Cox, K., Hicks, W., Bursey, M., Banfield, C.: EMPAware: analyzing changes in user perceptions of mobile privacy on iOS with enhanced awareness. In: Proceedings of the 2021 ACM Workshop on Security and Privacy Analytics, IWSPA 2021, pp. 15–24. Association for Computing Machinery, New York (2021). https://doi.org/10.1145/3445970.3451153

29. Memon, A.M., Anwar, A.: Colluding apps: tomorrow's mobile malware threat. IEEE Secur. Priv. **13**(6), 77–81 (2015). https://doi.org/10.1109/MSP.2015.143

30. Newman, J.: Apple and Google's tough new location privacy controls are working, January 2020. https://www.fastcompany.com/90454921/apple-and-googles-tough-new-location-privacy-controls-are-working

31. Peruma, A., Palmerino, J., Krutz, D.E.: Investigating user perception and comprehension of android permission models. In: Proceedings of the 5th International Conference on Mobile Software Engineering and Systems, MOBILESoft 2018, pp. 56–66. ACM, New York (2018). https://doi.org/10.1145/3197231.3197246. http://doi.acm.org/10.1145/3197231.3197246

32. Reardon, J., Feal, Á., Wijesekera, P., On, A.E.B., Vallina-Rodriguez, N., Egelman, S.: 50 ways to leak your data: an exploration of apps' circumvention of the android permissions system. In: 28th USENIX Security Symposium (USENIX Security 19), Santa Clara, CA, pp. 603–620. USENIX Association, August 2019

33. Song, Y., Hengartner, U.: PrivacyGuard: a VPN-based platform to detect information leakage on android devices. In: Proceedings of the 5th Annual ACM CCS Workshop on Security and Privacy in Smartphones and Mobile Devices, SPSM 2015, pp. 15–26. ACM, New York (2015). https://doi.org/10.1145/2808117.2808120. http://doi.acm.org/10.1145/2808117.2808120

34. Wang, H., Hong, J., Guo, Y.: Using text mining to infer the purpose of permission use in mobile apps. In: Proceedings of the 2015 ACM International Joint Conference on Pervasive and Ubiquitous Computing, UbiComp 2015, pp. 1107–1118. Association for Computing Machinery, New York (2015). https://doi.org/10.1145/2750858.2805833

35. Werthmann, T., Hund, R., Davi, L., Sadeghi, A.R., Holz, T.: PSiOS: bring your own privacy & security to iOS devices. In: Proceedings of the 8th ACM SIGSAC Symposium on Information, Computer and Communications Security, ASIA CCS 2013, pp. 13–24. ACM, New York (2013). https://doi.org/10.1145/2484313.2484316. http://doi.acm.org/10.1145/2484313.2484316
36. Westermann, T., Wechsung, I.: Empowering users to make informed permission request choices. In: Proceedings of the 17th International Conference on Human-Computer Interaction with Mobile Devices and Services Adjunct, MobileHCI 2015, pp. 1123–1125. ACM, New York (2015). https://doi.org/10.1145/2786567.2794333. http://doi.acm.org/10.1145/2786567.2794333
37. Zhou, Y., Zhang, X., Jiang, X., Freeh, V.W.: Taming information-stealing smartphone applications (on Android). In: McCune, J.M., Balacheff, B., Perrig, A., Sadeghi, A.-R., Sasse, A., Beres, Y. (eds.) Trust 2011. LNCS, vol. 6740, pp. 93–107. Springer, Heidelberg (2011). https://doi.org/10.1007/978-3-642-21599-5_7. http://dl.acm.org/citation.cfm?id=2022245.2022255

Interdependent Privacy Issues Are Pervasive Among Third-Party Applications

Shuaishuai Liu[(✉)], Barbara Herendi, and Gergely Biczók[(✉)]

Department of Networked Systems and Services, CrySyS Lab,
Budapest University of Technology and Economics, Budapest, Hungary
{sliu,biczok}@crysys.hu

Abstract. Third-party applications are popular: they improve and extend the features offered by their respective platforms, whether being mobile OS, browsers or cloud-based tools. Although some privacy concerns regarding these apps have been studied in detail, the phenomenon of *interdependent privacy*, when a user shares others' data with an app without their knowledge and consent. Through careful analysis of permission models and multiple platform-specific datasets, we show that interdependent privacy risks are enabled by certain permissions in all platforms studied, and actual apps request these permissions instantiating these risks. We also identify potential risk signals, and discuss solutions which could improve transparency and control for users, developers and platform owners.

Keywords: Interdependent privacy · Third-party apps · Permissions · Android · Browser extensions · Google Workspace · Risk signal

1 Introduction

Third-party applications (apps) occupy a prominent position in the current Internet ecosystem; such apps add extra features and functionality to already popular platforms, e.g., mobile operating systems, social networks, browsers, storage clouds, etc. Data sharing is the foundation of the ever-increasing number of third-party apps and their respective platforms. Faced with the large-scale, diverse and virtually non-stop data exchange, privacy issues have become even more pressing.

Nowadays, various application platforms are stepping up to improve the data privacy mechanisms; e.g., as of iOS v14.5[1], applications must obtain user consent to track user data from other applications and websites. Furthermore, A new privacy dashboard has been added to Android v12[2], which allows users to monitor the usage of app permissions more accurately. These updates are welcome efforts

---

[1] https://developer.apple.com/app-store/user-privacy-and-data-use/.
[2] https://www.androidauthority.com/android-privacy-dashboard-1233846/.

J. Garcia-Alfaro et al. (Eds.): DPM 2021/CBT 2021, LNCS 13140, pp. 70–86, 2022.
https://doi.org/10.1007/978-3-030-93944-1_5

in the quest for enhancing transparency, user control and privacy in general; yet, none of these current developments addresses *interdependent privacy* [2], where others might share your data without your knowledge and control. Especially pronounced in the third-party app scenario, data shared with the app by a single user might also contain personal and, potentially, sensitive information on their friends, contacts or colleagues.

The highest profile recent cases featuring interdependent privacy are connected to Facebook. The best-known is the Cambridge Analytica scandal [22], where 87 million Facebook profiles were harvested by an app called "thisisyourdigitallife", then used to build detailed personal psychological profiles, and, consequently, the users were targeted with personalized political ads to affect the outcome of the 2016 US presidential elections. The app in question exploited the *collateral information collection* mechanism on Facebook, where it was installed by 270,000 users but reached tens of millions of friend profiles through the controversially designed permission system [22] that allowed for harvesting friend profiles. More recently, on February 08, 2021, Facebook compensated more than 1.6 million users to the amount of $650 million, one of the largest privacy-related settlements to date, owing to creating and storing scans of their faces without permission. The class action lawsuit was initiated in Illinois in 2015, and involved Facebook's use of facial recognition technology in its photo tagging function. The photo tagging feature allowed users to tag friends in photos they had uploaded to Facebook, creating a personal link to the friends' profile without their consent[3]. In this case, a vivid example of interdependent privacy, the uploading user consciously granted Facebook the permission to display his photo, but the users who were tagged automatically in the photo suffered a privacy loss without even being aware of it.

However, there have been less publicized interdependent privacy incidents, as well. A security bug allowed third-party apps to access Google+ user profile data since 2015 until Google discovered and patched it in March 2018[4]. When a user gave permission to an app to access their public profile data, the bug also enabled developers pull their and their friends' non-public profile fields; around 500,000 profiles were affected. To make matters worse, Google decided not to inform the world on this issue. In another unfortunate case, the popular True-Caller Android app, used for blacklisting spam numbers, came under scrutiny. In addition to uploading the address book of the installing user to its servers (an interdependent privacy issue in itself as noted by the Article 29 Working Party in 2017[5]), TrueCaller allows its users to tag unknown numbers after taking the call, and to upload them to the servers for all other users to see the information. In 2019, this feature blew the cover of an investigative journalist in a hostile

---

[3] https://www.theguardian.com/technology/2021/feb/27/facebook-illinois-privacy-lawsuit-settlement.

[4] https://www.wsj.com/articles/google-exposed-user-data-feared-repercussions-of-disclosing-to-public-1539017194.

[5] https://ec.europa.eu/newsroom/article29/items/610173.

country; luckily, no actual harm has been inflicted, but there was a non-negligible threat to the physical well-being of the journalist and her sources[6].

The above incidents naturally invite the question *(RQ1): are interdependent privacy issues pervasive among third-party app platforms?* Moreover *(RQ2), do actual apps request the permissions enabling collateral information collection on their respective platforms?* In this paper, we answer *RQ1* and *RQ2* affirmatively. Specifically, the contribution of this paper is threefold. First, we analyze the permission systems of multiple third-party app platforms of different types, and identify permissions for each of them which can potentially cause interdependent privacy issues. Second, through analyzing freshly collected datasets from the respective platforms, we demonstrate and quantify the extent to which real-world apps request these permissions. Pointedly, we show that the type (i.e., category) of the app is a good predictor for the number of potentially interdependent privacy related permissions requested. Finally, we briefly discuss potential measures which can augment and/or improve the current, permission-based access control mechanisms with regard to transparency and control.

The rest of this paper is organized as follows. Section 2 lays out the related work. Section 3 analyzes the permissions of the studied third-party app platforms, and identifies interdependent privacy invoking permissions. Section 4 introduces our dataset, and quantifies the proliferation of such permissions requested by actual apps from their respective platforms. Section 5 briefly touches upon prospective transparency and control enhancing techniques. Finally, Sect. 6 reflects on our contributions and concludes the paper.

2   Related Work

Here we briefly summarize related work in the intersection of interdependent privacy and third-party apps.

Interdependent privacy captures the networked characteristics of privacy-related decisions. Owing to this networked nature, the privacy of individuals are bound to be affected by the actions of others, e.g., Facebook users sharing the data of their friends' [2]. In economic terms, unaware fellow users fall victim to a negative externality. Extending this interpretation, a data entry, seemingly concerning a single individual, may actually be also related to (multiple) others because of data correlation [15]. Note that the same concept is known under different monikers, such as collective privacy [20], networked privacy [3] and multiple-subject privacy [7], among others. For a comprehensive overview, we refer the interested reader to [10].

Interdependent privacy affects different types of data and data sharing scenarios. A subset of attributes from the profile of a social network user may be harvested [2]. The location privacy of certain individuals may be threatened by sharing co-location information [16]. Photo sharing may affect the privacy of friends and bystanders captured in the photo [15]. Even the genetic profile of

---

[6] https://privacyinternational.org/node/2997.

an individual and associated inferrable medical information might get exposed by an eager relative (i.e., kin genomic privacy) [9]. A common trait among the aforementioned scenarios is that all of them could be instantiated through a variety of third-party apps.

General privacy considerations regarding third-party apps, platforms, permissions and ecosystems have been a strong focus area of researchers in the last decade. We do not even attempt to give a comprehensive overview here, rather, we highlight a few studies with close relations to this paper. Wang et al. studied the data collection practices of Facebook third-party apps and proposed control mechanisms which can increase transparency [23]. King et al. conducted an exploratory survey on how Facebook users interact with apps, and how much they understand the privacy implications of such interaction [14]. Androidleaks uncovered how sensitive data is used once the user gave the required permissions and the Android app was installed [6]. Chia et al. studied app permissions, privacy risk signals and community ratings on multiple app platforms [4]. FlowDroid and its follow up works provided taint analysis for Android apps that sheds light on potential unintended and malicious data leaks [1]. Reardon et al. explored the many ways apps can circumvent the Android permission system [19]. Finally, Kelley et al. (and many others building on their study) showed that users actually factor in their privacy concerns when choosing between apps if they are presented with easy-to-understand privacy facts before installation [13]. The above selection of studies clearly demonstrate that i) permission models are imperfect, ii) various privacy leaks do occur in apps, and iii) users act on their concerns when presented with tractable information on app privacy.

Yet, there are only a handful of scientific studies dealing explicitly with interdependent privacy situations regarding third-party apps. Biczok and Chia showed that the personal, relational and spatial privacy of Facebook users are threatened by their friends [2]. Pu and Grossklags investigated the effect of selfish and other-regarding preferences in social app adoption [18]. Harkous and Aberer analyzed Google Drive apps, and pointed out that users suffer more privacy loss owing to their collaborators than their own actions [8]. Finally, Symeonidis et al. presented a comprehensive data analytics, modeling and legal study on the *collateral information collection* practices of Facebook apps affecting the friends of the user [22]. While both these studies and further anecdotal evidence suggest that interdependent privacy issues might be the norm rather than the exception on most third-party app platforms, the research community lacks a data-driven study for available, active, but previously uncharted platforms, such as Android, Google Chrome and other browsers, and cloud services. This paper aims at filling this gap.

3 Platforms, Permissions and Interdependent Privacy

3.1 Permissions and Interdependent Privacy

Permission-Based Access. Third-party app platforms share a common security model which is based on requesting and granting permissions. App permissions guard the access to i) restricted data, such as location or contact information, and ii) restricted actions, such as taking photos or connecting to the Internet. Generally, the main objectives of app permissions include: i) enabling user control over data shared, ii) achieving transparency, so that the user understands what data an app is using and why, and iii) promoting data minimization, so that the app accesses and utilizes only the data absolutely required for a specific task the user invokes.

Platforms, e.g., Google's Android, have evolved significantly since their inception to achieve these objectives. Android has introduced install-time and run-time permissions; the latter group includes all individual permissions deemed *dangerous* by the platform. Run-time permissions can be explicitly granted (or denied) by the user through a dedicated pop-up window, shown when the execution of the app reached a state where the permission is required. On top of this, very recently, Android has included a *privacy dashboard* that shows which apps had used sensitive permissions and for how long in the last 24 h; also, with easy access to revoke said permissions if so desired. Despite all these improvements in Android and other permission mechanisms, there are still no specific (neither transparency, nor mitigation) measures targeted at interdependent privacy.

Rubbing salt into the wound, app platforms' definition of certain permissions are vague, as to what extent the app will obtain and use sensitive private information. Combining this more general transparency issue with the specific flaws mentioned above, two sub-optimal privacy outcomes emerge. First, the user does not have sufficient knowledge on the scope of the information to be shared: others' private data might be transferred to the app without even their knowledge. Second, the user might grant excessive permissions to the app to preserve full functionality. Although this latter has been shown to be an issue with respect to one's own sensitive attributes, it could induce an even more negative impact in the context of interdependent privacy.

Permissions Related to Interdependent Privacy. Corresponding to the above two points, when the permission involved is ambiguous, users pay more attention to protecting their own privacy while ignoring the privacy of their friends [18]. When the number of permissions granted by users to apps becomes larger, interdependent privacy issues often emerge. An obvious example is a top-rated Firefox extension called *AdBlocker Ultimate*. The permission-related warnings of this app are the following: W1) "Access browser tabs", W2) "Store unlimited amount of client-side data", W3) "Access browser activity during navigation", and W4) "Access your data for all websites". Plausibly, the combination of W1, W3 and W4 enables the extension to read the website, detect ads, and replace them with blank boxes. However, the same permissions enable the app to collect, e.g., messages sent to and received from a web-based chat; an outcome that could cause privacy loss to the communication partners of the user, an obvious interdependent privacy scenario, no user would prefer to experience.

Furthermore, W2 enables the storage of unlimited personal data collected through W1, W2 and W4; this can allow for observing, e.g., personal communications over a longer period of time. Yet, not granting these requested permission makes it impossible to install and use the app.

As we would like to quantify the extent to which interdependent privacy issues are present in third-party app platforms, we classify permissions into three pre-defined categories: invoking interdependent privacy (IDP), potentially invoking interdependent privacy (PIDP), and not invoking interdependent privacy (NIDP). If a permission *directly* enables access to private data related to a natural person other than the user herself, it is in IDP; e.g., the READ_CONTACTS permission in Android. If a permission *potentially* enables access to private data related to a natural person other than the user herself, it is in PIDP. Such risk can be realized through i) accessing data that *may* implicate multiple parties, such as photos or documents (e.g., READ_EXTERNAL_STORAGE in Android); ii) enabling a restricted action that *may create* multi-party data, such as photos or audio recordings (e.g., RECORD_AUDIO in Android); and iii) enabling *inference* of other's private data with reasonable effort, such as location via co-location information from other sources (e.g., ACCESS_FINE_LOCATION in Android). Note that granting a PIDP permission does not automatically constitute privacy loss for a third party; the loss is context-dependent and may require additional effort from the app developer or an adversary. If a permission does not belong either to IDP or PIDP, then it is in NIDP, and not in our focus.

3.2 Platform Specifics

Here we briefly introduce the app platforms we investigated. For practical data availability reasons, we targeted the most popular mobile app platform Android, two well-known browsers providing an API for third-party extensions (Mozilla Firefox and Opera), and Google Workspace, a cloud-based enterprise collaboration tool bundle. Although these 4 platforms vary greatly in both their functionality and technical mechanisms, all of them offer the equivalent of an app store, where the access control of apps is based on the user granting permissions.

Android. Android users can download and install more than 3 million apps from the Google Play store, making Android the largest third-party app platform, both by user base and the set of available apps. This popularity has made the platform's permission model change continuously over time, while trying to keep a balance between being appealing to both users and third-party developers alike. The current stable OS is v11 (with v12 right around the corner), while the API version, also defining the current permission model, is level 30. Android has evolved into a general purpose OS with plenty of protected data objects and actions; this amounts to 91 permissions in total, offered to third-party apps). We make 91 our baseline for the total number of relevant permissions. Out of these 91, there are 4 which explicitly and 16 which potentially interfere with others' personal data instantiating interdependent privacy, see Table 1. Note that the

Table 1. Android permissions: IDP and PIDP

IDP	PIDP
read call log_Phone	read the contents of your USB storage_Photos/Media/Files
read your contacts_Contacts	modify or delete the contents of your USB storage_Photos/Media/Files
modify your contacts_Contacts	approx. location (network-based)_Location
read your text messages (SMS or MMS)_SMS	precise location (GPS and network-based)_Location
	access extra location provider commands_Location
	take pictures and videos_Camera
	read sensitive log data_Device & app history
	read your Web bookmarks and history_Device & app history
	record audio_Microphone
	read the contents of your USB storage_Storage
	modify or delete the contents of your USB storage_Storage
	find accounts on the device_Contacts
	read cal events plus confidential information_Calendar
	add or modify cal events and send email to guests w/o owners' knowledge_Calendar
	read cell broadcast messages_SMS
	find accounts on the device_Contacts

pop-up messages, appearing when installing an app from Google Play, contain warnings which can be mapped directly to API-level permissions with reasonable effort.

Browser Extensions: Permissions and Warnings. Although referred to differently, browser extensions are very similar to apps. Extensions usually expand browser functionality, and manage user operations. Owing to their objectives and architecture, browser extensions are all about interacting with their respective platforms, often times resulting in obtaining large amounts of information about user operations in the browser in real time, but also about content downloaded by the browser. Note that browsers are also used to access intranets and other non-public resources, therefore, they might leak a variety of personal (and other confidential) information if something goes wrong. Both Firefox and Opera are based on Chromium, therefore their APIs and permission models facing third-party extensions are all based on the Chrome API (along with Chrome, Edge, Brave and Safari, to be correct). Both browsers have their own extension store.

Albeit they are based on the same APIs, Firefox and Opera have some unique characteristics. They both support the majority of permissions but not all[7], and they both define their own warning messages that users can see before/when they install an extension[8]. In fact, Opera does not show these warnings when installing; they are only visible on their dedicated page in the extension store. Making things more complicated, i) not all permission requests generate warning messages, and ii) warning messages and API-level permissions are not totally consistent: the platforms have decided to simplify warnings for the sake of clarity to the average user. While this is laudable from one aspect, these explanations sometimes do not fully reflect the risks of granting the requested permissions. Exact mappings between permissions and user warnings are hard to find, but may be extrapolated from Chrome's official documentation[9]. Since it is only feasible to scrape the extension stores for per app warnings (and not for API-level permissions), we base our analysis on these. Note that our datasets contain information on Manifest V2 extensions; however, the changes introduced in Manifest V3 do not have a significant impact on interdependent privacy[10].

Firefox has 26 different warning messages, 19 of which are potential culprits for interdependent privacy violations, see Table 2. Opera extensions make use of 20 types of warning messages, 13 of which pose a potential threat owing to privacy interdependence, see Table 2. Note that all affected warnings (and their corresponding permissions) are in PIDP, and we omit NIDP due to space constraints. Also, note that all Opera warnings start with "This extension (can/will)".

Google Workspace (Formerly GSuite). GSuite is a collaborative enterprise office platform launched by Google in September 2016, that was rebranded to Google Workspace in 2020, when it already had more than 2 billions users. Users do not need to download applications, they only need to edit and share files in the cloud, realizing remote collaboration. The platform has an app store, the Marketplace[11], where business, productivity and educational tools are offered by third-party developers. One of Workspace's subsystems, Google Drive, has already been shown to leak others' personal information through apps owing to its collaborative nature [8]; however, its permission model has changed completely due to the integration of various Google subsystems into the Workspace. The platform has many specialized permissions catering to its intended usage

---

[7] https://developer.mozilla.org/en-US/docs/Mozilla/Add-ons/WebExtensions/manifest.json/permissions#browser_compatibility.

[8] e.g. Firefox: https://support.mozilla.org/en-US/kb/permission-request-messages-firefox-extensions.

[9] https://developer.chrome.com/docs/extensions/mv2/permission_warnings/#permissions_with_warnings.

[10] https://developer.chrome.com/docs/extensions/mv3/intro/mv3-overview/.

[11] https://workspace.google.com/marketplace.

Table 2. Browser extension permissions: PIDP

Firefox	Opera
Access browser tabs	Access your data on all websites
Access browser activity during navigation	Access your tabs and browsing activity
Access your data for named site	Access your data on some websites
Exchange messages with programs other than Firefox	Exchange messages with programs other than Opera
Download files and read and modify the browser's download history	Capture the content of the entire screen or of individual tabs and windows
Access your location	Access data you copy and paste
Access recently closed tabs	Allows other installed extensions and web pages to communicate with this extension
Access your data for all websites	Detect your physical location
Store unlimited amount of client-side data	Manipulate privacy-related settings
Access your data for sites in the named domain	Know which sites you're visiting most often
Read and modify bookmarks	Read and modify bookmarks
Access your data on # other sites	Store an unlimited amount of client-side data
Get data from the clipboard	Read and modify your browsing history
Extend developer tools to access your data in open tabs	
Read the text of all open tabs	
Access browsing history	
Access your data in # other domains	
Access browsing history	
Read and modify browser settings	

as a collaborative office productivity solution. Specifically, there are 87 different permissions, out of which 3 are IDP ("See and download your contacts", "View customer related information" and "View, edit, or permanently delete contacts" and 71 are PIDP (which we omit due to the lack of space). Note that, although Workspace is a subscription-based service for enterprises and universities, it hosts huge amounts of private data. What is more, if an employee (usually a system administrator) installs a third-party app resulting in a privacy violation for other natural persons, the company can be held responsible as per the GDPR.

Table 3. Summary: IDP and PIDP permissions/warnings

Platform	No. of permissions/warnings	IDP + PIDP	Ratio
Android	91	20	21.98%
Firefox	26	19	73.08%
Opera	20	13	65%
Google Workspace	87	74	85.06%

It is straightforward to see that each platform has a significant proportion of its permissions and warnings connected to interdependent privacy; see Table 3. This answers *RQ1* affirmatively: *interdependent privacy issues are indeed pervasive among third-party app platforms.*

4 Application-Level Statistics

4.1 Data Collection

We collected datasets by scraping the app stores of 4 different third-party app platforms in late 2020 and early 2021: Android ($10,589$ apps), Mozilla ($16,546$), Opera ($1,682$)) and Google Workspace (882). Each record contains all available meta-data, e.g., app name, category, permissions/warnings, number of users, rating, etc., depending on the actual platforms. Due to the app stores' protection against scraping i) we did not manage to collect enough data for Chrome and Edge extensions, therefore we omit these platforms from our analysis; ii) our Android dataset contains only a fragment of the millions of available apps (yet, large and random enough to be significant). To the best of our knowledge, we collected complete datasets for Firefox, Opera and Google Workspace. Note that automatic scraping was infeasible for Google Workspace; we collected information on all available apps manually. Both datasets and scraping scripts are available for download[12].

4.2 Do Real Apps Request IDP/PIDP Permissions?

Table 4 shows the number of apps that requested at least one IDP or PIDP permission. The last column calculates the proportion of the union of these apps versus all the apps in the dataset. It is clear that the vast majority of apps are affected as evidenced by proportion larger than 80% for all platforms. Note that the browser platforms offer only PIDP permissions.

To further study the privacy protection permissions of apps, we calculated the permissions requested by each app. Regarding Android (Google Play store), 17.2% of apps requested the permission "Contacts", which means that their users

---

[12] https://www.dropbox.com/s/iz9kedsbzaw2vn1/liu_dpm2021_data.zip?dl=0.

Table 4. Number of apps with IDP/PIDP

Platform	Apps with IDP	Apps with PIDP	Total Apps	Ratio
Android	1029	8307	10589	78.66%
Firefox	0	13704	16546	82.82%
Opera	0	1421	1682	84.48%
Google Workspace	29	845	882	97.62%

have shared their contact list with the third-party developer, directly exposing others' personal data without their knowledge. Besides, 78.66% of apps have the potential to leak private information owing to interdependent privacy. On average, each app requests 11.21 permissions, out of which 4.4 are IDP or PIDP.

Mozilla and Opera extensions, despite their similar architecture, differ significantly in terms of PIDP warning types (0.83 vs. 3.93 on average) and total warning types (0.85 vs. 4.63) displayed. Note that, although here we observe warning instead of permissions, the difference holds, as warning-permission mappings are alike on both platforms. One reason could be that more Mozilla extensions make use of the `active_tab` permission (which does not generate a warning) instead of `_url` type permissions[13]. Some other permissions also do not generate warnings, therefore the total number of permissions requested in Table 5 is underestimated, while the proportion in the last column is overestimated for browser extensions.

Google Workspace is dedicated to collaborative enterprise features with a lot of PIDP permissions, therefore we expected a high proportion of those requested by apps. Indeed, 85% of total permissions requested (2.04 out of 2.42) are IDP or PIDP. We also observed that a majority of permissions are requested only by a few apps. This can be explained by the relatively low number of available apps, and the fact that permissions are very specific (especially compared to browser extensions), e.g., "View and manage your Google Slides presentations" instead of "View and manage your documents".

Based on the results above, we can also answer *RQ2* affirmatively: *actual apps do request IDP/PIDP permissions enabling collateral information collection on all studied platforms.*

4.3   Risk Signals

Users can obtain limited information when deciding upon installing third-party apps, such as category, number of users, user ratings, and permission types. Taking the Google Play store as an example, here we investigate whether the user can interpret these pieces information as risk signals towards interdependent privacy. Previous studies found that neither popularity (number of users), nor

---

[13] https://developer.mozilla.org/en-US/docs/Mozilla/Add-ons/WebExtensions/manifest.json/permissions#activetab_permission.

Table 5. Average number of IDP&PIDP permissions per app

Platform	IDP/PIDP permissions	Total permissions	Proportion
Android	4.40	11.21	39.3%
Firefox	0.83	0.85	97.6%
Opera	3.93	4.63	84.9%
Google Workspace	2.04	2.42	84.3%

community ratings (stars) are good indicators for privacy-conscious app behavior [4]. We also found evidence supporting this hypothesis. In fact, community ratings show a weak positive correlation with both the number of total permissions and the number of IDP/PIDP permissions requested: favorable ratings are mostly based on advanced functionality requiring more permissions.

The only promising indicator for an app to enable collateral information collection is its category. In order to demonstrate this, we select 2,043 apps from the Google Play dataset randomly, with the constraint of around 200 samples should belong to each of the 10 major categories. The average number of total permissions (left) and IDP/PIDP permissions (right) can be seen in Fig. 1.

The number of permissions varies greatly across categories. Apps belonging to "Business" and "Communication" request an average of 14.74, 19.92 permissions, while "Art&Design" and "Comics" only have 8.26, 6.71. A reasonable explanation to this result is that communications and business apps have more advanced features requiring more permissions. Interestingly, the same result holds for IDP/PIDP permissions. Categories with a high number of total permissions have a high number of IDP/PIDP permissions, and vice versa. The reasoning above can explain this result partially, but we argue that it is also in the characteristics of communication/business apps to involve more collaboration and multi-party interaction, a main theme behind permissions invoking interdependent privacy.

To illustrate this observation, we turn to the distribution of the number of IDP/PIDP permissions across all apps in a given category. Figure 2 shows the histogram for this metric for the categories "Art&Design" (left) and "Communication" (right). The difference between the two plots are striking: both the average number of IDP/PIDP permissions (2.95 vs. 6.41), and the shape of the histograms (top-heavy vs. normal-like) are very different. These patterns are mostly consistent for categories with a low and high number of permissions, respectively. This corroborates our previous observation, as more interactive/collaborative categories have more apps requesting a large number of IDP/PIDP permissions.

Naturally, our observations on risk signals can be Android-specific. It constitutes important future work for us to investigate these signals with respect other platforms.

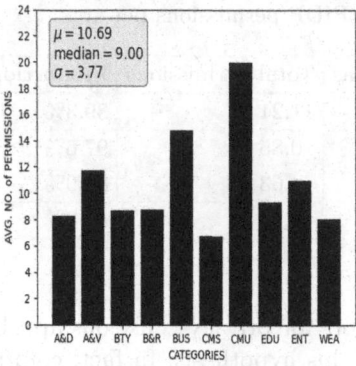 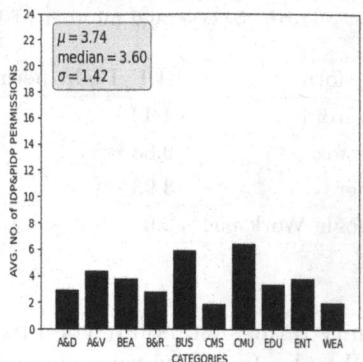

Fig. 1. Average number of permissions per app with different categories; Average number of IDP/PIDP permissions per app with different categories. Art&Design, Auto&Vehicles, Beauty, Books&Reference, Business, Comics, Communication, Education, Entertainment, Weather

5   Discussion: Avoidance, Transparency and Control

In Sect. 3 and 4 we observed that i) all observed platforms offer permissions potentially invoking interdependent privacy, and ii) real apps do request a number of these permissions. Users are not particularly aware of interdependent privacy risks [22], and app platforms neither i) do a good job of informing the installing user and other persons affected by this issue, nor ii) offer control levers to influence such sharing. Therefore, it is up to the individual privacy awareness of installing users (acting as "amateur data controllers" [22]) and blind luck, that none of these platforms will experience its own Cambridge Analytica moment. Naturally, these options are neither satisfactory, nor systemic; in the following we discuss potential mitigation mechanisms, promoting risk avoidance, transparency and control.

Risk Avoidance. A visceral response by app platforms to avoid exposed interdependent privacy risks could be to banish (most) IDP/PIDP permissions from their API. In fact, this is exactly what Facebook did in 2018, in response to the Cambridge Analytica scandal: it gutted its API for third-party apps, and introduced strict manual app review (hiring thousands of new employees)[14]. As evidenced by the declining popularity of Facebook apps, this might not be the most efficient way to deal with such risks. Indeed, the strong two-sided network effects characterizing app platforms require catering for both users and developers [17].

Transparency. Inspired by the GDPR and defined eloquently by Kamleitner's 3R insight framework [12], the sharing party (i.e., the amateur controller) can

---
[14] https://about.fb.com/news/2018/04/restricting-data-access/.

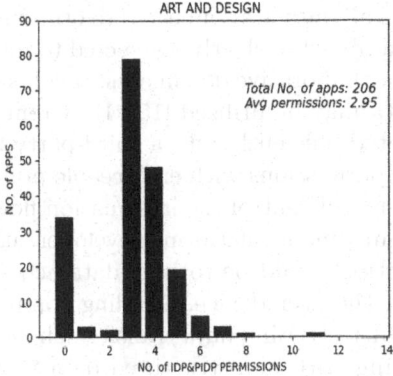
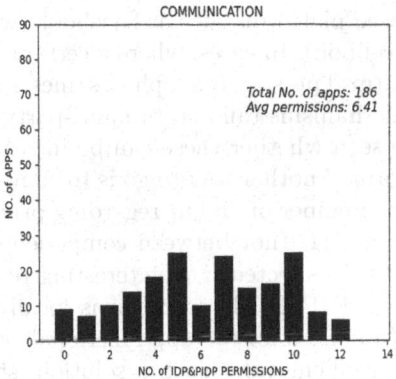

Fig. 2. Number of apps with different number of IDP/PIDP permissions in ART&DESIGN; Number of apps with different number of IDP/PIDP permissions in COMMUNICATION.

take 3 steps to reduce interdependent privacy risks: realize that there is a data transfer, recognize others' rights and respect others' rights. It is clear that transparency enhancing technologies can facilitate the first two steps. A potential way to make the sharer aware of interdependent privacy is to add a special warning sign to the already existing permission notification dialogues. Such a solution has to be platform-specific, and needs the co-operation of the platform owner. If such co-operation is unlikely, a dedicated interdependent privacy dashboard app can be implemented, in the manner of proposed dashboard designs for Facebook apps [22]. Note that an exact public mapping of API-level permissions to user warnings could also improve awareness (especially for browser extensions).

Following the opinion of the Article 29 Working Party and the subsequent recommendations of Privacy International[15] in the TrueCaller case, affected data subjects (i.e., "others") should/could also be notified by the app developer using SMS, using the very data it acquired unlawfully (i.e., contact list). Such notification, however, is not a general possibility: it depends on the platform and the actual data collected.

Control. There are some privacy best practices that, when adhered to, would improve the situation on the developer and the platform owner side. These include requesting the exact minimum privileges an app needs (developer), and introducing well-defined, fine-grain permissions to enable asking for the minimum privilege (platform owner, especially for browser extensions).

Best practices aside, there is potential for interdependent privacy specific solutions that can enable better control of personal information both for affected users, privacy-conscious apps and platforms. Notifying affected data subjects and asking for their consent can be feasible for i) specific data types (e.g., contact list)

---

[15] https://privacyinternational.org/node/2997.

or closed platforms such as Facebook (where all data are connected to other users of Facebook). In cases, where a certain data object is clearly connected to multiple natural persons (e.g., photos, messages, collaborative documents, calls), sharing mechanisms tailored to multi-party data may be utilized [15,21]. It remains to be seen whether these can be incorporated efficiently into a third-party app platform. Another way to go is to combine permissions with enforceable policies (in the manner of [5] but regarding privacy), and control the information flow in run-time [11] (not between components, but among platform, developer, users and others affected). An interesting restriction would be to keep data acquired through IDP/PIDP permissions locally on the user device, enabling computation (if needed for full app functionality) but restricting data transfer. There are many challenges for such a solution, starting with non-structured data that is hard to label as "multi-party".

Indeed, we can make a case for interdependent privacy being inherently present in current app platforms. A radical solution to mitigate this situation would be to completely redesign the currently widespread permission-based access for app platforms, and try different alternatives.

6   Conclusion

In this paper, we have investigated whether interdependent privacy issues are present in popular third-party application platforms, such as Android, browser extensions and Google Workspace. Specifically, we have shown that there exist a significant number of permissions in all platforms that, directly or with reasonable probability, invoke interdependent privacy (RQ1). Moreover, via datasets collected from multiple platforms, we have demonstrated that actual apps do request these permissions (RQ2). We also found that the category of apps can be used as a risk signal for interdependent privacy. Finally, we have discussed potential solutions which could help in enhancing transparency and control. In our future work, we will aim at i) a comprehensive analysis of permission models in browser platforms, and ii) implementing the most promising of the potential transparency and control enhancing solutions discussed above.

References

1. Arzt, S., et al.: FlowDroid: precise context, flow, field, object-sensitive and lifecycle-aware taint analysis for Android apps. ACM SIGPLAN Not. **49**(6), 259–269 (2014)
2. Biczók, G., Chia, P.H.: Interdependent privacy: let me share your data. In: Sadeghi, A.-R. (ed.) FC 2013. LNCS, vol. 7859, pp. 338–353. Springer, Heidelberg (2013). https://doi.org/10.1007/978-3-642-39884-1_29
3. Boyd, D.: Networked privacy. Surveill. Soc. **10**(3/4), 348 (2012)
4. Chia, P.H., Yamamoto, Y., Asokan, N.: Is this app safe?: a large scale study on application permissions and risk signals. In: Mille, A., Gandon, F., Misselis, J., Rabinovich, M., Staab, S. (eds.) Proceedings of the 21st World Wide Web Conference 2012, WWW 2012, Lyon, France, 16–20 April 2012, pp. 311–320. ACM (2012). https://doi.org/10.1145/2187836.2187879

5. Fragkaki, E., Bauer, L., Jia, L., Swasey, D.: Modeling and enhancing Android's permission system. In: Foresti, S., Yung, M., Martinelli, F. (eds.) ESORICS 2012. LNCS, vol. 7459, pp. 1–18. Springer, Heidelberg (2012). https://doi.org/10.1007/978-3-642-33167-1_1

6. Gibler, C., Crussell, J., Erickson, J., Chen, H.: AndroidLeaks: automatically detecting potential privacy leaks in Android applications on a large scale. In: Katzenbeisser, S., Weippl, E., Camp, L.J., Volkamer, M., Reiter, M., Zhang, X. (eds.) Trust 2012. LNCS, vol. 7344, pp. 291–307. Springer, Heidelberg (2012). https://doi.org/10.1007/978-3-642-30921-2_17

7. Gnesi, S., Matteucci, I., Moiso, C., Mori, P., Petrocchi, M., Vescovi, M.: My data, your data, our data: managing privacy preferences in multiple subjects personal data. In: Preneel, B., Ikonomou, D. (eds.) APF 2014. LNCS, vol. 8450, pp. 154–171. Springer, Cham (2014). https://doi.org/10.1007/978-3-319-06749-0_11

8. Harkous, H., Aberer, K.: "If you can't beat them, join them": a usability approach to interdependent privacy in cloud apps. CoRR abs/1702.08234 (2017). http://arxiv.org/abs/1702.08234

9. Humbert, M., Ayday, E., Hubaux, J., Telenti, A.: Addressing the concerns of the lacks family: quantification of kin genomic privacy. In: Sadeghi, A., Gligor, V.D., Yung, M. (eds.) 2013 ACM SIGSAC Conference on Computer and Communications Security, CCS 2013, Berlin, Germany, 4–8 November 2013, pp. 1141–1152. ACM (2013). https://doi.org/10.1145/2508859.2516707

10. Humbert, M., Trubert, B., Huguenin, K.: A survey on interdependent privacy. ACM Comput. Surv. **52**(6), 122:1–122:40 (2020). https://doi.org/10.1145/3360498

11. Jia, L., et al.: Run-time enforcement of information-flow properties on Android. In: Crampton, J., Jajodia, S., Mayes, K. (eds.) ESORICS 2013. LNCS, vol. 8134, pp. 775–792. Springer, Heidelberg (2013). https://doi.org/10.1007/978-3-642-40203-6_43

12. Kamleitner, B., Mitchell, V.: Your data is my data: a framework for addressing interdependent privacy infringements. J. Public Policy Market. **38**(4), 433–450 (2019)

13. Kelley, P.G., Cranor, L.F., Sadeh, N.: Privacy as part of the app decision-making process. In: Proceedings of the SIGCHI Conference on Human Factors in Computing Systems, pp. 3393–3402 (2013)

14. King, J., Lampinen, A., Smolen, A.: Privacy: is there an app for that? In: Proceedings of the Seventh Symposium on Usable Privacy and Security, pp. 1–20 (2011)

15. Olteanu, A., Huguenin, K., Dacosta, I., Hubaux, J.: Consensual and privacy-preserving sharing of multi-subject and interdependent data. In: 25th Annual Network and Distributed System Security Symposium, NDSS 2018, San Diego, California, USA, 18–21 February 2018. The Internet Society (2018). http://wp.internetsociety.org/ndss/wp-content/uploads/sites/25/2018/07/ndss2018_06B-1_Olteanu_paper.pdf

16. Olteanu, A., Huguenin, K., Shokri, R., Humbert, M., Hubaux, J.: Quantifying interdependent privacy risks with location data. IEEE Trans. Mob. Comput. **16**(3), 829–842 (2017). https://doi.org/10.1109/TMC.2016.2561281

17. Parker, G.G., Van Alstyne, M.W.: Two-sided network effects: a theory of information product design. Manag. Sci. **51**(10), 1494–1504 (2005)

18. Pu, Y., Grossklags, J.: Towards a model on the factors influencing social app users' valuation of interdependent privacy. Proc. Priv. Enhancing Technol. **2016**(2), 61–81 (2016). https://doi.org/10.1515/popets-2016-0005

19. Reardon, J., Feal, Á., Wijesekera, P., On, A.E.B., Vallina-Rodriguez, N., Egelman, S.: 50 ways to leak your data: an exploration of apps' circumvention of the android permissions system. In: 28th USENIX Security Symposium (USENIX Security 2019), pp. 603–620 (2019)
20. Squicciarini, A.C., Shehab, M., Paci, F.: Collective privacy management in social networks. In: Quemada, J., León, G., Maarek, Y.S., Nejdl, W. (eds.) Proceedings of the 18th International Conference on World Wide Web, WWW 2009, Madrid, Spain, 20–24 April 2009, pp. 521–530. ACM (2009). https://doi.org/10.1145/1526709.1526780
21. Such, J.M., Porter, J., Preibusch, S., Joinson, A.: Photo privacy conflicts in social media: a large-scale empirical study. In: Proceedings of the 2017 CHI Conference on Human Factors in Computing Systems, pp. 3821–3832 (2017)
22. Symeonidis, I., Biczók, G., Shirazi, F., Pérez-Solà, C., Schroers, J., Preneel, B.: Collateral damage of Facebook third-party applications: a comprehensive study. Comput. Secur. **77**, 179–208 (2018). https://doi.org/10.1016/j.cose.2018.03.015
23. Wang, N., Xu, H., Grossklags, J.: Third-party apps on Facebook: privacy and the illusion of control. In: Proceedings of the 5th ACM Symposium on Computer Human Interaction for Management of Information Technology, pp. 1–10 (2011)

DPM Workshop: Privacy and Learning

SPGC: An Integrated Framework of Secure Computation and Differential Privacy for Collaborative Learning

Kazuki Iwahana[✉][ID], Naoto Yanai[ID], Jason Paul Cruz, and Toru Fujiwara

Osaka University, 1-5 Yamadaoka, Suita, Osaka, Japan
k-iwahana@ist.osaka-u.ac.jp

Abstract. Achieving *differential privacy* and utilizing *secure multiparty computation* are the two major approaches used for ensuring privacy in privacy-preserving machine learning. However, the privacy guarantee by existing integration protocols of both approaches for collaborative learning weakens when more participants join the protocols. In this work, we present *Secure and Private Gradient Computation (SPGC)*, a novel collaborative learning framework with a strong privacy guarantee independent of the number of participants while providing high accuracy. The main idea of SPGC is to *create noise for the differential privacy within secure multiparty computation*. We also created an implementation of SPGC and used it in experiments to measure its accuracy and training time. The results show that SPGC is more accurate than a naive protocol based on local differential privacy by up to 5.6%.

Keywords: Collaborative learning · Privacy-preserving machine learning · Secure multiparty computation · Differential privacy

1 Introduction

1.1 Backgrounds

Collaborative learning as known as federated learning is a kind of machine learning where multiple participants pool all training data, and a model is trained on this communal pool. In general, each participant trains a local model with its data and then periodically exchanges and updates model parameters with other participants. Therefore, privacy is an important issue in collaborative learning because training data are collected and pooled from many sources. When sensitive data, such as genome data, are utilized as training data, their privacy should be protected. Inference attacks on training data privacy that reveal information about the training data [13,14] have been found in the past years.

A typical approach to guarantee privacy in collaborative learning is to achieve *differential privacy* [5], i.e., informally, each participant gives data noise in local [3,20] and then updates a model with the data from all participants. However, such an approach often generates significant amounts of noise that degrade

© Springer Nature Switzerland AG 2022
J. Garcia-Alfaro et al. (Eds.): DPM 2021/CBT 2021, LNCS 13140, pp. 89–105, 2022.
https://doi.org/10.1007/978-3-030-93944-1_6

the accuracy of its resultant model. In contrast, the privacy guarantee weakens when the noise generated in local is slight because the training data can be inferred from model parameters [13,14].

A potential solution to the privacy issues mentioned above is the integration [16] of differential privacy and *secure multiparty computation*, which computes a function on inputs given by participants without revealing the inputs themselves. In the integration approach, model parameters are protected by the use of secure multiparty computation before they are exchanged among participants, and small amounts of noise for the differential privacy are generated and added when the model is updated [24,25]. Intuitively, the integration approach enables participants to adjust the total amount of noise they generate and thus supports both the privacy guarantee and the inference accuracy.

However, the privacy guarantee in existing integration protocols [24,25] on collaborative learning weakens when the number of participants increases. In collaborative learning, many participants are expected to join the network, given that the primary motivation for collaborative learning is to collect data from many sources. Therefore, a protocol that offers a privacy guarantee independent of the number of participants is desirable. This paper aims to answer the following key question: *Can a new integrated protocol of differential privacy and secure multiparty computation for collaborative learning which maintains a strong privacy guarantee and accuracy without depending on the number of participants be constructed?*

1.2   Contribution

In this paper, we present *SPGC (Secure and Private Gradient Computation; SPGC is pronounced as "speak")*, an integrated protocol of differential privacy and secure multiparty computation for collaborative learning that provides privacy guarantee independent of the number of participants. As another contribution, we conducted extensive experiments on SPGC with academic and medical diagnosis datasets to measure its performance.

The construction of SPGC is significantly different from existing works [24, 25]. Existing works adopt local differential privacy [3] (LDP) in which each participant generates noise in local and then *removes* the noise via secure multiparty computation. However, an LDP-based construction will weaken the privacy guarantee even by the use of *any* secure multiparty computation. In contrast, the main idea behind SPGC is the *creation of noise within secure multiparty computation*. This idea was inspired by the collaborative gradient computation (CGC) protocol of Chase et al. [2], in which the noise is generated by using secure multiparty computation. However, Chase et al. discussed neither any key insight for constructing an integration protocol based on differential privacy and secure multiparty computation nor evaluation, including communication overhead which is significant in using the secure multiparty computation. Moreover, we found a negative case in the training method of CGC where the positive and negative gradients become indistinguishable from each other. SPGC can avoid such an issue, i.e., resultant gradients can be recovered correctly by restricting the range of gradients in the use of secure multiparty computation.

2 Preliminaries

This section provides backgrounds on deep learning, collaborative learning, differential privacy, and secure multiparty computation.

Deep Learning and Collaborative Learning: Deep learning is composed of a *training* phase to find optimal weight parameters on a model to be trained and an *inference* phase to solve a task via inference on the trained model. The goal of the training phase is to find weight parameters that yield an acceptably small loss on a loss function between an output of the model and its training data. Let the current weight parameters be w_t. A loss function L is defined as an average of outputs of the function with data samples $\{x_1, x_2, \cdots, x_u\}$, and thus the function is defined as $L(w_t) = \frac{1}{u}\sum_{i=1}^{u} L(w_t, x_i)$. The stochastic gradient descent (SGD) algorithm is often utilized to minimize L. The SGD algorithm computes a gradient $g = \frac{1}{u}\sum_{x_i \in X} \nabla_{w_t} L(w_t, x_i)$ and updates the current weight parameter w_t to $w_{t+1} = w_t - \eta g$, where η is a learning rate. In general, the update process of weight parameters is done for each data group called a *batch*.

Collaborative learning is a deep learning algorithm that trains a model distributively by multiple participants. The motivation of collaborative learning is to train a model in a way that, even if training data is distributed to multiple participants, each participant trains a local model on its data and then exchanges model parameters with other participants.

Differential Privacy: Differential privacy [5] is a mathematical notion that guarantees privacy theoretically. Recall the definition below. A randomized mechanism $M : D \rightarrow R$ with domain D and range R satisfies (ϵ, δ)-differential privacy if, for any two adjacent inputs $d, d' \in D$ and for any subset of outputs $S \subseteq R$, the following equation holds: $\Pr(M(d) \in S) \leq \exp(\epsilon)\Pr(M(d') \in S) + \delta$.

Note that ϵ-differential privacy is identical to a particular case for $\delta = 0$ in the definition above. When a deterministic real-valued function is defined as $f : D \rightarrow R$, a typical way to satisfy the differential privacy for f is to perturb the output of a function f by adding noise. More precisely, a mechanism M is instantiated via additive noise calibrated to f's sensitivity S_f, which is defined as the maximum of the absolute distance $|f(d) - f(d')|$ where d and d' are adjacent inputs. The Gaussian mechanism or the Laplace mechanism is often utilized for generating noise. Hereafter, we focus on the Gaussian mechanism which is defined by $M(d) = f(d) + \mathcal{N}(0, (S_f\sigma)^2)$, where $\mathcal{N}(0, (S_f\sigma)^2)$ is the normal distribution with mean 0 and standard deviation $S_f\sigma$. According to Theorem 3.22 in [6], the Gaussian mechanism to function f of the sensitivity S_f satisfies (ϵ, δ)-differential privacy for $\delta \leq \frac{4}{5}\exp\left(-(\sigma\epsilon)^2/2\right)$ and $\epsilon < 1$.

Secure Multiparty Computation: Secure multiparty computation is a cryptographic tool that is commonly used for evaluating a function between multiple participants without leaking any information beyond what is revealed by the output of the computation. We describe garbled circuits and secret sharing as building blocks of the secure multiparty computation below. A garbled circuit is a secure multiparty computation protocol used for evaluating any function as well as preserving the privacy of inputs. Garbled circuits are often utilized in a two-party setting. In this protocol, a function is presented as Boolean circuits to be encrypted. TinyGarble [23] is a publicly available library of garbled circuits. On the other hand, secret sharing is a cryptographic tool used for encoding data into multiple shares such that each share reveals nothing about the original data. The original data itself can then be recovered only when shares more than a threshold designated in advance are gathered.

3   Problem Description

This section describes privacy-preserving collaborative learning and its technical difficulty.

3.1   Privacy-Preserving Collaborative Learning

Privacy-preserving collaborative learning is collaborative learning where the privacy of training data provided by k participants $P = \{p_1, \cdots, p_k\}$ is preserved against n servers in the training phase and a client in the inference phase. For a privacy-preserving mechanism M and a model $Y = f(g(X_{p_1}), g(X_{p_2}), \cdots, g(X_{p_k}))$ trained by collaborative learning for the entire training datasets $X = \{X_{p_1}, X_{p_2}, \cdots, X_{p_k}\}$, all participants compute $M(Y)$ and a client can utilize $M(Y)$ for an inference on any chosen input z, i.e., computation of $M(Y(z))$ to the client.

In this paper, the requirements for achieving training data privacy against an adversary are described below. These requirements are the same as in Hybri-dAlpha [25]. In the following requirements, we assume that a participant p_1 and a server H_1 are honest for the sake of convenience.

Privacy of Computation: An adversary can collude with $n-1$ servers and $k-1$ participants in the training phase, and the servers and participants follow a protocol, i.e., the honest-but-curious setting. Then, any information except for $M(Y)$ with respect to training data X_{p_1} provided by an honest participant p_1 is not revealed to the adversary.

Privacy of Output: An adversary can collude with a client who follows a protocol, i.e., the honest-but-curious setting, in the inference phase. Then, any information with respect to training data X_{p_1} provided by p_1 is not revealed against the adversary except for $M(Y(z))$ for any chosen z.

As discussed in Sect. 1, attacks that infer training data from gradients during training have been proposed [13,14]. To protect training data from such attacks, the privacy to protect gradients in the training phase, i.e., the privacy of computation, is necessary. In addition, even when the privacy of computation is achieved, some attacks [7, 21] can reveal the original training data from inference results. This means that the privacy should be guaranteed in the inference phase, i.e., the privacy of output, to protect the training data. Therefore, by achieving both the privacy of computation and the privacy of output, a collaborative learning algorithm that achieves the privacy guarantee for training data in the training and inference phases can be realized.

3.2   Technical Difficulty

The privacy guarantee of existing integration protocols [24, 25] of secure multiparty computation and differential privacy for collaborative learning weakens as the number of participants increases. These protocols allow each participant to perturb model parameters locally by adding noise to these parameters. They then require a central server to compute the mean of the perturbed parameters via secure multiparty computation. Then, the amount of noise in the existing protocols is often reduced overly, instead of improving accuracy. In other words, the privacy guarantee becomes weakened in exchange for accuracy improvement. However, the privacy need to be guaranteed to prevent inference attacks [7, 21] as described in Sect. 3.1.

This problem with existing works [24, 25] is challenging to solve. In general, local differential privacy is used to guarantee privacy in collaborative learning [3] although the accuracy decreases due to the noise. Indeed, the existing works [24, 25] are extensions of local differential privacy. More specifically, the existing works have utilized secure multiparty computation to remove the noise of local differential privacy. In other words, if local differential privacy is adopted, then removing noise by the use of secure multiparty computation is necessary to maintain accuracy. Thus, besides the existing works [24, 25] described above, any protocol based on local differential privacy will sacrifice either the privacy guarantee or the accuracy *even if it will use secure multiparty computation.*

4   Design of SPGC

This section presents SPGC, a privacy-preserving collaborative deep learning protocol based on the integration of differential privacy and secure multiparty computation. We first describe an overview of SPGC, including the main idea to overcome the difficulty described in the previous section, and then show its construction and privacy analysis.

4.1   Overview

The key insight of SPGC is to perturb gradients by *generating noise and adding it to gradients within secure multiparty computation* in contrast to the existing works [24, 25] which *remove* the noise via secure multiparty computation. Intuitively, SPGC can avoid the possible weakening of the privacy guarantee because

---

Algorithm 1. Participant Side of SPGC

Input: The current batch B_{t,p_j} in a training step, the current weight w_t in a training step, the entire batch size m, gradient norm bound $C > 0$, modulus 2^N where $N > \log_2(mC + 1)$, loss function $L(\cdot, \cdot)$ used in training.

Output: $\langle G \rangle_1$ sent to a server H_1, $\langle G \rangle_2$ sent to a server H_2.

1: **for** $x_i \in B_{t,p_j}$ **do**
2:     $\overline{g}(x_i) = \nabla_{w_t} L(w_t, x_i)$
3:     $\tilde{g}(x_i) = \min(1, \frac{C}{||\overline{g}(x_i)||_2})\overline{g}(x_i)$
4: **end for**
5: $g = \sum_{x_i \in B_{t,p_j}} \tilde{g}(x_i)$
6: $G = \frac{2^N - 1}{mC} g$
7: $r = Uniform[-2^N, 2^N)$
8: $\langle G \rangle_1 = G + r$ smod 2^N
9: $\langle G \rangle_2 = r$ smod 2^N

---

it does not include a process for removing noise. Thus, SPGC can maintain a strong privacy guarantee even if many participants join the protocol.

The idea described above was inspired by the collaborative gradient computation (CGC) by Chase et al. [2], but they did not present any generalized discussion about the construction of collaborative learning. Furthermore, CGC cannot distinguish the positive and negative gradients from each other when a gradient is equal to a modulus of the protocol, although we omit the detail due to the space limitation. In contrast, SPGC is constructed in a manner where the gradients are *always* smaller than the value of a modulus, and therefore it can train a model correctly.

4.2 Construction

SPGC consists of two algorithms, i.e., one for the participant side and another for the server-side. Hereafter, we assume the following preconditions of SPGC: (1) each participant $p_j \in P$ utilizes a dataset X_{p_j} as a form of batches $\{B_{1,p_j}, B_{2,p_j}, ..., B_{\ell,p_j}\}$ of random examples where ℓ is the number of batches; (2) let the entire batch size m obtained from P be $\sum_{j \in [1,k]} |B_{t,p_j}|$ for any $t \in [1, \ell]$; (3) each participant p_j owns an initial model, whose weights w_0 and architecture are common for all the participants. The update of weights, i.e., the update of the model itself, is conducted on each batch. In other words, we describe only a gradient computation for a single step as the algorithms of SPGC below.

We also describe how the smod operations defined by Chase et al. [2] can be computed with secret sharing below. Smod is defined as x smod $C = ((x + C) \bmod 2C) - C$. For instance, for any integer $x \in [-C, C)$, shares of x are generated by $\langle x \rangle_1 = (x + \langle x \rangle_2)$ smod C, where $\langle x \rangle_2$ is uniformly distributed in $[-C, C)$. The resulting share $\langle x \rangle_1, \langle x \rangle_2$ then reveals nothing about x. x is recovered by computing $x = \langle x \rangle_1 - \langle x \rangle_2$ smod C.

Algorithm 2. Server Side of SPGC

Input: The participant sets P, $\langle G^{p_j} \rangle_1$ output from participant $p_j \in P$, $\langle G^{p_j} \rangle_2$ output from participant $p_j \in P$, the deviation σ of the normal distribution, the entire batch size m, gradient norm bound $C > 0$, modulus 2^N where $N > \log_2(mC + 1)$.
Output: $g^{DP} = \sum_{p_j \in P} g^{p_j} + \mathcal{N}(0, C^2\sigma^2)$
1: H_1 : $\langle G_{H_1} \rangle_1 = \sum_{p_j \in P} \langle G^{p_j} \rangle_1$ smod 2^N
2: H_1 : generate a random seed s_1
3: H_2 : $\langle G_{H_2} \rangle_2 = \sum_{p_j \in P} \langle G^{p_j} \rangle_2$ smod 2^N
4: H_2 : generate a random seed s_2
5: $G^{DP} = \left(\langle G_{H_1} \rangle_1 - \langle G_{H_2} \rangle_2 \text{ smod } 2^N \right) + \mathcal{N}_{s_1 \oplus s_2}\left(0, \left(\frac{2^N-1}{m}\sigma\right)^2\right)$
6: $g^{DP} = \frac{mC}{2^N-1}G^{DP}$

Participant Side: All the participants run Algorithm 1 in parallel. A participant $p_j \in P$ computes his/her per-example gradient $\overline{g}(x_i)$ in local. Then, p_j clips the L_2 norm for each gradient $\overline{g}(x_i)$ and computes a summation g of the gradients. This clipping decides the sensitivity S_f, which is utilized for the range of noise, i.e., $S_f = C$ in SPGC. Then, p_j converts a floating-point gradient g into a fixed-point gradient G in line 8 because of secret sharing for training. Therefore, p_j encodes G into two shares, i.e., $\langle G^{p_j} \rangle_1$ and $\langle G^{p_j} \rangle_2$. Finally, outputs of Algorithm 2, i.e., $\langle G^{p_j} \rangle_1$ and $\langle G^{p_j} \rangle_2$, are sent to servers H_1 and H_2, respectively.

Server Side: After all the participants have run Algorithm 1, H_1 and H_2 run Algorithm 2. H_1 and H_2 receive shares, i.e., $\langle G^{p_j} \rangle_1$ and $\langle G^{p_j} \rangle_2$, from each participant p_j, respectively. In doing so, H_1 and H_2 need to wait until they receive the shares from all participants. Moreover, H_1 and H_2 compute $\langle G_{H_1} \rangle_1$ and $\langle G_{H_2} \rangle_2$, respectively. Then, H_1 and H_2 execute garbled circuits.

Next, in line 5, both the recovery of gradients and the generation of noise are executed within the garbled circuits. In particular, the gradients are recovered by computing $(\langle G_{H_1} \rangle_1 - \langle G_{H_2} \rangle_2)$ smod 2^N. Simultaneously, via a xor computation of s_1 and s_2, a seed for generating noise of the differential privacy is computed. The xor computation within the garbled circuit is done to conceal the generated noise itself against each server. G^{DP} is then obtained with a noise generated from the seed $s_1 \oplus s_2$ and the recovered gradient $(\langle G_{H_1} \rangle_1 - \langle G_{H_2} \rangle_2)$ smod 2^N. Finally, g^{DP} is obtained as a floating-point value.

Note: SPGC may look similar to CGC [2], but its construction is strictly different from CGC, which contains a theoretical problem. CGC may compute a gradient imprecisely when the value of a gradient is equal to a modulus α. To overcome this problem, SPGC restricts a range of fixed-point gradients to be smaller than a modulus, i.e., $2^N > mC + 1$. Therefore, SPGC can always compute gradients because their values are not equal to a modulus. We also prove in Theorem 1 that SPGC can compute gradients precisely. Our idea enables SPGC to achieve higher accuracy than CGC as well. Furthermore, by creating a modulus in the smod operation in the form of 2^N, the smod operation within garbled circuits becomes faster.

Correctness: We show the following theorem as the correctness of SPGC.

Theorem 1. *For any modulus $\alpha \in \mathbb{N}$ such that $\alpha > mC > 1$ holds, $G' = |\sum_{i=1}^{m} \frac{\alpha-1}{mC} \tilde{g}(x_i)| < \alpha$ holds.*

Proof. From the assumption where $\alpha > mC > 1$ holds, $\frac{\alpha-1}{mC} > 0$ holds. Then, because $|\tilde{g}(x_i)| \leq C$ holds, the following relationship holds for $\tilde{g}(x_i)$:

$$-C \leq \tilde{g}(x_i) \leq C \Leftrightarrow -\frac{(\alpha-1)}{m} \leq \frac{\alpha-1}{mC}\tilde{g}(x_i) \leq \frac{(\alpha-1)}{m}.$$

Then, on a summation of gradients, the following relationship holds from the relationship described above:

$$-\alpha + 1 \leq \sum_{i=1}^{m} \frac{\alpha-1}{mC}\tilde{g}(x_i) \leq \alpha - 1 \Leftrightarrow -\alpha < \sum_{i=1}^{m} \frac{\alpha-1}{mC}\tilde{g}(x_i) < \alpha.$$

Therefore, for any $\alpha \in \mathbb{N}$ such that $\alpha > mC > 1$ holds, $|\sum_{i}^{m} \frac{\alpha-1}{mC}\tilde{g}(x_i)| < \alpha$ holds. $\qquad\square$

The above theorem restricts a summation of gradients in SPGC to the range of values less than $\pm\alpha$. Here, α is defined as 2^N in SPGC. Then, $\langle G_{H_1} \rangle_1 - \langle G_{H_2} \rangle_2$ smod $2^N = G'$ holds. Thus, the encoded gradient is correctly recovered.

4.3   Privacy Analysis

We analyze the privacy of computation and the privacy of output for SPGC, which were defined in Sect. 3.

Privacy of Computation: First, we assume that both the garbled circuits and secret sharing achieve the privacy of computation. Then, the privacy of computation in the training phase of the SPGC protocol can be achieved following the composition theorem by Kushilevitz et al. [11]. In other words, in Algorithm 2, the computations in lines 1 and 3 are executed via secret sharing, while the computation in line 5 is executed within a garbled circuit. Unless an adversary colludes with both H_1 and H_2, the adversary cannot identify any value except for g^{DP}. In addition, since noise with differential privacy is generated within garbled circuits, an adversary cannot know the accurate noise value. Consequently, no information with respect to training data X_{p_1} is revealed even if an adversary colludes with either H_1 or H_2 and any participant $p_{j\neq1}$. More formally, following the proof of CGC [2], we can prove the following theorem.

Theorem 2. *If all servers and participants follow the protocol, no information except for an output $g^{DP} = \sum_{p_j \in P} g^{p_j} + \mathcal{N}(0, C^2\sigma^2)$ of Algorithm 2 is revealed to an adversary.*

Proof. In this proof, we discuss from two standpoints, i.e., participant-side and server-side. On the participant-side, any participant will obtain the end result

g^{DP} from H_1, H_2 and nothing else. Hence, without colluding with H_1 and H_2, an adversary cannot reveal any information about g^{p_1}. On the server-side, $\langle G^{p_j} \rangle_1 = G^{p_j} + r^{p_j}$ smod 2^N and $\langle G^{p_j} \rangle_2 = r^{p_j}$ smod 2^N are uniformly distributed values by virtue of secret sharing as shown in Sect. 2. If there exists a mechanism M' controlled by an adversary, which is given g^{DP} and $G^{p_j} + r^{p_j}$ and then predicts any property p about G^{p_1}, then the following distribution is obtained from the view of the adversary:

$$\Pr[M'(g^{DP}, \langle G^{p_j} \rangle_1) = p(G^{p_1})] = \Pr\left[M'(g^{DP}, \langle G^{p_j} \rangle_1) = p(G^{p_1}) | \langle G^{p_j} \rangle_1\right]$$
$$= \Pr\left[M('g^{DP}, \langle G^{p_j} \rangle_1) = p(G^{p_1}) | \langle G^{p_j} \rangle_1 \sim \text{Uniform}[-2^N, 2^N)]\right].$$

Therefore, any mechanism M' cannot reveal information more than that viewed by any participant and server, who observe only g^{DP}.   □

Privacy of Output: To achieve the privacy of output, SPGC needs to satisfy the differential privacy [15,17]. When adding noise with (ϵ, δ)-differential privacy, SPGC satisfies constantly $(\tilde{\epsilon}, \tilde{\delta})$-differential privacy for the number of participants k based on the Theorem 3. In contrast, the existing works [24,25] satisfy $(\sqrt{k}\tilde{\epsilon}, \tilde{\delta})$-differential privacy. In other words, different from existing works, SPGC can guarantee privacy independent of the number of participants.

Theorem 3. *If all servers and participants follow the protocol and (ϵ, δ)-differential privacy at each batch of the training, SPGC satisfies $(\tilde{\epsilon}, \tilde{\delta})$-differential privacy in the entire process of the training after T epochs, where*

$$\tilde{\delta} = 1 - (1 - \delta)^T (1 - \delta),$$

$$\tilde{\epsilon} = \min\left\{ T\epsilon, \frac{(e^\epsilon - 1)T\epsilon}{e^\epsilon + 1} + \epsilon\sqrt{2T\log(e + \frac{\sqrt{T\epsilon^2}}{\tilde{\delta}})}, \frac{(e^\epsilon - 1)T\epsilon}{e^\epsilon + 1} + \epsilon\sqrt{2T\log(\frac{1}{\tilde{\delta}})} \right\}.$$

Proof. For computation on each batch, $\sum_{p_j \in P} g^{p_j} + \mathcal{N}(0, C^2\sigma^2)$ is obtained from an output of Algorithm 2. In doing so, σ is chosen so that (ϵ, δ)-differential privacy is satisfied with each batch. Since a training dataset for each participant is disjointedly divided into ℓ batches, each sample appears in a batch at once. Then, a perturbed gradient based on (ϵ, δ)-differential privacy is computed for each batch, and then a model is updated with the gradient. In doing so, SPGC satisfies (ϵ, δ)-differential privacy for each epoch following the parallel composition theorem [9,12]. Therefore, from Theorem 3.4 by Kairouz et al. [10], an output of the algorithms of SPGC after T epochs satisfies the $(\tilde{\epsilon}, \tilde{\delta})$-differential privacy described above.   □

5   Experiments

This section presents the experiments to measure the accuracy and training time of SPGC.

5.1 Experimental Setup

Implementation: All the experiments were conducted on a computer equipped with Ubuntu 18.04, 83GB RAM, Intel Xeon(R) CPU E5-2630 v3 2.40GHz, and no GPU. SPGC is implemented mainly with the TensorFlow library in python, which is an open-source platform developed by Google. Meanwhile, secret sharing is implemented with the NumPy library, and garbled circuits used between servers are implemented with the TinyGarble library [23] in C++.

Purpose of Experiments: The purpose of our experiments is to evaluate the accuracy and the training time of SPGC for academic and medical diagnosis datasets. To do this, we first evaluate the accuracy and training time of SPGC with respect to the amount of noise for differential privacy. Then, we compare the accuracy and training time of SPGC with the baselines, i.e., non-privacy setting, the use of differential privacy, and secure multiparty computation.

Baseline: The following settings are utilized as baselines to compare with the performance of SPGC.

Non-privacy: Train a model without the privacy guarantee. The Non-privacy setting significantly differs from the setting of SPGC in that it assumes the use of a single server, which aggregates gradients sent from participants.

Local Differential Privacy (LDP): Train a model with a mechanism satisfying local differential privacy (LDP) [3]. Concretely, each participant gives his/her gradients noise for differential privacy in local. LDP is a trivial way for guaranteeing privacy in collaborative learning and is also faster than SPGC because it does not use secure multiparty computation.

Only Secure Multiparty Computation (Only-MPC): It is the same setting as SPGC except that noise is non-generated within garbled circuits.

Choice of Parameters in SPGC: On Algorithm 1 and Algorithm 2, let the number of participants be 3, the gradient norm bound C be 1, and N be 16, i.e., a 16-bit integer is utilized. The standard deviation of a noise for differential privacy is computed as $\sigma = \sqrt{2\log(\frac{1.25}{\delta})}/\epsilon$ with respect to parameters ϵ and δ of the differential privacy [6]. Meanwhile, noise parameters are $\epsilon = 0.5, 2.0$, and 8.0, which are in common with CGC. [2]. Likewise, let δ be 10^{-3}. Parameters ϵ and δ in SPGC indicate the privacy level at one step in training. Meanwhile, ϵ and δ in LDP indicate the privacy level when a participant generates noise locally. The privacy levels in both settings may seem to have different values, but an adversary can reveal a perturbed gradient by an honest participant in SPGC if he/she colludes with all participants except for the honest participant. In particular, SPGC provides the same privacy level as when only an honest participant adds noise with a gradient with LDP. We can, therefore, fairly compare the privacy level of SPGC with that of LDP at one step in training.

Datasets and Their Architectures: The datasets used in the experiments and their architectures are shown below.

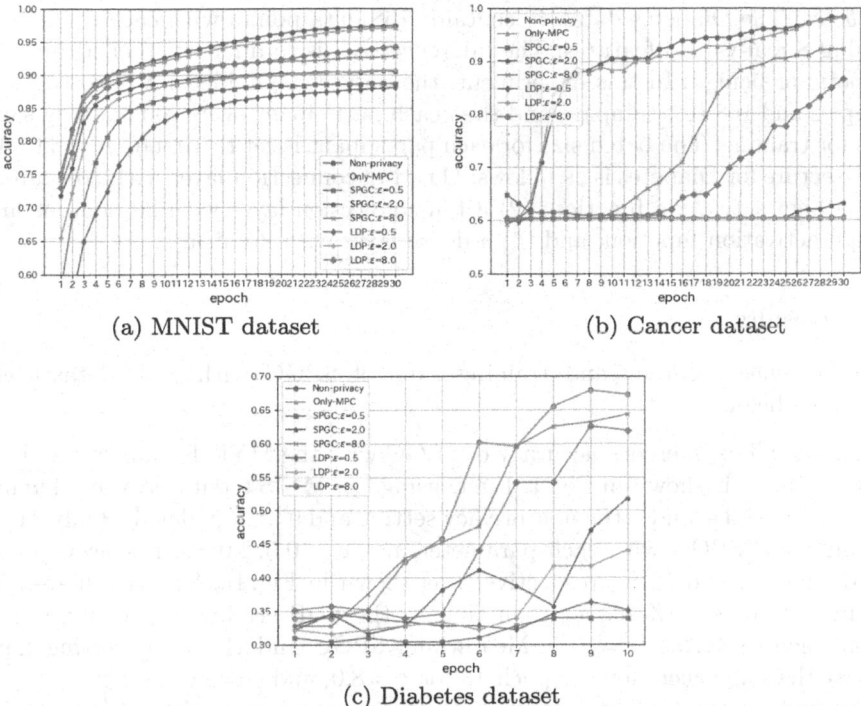

(a) MNIST dataset   (b) Cancer dataset

(c) Diabetes dataset

Fig. 1. Inference accuracy of each baseline

MNIST: The MNIST dataset contains 70,000 images of handwritten digits from 0 to 9. In particular, the dataset has 60,000 training samples and 10,000 test samples, each with 784 features representing 28×28 pixels in the image. In this experiment, the training samples are divided by three participants, i.e., 20,000 samples per participant for training. Furthermore, the batch size for each participant is set to 1,000, i.e., the entire batch size $m = 3,000$. An architecture is as follows: (1) a 5×5 convolution layer with 16 outputs per window, a $2 - 2$ stride, ReLU activation function, and padding; (2) a $1 \times 5 \times 5$ convolution layer with 32 neurons, a $1 - 2 - 2$ stride, no weight sharing on the first axis, and ReLU activation function; and (3) a dense layer with 10 neurons.

Cancer: The Cancer dataset[1] contains 569 data points with each point containing 30 real-valued features. The inference task is to infer whether a tumor is cancerous or benign. In this experiment, the dataset is divided into 390 training samples and 179 test samples, and then each participant owns 130 training samples for training. The batch size for each participant is set to 10, i.e., $m = 30$. We utilized a single full connection layer from 90 to 2 neurons.

---

[1] Cancer: https://www.kaggle.com/uciml/breast-cancer-wisconsin-data.

Diabetes: The Diabetes dataset[2] contains 768 data points with each point containing 8 real-valued features. The inference task is to infer whether a tumor is diabetic or benign. In this experiment, the dataset is divided into 600 training samples and 168 test samples, and then each participant owns 200 training samples for training. The batch size for each participant is set to 10, i.e., $m = 30$. An architecture for Diabetes is as follows: (1) a full connection layer with 20 neurons and a Sign activation function; (2) a full connection layer with 20 neurons and a Sign activation function; and (3) a dense layer with 2 outputs.

5.2   Results

The inference accuracy and training time of SPGC with each dataset are described below.

Accuracy: The inference accuracy of SPGC with the MNIST, Cancer and Diabetes datasets is shown in Fig. 1. First, using the MNIST dataset, the inference accuracy is 97.4% under the non-privacy setting and 97.1% under the Only-MPC setting while SPGC with each parameter, i.e., $\epsilon = 0.5, 2.0, 8.0$ has accuracy of 88.6%, 90.5%, and 92.8%,respectively, as shown in Fig. 1a. SPGC achieved an accuracy that is 0.4% higher than that in the LDP setting, especially with a strong noise such as $\epsilon = 0.5$. Meanwhile, SPGC and the LDP setting have almost the same accuracy at epoch 18 for $\epsilon = 8.0$, and $\epsilon = 2.0$.

Second, on the Cancer dataset, both the non-privacy setting and the Only-MPC setting have 98.3% accuracy, while SPGC for $\epsilon = 0.5, 2.0, 8.0$ has 60.3%, 63.1%, and 92.1% accuracy, respectively, as shown in Fig. 1b. SPGC achieved an accuracy that is 5.6% higher than the LDP setting for $\epsilon = 8.0$.

Finally, on the Diabetes dataset, both the non-privacy setting and the Only-MPC setting have 67.2% accuracy while SPGC for $\epsilon = 0.5, 2.0, 8.0$, has 33.9%, 51.8%, and 61.9% accuracy, respectively, as shown in Fig. 1c. SPGC achieved an accuracy that is 2.3% higher than that in the LDP setting for $\epsilon = 8.0$, but 2.8% lower for $\epsilon = 0.5$.

Training Time: The training time of SPGC with the MNIST, Cancer and Diabetes datasets is shown in Table 1. To clarify the differences in the training time of SPGC between each parameter, we conducted additional experiments for $\epsilon = 0.01$ and $\epsilon = 0.1$.

First, in terms of training time with the MNIST dataset, SPGC needed 115.7 h while the Only-MPC setting required only 70.1 h, i.e., a difference of 45.6 h. Meanwhile, there was a 3-hour difference in the training time between $\epsilon = 8.0$ and $\epsilon = 0.01$. Entirely, the training time of SPGC is 72 times longer than that of LDP.

Second, in terms of training time with the Cancer dataset, SPGC required 10.8 h for the training while the Only-MPC setting required 6.5 h, i.e., a difference of 4.3 h. Meanwhile, there was a 0.4 h difference in the training time between

---

[2] Diabetes: https://www.kaggle.com/uciml/pima-indians-diabetes-database.

$\epsilon = 8.0$ and $\epsilon = 0.01$. Entirely, the training time of SPGC is 98 times longer than that of LDP.

Finally, in terms of training time with the Diabetes dataset, SPGC required 1.23 h for the training while the Only-MPC setting required 0.80 h, i.e., a difference of 0.44 h. Meanwhile, there was a 0.05 h difference in the training time between $\epsilon = 8.0$ and $\epsilon = 0.01$. Entirely, the training time of SPGC is 21 times longer than that of LDP.

Table 1. Training time and communication overhead: for each dataset, let Training(h) be the training time until convergence, Offline(h) be gradient computation time, i.e., the lines 1–5 of Algorithm 1, Online(h) be the remaining time of Algorithm 1 and Algorithm 2, and CO(GB) be the communication overhead between H_1 and H_2. The values enclosed in ( ) are under the LDP setting.

	MNIST				Cancer			
	Offline	Online	Training	CO	Offline	Online	Training	CO
$\epsilon = 0.01$	1.69(1.53)	115.77(0.04)	117.45(1.57)	7758.0(-)	0.11(0.11)	10.93(0.01)	11.03(0.12)	736.9(-)
$\epsilon = 0.1$	1.66(1.53)	114.47(0.04)	116.13(1.57)	7746.9(-)	0.11(0.10)	10.50(0.01)	10.61(0.11)	707.8(-)
$\epsilon = 0.5$	1.67(1.55)	114.05(0.04)	115.7(1.59)	7641.9(-)	0.11(0.10)	10.65(0.01)	10.76(0.11)	711.7(-)
$\epsilon = 2.0$	1.67(1.55)	113.45(0.04)	115.1(1.59)	7641.9(-)	0.11(0.09)	10.52(0.00)	10.63(0.10)	699.8(-)
$\epsilon = 8.0$	1.67(1.55)	112.78(0.04)	114.5(1.59)	7528.2(-)	0.11(0.09)	10.53(0.00)	10 63(0.10)	698.8(-)
Only-MPC	1.66	70.16	71.82	289.2	0.11	6.40	6.51	39.5
Non-privacy	1.68	0.05	1.73	-	0.10	0.01	0.11	-

	Diabetes			
	Offline	Online	Training	CO
$\epsilon = 0.01$	0.07(0.07)	1.19(0.00)	1.26(0.07)	81.6(-)
$\epsilon = 0.1$	0.07(0.06)	1.20(0.00)	1.27(0.06)	78.4(-)
$\epsilon = 0.5$	0.07(0.06)	1.16(0.00)	1.23(0.06)	78.9(-)
$\epsilon = 2.0$	0.07(0.06)	1.15(0.00)	1.22(0.06)	77.5(-)
$\epsilon = 8.0$	0.07(0.06)	1.14(0.00)	1.21(0.06)	77.5(-)
Only-MPC	0.07	0.73	0.80	4.4
Non-privacy	0.06	0.00	0.06	-

5.3 Discussion

In this subsection, we discuss considerations on the accuracy and training time of SPGC and the effect on the number of participants.

Accuracy: We first discuss the accuracy of SPGC with respect to noise parameters for each dataset and then compare it with that of the LDP setting. According to Fig. 1, the decrease in the accuracy by noise is different for each dataset. This might be caused by the number of data in each dataset. The effect of noise on the model becomes more prominent as the number of training data is smaller. Meanwhile, the LDP setting achieves higher accuracy in evaluating the MNIST and Diabetes datasets than SPGC with $\epsilon = 8.0$, $\epsilon = 2.0$. The decrease in accuracy of SPGC is greatly affected by the bit truncation by a modulo operation with $\epsilon = 8.0$, $\epsilon = 2.0$. In contrast, the decrease in accuracy is restricted because the bit truncation by a modulo operation is unnecessary for the LDP setting.

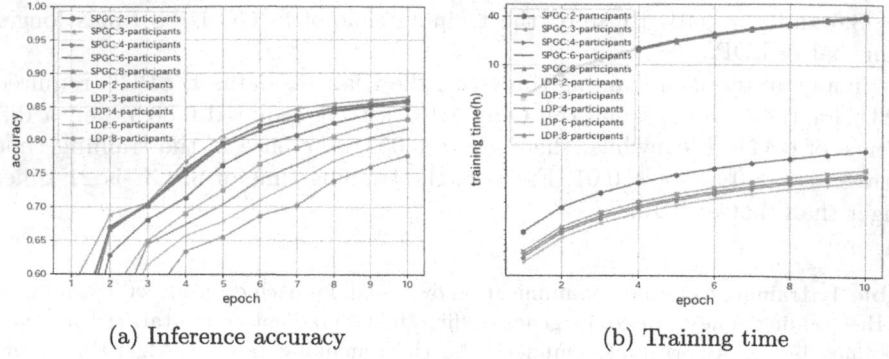

(a) Inference accuracy   (b) Training time

Fig. 2. Effect of the number of participants to accuracy and training time: We measured the accuracy and the training time for a noise parameter $\epsilon = 0.5$ on the evaluation of the MNIST dataset by changing the number of participants.

We also found a case that the accuracy of SPGC outperforms that of the LDP setting. Specifically, a sufficient number of participants is needed to improve the accuracy of the LDP setting. Since noise is generated from the Gaussian distribution with a mean of zero, the amount of noise becomes close to zero when a large number of participants join the protocols. In the experimental setting, the number of participants is three, and it is insufficient to become zero. Therefore, the accuracy of SPGC became higher than that of the LDP setting.

Training Time: We discuss the inflection of the training time for each noise. The training time of SPGC is directly proportional to the mounting noise as shown in Table 1. This is a result of the communication overhead of garble circuits shown as "CO" column in Table 1. Notably, the communication overhead for SPGC increases significantly in comparison with the Only-MPC setting. This is caused by the garbled circuits which generate a noise from $N(0, (\frac{2^N - 1}{m}\sigma)^2)$ with differential privacy. The communication overhead increases in proportion to noise because the structure of garbled circuits depends on the noise deviation σ. The relationship between communication overhead and noise was also discussed in work by Dwork et al. [4] in the combination of secret sharing and differential privacy. Dwork et al. also showed that the communication overhead in secret sharing increases in proportion to noise with differential privacy.

Number of Participants: To understand the effect of the number of participants on accuracy and training time, we evaluate SPGC with various numbers of participants. In our additional experiment, following the experiments presented in HybridAlpha [25], the accuracy and the training time are measured on the MNIST dataset for 3, 6, and 8 participants. Furthermore, we additionally measure for 2 and 4 participants. In doing so, the training data is divided equally among the participants, e.g., 10,000 data per participant for the 6-participant setting, and $\epsilon = 0.5$ is utilized as the noise parameter. The experiment results, which are measured until 10 epochs, are then compared with the accuracy and the training time on LDP.

The results on the accuracy are shown in Fig. 2a. The accuracy of SPGC is almost stable with respect to the number of participants at epoch 10, while the accuracy on the LDP setting is worsening. This confirms that the accuracy of SPGC is independent of the number of participants. The results on the training time are shown in Fig. 2b. The training time of SPGC is stable with respect to the number of participants because of the following reasons: (1) the total size of the dataset is the same for all settings, and thus the computational complexity is constant; and (2) all experiments were conducted on virtual machines via a physical computer, and thus the process synchronization is not affected. The results on the training time of SPGC may be different if multiple physical machines and the WAN environment are utilized. In contrast, the training time of LDP becomes shorter in proportion to the number of participants because the number of training data each participant owns becomes smaller.

6   Related Works

Many subsequent works on the integration of secure multiparty computation and differential privacy have focused on basic computations, such as median [1,16,22] and summation [8,18,19] with respect to the integration of secure multiparty computation and differential privacy. In recent years, applications of privacy-preserving methods to deep learning [2,24,25] have been presented. We describe details of existing protocols below. SPGC was inspired by CGC [2], which is the closest work to ours. We found a pitfall in CGC where the training fails as described in Sect. 4 and revised it, and thus SPGC is significantly better. Also, SPGC can shorten the training time potentially compared to CGC by virtue of the fixed-point gradients. This rigorous comparison is conducted in future work. Finally, HybridAlpha [25] and the work by Truex et al. [24] aim to optimize noise for differential privacy and mitigate the risks of privacy leakage. However, as discussed in this paper, the privacy guarantee of these works weakens as the number of participants increases, and thus the noise is uncontrollable. In addition, they did not give clear consideration about the differences in the performance of protocols with and without differential privacy.

7   Conclusion

This paper presented SPGC, a collaborative learning framework integrating secure multiparty computation and differential privacy. While existing protocols [24,25] remove noise for differential privacy via secure multiparty computation, SPGC creates the noise within the secure multiparty computation. Moreover, SPGC has overcome the pitfall of CGC [2], in which the training fails. We also conducted extensive experiments with academic and medical diagnosis datasets. The training time of SPGC with the Cancer dataset was carried out in about 10.8 h until convergence of training, and SPGC achieved an accuracy of 92.1%, which is 5.6% higher than that of the naive LDP-based approach. We identified that the training time becomes longer in proportion to the amount of noise as well. In the future, we plan to conduct additional experiments with more complicated and deeper architectures, e.g., CIFAR-10.

Acknowledgement. This work is supported by the Cabinet Office (CAO), Cross-ministerial Strategic Innovation Promotion Program (SIP), Cyber Physical Security for IoT Society (funding agency: NEDO).

References

1. Bohler, J., Kerschbaum, F.: Secure sublinear time differentially private median computation. In: Proceedings of NDSS. Internet Society (2020)
2. Chase, M., Gilad-Bachrach, R., Laine, K., Lauter, K., Rindal, P.: Private collaborative neural network learning. Cryptology ePrint Archive, Report 2017/762 (2017). https://eprint.iacr.org/2017/762
3. Duchi, J.C., Jordan, M.I., Wainwright, M.J.: Local privacy and statistical minimax rates. In: Proceedings of FOCS, pp. 429–438. IEEE (2013)
4. Dwork, C., Kenthapadi, K., McSherry, F., Mironov, I., Naor, M.: Our data, ourselves: privacy via distributed noise generation. In: Vaudenay, S. (ed.) EUROCRYPT 2006. LNCS, vol. 4004, pp. 486–503. Springer, Heidelberg (2006). https://doi.org/10.1007/11761679_29
5. Dwork, C., McSherry, F., Nissim, K., Smith, A.: Calibrating noise to sensitivity in private data analysis. In: Halevi, S., Rabin, T. (eds.) TCC 2006. LNCS, vol. 3876, pp. 265–284. Springer, Heidelberg (2006). https://doi.org/10.1007/11681878_14
6. Dwork, C., Roth, A.: The algorithmic foundations of differential privacy. Found. Trends Theor. Comput. Sci. **9**(3–4), 211–407 (2014)
7. Fredrikson, M., Jha, S., Ristenpart, T.: Model inversion attacks that exploit confidence information and basic countermeasures. In: Proceedings of CCS, pp. 1322–1333. ACM (2015)
8. Goryczka, S., Xiong, L.: A comprehensive comparison of multiparty secure additions with differential privacy. IEEE Trans. Dependable Secure Comput. **14**(5), 463–477 (2017)
9. Hsu, J.: Composition, verification, and differential privacy. Invited Talk on TPDP 2018 (2018). https://justinh.su/files/slides/tpdp18-invited.pdf
10. Kairouz, P., Oh, S., Viswanath, P.: The composition theorem for differential privacy. IEEE Trans. Inf. Theory **63**(6), 4037–4049 (2017)
11. Kushilevitz, E., Lindell, Y., Rabin, T.: Information-theoretically secure protocols and security under composition. SIAM J. Comput. **39**, 2090–2112 (2010)
12. McSherry, F.D.: Privacy integrated queries: an extensible platform for privacy-preserving data analysis. In: Proceedings of SIGMOD 2009, pp. 19–30. ACM (2009)
13. Melis, L., Song, C., De Cristofaro, E., Shmatikov, V.: Exploiting unintended feature leakage in collaborative learning. In: Proceedings of IEEE S&P, pp. 691–706. IEEE (2019)
14. Nasr, M., Shokri, R., Houmansadr, A.: Comprehensive privacy analysis of deep learning: passive and active white-box inference attacks against centralized and federated learning. In: Proceedings of IEEE S&P, pp. 739–753. IEEE (2019)
15. Park, C., Hong, D., Seo, C.: An attack-based evaluation method for differentially private learning against model inversion attack. IEEE Access **7**, 124988–124999 (2019)

16. Pettai, M., Laud, P.: Combining differential privacy and secure multiparty computation. In: Proceedings of ACSAC, pp. 421–430. ACM (2015)
17. Rahman, M.A., Rahman, T., Laganière, R., Mohammed, N., Wang, Y.: Membership inference attack against differentially private deep learning model. Trans. Data Priv. **11**(1), 61–79 (2018)
18. Rastogi, V., Nath, S.: Differentially private aggregation of distributed time-series with transformation and encryption. In: Proceedings of SIGMOD, pp. 735–746. ACM (2010)
19. Shi, E., Chan, T.H., Rieffel, E., Chow, R., Song, D.: Privacy-preserving aggregation of time-series data. In: Proceedings of NDSS, pp. 1–17. Citeseer (2011)
20. Shokri, R., Shmatikov, V.: Privacy-preserving deep learning. In: Proceedings of CCS, pp. 1310–1321. ACM (2015)
21. Shokri, R., Stronati, M., Song, C., Shmatikov, V.: Membership inference attacks against machine learning models. In: Proceedings of IEEE S&P, pp. 3–18. IEEE (2017)
22. Smith, A., Thakurta, A., Upadhyay, J.: Is interaction necessary for distributed private learning? In: Proceedings of IEEE S&P, pp. 58–77. IEEE (2017)
23. Songhori, E.M., Hussain, S.U., Sadeghi, A.-R., Schneider, T., Koushanfar, F.: TinyGarble: highly compressed and scalable sequential garbled circuits. In: Proceedings of IEEE S&P, pp. 411–428. IEEE (2015)
24. Truex, S., et al.: A hybrid approach to privacy-preserving federated learning. In: Proceedings of AISec, pp. 1–11. ACM (2019)
25. Xu, R., Baracaldo, N., Zhou, Y., Anwar, A., Ludwig, H.: HybridAlpha: an efficient approach for privacy-preserving federated learning. In: Proceedings of AISec, pp. 13–23. ACM (2019)

A k-Anonymised Federated Learning Framework with Decision Trees

Saloni Kwatra$^{(\boxtimes)}$ and Vicenç Torra

Department of Computing Science, Umeå University, Umeå, Sweden
{salonik,vtorra}@cs.umu.se

Abstract. We propose a privacy-preserving framework using Mondrian k-anonymity with decision trees in a Federated Learning (FL) setting for the horizontally partitioned data. Data heterogeneity in FL makes the data non-IID (Non-Independent and Identically Distributed). We use a novel approach to create non-IID partitions of data by solving an optimization problem. In this work, each device trains a decision tree classifier. Devices share the root node of their trees with the aggregator. The aggregator merges the trees by choosing the most common split attribute and grows the branches based on the split values of the chosen split attribute. This recursive process stops when all the nodes to be merged are leaf nodes. After the merging operation, the aggregator sends the merged decision tree to the distributed devices. Therefore, we aim to build a joint machine learning model based on the data from multiple devices while offering k-anonymity to the participants.

Keywords: Federated learning · Privacy · Decision tree · Aggregation

1 Introduction

The European General Data Protection Regulation (GDPR) is a turning point in the history of the European privacy framework. It was founded on the notion of **privacy** as a fundamental human right. Both the data controller and the data processor must follow a number of policies to ensure compliance with the law, even before the data is processed. It's not simple to come up with the proper definitions and legal interpretations. These concerns can be alleviated if all acquired data is anonymised, therefore avoiding GDPR in the first place, but this is not always achievable [1]. Data anonymisation is the process of protecting an individual's identity, such that the Personally Identifiable Information (PII) is irreversibly modified so that a data subject can no longer be identified directly or indirectly, either by the data controller alone or in collaboration with any other party. The data must be difficult or impossible to link to a specific individual to fulfill the standards of data anonymisation [2]. The critical feature that can be

This study was partially funded by the Wallenberg AI, Autonomous Systems and Software Program (WASP) funded by the Knut and Alice Wallenberg Foundation.

J. Garcia-Alfaro et al. (Eds.): DPM 2021/CBT 2021, LNCS 13140, pp. 106–120, 2022.
https://doi.org/10.1007/978-3-030-93944-1_7

extracted from this definition is that identifying information must be irrevocably modified so that the individual cannot be identified directly or indirectly. There are a plethora of anonymisation techniques. In our framework, we provide k-anonymity to data subjects by using Mondrian k-anonymity [7].

Today, humans are surrounded by AI-driven systems. With the spread of AI, users/data subjects are becoming increasingly worried about how their personal information is being used or even exploited without their permission for commercial and political objectives. Because diverse individuals and organizations generate and own data, the old and naive method of transferring all data to a single location where powerful systems can train machine learning models is no longer desirable, as it is not efficient and violates data privacy. Federated Learning (FL) is an wonderful answer to this problem in this situation. The aim is to train a model at each device where a data source is located, then let the devices communicate their models to establish a global model consensus. FL architecture may or may not have a central coordinating computer or an aggregation server to obtain a global model, depending on the application. In the presence of aggregation server, the devices train a model using their respective data, and submit the model updates to the aggregator. The aggregator then combines the model updates received from different devices, and sends the combined model updates back to the distributed devices. The process is continued until the model reaches a point of convergence or until the maximum number of iterations has been achieved. For e.g., McMachan et al. [3] uses this architecture in Federated Averaging algorithm. Also, the communication between the distributed devices and aggregation server can be encrypted using homomorphic encryption to protect against privacy leakage. In a peer to peer FL architecture (no aggregation server), distributed parties communicate directly with each other. Peer to peer FL is more secure than the previous approach. However, encrypting and decrypting messages has a computational overhead. As a summary, FL provides a distributed solution for building accurate data-driven models from multiple devices avoiding data sharing and providing different privacy guarantees.

The original definition of federated learning is about building deep learning models. It is well known that deep learning models are in, most contexts, the most effective and with the best accuracy among other alternative data-driven models. Nevertheless, they are not so good with respect to their explainability. In contrast, other models and, specially, decision trees, provide explainability. The majority of Artificial Intelligence (AI)-based healthcare diagnostics are black boxes, which means that the results don't explain why the machine thinks a patient has a specific disease or problem. While AI technologies are powerful, their acceptance in health care has been slowed down because of the inability of doctors to validate their results. Because of that, in this paper we propose a framework for federated learning to build decision trees. Our approach will also incorporate privacy guarantees.

In our work, we implement federated learning using **Decision Tree** models. Decision trees, as the name indicates, make decisions using tree-like structures that can be explained. The creation of decision trees is based on identifying the most significant feature related to the target feature and then partitioning the dataset based on the values of these features. While constructing the decision tree, we select the locally optimum choice for each split, making the root node the best predictor. The decision tree algorithms identify the most significant feature using Information Gain (in e.g. Iterative Dichotomiser 3 or ID3 [5]) and Gini Index (in e.g. Classification and Regression Tree or CART [6]). The ID3 and CART algorithms are recursive because the groups formed can be subdivided again using the same policy.

Data heterogeneity is a core problem of FL. In federated learning, data owned by various participants may follow entirely different distributions. Observe that different devices may correspond to mobile phones with individuals gathering and producing data according to different patterns (e.g., using different languages, accessing different social networks, having different interests, etc.). Hence, we are, in general, unable to make IID assumptions about the data in FL. Furthermore, various participants in FL have varying volumes of training data, i.e., some individuals may have only a few data samples while others may have enormous amounts of data. According to how the data is partitioned among multiple parties in the feature and sample spaces, researchers classified FL into Horizontal Federated Learning (HFL), Vertical Federated Learning (VFL), and Federated Transfer Learning (FTL). HFL is a sample-partitioned FL, which means that datasets on various devices share the overlapping feature space but have separate sample space. VFL is a feature-partitioned FL, which is just the opposite of HFL. FTL can be used in situations when neither the features nor the data samples overlap.

Hence, taking inspiration from FL and its categories, we propose a framework for implementing HFL with decision trees. The main **contributions** in this paper are as follows:

- The framework implements Horizontal Federated Learning (HFL) with decision trees.
- The proposed FL framework uses the tree merging algorithm introduced in the paper [10], in which each decision tree defines a set of regions in the space of data. Then, aggregation of decision trees is defined in terms of an aggregation of these regions. We used their approach to implement the aggregation step of FL.
- The proposed FL framework utilizes a novel approach for generating non-IID partitions of the data, which is mathematically proved. It is described in Sect. 4.
- The proposed FL framework provides k-anonymity to its participants. We use Mondrian k-anonymity algorithm [7] to reduce the granularity of data prior using Machine Learning classifier on the data. The reason to select Mondrian is that in [8] and [9], the authors investigated the impact of data anonymisation on machine learning classifiers. Both the papers concluded that Mondrian can be considered as the method with the most appropriate qualities for subsequent classification.

- Our results show that for Mondrian the performance loss is acceptable for particular datasets even for huge values of the size of the anonymised group k, e.g., up to 50 (which are relatively larger than the numbers used in reality).
- Our experimental results show that the method is effective in the non-IID setting too.

The structure of the paper is as follows. In Sect. 2, we review some concepts that are needed in the rest of the paper. In particular, we discuss Mondrian k-anonymity, and aggregation of decision trees, and some key insights of the tree aggregation algorithm. In Sect. 3, we state the problem and propose a workflow for HFL with decision trees. Section 4 discusses the creation of non-IID partitions, an approach we use later to generate the data to perform our experiments, as described in Sect. 5.4. Section 5 gives a brief about the datasets and our experimental settings. In Sect. 6, we present our results in the IID and non-IID setting and analyze the results. Section 7 gives the conclusion.

2 Preliminaries

2.1 Mondrian *k*-Anonymity

k-anonymity [15–18], is a popular privacy concept suggested by Samarati and Sweeney. k-Anonymity involves the manipulation of Quasi-Identifiers or QID (QID is a set of attributes, which are available to attacker, such as gender, birth date, but a combination of the attributes in QID can potentially identify an individual, while sensitive attributes contain the information, which we want to hide, such as disease, salary). The essential concept of k-anonymity is group safety, which implies you are safe if you are in a group of individuals with the same QID (i.e., an anonymity set). For a dataset with k-anonymity, each quasi-identifier tuple appears in at least k records. Generalisation, Suppression, microaggregation and bucketisation are some of the ways for masking QID's.

In our experiments, we use Mondrian k-anonymity anonymisation algorithm to transform raw dataset into an anonymised dataset. It is a greedy multi-dimensional method that, according to previous research, produces more desired anonymisations than optimum single-dimensional algorithms [7]. We summarize the steps of Mondrian k-anonymity algorithm as follows:

- Each attribute in Quasi Identifier (Q.I.D.) represents a dimension.
- Each tuple denotes a point in a space defined by Quasi Identifier.
- A multi-dimensional space is formed by plotting the tuples in the dimensions.
- Multi-dimensional space is partitioned by splitting the dimensions.
- Splitting is done in such a way that the region formed after splitting will have at least k-points to follow the k-anonymity principle.
- The tuples corresponding to the points are replaced with the generalized values.
- For selecting splitting value for the attributes, a median value is used, which is called as median partitioning method.

- For selected splitting value, it is checked whether it is an allowable cut. There is an allowable cut, if and only if the number of points in the region that are less than the split value and the number of points greater than the split value is at least k to satisfy the k-anonymity principle.
- If there is an allowable cut, the space is split into two regions.
- The process is repeated until all the regions are examined and there is no allowable cut in all regions.
- If x_i is a splitting value, there is allowable cut, if and only if Count(Number of points $< x_i$)) $\geq k$ and Count(Number of points $\geq x_i$)) $\geq k$ (to obey the k-anonymity principle).

There are two versions of Mondrian algorithm: relaxed and strict. In strict Mondrian, left partition has no intersection with right partition. But in relaxed Mondrian, the points in the middle are evenly divided between left and right partition to ensure number of points in left partition = number of points in right partition (+1 where number of partitions is odd). So in Mondrian, the generalized result of left and right partition may have intersection. We use strict version of Mondrian in our implementation.

2.2 Aggregation of Decision Trees

Fan and Li addressed [10] the problem of merging decision trees: Given d decision trees T_1, T_2, T_3 ..., T_d, these d trees are merged into one super tree T. They called it a lossless compression of a random forest. By lossless, they mean that the prediction performance remains the same when we use a merged super tree instead of Random Forest consisting of T_1, T_2, T_3 ..., T_d to predict for a test instance. Their approach defines the aggregation of decision trees in terms of the aggregation of decision regions. For a given tree, each region has associated a class. Then, the regions of different trees are combined using the majority rule. The aggregated tree represents the aggregated regions. This kind of approach is also followed by Hall, Chawla and Bowyer [11], Bursteinas and Long [12] (regions are called hypercubes), Andrzejak, Langner and Zabala [13] (sets of iso-parallel boxes), and Strecht, Moreira, and Soares [14] (decision regions). The authors of the paper [10] prove mathematically that the time complexity to merge d trees is $O(d|T|)$, where $|T|$ is the number of leaves of tree T, which means that the approach is scalable for aggregating decision trees in the FL framework.

We utilize this algorithm by Fan and Li [10] for merging decision trees for the aggregation step of FL. The aggregator merges the decision tree models of the local devices, and sends the merged tree or global tree T to the devices. The algorithm for merging trees we selected to do HFL with decision trees has a very logical flow. The algorithm is recursive until it meets the stopping or base condition. The summary of the decision tree merging algorithm is as follows:

- Find the split attribute of the merged decision tree: The split attributes of the roots of decision trees T_1, T_2, ..., T_d are denoted by X_1, X_2, ... X_d. A node whose split attribute X_{freq} is the most frequent attribute among X_1, X_2, ... X_d is the root of the merged decision tree model.

- Create condition trees: Remove the duplicate split values, sort them and make condition intervals using the split values. Create the condition trees, whose number of branches is equal to the number of conditions in the condition intervals. e.g., If s_1, s_2, and s_3 are the split values of the attributes X_1, X_2, and X_3 for decision trees T_1, T_2, and T_3. The split condition intervals are as follows: $\leq s_1$, $(s1, s_2]$, $(s_2, s_3]$, $\geq s_3$.
- Determine the pruned condition trees: For each condition tree, when there is only a single branch connecting the child node to the parent node, delete the inner nodes.
- Stopping/Base condition: Repeat the above steps until we get all the pruned condition trees as leaf nodes. If all the pruned condition trees are leaf nodes, find the label of the leaf node of merged tree T using majority voting.

2.3   Critical Insights of Tree Merging Algorithm

Fan and Li [10] propose two main algorithms for merging decision trees in their paper. They are mergeDecisionTrees and computeBranch. The algorithm mergeDecisionTrees takes the roots of the decision trees to be merged and the number of decision trees to be merged (i.e., d) as an input, and outputs the merged decision tree T. It works out by finding the most frequent split attribute, and makes the condition intervals according to the split values of the most frequent split attribute, and then the computeBranch algorithm is called for each decision tree to obtain the part branch trees. The algorithm mergeDecision-Trees obtains the children for each condition in condition interval, and obtains the merged super tree T. The algorithm computeBranch has three conditional checks:

- If the node of the decision tree is a leaf
- If the split attribute of the node of the decision tree is not the most frequent attribute
- If the split attribute of the node of the decision tree is the most frequent attribute

If the number of records connected with a node is too small, we can ask the device if it wishes to provide more information about the decision tree structure. If yes, go ahead; otherwise, we recommend discarding that tree. Depending on the risk-utility trade-off, various devices may have different policies for dealing with this circumstance, allowing or disallowing information exchange. We did not implement this approach in our experiments and has been left for future work. Nonetheless, we highly advise to do so in real circumstances.

3   Problem Statement

FL implements on-device learning, which means that the data never leaves the device. We begin by introducing the notations utilized in our proposed FL architecture to define our problem statement. Suppose, we are given with a set of d

devices, and $\mathcal{D}_i$ represents the data held by the ith device. Let $\mathcal{X}$ denotes the feature space, $\mathcal{Y}$ denotes the label space, and $\mathcal{S}$ denote the sample ID space. Hence, we represent the complete training dataset as $(\mathcal{S}, \mathcal{X}, \mathcal{Y})$. We consider that $\mathcal{D}_i$ is a horizontal partitioning of the training data set. In FL set up, the owners of d devices desire to collaboratively train an ML model, T_{global} without accumulating their individual datasets $\{\mathcal{D}_i\}_{i=1}^d$ at one location. Since, in our proposed framework, we perform experiments with decision trees models, T_{global} symbolizes the global decision tree model, which should be a decent approximation of the model built with all the data transmitted to a single location.

3.1 Proposed Scheme for HFL with Decision Trees

We propose an FL framework based on the assumption that data is horizontally partitioned among devices. We depict our suggested framework in Fig. 1, and describe each stage of Fig. 1 as follows:

- Since, we are doing simulation of FL, we do not have real d devices, each with its own data partition. Therefore, to evaluate our proposed FL approach, we generate non-IID partitions from publicly available data from the UCI Machine Learning Repository and then we use the approach described in Sect. 4 to construct these non-IID partitions to assign records to devices. For detailed description, refer [20].
- Each of the d devices discards certain features of its data by determining the correlation of input features with the output class label. We apply this step because not all input features contribute equally to the building of decision trees. That is, we apply a dimensionality reduction process. This step greatly cuts the time it takes to build decision trees while maintaining the accuracy of our proposed FL system.
- Then, utilizing strict version of Mondrian k-anonymity [7], each device converts its raw data into anonymized data. As we discuss later in more detail, we do our experiments considering various k values ranging from 0 to 50. Also, in our experiments, we first do a correlation analysis on the entire dataset to reduce its dimensionality before applying Mondrian k-anonymity to the data.
- Each of the d devices trains a decision tree classifier, on each masked data partition. Hence, we obtain d decision trees.
- The aggregator uses the algorithm described in [10] to combine the decision trees. The procedure takes the decision trees from each partition (or device in the real world) and combines them into a merged super tree or a global decision tree T_{global}. The tree merging method works top-down.
  From the federated learning perspective, the aggregation is seen as follows. Devices share the root node of their trees (a node of the decision tree contains split attribute and split value). Then, the aggregator (central coordinating computer) selects the node with the most often split attribute. This process is repeated recursively until the merging is completed, i.e., all of the devices remain with leaf nodes. At each point, devices need to supply the appropriate nodes, and the algorithm selects the most often split attribute and builds its

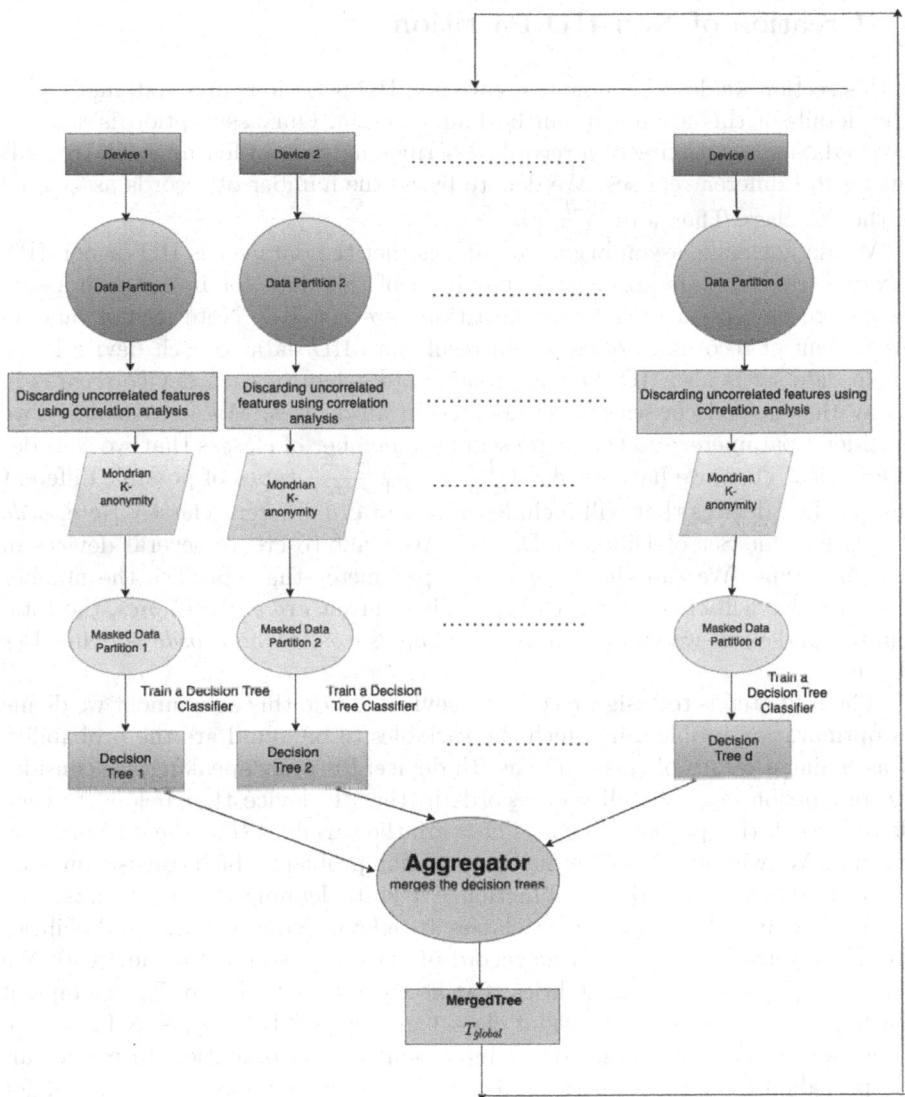

Fig. 1. Research flowchart

branches based on the split values of the most frequently split attribute. In our implementation, devices share all nodes, nevertheless, devices may have individual privacy policies about what to share.
- The aggregation server distributes the T_{global} to all the device, so that they can apply it to an unknown data instance for inference.

4   Creation of Non-IID Partitions

In this section we describe how to create non-IID partitions in a systematic way. The details of this approach can be found in [20]. Our assumption is that we have a data set consisting of n records described in terms of features. The records belong to l different classes. We denote by n_j the number of records associated to the jth class. Therefore, $\sum_{j=1}^{l} n_j = n$.

We do not make assumptions about whether the data set is IID or non-IID. Nevertheless, we want to create a partition of this data set in order to assign records to devices in a way that partitions are non-IID. Note that a random assignment of records to devices will result into IID data to each device if the whole data set is also IID. Our approach is to assign to each device records in a way that not all classes are represented in all devices. More particularly, we consider a parameter cxd that represents the number of classes that we consider in a device. Then, we have $osdd = \binom{l}{cxd} = \frac{l!}{cxd!(l-cxd)!}$ types of possible different devices. I.e., devices that will include records of cxd different classes. Here, $osdd$ stands for One Set of Different Devices. We want to create several devices of the same type. We call the $nCopies$ the parameter that specifies the number of devices we will create for each type. Then, given cxd and $nCopies$, the total number of devices we will create is $d = nCopies \cdot osdd$ where $osdd$ is defined as above.

The next step is to assign records to devices. To do this assignment we define an optimization problem in which the variables to be found are the probability of assigning a record of class j to the ith device. Properly speaking, we consider the proportion or probability of records in the ith device that belong to each class. We call this probability p_{ij}. These are the variables that the optimization will find. We will now describe the optimization problem which consists on a set of constraints and an objective function. We start defining the constraints.

As for a given device only a few classes are allowed, some of these probabilities should be zero (i.e., $p_{ij} = 0$ if no record of class j is assigned to device i). We denote by N the set of probabilities that needs to be set to zero. For example if the first device has only records of class 1 and class 2 then $p_{1j} \in N$ for $j \geq 3$. Then, we can consider some constraints about the probabilities. In particular, the probabilities of each device needs to add to one. That is, $\sum_{j=1}^{l} p_{ij} = 1$ for all devices $i = 1, \ldots, d$. In addition, the probabilities associated to a class also need to satisfy a constraint. Basically, if in the original data set we have a class that has twice as many records as another class, the probabilities associated to the first class need to be the double of the probabilities associated to the second class. Expressed in another way, the probabilities associated to class j should be proportional to the number of records in the class (with respect to the total number of records). This corresponds to the following mathematical expression: $\sum_{i=1}^{d} p_{ij} = dn_j/n$ which needs to hold for each $j = 1, \ldots, l$. In this expression d is the number of devices, as we have seen above. We need in addition that all probabilities are positive. That is, $p_{ij} \geq 0$ for all i, j. These are all the constraints to be considered in the problem.

In most of the cases, there are multiple (infinite!) assignments of probabilities that satisfy these constraints. Because of that we consider an objective function to select a *good* one. In general, given two possible assignments, we prefer one in which probabilities are better distributed. That is, when two classes are allowed for a device, we prefer 0.5 to the first class and 0.5 to the second that 1 to the first and 0 to the second. From an optimization perspective, this means that we prefer solutions that are not in the vertices of the feasible polyhedron. In addition, when *nCopies*> 1 we want that the different devices have different probabilities for the different classes. In order to have a solution with this property we consider a quadratic objective function of the form $OF(p; \alpha_{ij}) = (p_{ij} - \alpha_{ij})^2 = (p_{ij}^2 - 2\alpha_{ij}p_{ij} + \alpha_{ij}^2)$. In this expression, α_{ij} is a random number taken from a uniform distribution in $[0, 1]$. If α_{ij} is $1/cxd$, we would have solutions that are as near as possible to equally distributed probabilities (taking into account the required constraints). When random number are used, different devices of the same type will have different probabilities (as similar as possible to the random numbers) and satisfying the constraints. We can rewrite this quadratic objective function using the square matrix $Q = Id$ (i.e., the identity matrix of size $d \cdot l$) and the vector $L = -2A$ where $A = (\alpha_{11}, \alpha_{12}, \dots, \alpha_{dl})$. Therefore, we have $OF(p; A) = p^T Q p + p^T L$, where p^T denotes the transpose of p.

Now, as a summary, we write all the constraints and the objective function together. This results into the following optimization problem.

$$
\begin{aligned}
\text{Minimize} \quad & p^T Q p + p^T L \\
\text{subject to} \quad & \\
& \sum_{i=1}^{d} p_{ij} = dn_j/n \ \text{ for each } \ j = 1, \dots, l \\
& \sum_{j=1}^{l} p_{ij} = 1 \ \text{ for each } \ i = 1, \dots, d \\
& p_{ij} \geq 0 \ \text{ for each } \ i = 1, \dots, d \text{ and } j = 1, \dots, l \\
& p_{ij} = 0 \ \text{ for each } \ p_{ij} \in \mathcal{N}
\end{aligned}
\tag{1}
$$

5   Experimental Settings

We explain each step of our experiment, one by one, in the next sections.

5.1   Datasets

We perform our experiments using datasets available on UCI Machine Learning Repository [4]. We show the specification of datasets in Table 1. We perform our experiments on four datasets, namely Car, Adult, Magic, and Bank. The bank dataset has two folders, bank-full.csv and bank.csv. We use the bank-full.csv file in our experiments, which has 45211 instances. Note that all the datasets are for binary classification. We show FL on the data for binary classification.

5.2   Dimensionality Reduction of Data

The goal of this phase is to reduce the dimensionality of the data. In general, there are two types of approaches for decreasing the dimensionality of data.

One is by performing feature selection, which preserves the most important features from the original dataset, and the other one is by reducing the number of features to a smaller number, each of which is a combination of (some of) the input features and contains essentially the same information as the original input features. There are more sub-categories of these categories. We perform in our work feature selection by obtaining the correlation between each input feature and output label. The advantage of executing this step is that it reduces the construction time of decision trees considerably.

5.3 Anonymisation of Data

After reducing the dimension of the data, we use Mondrian k-anonymity [7] for anonymising the data. It divides, in an iterative process, the original data into smaller and smaller groups using a greedy search method. We anonymise the data with different values of k ranging from 0 to 50. We take inspiration from the jupyter notebook[1] for our code.

5.4 Generation of IID and Non-IID Partitions

Given a dataset $\mathcal{D}$, we use 30 % of the dataset $\mathcal{D}$ as the test set, and the remaining as the train data. Then, we consider the generation of IID and non-IID partitions to produce the data associated to each device.

- IID Partitions: The subsamples S_i are generated by sampling from the whole training data. The size of subsamples is likewise fixed. If the dataset is large, such as a bank or an adult dataset, we limit each subsample size to 15% of the total data. If the dataset is tiny, such as a Car dataset, we set the size of each subsample to 30% of the total data.
- Non-IID Partitions: For a given device i, we obtain the probability p_{ij} of records allocated to each class j by solving the optimization problem described in Sect. 4. We must calculate the average number of records for each pair of (device, class) using these probabilities. This was accomplished by multiplying p_{ij} by n/d, where n is the total number of samples, and d is the number of devices or number of partitions we are creating in our experiments. After knowing the number of records per class for each device i, we use the `random.choice` Python function from the `numpy` module for assigning the records to devices.

In the experiment section, we show our results for 50 partition for both IID and non-IID settings.

5.5 Building Decision Trees

For each partition, we train a decision tree classifier [19]. We use Gini Index for finding the most significant attribute for each split. The attribute with the lowest Gini Index is the most relevant attribute for splitting the data into smaller groups. We got the best results when the depth of the decision tree = 3 or 4.

[1] https://github.com/Nuclearstar/K-Anonymity.

5.6 Aggregation Algorithm

For merging the decision trees, we use the aggregation algorithm suggested by [10] (described in detail in Sect. 2.2). The tree aggregation algorithm builds the merged decision tree by finding the most occurred split attribute at a specific level and computes the number of branches of the merged tree based on the split values of the most occurred attribute at a specific level of the decision tree. The merged decision tree grows until all the nodes of the trees to be merged are leaves.

5.7 Testing

To obtain the class label of a test instance, we traverse the merged decision tree, which we obtained as an output after performing the aggregation technique. The following is a brief explanation of how the prediction function of merged tree works. Return the predicted class label associated with the node, if we reached the base or stopping condition (implying the merged tree node is a leaf node); otherwise, for the split attribute of the tree node, we check its split value with the feature value of the test instance and continue traversing the merged tree's children recursively until we get the base condition.

5.8 Implementation Details

We use Python 3.8.1 for writing our code. We make use of Python packages such as `scipy`, `cvxopt`, `numpy`, and `pandas`.

Table 1. Description of datasets

Dataset	Number of samples	Number of attributes
Car	1728	6
Adult	32580	14
Magic	19020	11
Bank	45211	14

6 Results and Analysis

The experiments performed as described in the previous section lead to the following results.

- Figure 2 shows the results on UCI datasets when the datasets associated to devices correspond to IID data partitions. The figure depicts how the accuracy changes with increasing the size of k (size of the anonymised groups) in Mondrian k-anonymity. From Fig. 3, we observe that the accuracy remains in acceptable limits, even when we did our experiment with a large value of $k = 50$.

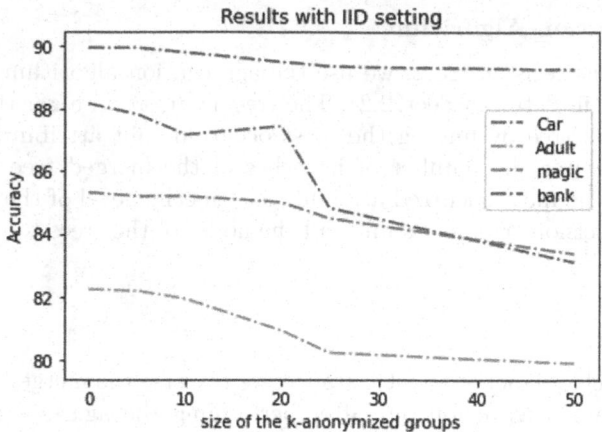

Fig. 2. Results of our proposed framework in a an IID setting with different size of anonymised groups on Car, Adult, Bank and Magic dataset from UCI Machine Learning Repository

- For Bank dataset, the accuracy remains almost the same for any value of k. For Adult, and Magic dataset, we observed a minor drop in accuracy. For Car dataset, there is a 3% drop in accuracy, from $k = 0$ (without anonymisation) to $k = 50$.
- The results show the efficacy of our approach. This is consistent with previous research in the field of data privacy, which also showed that the results remain almost consistent, when a strict version of Mondrian anonymisation [7] technique is used.
- Figure 3 shows the results when the devices use data from the UCI datasets and where the databases follow non-IID data partitions of the whole dataset. We observe a drop of 2% in accuracy in the non-IID setting compared with the IID setting, when $k = 0$ ($k = 0$ means without anonymisation). This shows that the case of non-IID partitioning of data has some effect on the performance of our framework. From our perspective, this behavior is due to the fact that different devices have data with different probability distributions.
- Even in the non-IID case, the classification accuracy remains acceptable in the non-IID case, even when the value of k is as big as 50. So, this is similar to the IID setting.

As a conclusion of our experiments, we consider that the proposed framework, and the novel technique to create non-IID partitions, has potential to contribute in the domain of FL with Decision Trees.

7   Conclusion and Future Works

The paper presents an approach for implementing FL with decision trees on a horizontally partitioned data. Our proposed FL framework also provides k-anonymity to distributed clients. Also, the aggregation technique is lossless,

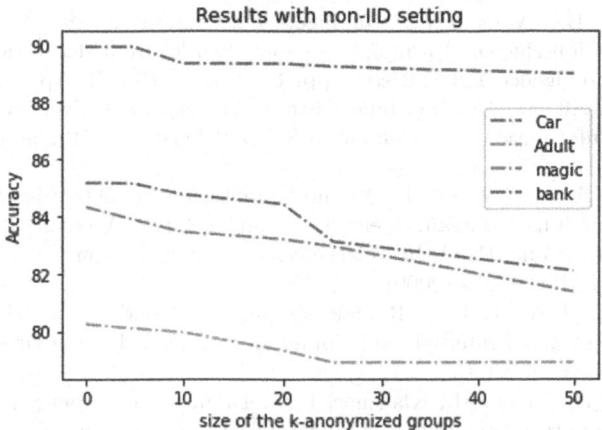

Fig. 3. Results of our proposed framework in a non-IID setting with different size of anonymised groups on Car, Adult, Bank and Magic datasets from UCI Machine Learning Repository

which means that the results would have been the same, if all the data is present in one centralised location. We present the detailed analysis of the tree aggregation algorithm and propose some interesting ideas to avoid privacy breaches of the data corresponding to each distributed client. We executed a novel way to generate non-IID datasets for our experiments in an FL scenario, which is mathematically proven in Sect. 4.

In our implementation, all devices have the policy of sharing all their nodes with the aggregator. Nevertheless, it would be possible that different devices have different policies about sharing (or not) their nodes. This is left as future work. Also, our FL approach does not consider retraining the decision trees. That is, node sharing is based on the decision tree learned with the original data. If partial decision trees are shared by the central computer (the aggregator), devices can recompute their trees at each iteration. This is another direction for future work.

It is well known that FL is prone to membership inference attacks, linkage attacks, and backdoor attacks. A direction for future work is to examine the robustness of our approach under the influence of these attacks. Another direction is the application of the proposed method in a real-life medical domain.

References

1. Dode, A.: The challenges of implementing general data protection law (GDPR). In: 14th International Conference "Standardization, Protypes and Quality: A Means of Balkan Countries'collaboration", p. 65 (2018)
2. Anonymisation and GDPR compliance; an overview - GDPR Summary (2021). https://www.gdprsummary.com/anonymisation-and-gdpr/. Accessed 27 June 2021

3. McMahan, B., Moore, E., Ramage, D., Hampson, S., y Arcas, B.A.: Communication-efficient learning of deep networks from decentralized data. In: Artificial Intelligence and Statistics, pp. 1273–1282. PMLR, April 2017
4. Dua, D., Graff, C.: UCI machine learning repository. University of California, School of Information and Computer Science, Irvine (2019). http://archive.ics.uci.edu/ml
5. Peng, W., Chen, J., Zhou, H.: An implementation of ID3-decision tree learning algorithm. arch.usyd.edu.au/wpeng/DecisionTree2.pdf. Accessed 13 May 2009
6. Steinberg, D., Colla, P.: CART: classification and regression trees. Top Ten Algorithms Data Min. **9**, 179 (2009)
7. LeFevre, K., DeWitt, D.J., Ramakrishnan, R.: Mondrian multidimensional k-anonymity. In: 22nd International Conference on Data Engineering (ICDE 2006), p. 25. IEEE, April 2006
8. Slijepčević, D., Henzl, M., Klausner, L.D., Dam, T., Kieseberg, P., Zeppelzauer, M.: k-anonymity in practice: how generalisation and suppression affect machine learning classifiers. arXiv preprint arXiv:2102.04763 (2021)
9. Buratović, I., Miličević, M., Žubrinić, K.: Effects of data anonymisation on the data mining results. In: 2012 Proceedings of the 35th International Convention MIPRO, pp. 1619–1623. IEEE, May 2012
10. Fan, C., Li, P.: Classification acceleration via merging decision trees. In: Proceedings of the 2020 ACM-IMS on Foundations of Data Science Conference, pp. 13–22 (2020)
11. Hall, L., Chawla, N., Bowyer, K.: Combining decision trees learned in parallel. In: Working Notes of the KDD-97 Workshop on Distributed Data Mining, pp. 10–15 (1998)
12. Bursteinas, B., Long, J.: Merging distributed classifiers. In: Proceedings of 5th World Multi-conference on Systemics, Cybernetics and Informatics (2001)
13. Andrzejak, A., Langner, F., Zabala, S.: Interpretable models from distributed data via merging of decision trees. In: Proceedings of 2013 IEEE Symposium on Computational Intelligence and Data Mining (CIDM) (2013)
14. Strecht, P., Mendes-Moreira, J., Soares, C.: Merging decision trees: a case study in predicting student performance. In: Luo, X., Yu, J.X., Li, Z. (eds.) ADMA 2014. LNCS (LNAI), vol. 8933, pp. 535–548. Springer, Cham (2014). https://doi.org/10.1007/978-3-319-14717-8_42
15. Sweeney, L.: k-anonymity: a model for protecting privacy. Int. J. Uncertain. Fuzziness Knowl.-Based Syst. **10**(05), 557–570 (2002)
16. Samarati, P., Sweeney, L.: Protecting privacy when disclosing information: k-anonymity and its enforcement through generalization and suppression (1998)
17. Samarati, P.: Protecting respondents identities in microdata release. IEEE Trans. Knowl. Data Eng. **13**(6), 1010–1027 (2001)
18. Sweeney, L.: Achieving k-anonymity privacy protection using generalization and suppression. Int. J. Uncertain. Fuzziness Knowl.-Based Syst. **10**(05), 571–588 (2002)
19. Hastie, T., Tibshirani, R., Friedman, J.: The Elements of Statistical Learning. Springer, Heidelberg (2009). https://doi.org/10.1007/978-0-387-84858-7
20. Torra, V.: A systematic construction of non-I.I.D. data sets from a single dataset, manuscript (2021)

Anonymizing Machine Learning Models

Abigail Goldsteen$^{(\boxtimes)}$, Gilad Ezov, Ron Shmelkin, Micha Moffie,
and Ariel Farkash

IBM Research - Haifa, Haifa University Campus, Haifa, Israel
{abigailt,ronsh,moffie,arielf}@il.ibm.com, Gilad.Ezov@ibm.com
http://www.research.ibm.com/labs/haifa/

Abstract. There is a known tension between the need to analyze personal data to drive business and the need to preserve the privacy of data subjects. Many data protection regulations, including the EU General Data Protection Regulation (GDPR) and the California Consumer Protection Act (CCPA), set out strict restrictions and obligations on the collection and processing of personal data. Moreover, machine learning models themselves can be used to derive personal information, as demonstrated by recent membership and attribute inference attacks. Anonymized data, however, is exempt from the obligations set out in these regulations. It is therefore desirable to be able to create models that are anonymized, thus also exempting them from those obligations, in addition to providing better protection against attacks.

Learning on anonymized data typically results in significant degradation in accuracy. In this work, we propose a method that is able to achieve better model accuracy by using the knowledge encoded within the trained model, and guiding our anonymization process to minimize the impact on the model's accuracy, a process we call *accuracy-guided anonymization*. We demonstrate that by focusing on the model's accuracy rather than generic information loss measures, our method outperforms state of the art k-anonymity methods in terms of the achieved utility, in particular with high values of k and large numbers of quasi-identifiers.

We also demonstrate that our approach has a similar, and sometimes even better ability to prevent membership inference attacks as approaches based on differential privacy, while averting some of their drawbacks such as complexity, performance overhead and model-specific implementations. In addition, since our approach does not rely on making modifications to the training algorithm, it can even work with "black-box" models where the data owner does not have full control over the training process, or within complex machine learning pipelines where it may be difficult to replace existing learning algorithms with new ones. This makes model-guided anonymization a legitimate substitute for such methods and a practical approach to creating privacy-preserving models.

Keywords: GDPR · Anonymization · k-anonymity · Compliance · Privacy · Machine learning

© Springer Nature Switzerland AG 2022
J. Garcia-Alfaro et al. (Eds.): DPM 2021/CBT 2021, LNCS 13140, pp. 121–136, 2022.
https://doi.org/10.1007/978-3-030-93944-1_8

1   Introduction

The EU General Data Protection Regulation (GDPR)[1], and similarly, the California Consumer Protection Act (CCPA)[2], as well as the superseding California Privacy Rights Act (CPRA), set out many restrictions on the processing of personal data. Similar laws and regulations are being enacted in additional states and countries around the world. Adhering to these regulations can be a complex and costly task.

However, these regulations specifically exempt anonymized data. Recital 26 of GDPR states that the principles of data protection should not apply to personal data rendered anonymous in such a manner that the data subject is no longer identifiable. CCPA, in its article 1798.145 (a), affirms that the obligations imposed by the title shall not restrict the use of consumer information that is deidentified or aggregate information; meaning information that cannot reasonably identify, relate to, describe, be capable of being associated with, or be linked, directly or indirectly, to a particular consumer. It is therefore very attractive for data collectors to be able to perform their processing tasks on anonymized data.

Many data processing tasks nowadays involve machine learning (ML). In recent years, several attacks have been developed that are able to infer sensitive information from trained models, including *membership inference attacks*, *model inversion attacks* and *attribute inference attacks*. This has led to the conclusion that machine learning models themselves should, in some cases, be considered personal information [14,29], and therefore subject to GDPR and similar laws. The 2020 study of the European Parliamentary Research Service (EPRS) on the impact of GDPR on artificial intelligence[3] found that, although AI is not explicitly mentioned in the GPDR, many provisions in the GDPR are relevant to AI. The authors note that an item may be linked to a person with a certain degree of probability, and propose to address this by ensuring that data is deidentified in ways that make it more difficult to re-identify the data subject.

It is therefore desirable to be able to anonymize the ML models themselves, i.e., ensure that the personal information of a specific individual that participated in the training set cannot be re-identified. Most existing work on protecting the privacy of ML training data, including differential privacy, typically requires making changes to the learning algorithms themselves, as they incorporate perturbations into the model training process [1,23]. They are thus not suitable for scenarios in which the learning process is performed by a third party and is not under the control of the organization that owns (and wants to anonymize) the private data. They may also be extremely difficult to adopt in organizations that employ many different ML models of different types. Moreover, when applying

---

[1] https://ec.europa.eu/info/law/law-topic/data-protection/data-protection-eu_en.

[2] https://leginfo.legislature.ca.gov/faces/billTextClient.xhtml?bill_id=201720180AB 375.

[3] https://www.europarl.europa.eu/thinktank/en/document.html?reference=EPRS_ STU(2020)641530.

this type of method, any effort already invested in model selection and hyper-parameter tuning may need to be redone, since the learning algorithm itself is replaced. In this paper, we present a practical solution for anonymizing ML models that is completely agnostic to the type of model trained.

Akin to some previous efforts, our method is based on applying k-anonymity to the training data and then training the model on the anonymized dataset to yield an anonymized model. Past attempts at training ML models on anonymized data have resulted in very poor accuracy [19,25]. This approach is therefore typically not employed in practice. However, our anonymization method is guided by the specific ML model that will be trained on the data. We use the knowledge encoded within the model to produce an anonymization that is highly tailored to the model. We call this method *accuracy-guided anonymization*. We demonstrate that this approach outperforms state of the art anonymization techniques in terms of the achieved utility, as measured by the resulting model's accuracy. We also show that our proposed approach can preserve an acceptable level of accuracy even with fairly high values of k and larger numbers of quasi-identifier attributes, making anonymous machine learning a feasible option for many enterprises.

We also tested the effectiveness of our method as a mitigation against membership inference attacks and compared it against existing implementations of differentially private models. We found that the results achieved using our anonymization were comparable to, sometimes even slightly better than, differential privacy in terms of the achieved model accuracy for the same level of protection against attacks. This shows that model-guided anonymization can, in some cases, be a legitimate substitute for such methods, while averting some of their inherent drawbacks such as complexity, performance overhead and the need for different implementations for each model type.

Our approach is generic and can be applied to any type of ML model. Since it does not rely on making modifications to the training process, it can be applied in a wide variety of use cases, including integration within existing ML pipelines, or in combination with machine learning as a service (ML-as-a-service or MLaaS in short). This setting is particularly useful for organizations that do not possess the required computing resources to perform their training tasks locally. It can even be applied to existing models, reusing the same architecture and hyperparameters and requiring only retraining the model. Similar to classic k-anonymity methods, our method can only be applied to structured data, including numeric, discrete and categorical features, not image data. It also does not work well for very high-dimensional data, or data with a very high degree of uniqueness.

In the remainder of the paper we present the most relevant related work in Sect. 2, describe the details of our method in Sect. 3, present experimental results in Sect. 4 and finally conclude in Sect. 5.

2   Related Work

2.1   K-anonymity

K-anonymity was proposed by L. Sweeney [28] to address the problem of releasing personal data while preserving individual privacy. It is a method to reduce the likelihood of any single person being identified when the dataset is linked with external data sources. The approach is based on generalizing attributes, and possibly deleting records, until each record becomes indistinguishable from at least $k - 1$ others. A generalization of a numeric attribute typically consists of a range of consecutive values, whereas the generalization of a categorical attribute consists of a sub-group of categories. Generalization is applied only to attributes that can be used in combination, or when linked with other data sources, to enable re-identifying individuals. Such attributes are called quasi-identifiers (QI).

There has been some criticism of anonymization methods in general and k-anonymity in particular, mostly revolving around possible re-identification even after a dataset has been anonymized. Cases such as the Netflix recommendation contest dataset [21] have been used to justify the need for new, more robust methods. However, a deeper analysis of these cases reveals that this typically occurs when poor anonymization techniques were applied [27] or when the chosen list of quasi-identifiers was not exhaustive, leaving some attributes that could potentially be linked to external datasets unaccounted for. When correctly applied, the re-identification risk in a k-anonymized dataset is at most $1/k$ [4].

Another shortcoming of basic k-anonymity is that even though it prevents identity disclosure (re-identification), it may fail to protect against attribute disclosure if all (or most of) the k records within a similarity group share the same value of a sensitive attribute [3]. For example, in the case of health records, if all k records within a group share the same disease, knowing that an individual belongs to that group automatically discloses their medical condition. To this end, extensions such as l-diversity [18] and t-closeness [17] were developed.

Many heuristics have been proposed for achieving k-anonymity [8,10,15]. The spatial indexing (or R+ tree based) method [11] suggests multi-dimensional spatial indexing, and in particular the R+-tree, as the basis for anonymization. This approach is somewhat similar to building a decision tree, as in our method (described in Sect. 3). However, it is focused on finding minimal bounding boxes for the data, as opposed to building the tree in a manner that is optimized for solving a machine learning (classification) task. In other words, this method is not tailored in any way to the downstream task of training a model.

2.2   Protecting Machine Learning Training Sets

Several attacks have been able to reveal either whether an individual was part of the training set (membership inference attacks) or infer certain possibly sensitive properties of the training data (attribute inference attacks) [6,7,24,26]. As a result, a lot of work has focused on protecting the privacy of datasets used to train machine learning models.

One straightforward approach to applying the concept of k-anonymity to machine learning is to perform anonymization on the training data prior to training the model. When these methods are applied without considering the intended use of the data, they tend to yield poor accuracy results [19,25]. Iyengar [12] and LeFevre et al. [16] were the first to propose *tailored anonymization* that takes into consideration the intended use of the data, e.g., training an ML model. They do not, however, tailor their methods to a specific ML model, since their goal is to publish the anonymized dataset. Rather they use either a generic "classification metric" [12] or simply use the label that is the target of classification [16]. In our work, we use an initial, trained model as a starting point for the anonymization process, using the model's predictions on the data as our similarity measure, as described in detail in Sect. 3. For different target models, a different version of the anonymized dataset will be created, thus yielding an anonymization that is truly tailored to the model.

In addition, the approach described in [16] for mapping the resulting regions to a set of features on which to train the model forces them to apply the same recoding mechanism to any test data before the model can be applied to it. This may make applying the method more difficult in practice. In our method, test data can be used as is in the anonymized model, without having to apply any special transformation to it.

More recently, approaches based on *differential privacy* (DP), have been used to add noise during training to protect training sets and counter membership attacks [1,5]. The idea behind this approach is to reduce the effect of any single individual on the model's outcome. These techniques tend to be highly tailored to specific ML algorithms, including internal implementation details such as the choice of loss function or optimization algorithm.

Another significant challenge when using DP in practice is the choice of privacy budget (ϵ value). A recent survey of techniques based on differential privacy [13] analyzed various variants of DP that differ in their analysis of the cumulative privacy loss, and thereby in the amount of noise added during training to satisfy a particular privacy budget. They found that the level of privacy leakage (measured by the success of inference attacks) for each variant accords with the actual amount of noise added to the model, and not necessarily with the absolute ϵ value, indicating that ϵ alone is not a good indicator for the degree of privacy achieved. Their main finding is that current mechanisms for differentially private machine learning rarely offer acceptable utility-privacy trade-offs for complex learning tasks. Moreover, Bagdasaryan et al. [2] and Mclis et al. [20] showed that differentially private training may fail to converge in some cases.

PATE [23] transfers to a "student" model the knowledge of an ensemble of "teacher" models, with privacy guaranteed by noisy aggregation of teachers' answers. However, this approach assumes the availability of a public or non-sensitive dataset with a similar distribution to the private dataset on which the student model can be trained. This may be very difficult to achieve in practice, especially when dealing with highly sensitive and unique datasets collected exclusively by governmental agencies, pharmaceutical companies, etc.

The most significant difference between approaches based on differential privacy or ensemble aggregation and our approach is that they require complete control over the learning process. The learning algorithms themselves must be modified to guarantee the desired privacy properties. These approaches cannot be applied at all in cases where the learning process occurs outside the hands of the private data owner, such as with ML-as-a-service. Since our method does not rely on making modifications to the training process, it is much better suited for such (and similar) scenarios.

3   Model-Guided Anonymization

In this section we describe in more detail the proposed approach for ML model anonymization. Our implementation is based on k-anonymity, but could possibly be extended to cover additional guarantees such as l-diversity and t-closeness. Many typical k-anonymity algorithms rely on finding groups of k (or more) similar records that can be mapped together to the same generalized value (on the quasi-identifier attributes), thus fulfilling the requirement that these k records are indistinguishable from each other. Some do this by iteratively choosing a feature and splitting the domain of the feature along a chosen split value. The resulting splits create a partitionning of the domain into groups of k or more records, which serve as the basis for the generalization.

The Median Mondrian method [15] chooses at each phase the split attribute with the widest normalized range and uses the median value as the split value. The Greedy algorithm [10] chooses the candidate split based on minimal information loss. In our case, we replace these criteria with minimal accuracy loss in the target model. The intuition behind this approach is that we want to find groups of records that the model sees as similar (i.e., makes the same decision for) so as to minimally impact the ability of the model to make correct predictions even after generalization.

The overall process of *accuracy-guided anonymization* is depicted in Fig. 1. The process starts with an initial model trained on the raw training data. This is the model whose accuracy we will try to preserve. To achieve this, we use the training data with the initial model's predictions on that data as input to the anonymization process.

Next we train an *anonymizer model* on the training data, using as labels the original model's predictions. That is, we train a new model to learn the target model's "decision boundaries". This is similar to the student-teacher training or knowledge distillation concept often employed as a means for model compression [9]. In use cases where the full model training is performed by a third (possibly untrusted) party, the initial model used to generate these predictions may be a simple, representative model, trained on a small subset of the data or a pre-trained model performing a similar classification task as the target model. If no pre-existing or minimally trained model is available, the target (class) labels may be used instead of model predictions.

For the anonymizer model we employ a decision tree model. We set the minimum number of samples required to be in each leaf node of the tree to k, and then use the leaves of the tree as the basis for generalization. The training samples mapped to each leaf constitute the group of records that are generalized to the same value. Since each leaf node contains at least k samples from the training set, and we generalize all of those samples in the same manner, they will be indistinguishable from each other, thus satisfying k-anonymity.

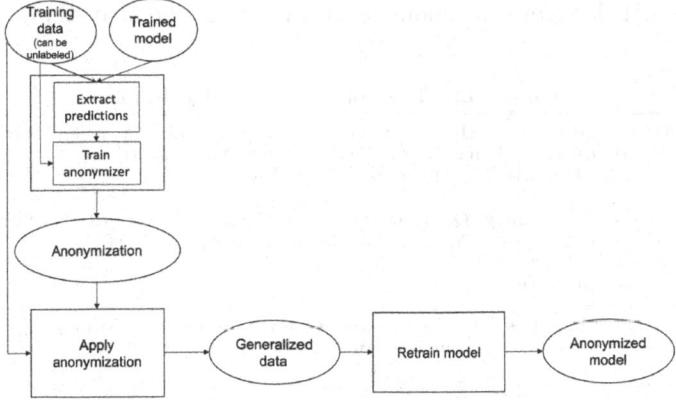

Fig. 1. Complete anonymization process

One common approach to generalize features for a group of records is to use a range (for numerical features) or sub-group (for categorical features) that covers all records in the group. For example, if we have three records with the age values 31, 32 and 34, these can be generalized to the age range 31–34. Similarly, if those three records have the occupation values "nurse", "teacher" and "engineer", these can be generalized to the group ["nurse","teacher","engineer"]. However, since we want to be able to retrain our ML model on the anonymized dataset, we need to map these ranges and sub-groups to numerical features on which the model can be trained.

In [16], the d-dimensional hyper-rectangle of each partition is represented as points in a 2-dimensional space. We adopted a different approach, where we map each sample to a concrete, representative point in the same domain as the original features. Having the anonymized records share the same domain as the original data enables using the model directly on any newly collected test data, without having to apply any special recoding dictated by the anonymization process. In other words, the rest of the ML lifecycle can remain unchanged.

There are several choices for mapping the data points in each leaf to a representative value. We opted to use an actual value that falls in the cluster as the representative point for that cluster, as we found that it entails higher prediction accuracy. We chose to use the point closest to the median of the cluster from the points with the majority label in that cluster. It is also possible to choose an actual value from each range/group separately. By mapping all records belonging to the same leaf node to the same concrete value, we still satisfy the k-anonymity requirement of indistinguishability.

Algorithm 1 describes the anonymization part of the algorithm.

Algorithm 1: Anonymization algorithm

Inputs: training data X labeled with original model's predictions y,
          list of quasi-identifiers QI, required k value
Output: anonymized training data $\overline{X}$

Separate X into X_{qi} (only QI features) and X_{rest} (rest of features)
Train decision tree T on (X_{qi}, y) with min_samples_leaf=k
foreach leaf node l *in* T:
        S $\leftarrow$ samples *in* l
        m $\leftarrow$ median(S)
        s $\leftarrow$ sample closest to m (using euclidean distance)
        S' $\leftarrow$ replace all samples *in* S with s
        X' $\leftarrow$ $\cup$ S'
Re-attach X' with X_{rest} $\rightarrow$ $\overline{X}$

Once each of the original records is mapped to its new, representative value, based on the leaf to which it belongs, the dataset is k-anonymized. In this implementation we did not consider the label itself as requiring anonymization, and therefore assigned each anonymized record its original label. However, we could also have assigned the leaf majority class as the label, if required. Finally, we retrain the model on the anonymized data, resulting in an anonymized model that is no loger considered personal information (e.g., under Recital 26 of GDPR) and can be stored and shared freely.

The described anonymization process is typically performed after applying feature selection. The motivation for this is that if there are features that are not needed at all, they should simply be removed from consideration rather than undergo anonymization. However, there are also advantages to applying our method before feature selection. When performing feature selection "blindly", without knowing which features are considered quasi-identifiers, the process may inadvertently select quasi-identiers as important features, even if other, non-identifying features could have been used instead. In these cases, it may be better to perform feature selection after anonymization, allowing features that have not been anonymized to be prioritized. In Sect. 4 we show results both with and without applying feature selection prior to the anonymization.

The code for our accuracy-guided anonymization method can be found on GitHub: https://github.com/IBM/ai-privacy-toolkit.

4   Results

Our evaluation method consists of the following steps. First, we select a dataset, train one or more original models on it (either applying feature selection or not), and measure their accuracy on a hold-out (test) set. We consider the resulting model and its accuracy as our baseline. We then perform the anonymization process described in Sect. 3 and retrain the model on the anonymized data. Finally, we measure the accuracy of the new model on the same test set.

We evaluated our method using two openly available datasets: Adult[4], an excerpt of the 1994 U.S. Census database, which is widely used to evaluate anonymization and generalization techniques; and Loan[5], an excerpt of the Lending Club loan data from 2015. This second dataset was chosen to demonstrate that our approach works for data with a larger number of attributes. The characteristics of each dataset are presented in Appendix A.

Both datasets were used for binary classification tasks. For the Adult dataset we trained neural network (NN) (86.5), XGBoost (XGB) (86.4), decision tree (DT) (88.78) and random forest (RF) (89.92) models (the test accuracy of each model is stated in parentheses). The last two were chosen because of their use in [16] and [12]. The neural network was composed of one hidden layer with 100 neurons, relu activation and adam optimizer, and a constant learning rate of 0.001. The random forest was composed of 100 trees using Gini impurity as the split criterion. Except for neural networks, in all other cases we performed feature selection prior to anonymization. We also chose several different sets of quasi-identifiers: we either used all 12 attributes, 10 attributes or 8 attributes (as detailed in Appendix A). The list of 8 attributes was chosen to be similar to the one used in [12]. Due to space constraints we show results for select runs. The remainder of the results follow similar patterns.

The data was divided into three subsets, used for: (1) training the original model (40%), (2) training the anonymizer decision tree model (40%), and (3) validation (20%). The 40% data that was used to train the original model is also the dataset that is eventually anonymized and then used to retrain the model. The validation set was used to measure the accuracy of both the original and the new, anonymized model. Each run of our accuracy-guided anonymization (AG) is compared with three "regular" anonymization methods: the Median Mondrain method [15], the Hilbert-curve based method [8] and the R+ tree based method [11]. The results of these runs can be found in Figs. 2 and 3.

For the Loan dataset we trained a neural network model (test accuracy: 93.32) with the same architecture and hyperparameters as the one used for Adult. For this dataset we used 18 attributes as QI (detailed in Appendix A). The results are presented in Fig. 4.

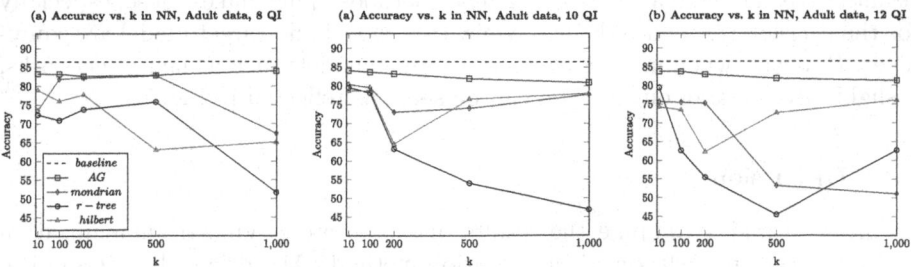

Fig. 2. Adult data with NN model, different sets of QI

---

[4] https://archive.ics.uci.edu/ml/datasets/adult.
[5] https://www.lendingclub.com/info/download-data.action.

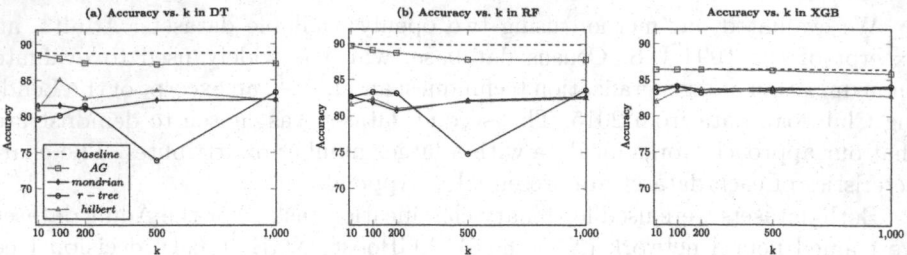

Fig. 3. Adult data with 8 QI+feature selection, different models

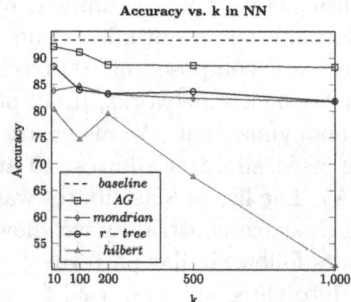

Fig. 4. Loan data with 18 QI, Neural Network model

Next we compare our method with one of the workload-aware approaches, namely [16]. Since their method is basically equivalent to training a decision tree on the data with the true labels using an entropy-based split criterion, we employed a regular decision tree model, similar to the one used for model-guided training, but using the true labels instead of the target model's classifications. Note that we did not use the method they described for mapping the resulting regions into 2d points, but rather employed the same method that we used for choosing representative values for each cluster.

For relatively simple models such as decision tree and random forest, the results were very similar between the two methods. This makes sense, especially for the decision tree, since the anonymization model and target model are equivalent. However, when moving to more complex models such as neural networks, a slight advantage of our method can be seen, as reflected in Fig. 5.

4.1 Discussion

Figures 2, 3 and 4 compare the results of our accuracy-guided anonymization method with three "classic" anonymization methods: Mondrian, Hilbert and R+ tree. These methods are not tailored for any specific analysis on the resulting dataset. It is clear that in all cases, our method outperforms these.

Figure 5 shows a comparison with workload-aware anonymization [16] that uses the label class value as an impurity measure when partitioning the data.

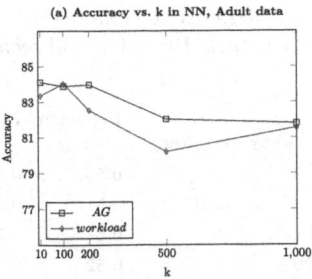
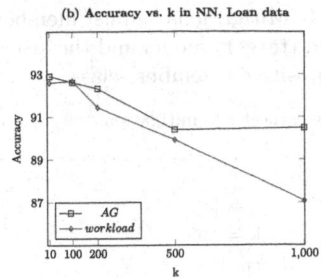

Fig. 5. Neural Network model, AG vs. workload-aware anonymization

Here, better accuracy was achieved mainly for complex models such as neural networks. It is possible that in these cases, learning the "decision boundaries" of an existing model is more effective than learning the task from scratch (based on the true labels). This technique has proven useful to help distill the knowledge of large, complex models into smaller, simpler models [9]. We therefore believe that our method is more advantageous when applied to more modern and complex models. It could be interesting to also compare the two methods of mapping clusters to features, but we leave this for future work.

It is noteworthy to point out that in many previous works on anonymization, results were demonstrated on relatively small values of k (up to 100) and small sets of quasi-identifiers (typically 8–10). In our evaluation, we demonstrated results for very high k values (up to 1000) and QI sets of up to 18 attributes, which, as far as we know, has not been attempted in the past. On one hand, as previously mentioned, it is critical to include as many QI attributes as possible to prevent re-identification. On the other hand, the more attributes are considered QI, the more generalization must be performed on the data and the higher the information loss. That said, using our method we were able to achieve satisfactory accuracy even with high numbers of quasi-identifiers. This enables providing a higher level of privacy without suffering too large an accuracy loss.

4.2 Defending Against Inference Attacks

Next, we demonstrate the effect of using our anonymization method to defend against membership inference attacks. We trained both a random forest and neural network model on the Adult and Loan datasets. The random forest has the same hyperparameters as in the previous experiment. The neural network architecture consists of three fully-connected layers of sizes 1024, 512 and 256, tanh activation, and Adam optimizer with learning rate 0.0001. We employed a more complex architecture this time, along with tanh activation, to make it easier to successfully apply membership inference to the model. Each model's initial accuracy is documented in Table 1.

The attack model consisted of an architecture similar to the one used by Nasr et al. [22] but slightly shallower and with smaller layers (see Appendix B). Also similar to the Nasr paper, we employed a **strong** attack, that assumes knowledge of (part of) the training data used to train the model.

Table 1. Mitigations against membership inference. The first two columns refer to the attacked (target) model and the last three refer to the attack. Precision and recall refer to the positive (member) class.

Dataset, model & mitigation	Train accuracy	Test accuracy	Attack accuracy	Precision	Recall
Adult, RF	0.98	0.83	0.58	0.56	0.78
Adult, RF, k = 50	0.85	0.83	0.51	0.51	0.33
Adult, RF, k = 100	0.85	0.81	0.5	0.5	0.76
Adult, RF, epsilon = 1	0.8	0.79	0.5	0.52	0.13
Adult, NN	0.96	0.89	0.53	0.52	0.6
Adult, NN, k = 25	0.84	0.82	0.5	0.5	0.71
Adult, NN, k = 50	0.84	0.81	0.5	0.5	0.32
Adult, NN, epsilon = 2.11, delta = e-05	0.83	0.83	0.5	0.5	0.14
Loan, RF	1.0	0.92	0.67	0.65	0.71
Loan, RF, k = 100	1.0	0.92	0.51	0.51	0.29
Loan, RF, epsilon = 10	0.82	0.81	0.5	0.66	0.0094
Loan, NN	0.95	0.95	0.54	0.53	0.67
Loan, NN, k = 200	0.95	0.92	0.5	0.5	0.46
Loan, NN, epsilon = 3.1, delta = e-05	0.87	0.87	0.5	0.5	0.47

After applying the attack to the original models, we then trained each of the models on different anonymized versions of the datasets, using different k values. For the Adult dataset we used all features as QI and for the Loan dataset we used the same set of 18 features as in previous experiments. Those results are presented in Table 1. It is clear from these results that the attack can be mostly prevented using our anonymization method, with a very low accuracy cost.

For comparison we also applied differential privacy (DP) as a possible mitigation against the membership attack. For the random forest model we used the implementation of Fletcher and Islam[6] [5]. For the neural network we used the torch-dp library[7], whose implementation is based on the principles of Abadi et al. [1]. The results achieved using differential privacy were comparable to our anonymization results in terms of the accuracy-privacy tradeoff. With the Loan dataset, there was a pretty significant 5–11% test accuracy gap in favor of our method. Those results can also be found in Table 1, the cells highlighted in blue indicating the cases where AG achieved better test accuracy for the same level of attack accuracy (note that in some cases DP achieved better attack recall).

It is worth noting that when using differential privacy there was an added complexity of having to use different implementations for the different model types and ML frameworks. In the case of our anonymization approach, the same method can be applied regardless of the ML model, framework and implementation details.

We also tested the efficiency of using our anonymization method to defend against attribute inference attacks, such as the one described in [6]. For this

---

[6] https://github.com/sam-fletcher/Smooth_Random_Trees.
[7] https://github.com/facebookresearch/pytorch-dp.

evaluation we used the Nursery dataset[8], and the 'social' feature as the attacked feature. Table 2 shows the effectiveness of the attack on a decision tree model, with and without applying anonymization to the dataset. These results show that our method can also be effective against attribute inference.

It is important to note that the anonymization-based method does not work well for highly dimensional datasets, especially with a high degree of uniqueness. This is typically true for k-anonymity based methods in general. For example, applying this method to the Purchase100 dataset from [26], we were not able to achieve more than 24% model accuracy, even using the smallest possible value of k (k = 2). In contrast, the DP implementation was able to achieve up to 42% accuracy (still significantly lower than the original 66%). First of all, since there is no real distinction between the features of this dataset, we considered all 100 as quasi-identifiers. Since purchase patterns are pretty unique, once each group of records was rendered identical, it seems the model no longer had enough information to distinguish between these patterns properly.

Table 2. Mitigation against attribute inference. The first column refers to the attacked model and the last three refer to the attack. Precision and recall refer to the 'problematic' value of the social feature. All features were used as quasi-identifiers.

Dataset, model & mitigation	Test accuracy	Attack accuracy	Precision	Recall
Nursery, DT	0.68	0.61	0.41	0.32
Nursery, DT, k = 100	0.74	0.56	0.31	0.21

5   Conclusions and Future Work

We presented a novel machine learning model anonymization method that applies a model-specific accuracy-guided anonymization to the training dataset, then retrains the model on the anonymized data to yield an anonymized model. This anonymized model no longer contains any personal data, and can be freely used or shared with third parties. Our method outperforms state-of-the-art anonymization techniques in terms of the achieved utility, as measured by the resulting model's accuracy. It also enables applying anonymization in previously unattainable situations: with complex machine learning models, large values of k and large numbers of quasi-identifiers. This provides stronger privacy than previously possible, without suffering from great accuracy loss.

In addition, this method is able to achieve a similar effect in preventing membership inference attacks as alternative approaches based on differential privacy, while being much less complex and resource-intensive. It does not assume the availability of similar public datasets, and does not require making changes to the training process. It is thus well suited for scenarios where the private data owner

---

[8] https://archive.ics.uci.edu/ml/datasets/nursery.

does not have complete control over the training process, or when employing many different ML models. The presented method can also defend against other classes of attacks such as attribute inference.

In this work, only the training data underwent anonymization, and the test (runtime) data remained unchanged. It could be interesting to investigate whether applying the same transformations to the test data as to the training data would improve the performance of the model. This could be accomplished by storing those transformations as part of the ML pipeline. Moreover, the use of decision trees and knowledge distillation may lend to relatively easily extending this work to support regression tasks. This can be achieved by employing a decision tree regressor as the anonymization model. In addition, we would like to investigate the generalizability of this approach to other domains, such as medical data. Finally, we would like to investigate how ML anonymization could potentially be integrated with other related technologies such as federated learning and homomorphic encryption.

A   Datasets and Quasi-identifiers

Table 3 describes the datasets used for evaluation. Table 4 presents the attributes used as quasi-identifiers in the different runs.

Table 3. Datasets used for evaluation

Name	# records	# total features	# features used	# categorical features	label feature
Adult	48842	14	12	7	income
Loan	421095	144	43	11	loan status

Table 4. Quasi-identifiers used for evaluation

Dataset	# QI	QI attributes
Adult	12	age, workclass, education-num, marital-status, occupation, relationship, race, sex, capital-gain, capital-loss, hours-per-week, native-country
Adult	10	age, workclass, education-num, marital-status, occupation, relationship, race, sex, hours-per-week, native-country
Adult	8	workclass, marital-status, occupation, relationship, race, sex, native-country, education-num
Loan	18	emp_length, home_ownership, annual_income, zip_code, purpose, dti, delinq_2yrs, inq_last_6mths, mths_since_last_delinq, open_acc, total_acc, mths_since_last_record, pub_rec, revol_bal, revol_util, hardship_flag, last_pymnt_amnt, installment

B   Attack Model

Figure 6 depicts the attack model employed for membership inference, trained with 50% members and 50% non-members. n represents the number of target classes in the attacked model, f(x) is the logit (for NN) or probability (for RF) of each class, and y is the one-hot encoded true label. This architecture was adapted from [22] and chosen empirically to yield better accuracy for the tested datasets and models.

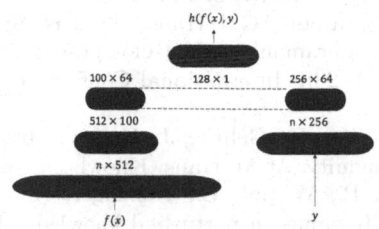

Fig. 6. Attack model

References

1. Abadi, M., et al.: Deep learning with differential privacy. In: Proceedings of the ACM SIGSAC Conference on Computer and Communications Security, pp. 308–318 (2016)
2. Bagdasaryan, E., Shmatikov, V.: Differential privacy has disparate impact on model accuracy. In: Advances in Neural Information Processing Systems, pp. 15453–15462 (2019)
3. Domingo-Ferrer, J., Torra, V.: A critique of k-anonymity and some of its enhancements. In: 3rd International Conference on Availability, Reliability and Security, pp. 990–993. ARES (2008). https://doi.org/10.1109/ARES.2008.97
4. Emam, K.E., Dankar, F.K.: Protecting privacy using k-anonymity. J. Am. Med. Inform. Assoc. **15**(5), 627–637 (2008)
5. Fletcher, S., Islam, M.Z.: Differentially private random decision forests using smooth sensitivity. Expert Syst. Appl. **78**(1), 16–31 (2017)
6. Fredrikson, M., Jha, S., Ristenpart, T.: Model inversion attacks that exploit confidence information and basic countermeasures. In: CCS (2015)
7. Fredrikson, M., Lantz, E., Jha, S., Lin, S., Page, D., Ristenpart, T.: Privacy in pharmacogenetics: an end-to-end case study of personalized warfarin dosing. In: USENIX Security Symposium, pp. 17–32 (2014)
8. Ghinita, G., Karras, P., Kalnis, P., Mamoulis, N.: Fast data anonymization with low information loss. In: Very Large Databases (2007)
9. Hinton, G., Vinyals, O., Dean, J.: Distilling the knowledge in a neural network. In: NIPS Deep Learning and Representation Learning Workshop (2015)
10. Huda, M.N., Yamada, S., Sonehara, N.: Recent Progress in Data Engineering and Internet Technology. Lecture Notes in Electrical EngineerinG, vol. 156. Springer, Heidelberg (2013)
11. Iwuchukwu, T., DeWitt, D.J., Doan, A., Naughton, J.F.: K-anonymization as spatial indexing: toward scalable and incremental anonymization. In: IEEE 23rd International Conference on Data Engineering (2007)

12. Iyengar, V.S.: Transforming data to satisfy privacy constraints. In: SIGKDD. Edmonton, Alberta (2002)
13. Jayaraman, B., Evans, D.: Evaluating differentially private machine learning in practice. In: Proceedings of the 28th USENIX Conference on Security Symposium, pp. 1895–1912. USENIX Association, Berkeley (2019)
14. Kazim, E., Denny, D.M.T., Koshiyama, A.: Ai auditing and impact assessment: according to the UK information commissioner's office. AI Ethics 1, 301–310 (2021)
15. Lefevre, K., Dewitt, D.J., Ramakrishnan, R.: Mondrian multidimensional k-anonymity. In: 22nd International Conference on Data Engineering (2006)
16. Lefevre, K., Dewitt, D.J., Ramakrishnan, R.: Workload-aware anonymization techniques for large-scale datasets. ACM Trans. Database Syst. 33(3), 1–47 (2008)
17. Li, N., Li, T., Venkatasubramanian, S.: t-closeness: privacy beyond k-anonymity and l-diversity. In: IEEE 23rd International Conference on Data Engineering, pp. 106–115 (2007)
18. Machanavajjhala, A., Kifer, D., Gehrke, J., Venkitasubramaniam, M.: L-diversity: privacy beyond k-anonymity. ACM Trans. Knowl. Discov. Data 1(1), 3-es (2007)
19. Malle, B., Kieseberg, P., Weippl, E., Holzinger, A.: The right to be forgotten: towards machine learning on perturbed knowledge bases. In: Buccafurri, F., Holzinger, A., Kieseberg, P., Tjoa, A.M., Weippl, E. (eds.) CD-ARES 2016. LNCS, vol. 9817, pp. 251–266. Springer, Cham (2016). https://doi.org/10.1007/978-3-319-45507-5_17
20. Melis, L., Song, C., Cristofaro, E.D., Shmatikov, V.: Exploiting unintended feature leakage in collaborative learning. In: IEEE Symposium on Security and Privacy, pp. 691–706 (2019)
21. Narayanan, A., Shmatikov, V.: How to break anonymity of the netflix prize dataset (2006). https://arxiv.org/abs/cs/0610105
22. Nasr, M., Shokri, R., Houmansadr, A.: Machine learning with membership privacy using adversarial regularization. In: Proceedings of the 2018 ACM SIGSAC Conference on Computer and Communications Security, pp. 634–646. ACM, New York (2018). https://doi.org/10.1145/3243734.3243855
23. Papernot, N., Abadi, M., Úlfar Erlingsson, Goodfellow, I., Talwar, K.: Semi-supervised knowledge transfer for deep learning from private training data. In: ICLR (2017). https://arxiv.org/abs/1610.05755
24. Salem, A., Zhang, Y., Humbert, M., Berrang, P., Fritz, M., Backes, M.: Ml-leaks: model and data independent membership inference attacks and defenses on machine learning models. In: Network and Distributed Systems Security Symposium, San Diego, CA, USA (2019). https://doi.org/10.14722/ndss.2019.23119
25. Senavirathne, N., Torra, V.: On the role of data anonymization in machine learning privacy. In: 2020 IEEE 19th International Conference on Trust, Security and Privacy in Computing and Communications (TrustCom), pp. 664–675. IEEE Computer Society, Los Alamitos, CA, USA (2020)
26. Shokri, R., Stronati, M., Song, C., Shmatikov, V.: Membership inference attacks against machine learning models. In: IEEE Symposium on Security and Privacy, San Jose, CA, USA, pp. 3–18 (2017)
27. Sánchez, D., Martínez, S., Domingo-Ferrer, J.: How to avoid reidentification with proper anonymization (2018). https://arxiv.org/abs/1808.01113
28. Sweeney, L.: k-anonymity: a model for protecting privacy. Int. J. Uncertain. Fuzziness Knowl.-Based Syst. 10, 557–570 (2002)
29. Veale, M., Binns, R., Edwards, L.: Algorithms that remember: model inversion attacks and data protection law. Philos. Trans. R. Soc. A 376, 20180083 (2018). https://doi.org/10.1098/rsta.2018.0083

DPM Workshop: Short Papers

A New Privacy Enhancing Beacon Scheme in V2X Communication

Takahito Yoshizawa$^{(\boxtimes)}$ ⓘ, Dave Singelée ⓘ, and Bart Preneel ⓘ

KU Leuven - imec - COSIC, Kasteelpark Arenberg 10 Bus 2452,
3001 Leuven, Belgium
{takahito.yoshizawa,dave.singelee,bart.preneel}@esat.kuleuven.be

Abstract. We propose a new privacy-enhancing beacon scheme in Vehicle-to-Everything (V2X) communication systems and evaluate its effectiveness based on a simulation. With this scheme, vehicles dynamically adjusts their periodic transmission of Cooperative Awareness Message (CAM) and Basic Safety Message (BSM) messages based on the observation of surroundings and transmit these messages only when it is necessary. This new scheme addresses the gap in standards where continuous transmission of broadcast-based unencrypted vehicle information is assumed but may not be needed under certain circumstances. Our beacon message does not convey any privacy-linking information. This way, this new scheme enhances privacy protection of vehicle owners by limiting the transmission of information that can be linked to a particular vehicle. The complexity of its processing in both transmitting and receiving ends is kept at minimum and is simpler than CAM and BSM processing. Our simulation result indicates that this new scheme is highly effective if the density of vehicles with V2X technology is limited.

Keywords: V2X · Vehicle communication · Privacy protection · Pseudonym · Pseudonym usage · Beacon message

1 Introduction

V2X communication offers a service in which vehicles periodically broadcast its presence to surrounding vehicles. These messages are defined as Cooperative Awareness Messages (CAMs) in ETSI EN 302 637.2 [10] in Europe and as Basic Safety Message (BSM) in SAE J2735 [18] in the US, respectively [5]. Vehicles within communication range exchange these messages to construct and maintain a dynamic map of the presence of vehicles. Vehicles' situational awareness as the result of these message exchanges leads to an overall improvement in road safety. To establish this awareness, CAM and BSM contain vehicle information

---

This work was supported in part by CyberSecurity Research Flanders with reference number VR20192203 and by the Research Council KU Leuven C1 project on Security and Privacy for Cyber-Physical Systems and the Internet of Things with contract number C16/15/058.

© Springer Nature Switzerland AG 2022
J. Garcia-Alfaro et al. (Eds.): DPM 2021/CBT 2021, LNCS 13140, pp. 139–151, 2022.
https://doi.org/10.1007/978-3-030-93944-1_9

such as position, speed, direction, and acceleration. In addition, they also contain vehicle's physical characteristics such as vehicle type, its length and width [9]. These messages are digitally signed using certificates issued by a management system for authenticity. From a privacy perspective, information in CAM and BSM allows receiving vehicles to discern the sending vehicle by examining the message content and correlate it with sensory observations. Due to its broadcast nature, these messages are sent in clear. It implies that any suitable device, legitimate or not, can receive them. This condition enables adversaries to receive, collect, and analyse these messages from all transmitting vehicles within communication range.

Vehicles exchange these messages to establish and maintain awareness of one another. In other words, CAM or BSM transmission is meaningful only when there are other vehicles within the communication range from a given vehicle. However, this is not always the case. For example, there are situations where no vehicle is present within the communication range for extended period of time. This no- or low-traffic condition includes scenarios such as: 1) late night, 2) small town and rural areas, 3) quiet residential areas, and 4) early days of V2X technology introduction. Under these conditions, transmitting CAMs or BSMs achieves no useful purpose. On the contrary, doing so may result in exposing vehicle information to passive adversaries. In this paper, we propose an alternative approach to this problem in such a way that the exposure of privacy information is prevented whenever possible. Our proposed beacon scheme does not contain any vehicle-specific information, not even a temporary identifier or pseudonym. Using extensive simulations, we show that the new approach is effective under various conditions.

The rest of the paper is organized as follows. Section 2 discusses the existing literature as a background information for Sect. 3 in which we describe the new beacon scheme. In Sect. 4, we discuss the simulation results to evaluate the effectiveness of the beacon scheme, followed by conclusion in Sect. 5.

2   Related Work

Various solutions for privacy protection and trustworthiness in V2X communication have been proposed in existing literature. Privacy protection hinges on the effective use of pseudonyms to prevent or minimize the leak of privacy-related information. It includes various pseudonym change schemes. A *mix zone* [4] is a defined area, such as an intersection. Vehicles within the mix zone collaborate and change pseudonyms at the same time. Presence of multiple vehicles moving in different directions around an intersection while changing pseudonyms makes tracking more difficult. In a *silent period* [11], a vehicle stops transmission for a pre-defined time period when a pseudonym is changed. Doing so prevents a change of pseudonym from being immediately observable. *Decoy traffic* [12] refers to transmitting CAMs for one or more non-existing vehicles to make it appear as if there are more vehicles. *Location obfuscation* [3] is a technique to intentionally report incorrect location information during the pseudonym change. Reporting fake location information thwarts adversaries from correlating pseudonyms before and after the change. In *Transmission range adjustment* [2], a vehicle reduces its transmission power to reduce the number of vehicles that can observe it.

From the trustworthiness perspective, multiple elaborate schemes have been proposed to ensure that received messages are trustable in V2X communication while protecting privacy of vehicles involved. Threshold anonymous announcement (TAA) [6] is a mechanism to verify uniqueness of message origin based on a message signature using direct anonymous attestation (DAA). It allows receiving vehicles to determine the message validity using threshold, i.e. the number of endorsement of a message by other receiving vehicles while remaining anonymous. Message linkable group signature (MLGS) [21] is a group signature scheme that also uses threshold as the measure of message trustworthiness. This scheme ensures that a vehicle can endorse a given received message only once, thus prevents from adversaries from artificially altering the endorsement outcome. Another group signature scheme in [16] enables efficiently sign and verify V2V messages while maintaining group members' privacy. A reputation-based scheme [14] is another approach. It allows vehicles to send feedback of whether they consider a given message by a sender as trustable or not. This feedback can be either positive or negative. Based on multiple such feedbacks, a sender's reputation is derived. Receiving vehicles consult this reputation upon determining whether accept messages from the sender or not. Balancing trust management and privacy preservation (BTMPP) [15] is another reputation-based scheme. It specifically focuses on the trustworthiness of emergency messages. Its reputation is also based on feedbacks from receiving vehicles while preserving privacy of them.

2.1 Our Contribution

The existing schemes we discussed above can be characterized as follows. For privacy protection, the overall approach revolves around pseudonym usage and how to obscure the change from one to another to maintain the unlinkability property. For trustworthiness, the focus is on addressing how receiving ends of the communication can determine whether to accept or reject received messages. Contrary to these solutions, we approach the privacy protection problem from a completely different angle. To the best of our knowledge, this is the first of its kind to propose this type of approach to this problem. In our new scheme, vehicles

- observe its surrounding to judge whether V2X transmission is warranted or not,
- refrain from transmission when observation indicates as such, thus minimizing potential exposure of privacy information,
- continue to observe its surrounding and adjust its transmission behavior as needed.

3 New Beacon Scheme

3.1 Overview

In our proposed beacon scheme, we apply the discovery concept in Proximity Service (ProSe) specified by the 3rd Generation Partnership Project (3GPP). ProSe allows direct communication between mobile devices [1]. Its original application was for public safety, but it was later extended to support V2X communication. Upon applying ProSe to V2X, some functionalities were removed to allow instantaneous communication with low overhead. This reduced functionality in ProSe in V2X is analogous to the relationship between the conventional IEEE 802.11 operation and 802.11 OCB mode (former 802.11p) [7]. Specifically, discovery, association, and security related procedures are omitted for V2X purpose in which communication duration among moving vehicles is expected to be short and the overhead to establish communication needs to be minimal.

In our proposed scheme, we apply the ProSe discovery model A (*"I am here."*) [1]. Its sole purpose is to announce the presence of a vehicle. Beacon messages sent by vehicles are identical; they contain no vehicle-specific or unique information. As with CAM, they are broadcast messages sent in clear. Therefore, this new beacon mechanism needs to ensure secure operation and should not negatively impact the exchange of CAMs.

At a high level, the proposed beacon scheme is a two-tier process – the first is beacon transmission and reception; the second is verification of vehicle presence and subsequent decision to select beacon or CAM transmission. In the first tier step, vehicles announce their presence by transmitting beacons, and detect the potential presence of other vehicles by receiving them. Because beacons are not unique per vehicle and can also be sent by adversaries, simply receiving them does not guarantee that vehicles are present. In the second tier step, vehicles verify actual presence of vehicles using opportunistic and provisional CAM transmission and reception. If the result of this verification indicates that at least a minimum number of vehicles are actually present, vehicles commit to CAM transmission (*CAM mode*). Otherwise, they fall back to beacon transmission (*beacon mode*). Vehicles continue to monitor incoming messages and adjust its transmission mode as needed. To avoid rapid and frequent changes in the vehicle's transmission mode due the dynamically changing RF environment in moving traffic, pre-determined threshold and hysteresis are used to make this decision.

3.2 Security Properties of the Beacon Scheme

From security perspective, we identify the following desired properties of the beacon operation in our analysis.

1. beacon messages need to accurately reflect the actual vehicle presence.
2. beacon messages transmitted by active adversaries do not negatively influence honest vehicles' behavior.
3. beacon messages enhance security and privacy protection compared to the current CAM transmission alone.

4. beacon message transmission does not introduce any new security issues or negative side effects to the V2X communication.
5. beacon message processing is no more complex than CAM processing.

Property 1 and 2 are closely related. The only purpose of beacon messages is to announce its presence to vehicles within the communication range. Therefore, they need to accurately reflect the actual vehicle presence. On the other hand, due to its nature of broadcasting identical unencrypted messages by all vehicles, active adversaries can also generate and transmit, or replay, beacons to make ghost vehicles appear. In this sense, it is important that adversaries do not negatively influence honest vehicles.

In addition, property 3 and 4 requires that there are clear benefits of introducing the new beacon scheme from security and privacy perspectives. Moreover, we need to ensure that the introduction of this scheme does not result in any negative side effect or new security issues.

Finally, property 5 requires the processing of beacon messages should be simple, lightweight, and no more complex than CAM processing for both transmitting and receiving vehicles. Strictly speaking, it does not fall under security or privacy. However, it is nonetheless important to prevent additional overhead.

3.3   Adversary Model

For real-world application, the solution needs to be resistant against adversaries. For this purpose, we assume the presence of Local Active Adversaries (LAA) with limited capabilities and Global Passive Adversaries (GPA).

An LAA has one or more devices installed at road side at fixed locations. They can actively transmit beacon messages to entice honest vehicles to transmit CAMs. A device can transmit beacons locally without coordinating with other devices, thus it is a local adversary. Further, we assume that they do not have access to the legitimate certificates and corresponding private keys, thus they cannot transmit valid CAMs. Hence the adversary is an LAA with limited capabilities

A GPA has a set of devices installed along roads at fixed locations. They can passively collect and analyse CAMs from vehicles within the communication range. When vehicles pass by one of these devices while transmitting CAM at regular intervals, the device detects the presence of these vehicles with specific information from received messages. Using timestamp, adversary devices may share and aggregate information over a wider area. This way, they may be able to construct the recurring appearance of a vehicle (i.e. pseudonym) at various locations and time, such as a commuting pattern. They are passive devices that only monitor incoming messages but collaborate with other devices at multiple locations, hence GPA.

3.4   Beacon Scheme Algorithm

Algorithm 1 illustrates the beacon operation. A vehicle starts with *beacon mode* by default, and hysteresis counter for CAM (d_{CAM}) and for beacon (d_{Beacon}) are

---

Algorithm 1: Switching between CAM and Beacon mode

Result: determine CAM or Beacon to send

```
1  txMode ← "Beacon";
2  d_CAM, d_Beacon ← 0;
3  repeat
4  |    monitor V2X channel for n seconds;
5  |    N_CAM ← number of CAMs received;
6  |    N_Beacon ← number of Beacon messages received;
7  |    if (txMode="Beacon") then
   |    |    // handling when current txMode="Beacon"
8  |    |    if (N_CAM > th_C) & (d_CAM > hy_C) then
9  |    |    |    txMode ← "CAM"; d_CAM ← 0; // switch to CAM
10 |    |    else if (N_CAM > th_C) & (d_CAM <= hy_C) then
11 |    |    |    d_CAM ← d_CAM + n;
12 |    |    else if (N_Beacon > th_B) & (d_Beacon > hy_B) then
13 |    |    |    nextMsg ← coinToss(p); d_Beacon ← 0;
14 |    |    |    if (nextMsg == "CAM") then
15 |    |    |    |    txMode ← "CAM"; // provisional switch to CAM
16 |    |    else if (N_Beacon > th_B) & (d_Beacon <= hy_B) then
17 |    |    |    d_Beacon ← d_Beacon + n;
18 |    |    else
19 |    |    |    d_Beacon, d_CAM ← 0;
20 |    |    end
21 |    else
   |    |    // handling when current txMode="CAM"
22 |    |    if (N_CAM <= th_C) & (d_CAM > hy_C) then
23 |    |    |    txMode ← "Beacon"; d_CAM ← 0; // switch to beacon
24 |    |    else if (N_CAM <= th_C) & (d_CAM <= hy_C) then
25 |    |    |    d_CAM ← d_CAM + n;
26 |    |    else
27 |    |    |    d_CAM ← 0;
28 |    |    end
29 |    end
30 |    switch txMode do
31 |    |    case "CAM" mode do send CAMs;
32 |    |    case "Beacon" mode do send Beacon messages;
33 |    end
34 until arrives at destination;
```

---

reset (line 1,2). The vehicle checks the presence of other vehicles by monitoring the channel for n seconds and count the number of received CAM (N_{CAM}) and beacon messages (N_{Beacon}) (line 4–6). Lines 8 through 20 describe the vehicle behavior when it is in *beacon mode*. If N_{CAM} is above threshold (th_C) for longer than hysteresis period (hy_C), then the vehicle switches to *CAM mode* (line 8–11). On the other hand, if N_{Beacon} is above threshold (th_B) for longer than hysteresis period (hy_B), then the vehicle transmits CAMs with probability p (line 12–17).

This is a provisional transition to *CAM mode*. If the detected number of vehicles (N_{Beacon} or N_{CAM}) falls below the threshold (th_B or th_C) before the hysteresis condition (hy_B or hy_C) is reached, then the hysteresis values (hy_C, hy_B) are reset (line 19).

The provisional transitions to *CAM mode* verifies the vehicle's existence to other vehicles. During the next monitoring period, vehicles verify that received CAMs from other vehicles which also transition to *CAM mode* provisionally or already in that mode. Using the certificate and vehicle-specific information contained in each CAM, receiving vehicles can deduce the actual number of vehicles present within the communication range. Under the assumption of LAAs with limited capabilities as stated in Sect. 3.3, all valid CAMs are considered as legitimate and honest vehicles.

Lines 21–29 describe the vehicle behavior when it is in *CAM mode* and is actively transmitting CAMs. If N_{CAM} falls below the threshold (th_C) longer than the hysteresis period (hy_C), then the vehicle falls back to *beacon mode*; otherwise, it stays in the *CAM mode*. If N_{CAM} exceeds the threshold before the hysteresis condition (th_C) is reached, then the hysteresis value (hy_C) is reset (line 27), avoiding rapid and frequent change of mode. Finally, the vehicle transmits the selected mode based on the previous steps (line 30–33). This cycle repeats until the vehicle reaches its destination.

3.5   Consideration on Security Properties

In this section, we discuss how the proposed beacon scheme addresses the stated security properties in Sect. 3.2. Property 1 and 2 are addressed by the two-tier process discussed in Sect. 3.1. LAAs may transmit fake beacons to entice honest vehicles to transmit CAMs. However, if the second tier process indicates that the actual number of vehicles does not meet the minimum threshold (th_C), vehicles remains in *beacon mode*. This way, the impact of LAAs can be mitigated. During this period, each vehicle in *beacon mode* provisionally transmits CAMs with a probability of p. If this value is set high, more vehicles will provisionally transmit CAMs, i.e. higher chance of honest vehicles falling victim to LAAs. Therefore, p needs to be sufficiently low. However, lower p value implies a situation where the number of detected vehicles will fall short of the actual vehicle presence. As p decreases, this condition is pronounced further. In this case, more honest vehicles need to be present to cross the threshold. Under a marginal situation where the detected number of vehicles is around the threshold, it may delay the CAM transmission with lower p value when ($N_{CAM} > th_C$) condition is already met in reality. This is a fine balance to attain as delayed transition implies potential impact to safety applications that rely on CAMs. This is a trade-off between privacy protection and safety applications to maximize the benefit of the former while minimizing impact on the latter.

Regarding property 3 and 4, beacon messages enhance privacy protection of vehicle as the beacon scheme ensures that CAMs are sent only when they are indeed necessary and useful to achieve its purpose, i.e. exchange information with other vehicles. If the number of vehicles does not meet the condition, no privacy-relevant information is transmitted. Regarding property 5, it is clear that beacon message processing is simpler from both transmitting and receiving vehicles' perspectives. Beacon messages is static and do not contain any vehicle-specific dynamic information, such as vehicle's speed and direction. Therefore, processing is much simpler than CAM processing.

4   Simulation

4.1   Approach

Table 1 lists the set of parameters used in our simulation. We conducted driving in two different settings: a large city and a small city. In both cases, we used values 1 through 7 for th_C. The average length for passenger vehicles was obtained by taking an average of full-size, mid-size, small, and mini vehicle lengths [8]. The average truck length was obtained from taking an average of class 1 and class 2 trucks [13]. We made an assumption that the ratio of passenger vehicles and trucks on the road is 80% to 20%, and each vehicle has a buffer space of 5 m in front of it. Using these values, the vehicle density is obtained as 95 vehicles/km/lane. We also assumed the number of lanes vary with the ratio of 1, 2, and 3-lane roads of 25%, 50%, and 25% of the travel.

We simulated a vehicle's behavior as described in Algorithm 1 in Sect. 3.4 in a round-trip drive with distance of 30.0 km one way. It transmits beacons at

Table 1. Simulation parameters

Parameter	Value
City size	Large, small
Opportunistic CAM transmission prob. (p)	30, 50, 70, 90%
Mode switch threshold (th_C)	1–7 vehicles
Average passenger vehicle length	4.18 m
Average truck length	10.71 m
Passenger vehicle vs. truck ratio	80%, 20%
Vehicle buffer space	5 m
Road capacity	95 vehicle/km/lane
Drive distance (1 way)	30.0 km
Number of lanes	1, 2, or 3
Ratio of 1/2/3-lane roads	25%, 50%, 25%
Beacon transmission rate	1 msg/s
Vehicle monitor interval	1 s
Mode switch hysterisis (hy_C)	3
Inter-GPA distance	800 m
V2X communication distance	300 m
Repeat per run	10 times

Table 2. Traffic congestion in brussels by time of the day (2019)

	Mon	Tue	Wed	Thu	Fri	Sat	Sun		Mon	Tue	Wed	Thu	Fri	Sat	Sun
0:00	4%	3%	4%	4%	5%	6%	7%	12:00	29%	30%	43%	37%	41%	28%	16%
1:00	1%	2%	1%	2%	2%	3%	5%	13:00	28%	29%	40%	36%	41%	28%	17%
2:00	1%	2%	1%	1%	1%	2%	3%	14:00	30%	32%	38%	38%	46%	30%	19%
3:00	0%	1%	1%	1%	1%	1%	2%	15:00	44%	47%	45%	53%	62%	30%	19%
4:00	0%	1%	1%	1%	1%	1%	1%	16:00	59%	66%	59%	72%	75%	29%	20%
5:00	3%	3%	3%	3%	3%	1%	1%	17:00	71%	80%	73%	86%	75%	30%	25%
6:00	22%	24%	22%	24%	18%	2%	1%	18:00	54%	64%	64%	72%	59%	31%	26%
7:00	56%	58%	52%	57%	45%	4%	1%	19:00	23%	30%	34%	38%	36%	26%	19%
8:00	77%	83%	70%	81%	63%	6%	2%	20:00	9%	12%	13%	14%	18%	16%	12%
9:00	50%	55%	46%	56%	41%	12%	5%	21:00	6%	8%	8%	9%	12%	11%	8%
10:00	30%	34%	31%	37%	32%	19%	10%	22:00	7%	9%	9%	11%	11%	11%	7%
11:00	28%	28%	32%	34%	35%	25%	14%	23:00	5%	7%	7%	9%	10%	10%	5%

(continue to the next column)

a rate of 1 message/s, and monitors the V2X channel for a period of 1 s. A hysteresis threshold (hy_C) of 3 is used. We assume a maximum V2X communication distance of 300 m [19]. For the large-city scenario, we used the actual data of weekly traffic congestion in Brussels in 24 h over a 7-day period. Table 2 shows this statistics [20] (green/yellow/red for low/medium/high density). For the small-city scenario, we scaled it down to model a city having one-tenth of the traffic in Brussels. Using these data, we simulated a round-trip drive for each hour over a 7-day period.

4.2 Discussion and Evaluation

Figures 1, 2 illustrate the use of CAM in a large and a small city for weekdays over 24 h period with decreasing value of p, respectively[1]. Lines in each figure represent th_C values. Table 2 shows low traffic period is between 9 PM and 5 AM next morning each day. Driving in this period makes vehicles switch to and stay in *beacon mode* as shown in these two figures, i.e. the main contributor to the reduced CAM usage. As th_C value increases from 1 to 7, vehicles switch to *beacon mode* progressively earlier in the evening. On the contrary, in Fig. 1, the use of CAMs continues throughout the day time in a large city irrespective of th_C value, while Fig. 2 shows that the traffic in a small city reduces between 10 AM to 2 PM to an extent that vehicles switch to *beacon mode* during this period. This further reduction of CAM usage in a small city indicates that our beacon scheme is more effective in lower traffic environment in reducing exposure of vehicle information to GPAs.

---

[1] Our simulation results also include weekend traffic pattern. However, as the result is similar to weekdays and does not add significant insights, we omit including the figures and discussion.

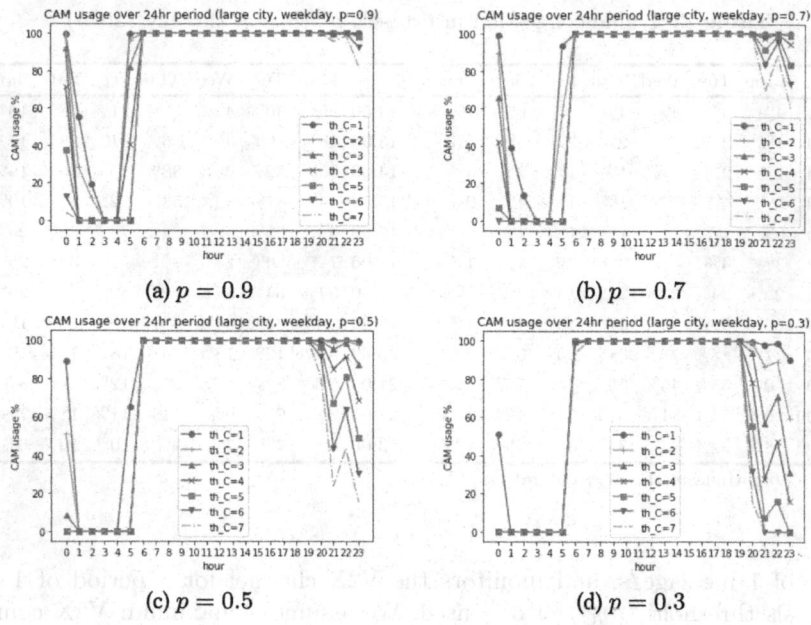

Fig. 1. CAM usage over 24 h period (large city, weekdays)

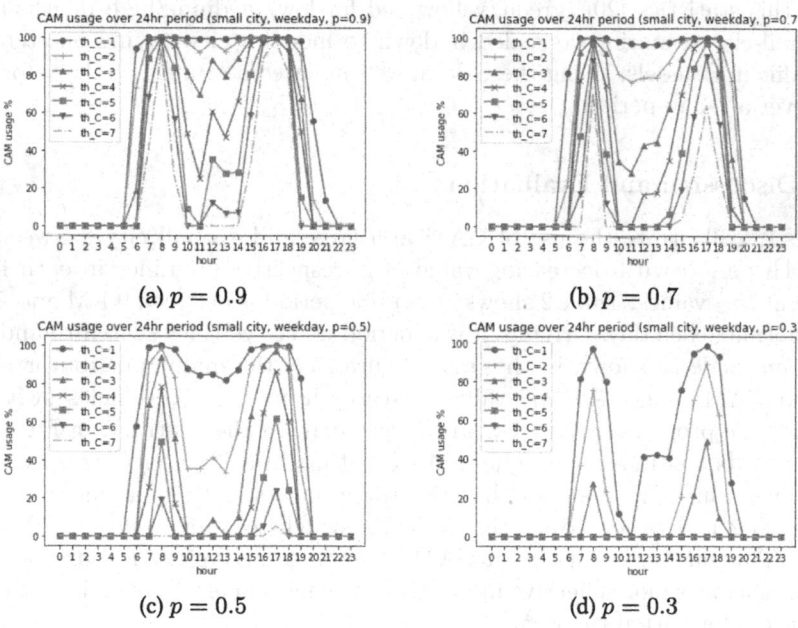

Fig. 2. CAM usage over 24 h period (small city, weekdays)

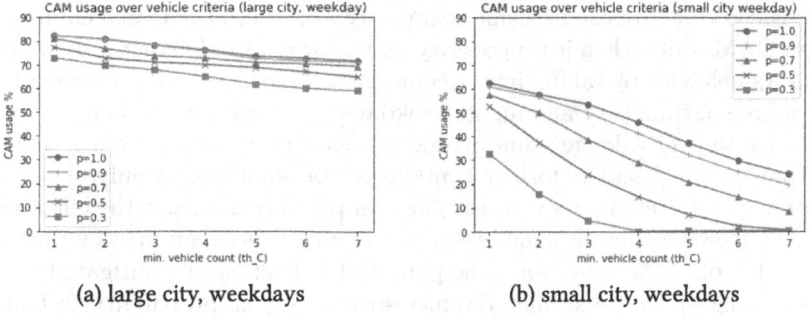

(a) large city, weekdays   (b) small city, weekdays

Fig. 3. CAM usage over varying provisional CAM probability (p)

Figure 3 summarizes the reduction of CAM transmission in both large and small cities during weekdays with the same set of p values as in previous two figures. Figure 3(b) clearly highlights a larger reduction of CAM in a small city. It reflects the lower traffic condition during late night and early afternoon period as shown in Fig. 2. On the contrary, CAM reduction in a large city is limited up to approximately 40% with increasing value of th_C as shown in Fig. 3(a). This limited effectiveness in a large city reflects the situation where use of beacons occurs in early morning hours only as seen in Fig. 1 where a lower p value has no influence to the consistent use of CAM throughout the day time. On the other hand, the CAM reduction in a small city in Fig. 3(b) is more significant. Even for $th_C = 1$ and $p = 0.9$, the CAM reduction already starts from approximately 40%. This is another data point showing that the beacon scheme is more effective in a reduced traffic environment. In other words, a lower traffic condition, such as in small cities, rural areas, and quiet residential areas, benefits more from the use of our beacon scheme. This is crucial as majority of the land in a country are small cities or rural environment. In addition, privacy concerns are higher in these environments as it is harder to disappear in the masses. Large cities have limited benefit. However, Fig. 3(a) clearly shows that there are benefits nonetheless.

Our solution is also effectiveness in the early days of V2X technology deployment where the proportion of V2X-capable vehicle is low in the total vehicle population. Because proliferation of new technology takes long time, especially durable goods such as passenger cars last as long as 9 to 23 years [17], this is a significant point. In our simulation, we assumed that all vehicles are V2X capable. However, during this period, the effective number of vehicles reduces as the proportion of the V2X-capable vehicles in the total vehicle population is low. In this case, the effectiveness of our beacon scheme increases further by refraining from possibly volunteering privacy-related information to GPAs.

5 Conclusions and Future Work

In this paper, we proposed a new beacon scheme for V2X communication. Through extensive simulations, we showed that our scheme reduces the exposure of vehicle information to potential adversaries when transmission of CAM is unnecessary. Our proposed scheme seamlessly adjusts to the traffic environment and use CAMs only when it is necessary and appropriate. Further it dynamically adjusts its behavior by taking into account geography (large city and small cities or rural areas), time (day and night, weekdays and weekend), as well as the V2X adoption rate over a longer time period. Beacon message processing is simpler than that of CAM as the former contains static information only. The potential latency of switching between the two can possibly influence the effectiveness of CAMs. However, our scheme presents a trade-off between privacy protection and benefits of CAM operation. The potential impact can be mitigated by carefully selecting optimal parameter values such as p (the probability to transmit CAMs) and th_C (CAM threshold). Studying the optimal values depending on the operational condition, such as traffic density and type of location, would be an interesting topic for future work.

References

1. 3GPP: TS 23.303 Technical Specification Group services and system aspects; Proximity-based services (ProSe); stage 2, ver.16.0.0. Standard 3GPP TS 23.303:2020, 3rd Generation Partnership Project (2020). https://www.3gpp.org/DynaReport/23303.htm
2. Babaghayou, M., Labraoui, N.: Transmission range adjustment influence on location privacy-preserving schemes in VANETs. In: 2019 International Conference on Networking and Advanced Systems (ICNAS), pp. 1–6. IEEE (2019)
3. Benarous, L., Kadri, B., Boudjit, S.: Alloyed pseudonym change strategy for location privacy in VANETs. In: 2020 IEEE 17th Annual Consumer Communications & Networking Conference (CCNC), pp. 1–6. IEEE (2020)
4. Beresford, A.R., Stajano, F.: Mix zones: user privacy in location-aware services. In: IEEE Annual Conference on Pervasive Computing and Communications Workshops, 2004. Proceedings of the Second, pp. 127–131. IEEE (2004)
5. Campolo, C., Molinaro, A., Scopigno, R.: Vehicular Ad Hoc Networks. Springer, Cham (2015). https://doi.org/10.1007/978-3-319-15497-8
6. Chen, L., Ng, S.L., Wang, G.: Threshold anonymous announcement in VANETs. IEEE J. Sel. Areas Commun. **29**(3), 605–615 (2011)
7. I.L.S. Committee: IEEE Standard for Information Technology-Telecommunication and Information Exchange between Systems-Local and Metropolitan Area Networks-Specific Requirements Part11: Wireless LAN Medium Access Control (MAC) and physical layer (PHY) Specifications Amendment1: Radio resource measurement of wireless LANs (2016)
8. Ekweghi, J.: Car length and width. https://autovfix.com/average-length-of-a-car-how-long-is-the-average-car/
9. ETSI: TS 102 894–2: Intelligent Transport Systems (ITS); Users and applications requirements; Part 2: Applications and facilities layer common data dictionary; v1.3.1. Standard, European Telecommunication Standard Institute (2018)
10. ETSI: EN 302 637–2: Intelligent Transport Systems (ITS); Vehicular Communications; Basic Set of Applications; Part 2: Specification of Cooperative Awareness Basic Service, v1.4.1. Standard, European Telecommunication Standard Institute (2019)

11. Huang, L., Matsuura, K., Yamane, H., Sezaki, K.: Enhancing wireless location privacy using silent period. In: IEEE Wireless Communications and Networking Conference, vol. 2, pp. 1187–1192. IEEE (2005)
12. Khodaei, M., Papadimitratos, P.: Cooperative location privacy in vehicular networks: why simple mix zones are not enough. IEEE Internet Things J. 8(10), 7985–8004 (2020)
13. Larsson, S.: Weight and dimensions of heavy commercial vehicles as established by directive 96/53/EC and the European Modular System (EMS). In: Workshop on LHVs, Bruxelles (2009)
14. Li, Q., Malip, A., Martin, K.M., Ng, S.L., Zhang, J.: A reputation-based announcement scheme for VANETs. IEEE Trans. Veh. Technol. 61(9), 4095–4108 (2012)
15. Liu, Z., et al.: BTMPP: balancing trust management and privacy preservation for emergency message dissemination in vehicular networks. IEEE Internet Things J. 8(7), 5386–5407 (2020)
16. Malina, L., Vives-Guasch, A., Castellà-Roca, J., Viejo, A., Hajny, J.: Efficient group signatures for privacy-preserving vehicular networks. Telecommun. Syst. 58(4), 293–311 (2015). https://doi.org/10.1007/s11235-014-9878-3
17. Oguchi, M., Fuse, M.: Regional and longitudinal estimation of product lifespan distribution: a case study for automobiles and a simplified estimation method. Environ. Sci. Technol. 49(3), 1738–1743 (2015)
18. SAE: J2735: Dedicated Short Range Communications (DSRC) message set dictionary. Standard SAE J2735:2009, SAE International (2009)
19. Schmidt, R.K., Lasowski, R., Leinmüller, T., Linnhoff-Popien, C., Schäfer, G.: An approach for selective beacon forwarding to improve cooperative awareness. In: 2010 IEEE Vehicular Networking Conference, pp. 182–188. IEEE (2010)
20. TomTom.com: Brussels traffic. https://www.tomtom.com/en_gb/traffic-index/brussels-traffic/
21. Wu, Q., Domingo-Ferrer, J., González-Nicolás, U.: Balanced trustworthiness, safety, and privacy in vehicle-to-vehicle communications. IEEE Trans. Veh. Technol. 59(2), 559–573 (2009)

Next Generation Data Masking Engine

Micha Moffie[✉], Dan Mor, Sigal Asaf, and Ariel Farkash

IBM Research - Haifa, Haifa University Campus, Haifa, Israel
{moffie,danm,arielf}@il.ibm.com

Abstract. This paper introduces Magen, an advanced masking engine. Magen is a policy-based masking engine that supports a wide range of payloads and use cases. Our graph-based policies and engine support the masking of composite payloads and recursively handles nested payloads based on their type (e.g., json in xml). The engine supports a myriad of advanced masking methods such as format preserving encryption and format preserving tokenization, enabling on-the-fly dynamic masking of payloads as well as the static masking of large data sets. Magen allows users to easily define their own policies for the masking process and specify their formats (data classes).

This engine was developed as part of a multi-year effort and supports real life scenarios such as: conditional masking, robustness to illegal values, enforcement of both format and masking restrictions, and semantic data fabrication. Magen has been integrated as a cloud SaaS within IBM Data and AI offerings and has proved its value in various use cases.

Keywords: Masking · Masking policy · Format preserving masking

1 Introduction

Data masking is the process by which sensitive data is replaced, possibly in a reversible manner, with data that is unintelligible to the receiver, addressing data security and privacy requirements and regulations. The process of masking may appear to be straightforward. If we are simply replacing an item with '***', this can be achieved with a simple regular expression. However, it is a more complex matter to build a generic, flexible, and powerful masking engine that can support composite payloads, advanced masking methods such as format preserving encryption (FPE) and format preserving tokenization (FPT) while addressing large data sets performance requirements.

We developed Masking Gateway for Enterprises, or Magen for short, to address two main use cases, among others. The first is to mask log files such as QRadar [11], allowing them to be exported for off-site analysis. The second case is the masking of DB tables to generate test DB tables.

This work was supported in part by the EU Horizon 2020 Research Fund, SUNFISH GA-644666 and SHIELD GA-727301.

S. Asaf—Work done while at IBM Research - Haifa.

J. Garcia-Alfaro et al. (Eds.): DPM 2021/CBT 2021, LNCS 13140, pp. 152–160, 2022.
https://doi.org/10.1007/978-3-030-93944-1_10

Although many masking tools exist, most of them address a particular payload such as database tables [7–10] or pdf [1,6] files for example. These tools fall short when the payloads are composite, such as a Json snippet within an XML document, or when advanced masking is required for user-defined data classes (e.g., proprietary organization ID). These types of scenario are common in industrial settings and are addressed by Magen.

2 Magen

Our analysis of different data masking use cases produced a set of requirements, which are the basis for the implementation of Magen. These requirements, commonly seen in industry, include the following:

1. Support a wide array of mechanisms to identify, select, and modify (rewrite) data elements within structured, unstructured, and composite documents, while keeping the original document structure.
2. Provide a selection of masking/unmasking operations that address different needs including reversibility, consistency (referential integrity), preservation of the format, validation of input, and importantly, provide the user with the ability to define his own formats (data classes).
3. Support conditional processing and fine-grained flow control.
4. Provide the user with the means to specify a policy to configure and control every aspect of the masking process.

Moving ahead from the requirements to implementation, Magen's architecture is composed of three main components. Each component addresses different aspects of the engine:

1. Core - Provides the engine's API and policy, responsible for parsing, conditional processing and selecting the items in different payloads.
2. Metal - Masking encryption and tokenization library, provides the encryption and tokenization functionality. In particular, it offers integer format preserving encryption and tokenization.
3. Format - Provides the means to create formats. Each format is responsible for implementing its own search and match operations, as well as ranking a string to integer and vice versa (unranking).

We built Magen upon the rank-then-cipher approach, which allows one to preserve the format by first mapping an instance (617-628-1047) in the format domain (phone) to an integer, encrypting or tokenizing it to another integer within the domain size (10^{10}), and finally, mapping the cipher integer back to an instance in the domain (234-345-3602). More details can be found in [2,12].

2.1 Core

Magen's core supports a policy-based, configurable, graph-based data flow. Each node in the graph is responsible for parsing the payload it has received, and then selecting and forwarding part(s) of the payload through different edge(s) to the next node(s). Essentially, this process identifies the sensitive elements that require masking, while parsing from the root node to the leaves. Each leaf node performs a masking operation and returns the masked value. Next, each node receives all updated results from its children, replaces the selected parts with the masked parts, produces an updated payload, and returns it. This process is supported by the following basic components:

- Processor - An element (node) responsible for parsing and selecting data, from a specific type of payload such as Json, CSV etc. Or, implement a masking operation such as redact or encrypt.
- Selector - An element (edge) related to a processor that is used to specify how the selection of a certain data element is executed. Examples include xpath or jpath selectors.
- Expression - A conditional function evaluated before selection, indicating whether processing should continue, and after processing returns indicating whether the updated result should be incorporated. Users can use these boolean expressions to control the execution based on external input or the payload content itself.

Below is an example from an actual composite document, where the goal is to mask a name (line 5).

```
1. <?xml version="1.0" encoding="utf-8"?>
2. <partial-response> ...
3.   <update ...>  <![CDATA[
4.     <table ..> ...
5.       <td ...>john doe</td>...
6. </update> ...
7. </partial-response>
```

Figure 1 shows a processing graph that was constructed for the example. The root of the engine is the XML processor on the left. The XML processor parses the XML payload, selects the xpath specified on the outgoing selector (*"/partial-response/update"*), and passes the selected CDATA node (as text) to the HTML processor. Next, an HTML processor parses the HTML table snippet, and the matching CSS selector (configured with *"table > tbody > tr > td:nth-child(2)"*) selects the name. The name is then passed to the Masking Processor (a leaf node), which is able to mask the text, e.g., replacing the text with '*'. Next, the updated value ('********') is returned from the Masking Processor to the HTML processor, which then replaces the original value with the updated text. Lastly, the updated HTML is returned to the XML processor, which updates the CDATA node and returns the updated XML to the caller.

Policy. The policy determines how a payload should be processed, elements selected and masked. This is done using a json file containing all the information

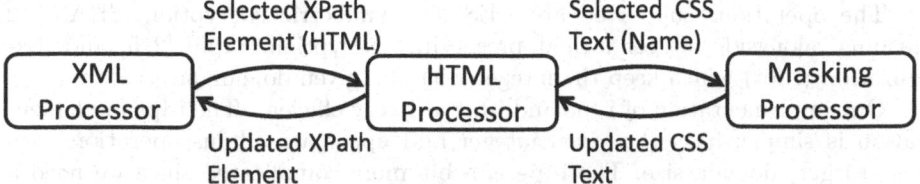

Fig. 1. An instance of Magen engine and processing graph

required to instantiate the engine. It includes the specification of the data flow in a graph, the configuration of each processor and selector, as well as expressions and user-defined formats.

API. Magen's API is simple. An instance of the engine can be created using a policy; this engine is then used to process one or more payloads:

```
Magen magen = new Magen(policy)
String masked = (String) magen.process(payload, metadata, state)
```

The payload is the document to be masked (json, xslx), the metadata is a simple key/value structure to support expressions (conditional execution), and the state can contain an encryption key and initial vector when needed. The call returns an almost identical copy of the payload; it is basically the same payload type with the selected items masked.

Service. On top of Magen, we developed an experimental service. The service exposes: (1) a RESTful API for managing policies and masking a payload, and (2) a graphical user interface (GUI) for creating and testing policies (including expressions and formats). The GUI is able to represent a json policy as a proper graph and support the visual creation of the policy using nodes and edges.

2.2   Metal

Metal is the component responsible for applying the cryptographic transformations; this is the *cipher* part of the rank-then-cipher approach. It includes the mechanisms to support the transformations needed for format preserving encryption and tokenization, format transforming encryption and tokenization, as well as random and repeatable format fabrication.

The engine performs format transforming operations by ranking the input format, performing the operation on the output domain size, and unranking on the output format. Format fabrication operations are done by replacing the ranking values of invalid instances, values that do not match the format, with the binary representation of the hashed input text. These transformations allow users to fabricate data (e.g., for testing) and provide robustness to illegal values.

The operations supported are AES-256 symmetric encryption, SHA3-512 hashing, alongside integer format preserving encryption (i-fpe) [2–5] and tokenization (i-fpt) which keep the integer within a given domain size.

Our implementation of i-fpe and i-fpt are very efficient. The i-fpt implementation is simple: hash the given integer and apply a modulus operation with the (target) domain size. The i-fpe is a bit more complicated since we need a one-to-one mapping. While several alternatives for performing i-fpe exist, we needed an *efficient* solution for large domains such as email addresses (3×10^{29}). Our i-fpe algorithm relies on a block cipher (e.g., AES), where the number of bits required to represent the largest value in the domain defines the number of blocks needed. This way, we can apply simple block encryption and decryption, which is very efficient. However, most domain sizes do not fit into blocks exactly. In these cases, the last block is padded with encrypted bits from the previous block to construct a full block for encryption, effectively encrypting part of the previous block twice.

2.3   Format

The format library is responsible for the *match*, *search*, and the *rank* part of the rank-then-cipher approach. The match and search capabilities are used by the engine to search for candidates in free text and to make sure they are valid format instances.

The library provides a flexible API that allows users to define their own formats, based on the compositions of various building blocks. Before delving into more detail, we provide an example of how a format can be defined. The following json definition of the IP format is also used below in our performance evaluation.

```
{"type": "Tiled",
 "configuration": { "subformats": [
   {"type": "Concatenation",
    "configuration": { "subformats": [
      {"type": "Integer",
       "configuration": {"min":0,"max":255}},
      {"type": "FixedLengthString",
       "configuration": {"alphabet":".","length":1}}
      ... ]}},
   {"type": "Concatenation",
     "configuration": { "subformats": [
       {"type": "RegularExpression",
        "configuration": {"regex":"[0-9a-fA-F]{4}"}},
       {"type": "FixedLengthString",
        "configuration": {"alphabet":":","length":1}}
       ... ]}}
 ]}
}
```

The definition above demonstrates how a user can easily define a new format by simply using compositions and building blocks. All building blocks are required to realize their own search, match, and rank functions. Composition blocks, such as concatenation, must construct search, match, and rank *automatically* based on their sub-formats. Table 1 lists several of the main building blocks and compositions available.

Table 1. Format blocks

Format basic building blocks	Ranking based on	Format composite building blocks	Ranking based on	Masking restriction
Integer	Integer range	Immutable	Subformat	✓
FixedLengthInteger	Integer range	Concatenation	Multiplication of sub-formats	
RealNumber	Integer range			
FixedLengthString	Lexicographic	Union	Addition of sub-formats	
VariableLengthString	Lexicographic			
RegularExpression	State machine	Tiled	Addition of sub-formats	✓
StringSet	Enumeration			

In defining a format, we must consider two types of restrictions. The format restriction defines the valid instances in the domain. These may include the text pattern as well as validity checks such as Luhn checksum. The masking restrictions limit the transformation of instances to a specific sub-domain. The target sub-domains are non-overlapping and cover the entire domain.

In the IP example above, both the IPv4 and IPv6 addresses are valid and will be matched. However, the tiled masking restriction limits IPv4 instance transformations to IPv4 and IPv6 instance transformations to IPv6.

3 Implementation

Magen has been designed and implemented to be stateless and thread safe. It is written in Java as a stand-alone library and includes over 400 predefined formats, such as CCN, IBAN, email, USFirstNames, etc. Table 2 lists the different payload types and accompanying selectors that are supported by the library. The library also supports user-defined code (JavaScript) to be inserted before or after each processor's main code allowing modification of the payload and metadata.

The masking methods are shown in Table 3. The table also indicates which formats are reversible (using a key), which employ input validation, and which are repeatable and support referential integrity.

4 Performance

Much work has been done to address the performance of Magen overall as well as FPE and FPT operations. Magen is able to handle large datasets, on-the-fly, with very little overhead.

Table 2. Masking support for different payload types

Payload type	Payload selectors
json	jpath
html	css
xml	xpath
xlsx, csv	table cell selector
text	regex, format
docx, pptx, pdf (Beta)	docPath

In this section we present select test cases showcasing the overall performance of Magen while focusing on (1) the cost of FPT/FPE cryptographic operations on different formats, (2) the overall masking performance for different payload types and (3) engine scalability. Table 4 shows the performance of FPE and FPT on the following formats: (Note that the overall time increases with the domain size while CCN's performance is lower due to the Luhn validation check.)

1. USLastNames (a dictionary of 88,799 entries)
2. US Phone - Regex + decorations (immutable)
3. Credit Card Number (CCN): 13–16 digits + decoration + **Luhn checksum**
4. IP - the composite IPv4 and IPv6 format shown above

Table 5 shows masking performance results, comparing different payloads and showcasing how well the engine scales. We compared the throughput of 2M records each containing a credit card number, IP, and last name, encoded in different payload types: text, json, CSV. The engine was required to mask (FPT) only the credit card numbers so we could showcase the overhead of parsing and selecting on top of Metal. Additionally, we measured the throughput when

Table 3. Masking methods

Method	Reversible	Input validation	Repeatable
Redaction	x	x	x
Tokenization	x	x	✓
Encryption	✓	x	✓
Random format fabrication[a]	x	x	x
Repeatable format fabrication	x	x	✓
Format preserving tokenization	x	✓	✓
Format preserving encryption	✓	✓	✓
Format transforming tokenization	x	✓	✓
Format transforming encryption	✓	✓	✓

[a]When the input matches the format, restrictions such as immutable/tiled will be enforced.

Table 4. Metal throughput, operation/sec

Format	FPT	FPE	Domain size
USLastNames	590K	2646K	8.879×10^4
US Phone	163K	171K	6.400×10^{11}
CCN	62K	63K	2.799×10^{16}
IP	62K	65K	3.402×10^{38}

Table 5. Masking E2E throughput, operation/sec (FPT on all CCNs)

Payload	Number of threads		
	1	2	4
Text	47K	85K	60K
CSV	57K	105K	174K
Json	53K	98K	149K

running the engine on 1, 2, and 4 threads in parallel to illustrate the engine's scalability.

All tests were conducted using Java OpenJDK 11.0.9, on a machine running MacOs BigSur with a 2.3 GHz 8-Core Intel core i9 and 64 GB of RAM. The resulting performance numbers show the masking efficiency and scalability supported by the engine. These results are well within the required performance boundaries for the use cases and customers we are currently working with including online dynamic data masking and large data sets masking for generating testing data.

5 Summary

We introduced Magen, an advanced masking engine, and demonstrated how it works. The advancements made in Magen, including support for composite payloads, advanced masking methods (e.g. FPE, FPT), flexible policies, support for user defined formats as well as its masking performance, make it very suitable for industry applications. Magen is already available for customers and is actively maintained and continuously improved to support additional use cases and increase adoption.

References

1. Adobe: Adobe redaction tool (2021). https://helpx.adobe.com/acrobat/using/removing-sensitive-content-pdfs.html
2. Bellare, M., Ristenpart, T., Rogaway, P., Stegers, T.: Format-preserving encryption. In: Jacobson, M.J., Rijmen, V., Safavi-Naini, R. (eds.) SAC 2009. LNCS, vol. 5867, pp. 295–312. Springer, Heidelberg (2009). https://doi.org/10.1007/978-3-642-05445-7_19
3. Bellare, M., Rogaway, P., Spies, T.: The FFX mode of operation for format-preserving encryption. NIST submission 20 (2010)
4. Brier, E., Peyrin, T., Stern, J.: BPS: a format-preserving encryption proposal (2020)
5. Dworkin, M.: Recommendation for block cipher modes of operation. NIST Special Publication 800, 38G (2016)
6. Evermap: Evermap data masking (2021). https://www.evermap.com/autoredact.asp

160   M. Moffie et al.

7. Imperva: Imperva data masking (2021). https://www.imperva.com/data-security/data-security-101/data-masking/
8. IBM InfoSphere: IBM infosphere data masking (2021). https://www.ibm.com/il-en/marketplace/infosphere-optim-data-privacy
9. Microsoft: Microsoft data masking (2021). https://docs.microsoft.com/en-us/sql/relational-databases/security/dynamic-data-masking
10. Oracle: Oracle data masking (2021). https://www.oracle.com/database/data-masking-subsetting/
11. QRadar: IBM QRadar (2021). https://www.ibm.com/security/security-intelligence/qradar
12. Weiss, M., Rozenberg, B., Barham, M.: Practical solutions for format-preserving encryption, June 2015

Towards a Formal Approach for Data Minimization in Programs (Short Paper)

Florian Lanzinger[✉][iD] and Alexander Weigl[iD]

Institute of Information Security and Dependability (KASTEL),
Karlsruhe Institute of Technology (KIT), Karlsruhe, Germany
{lanzinger,weigl}@kit.edu

Abstract. As more and more processes are digitized, the protection of personal data becomes increasingly important for individuals, agencies, companies, and society in general. One principle of data protection is data minimization, which limits the processing and storage of personal data to the minimum necessary for the defined purpose. To adhere to this principle, an analysis of what data are needed by a piece of software is required. In this paper, we present an idea for a program analysis which connects data minimization with secure information flow to assess which personal data are required by a program: A program is decomposed into two programs. The first projects the original input, keeping only the minimal amount of required data. The second computes the original output from the projected input. Thus, we achieve a program variant which is compliant with data minimization. We define the approach, show how it can be used for different scenarios, and give examples for how to compute such a decomposition.

Keywords: Secure information flow · Data minimization · GDPR

1 Introduction

Privacy and data protection are urgent topics as more and more processes in society are digitized. One consequence of this digitization is the increasing amount of stored and processed personal data. To ensure that users' privacy is respected and their data protected, the European legislator reacted with the General Data Protection Regulation (GDPR) [3] which regulates the collection and processing of personal data. One important principle is *data minimization*, which limits the collection and storage of personal data to those which are "necessary in relation to the purposes for which they are processed" [3, §5(1)(c)].

Therefore, authorities and companies must analyze which personal data are necessary for the conduct of their operation. This not only includes inspecting the accessed and used personal data, but also analyzing how they are involved in the

---

This work was supported by funding of the Helmholtz Association (HGF) through the Competence Center for Applied Security Technology (KASTEL).

J. Garcia-Alfaro et al. (Eds.): DPM 2021/CBT 2021, LNCS 13140, pp. 161–169, 2022.
https://doi.org/10.1007/978-3-030-93944-1_11

process and what decisions, if any, depend on them. For example, an authority may store the exact income of a person, but if it only needs to know that the income is above a certain threshold, it can just store this Boolean information. As a result of such an analysis, only the minimal necessary information should be collected.

Contribution. We sketch a formal approach to analyze and assess the data usage of algorithms (Sect. 2). The idea of the analysis is to decompose a given program into two parts: The first part projects the original input data onto the minimal set of data from which the result can be computed. The second part computes the original output from this minimal data. We discuss how this decomposition can be applied in different scenarios (Sect. 3) and which additional constraints are added to the base problem. Moreover, we give two examples of how such a decomposition can be computed with different precisions using syntactic or semantic analyses.

2   A Formal Approach to Data Minimization

For the presentation of the approach, we model a program as a function $f: I \rightarrow O$ which maps the given input $i \in I$ to an output $f(i) = o \in O$. The input space $I = H \times L$ is a combination of personal data H, which are **Highly** confidential, and **Low** confidential data L like configuration parameters. The high and low categorization is defined by the author or auditor. This modeling assumes that programs are side-effect free and that the output o is computed only by considering the inputs in $H \times L$. Figure 1

```
tax_rate(age, income: H,
          base: L) {
  if (age<18) return 0*base;
  if (age<25 && !(income>1000))
    return base;
  if (income<=1000)
    return 2*base;
  return 3*base; }
```

Fig. 1. An example program which computes someone's tax rate based on their age and income.

shows an example program whose output is the tax rate, whose confidential inputs H are the **age** and **income** of a person, and whose non-confidential input L is a base tax rate, from which the actual tax rate is computed.

Basic Idea. Given a program $f : H \times L \rightarrow O$, we want to find a decomposition into two programs (π, ρ) such that $f(h, l) = \rho(\pi(h), l)$ for all inputs $(h, l) \in H \times L$ and such that the information provided by $\pi(h)$ is minimal. We call π the *projection* and ρ the *reduction*.

The information provided by $\pi(h)$ can be described as the information leakage, a notion commonly used in quantitative information flow. Leakage is the amount of secret information (here, the amount of information about h) that is disclosed by a program [7]. The leakage is given in bits and computed from the entropy. Different entropy definitions reflect different attacker capabilities. For simplicity, we consider the min-entropy which reflects how well the input can be guessed by an attacker in one try. This leads to a minimization of the number of possible images of π for deterministic programs: $\min_\pi |\{\pi(h) \mid h \in H\}|$.

Our approach is also related to secure information flow, which analyses whether an attacker learns secret information by observing the exposed output. In some situations, secret information is declassified. For example, paper reviews are confidential until the final acceptance decision is drawn. By computing the decomposition, we want to infer the minimal amount of secret information that is declassified by f. This declassified information is represented by the image of π.

An additional benefit of our approach is that it allows for a comparison between programs. Given two programs f, f', we can compute both decompositions and compare the images of the projections π and π' to find out which version requires less information.

We assume that the decomposition of f into (π, ρ) is computed either by the author of f who honestly wants to observe the principle of data minimization or by an independent auditor with access to f's source code.

Unwanted Degenerate Solution. If all parameters are in H (e.g., if we replaced the parameter base in Fig. 1 with a constant), there is a trivial solution to the stated problem definition, where $\pi(h) = f(h)$ projects all inputs h to the output $f(h)$ and ρ is just the identity function $\rho = \mathrm{id}$. In our tax example, this represents a decomposition in which the applicants compute their tax rates by themselves and only submit these final tax rates to the authority. This solution is undesirable for various reasons: First, it does not provide any insight into which information is required by the computation. Second, from the viewpoint of the authority, the decision might not be auditable later, especially if the required personal information has changed. Collecting a rudimentary amount of personal data may be required to simplify later validation.

The given formalization thus requires further constraints to give useful results. The constraints depend on the operational purpose and the usage context in which the personal data should be minimized.

3   Usage Scenarios

In this section, we consider some usage scenarios, each of which leads to different additional constraints.

Paper-Based Form. Public authorities often ask applicants for personal data using paper-based forms. These forms are of course static; their contents cannot change depending on the user's input. Also, they should not require the applicant to do very complex computations.

Let us again consider Fig. 1. It shows a simple program which computes the tax rate based on the applicant's age and income, which are both in H. The authority wants to collect the minimal amount of personal information required by this program.

To keep the projection simple enough to compute for the person filling out the form, and to prevent degenerate solutions, we add the following constraint:

The projection π is only allowed to contain basic unary and binary expressions over a single variable, e.g., $x < 2$ or $\neg x$. In our example, the function which maps `age` and `income` to the three truth values $age < 18, age < 25, income > 1000$ is a valid projection.

The reduction ρ then only has to know the values of these Boolean expressions instead of the exact age and income. Indeed, it is common in tax applications that applicants only need to confirm that they qualify for some taxation rule without giving the exact reason why they qualify. Only in doubt does the tax office request further evidence to check the confirmation.

Web Form. Our second scenario uses the same setting, but instead of a paper-based form, we use a web form. In this case, the decomposition represents the system borders: π represents the web form in the browser, ρ the program on the authority's servers. The user can enter their complete personal information, but the browser will only send the required information to the authority. This allows π to synthesize expressions that would be too complex to put on a paper form. However, the actual decision-making should still be done in ρ, not in π. We thus modify the previously stated constraint: The program π is allowed to contain Boolean and arithmetic expressions over multiple variables, e.g., $x < y \wedge y < z$, $x + y$, or $x + y > 0$. This allows for a smaller information leakage between π and ρ, but the requirement that π only contain basic expressions (and not, for example, **if** or **while** statements) ensures that the actual computation is still done in ρ. One reason behind this requirement is that π runs on a non-trusted computer system, i.e., the browser of the customer or applicant. To ensure a proper evaluation of the personal data, we still need to transfer them to the trusted server where ρ is executed. Thinking beyond, we might want to decompose f into three programs, one that runs on the non-trusted platform and minimizes the data to be transferred to the server, one that runs on the server and minimizes the data to be stored, and one which computes the final decision from the storage. In general, we can extend the approach to a decomposition into an arbitrary number of program parts, as long as it is defined which computations must be done in which part.

Outsourcing Computation to the Cloud. We consider a company which wants to outsource expensive computations to the cloud while exposing as little internal data and computation as possible. The decomposition into π and ρ represents different environments. The program π is executed on the company's system—a trusted environment where sensitive computations can be executed—and ρ is executed in the cloud. Therefore, ρ should contain expensive computations on the minimal required sensitive data. Thus, in this scenario, π can be any arbitrary program. Additionally, we assign computation costs to each statement or expression in f. We want to keep sensitive computations from f from being moved into the cloud computation ρ. We thus receive new constraints: The program f is split into π and ρ, such that the computation cost of π is minimal, and no (or only a certain amount of) sensitive computation is done in ρ.

4   Approaches to the Computation of the Decomposition

In this section, we sketch some ideas how such a partitioning can be (approximately) computed. For now, we assume that f is loop-free and that all expressions are side-effect-free. We also assume that f is free of local variables; i.e., the only variables that occur are the parameters. We give some ideas of how these restrictions can be lifted at the end of this section.

The first approach works syntactically by collecting the set E of all expressions in f which contain at least one sensitive parameter in H. Choose a set $\Pi \subseteq E$ such that all expressions in E can be built up only from expressions in Π, low parameters in L, literals, and the basic binary operators. E.g., from the expressions a and b, we can build $a + b > 0$ and also $a + c > 0$ if $c \in L$. A function that maps f's parameters to such a subset Π is a valid projection π. The reduction ρ belonging to π is the function whose body is equal to f's body, except that every expression e in Π is substituted by a new variable, which represents the value of e as computed by π.

For example, a possible solution for Fig. 1 is $\Pi = \{\text{age} < 18, \text{age} < 25, \text{income} > 1000\}$. The program π maps age and income to the values of the expressions in Π, and ρ is identical to f except that all expressions in Π have been replaced by new variables, e.g., the expression age < 18 has been replaced by a new variable ageUnder18. If we allow π to contain expressions over multiple variables, as in our second scenario, we can also choose $\Pi = \{(\text{age} < 18), (\text{age} < 25 \land \neg\text{income} > 1000), (\text{income} > 1000)\}$.

The second approach works semantically: We collect the path conditions and returned expressions for each path by using symbolic execution, a common technique for program analysis and widely available for different programming languages. For Fig. 1, this yields the four conditions

$R1 = \text{age} < 18;$

$R2 = \neg(\text{age} < 18) \land \text{age} < 25 \land \neg(\text{income} > 1000)$

$R3 = \neg(\text{age} < 18) \land \neg(\text{age} < 25 \land \neg(\text{income} > 1000)) \land \text{income} \leq 1000$

$R4 = \neg(\text{age} < 18) \land \neg(\text{age} < 25 \land \neg(\text{income} > 1000)) \land \neg(\text{income} \leq 1000))$

and the four return expressions 0, base, $2 * \text{base}$ and $3 * \text{base}$. We choose a set of expressions Π from whose values the value of the path conditions and return expressions of all reachable paths can be computed (e.g., from a and b, we can compute $a + b > 0$, but also $a + b + c - c > 0$ for any c) and construct π, ρ as before.

For Fig. 1, this leads to the same solution(s) as the syntactic approach. However, the semantic approach has several advantages in comparison to the syntactic approach. First, it is robust against misleading syntactical constructs. A programmer may try to change a program's syntax to increase the required information in favor of the company. For example in Fig. 2,

```
tricky(a, b: H) {
  if(a != 0)
    if(b < 0) return a-b;
  else
    if(a != 0) return b;
  return a; }
```

Fig. 2. An example with unreachable code and misleading syntax which are undetectable by the syntactical approach.

the programmer split an expression a!=0 and b<0 into two if-statements. A syntactic analysis would include both expressions in the projection, missing the fact that they can be joined into a!=0 && b<0, Moreover, working on a semantic level makes the analysis aware of unreachable code. For example, the return b; in Fig. 2 is not reachable. A syntactic approach would include b in the projection, while a semantic approach could notice that this return statement is unreachable.

In general, semantic approaches track and extract the required information precisely. The disadvantage is the complexity and low scalability of the analysis. The halting problem is reducible to the computation of the exact minimizing decomposition. Thus, the exact decomposition is undecidable in general.

To allow local variables, we can transform a program into its *static single assignment (SSA)* form, in which every local variable is only assigned to exactly once. The SSA form allows us to expand the definitions of all variables and then delete all unnecessary assignments; e.g., the statements a=b;c=a can be transformed into c=b. We can then apply our—slightly adapted—approaches on this transformed program. For programs containing loops, we cannot expand variable definitions like this, since the correct expansion depends on which loop iteration we are in. One way to solve this may be to choose an upper bound for the number of loop iterations and unroll all loops.

5   Limitations

Our proposed approach has several limitations. First, we do not assess whether the given data are "adequate, relevant, and limited to what is necessary" for the stated purpose, as required by GDPR §5(1)(c). We only consider whether the data are required to compute the output of the given program. For example, the gender of a person may not be (legally) relevant for some application process, but if the program's output depends on it, our approach will mark it as required. This difference was discussed by Biega et al. [2], where you can also find a discussion on the wording of GDPR §5(1)(c), including the legal meaning of the term *relevant*.

Second, the approach is not aware of statistical correlations or dependencies between parameters. If two parameters are correlated, e.g., address and income, the approach is unable to infer that knowing a person's address may also allow one to draw conclusions about their income. Datta et al. [4] show how systems can be validated against this *proxy discrimination*.

Furthermore, this is a white-box approach which requires access to the source code and the program structure. On the one hand, this gives us the possibility to output either witnesses that show why certain data are indeed required by a program or formal guarantees that the date are not required. On the other hand, it limits the scalability of the approach, as it needs to scale with large source code. Also, we need to adapt the approach in situations where the source code may not be available (e.g., built-in library functions). As discussed in Sect. 4, using the source code of the program makes our approach, especially the syntactic variant, vulnerable to adversaries. Programmers may be able to exploit the program structure to increase the minimal required amount of information.

6   Related Work

Pfitzmann and Hansen [9] identify five concepts for data minimization: anonymity, unlinkability, undetectability, unobservability, pseudonymity, and authenticity. We follow a different approach and only consider whether personal data are required for the execution of a program. In detail, we try to find a *similar* program which is functionally equivalent and requires less personal data. Goldsteen et al. [5] present a method for the minimization of the required personal data in a machine learning model. Their approach removes and generalizes the input features. The features which promise the least degeneration of accuracy are identified in the learned model. Later in the application phase of the trained machine, only the survived features are collected. The other features are removed. Therefore, the training still requires personal data. A similar approach is followed by Biega et al. [2]. They investigate data minimization for recommendation systems under a global and per-user minimization strategy. Ramadan et al. [10] present a framework for modeling business processes that evaluates the security, data-minimization, and fairness requirements, and allows the detection of conflicts between them based on a catalog of domain-independent anti-patterns.

Program Slicing [1] is a technique to omit unnecessary statements from a program. A statement is unnecessary if it does not influence the output. We can compute a program's slice, in which every statement influences the output. In such a slice, the required data is easier to identify. Our approach goes further: Instead of just removing completely unnecessary statements, it is also able to replace expressions with less informative variants and thus actually decrease the amount of required information.

Kammüller [6] demonstrates the formalisation of the GDPR using the *Decentralized Label Model* (DLM) [8] in Isabelle. In DLM, data is labeled with owner and reader lists which define access rights. DLM allows multiple principles, i.e., users who are granted access rights. In contrast to DLM, our approach consumes only one algorithm as input and input categorization. It can be extended for multiple principles: If we consider each principle's information use separately, we can compute the minimal amount of required information for each principle.

Then, instead of granting a principle read access to the complete information, they only receive the required amount of information. In contrast to Kammüller, who checks for GDPR compliance, we focus on a program transformation which makes a program GDPR-compliant.

7   Conclusion

We present a novel connection between data minimization and secure information flow. The idea is to split a given program into two programs: one which projects the specified personal data to the minimal needed amount of data, and one which computes the original output from the minimized data. We elaborate various additional constraints on this formalization depending on different usage scenarios and also discuss the feasibility of the approximation of such a flow-minimizing program split.

In the future, we plan to extend our approach to programs with loops. We also plan to implement both a syntactic and a semantic approach as outlined in Sect. 4, which automatically computes (minimal or approximately minimal) projections and appropriate reductions for programs in a real-world programming language.

References

1. Beckert, B., Bormer, T., Gocht, S., Herda, M., Lentzsch, D., Ulbrich, M.: SEMSLICE: exploiting relational verification for automatic program slicing. In: Polikarpova, N., Schneider, S. (eds.) IFM 2017. LNCS, vol. 10510, pp. 312–319. Springer, Cham (2017). https://doi.org/10.1007/978-3-319-66845-1_20
2. Biega, A.J., Potash, P., Daumé, H.D., III, Diaz, F., Finck, M.: Operationalizing the legal principle of data minimization for personalization. In: Huang, J., et al. (eds.) Proceedings of SIGIR 2020, pp. 399–408. ACM (2020). https://doi.org/10.1145/3397271.3401034
3. Council of the European Union: General Data Protection Regulation (2016). https://eur-lex.europa.eu/eli/reg/2016/679
4. Datta, A., Fredrikson, M., Ko, G., Mardziel, P., Sen, S.: Proxy non-discrimination in data-driven systems. CoRR (2017). arXiv:1707.08120
5. Goldsteen, A., Ezov, G., Shmelkin, R., Moffie, M., Farkash, A.: Data minimization for GDPR compliance in machine learning models. CoRR (2020). arXiv:2008.04113
6. Kammüller, F.: Formal modeling and analysis of data protection for GDPR compliance of IoT healthcare systems. In: Proceedings of IEEE SMC, pp. 3319–3324. IEEE (2018). https://doi.org/10.1109/SMC.2018.00562
7. Klebanov, V., Manthey, N., Muise, C.: SAT-based analysis and quantification of information flow in programs. In: Joshi, K., Siegle, M., Stoelinga, M., D'Argenio, P.R. (eds.) QEST 2013. LNCS, vol. 8054, pp. 177–192. Springer, Heidelberg (2013). https://doi.org/10.1007/978-3-642-40196-1_16
8. Myers, A., Liskov, B.: Complete, safe information flow with decentralized labels. In: Proceedings of IEEE S&P, pp. 186–197 (1998). https://doi.org/10.1109/SECPRI.1998.674834

9. Pfitzmann, A., Hansen, M.: A terminology for talking about privacy by data minimization: anonymity, unlinkability, undetectability, unobservability, pseudonymity,
   and identity management (2010). http://dud.inf.tu-dresden.de/Anon_Terminology.
   shtml
10. Ramadan, Q., Strüber, D., Salnitri, M., Jürjens, J., Riediger, V., Staab, S.: A
    semi-automated BPMN-based framework for detecting conflicts between security,
    data-minimization, and fairness requirements. Softw. Syst. Model. **19**(5), 1191–
    1227 (2020). https://doi.org/10.1007/s10270-020-00781-x

CBT Workshop: Mining, Consensus and Market Manipulation

Virtual ASICs: Generalized Proof-of-Stake Mining in Cryptocurrencies

Chaya Ganesh[1], Claudio Orlandi[2], Daniel Tschudi[3(✉)], and Aviv Zohar[4]

[1] Indian Institute of Science, Bangalore, India
chaya@iisc.ac.in
[2] Concordium Blockchain Research Center, Aarhus University, Aarhus, Denmark
orlandi@cs.au.dk
[3] Concordium, Zurich, Switzerland
dt@concordium.com
[4] The Hebrew University of Jerusalem, Jerusalem, Israel
avivz@cs.huji.ac.il

Abstract. In proof-of-work based cryptocurrencies, miners invest computing power to maintain a distributed ledger. One known drawback of such a consensus protocol is its immense energy consumption. To prevent this waste of energy various consensus mechanism such as proof-of-space or proof-of-stake have been proposed. In proof-of-stake, block creators are selected based on the amounts of currency they stake instead of their expanded computing power,

In this work we study *Virtual ASICs*–a generalization of proof-of-stake. Virtual ASICs are essentially a virtualized version of proof-of-work. Miners can buy on-chain virtual mining machines which can be powered by virtual electricity. Similar to their physical counterparts, each powered virtual ASIC has a certain chance to win the right to create the next block. In the boundary case where virtual electricity is free, the protocol corresponds to proof-of-stake using an ASIC token which is separate from the currency itself (the amount of stake equals your virtual computing power). In the other boundary case where virtual computers are free, we get a proof-of-burn equivalent. That is, a consensus mechanism in which miners 'burn' currency to obtain lottery tickets for the right to create the next block.

C. Ganesh and D. Tschudi—Work partially done when authors were at Aarhus University supported by the Concordium Blockhain Research Center.

Claudio Orlandi is supported by: the Concordium Blockhain Research Center, Aarhus University, Denmark; the Carlsberg Foundation under the Semper Ardens Research Project CF18-112 (BCM); the European Research Council (ERC) under the European Unions's Horizon 2020 research and innovation programme under grant agreement No. 803096 (SPEC); the Danish Independent Research Council under Grant-ID DFF-6108-00169 (FoCC).

Aviv Zohar is supported by the Israel Science Foundation (grant 1504/17) and by a grant from the HUJI Cyber Security Research Center in conjunction with the Israel National Cyber Bureau.

© Springer Nature Switzerland AG 2022
J. Garcia-Alfaro et al. (Eds.): DPM 2021/CBT 2021, LNCS 13140, pp. 173–191, 2022.
https://doi.org/10.1007/978-3-030-93944-1_12

From a technical point of view, we provide the following contributions:
- We design cryptographic protocols that allow to sell Virtual ASICs in sealed-bid auctions on-chain. We ensure that as long as a majority of the miners in the system mine honestly, bids remain both private and binding, and that miners cannot censor the bids of their competitors;
- In order to implement our auction protocol, we introduce a novel all-or-nothing broadcast functionality in blockchains that allows to "encrypt values to the future" and could be of independent interest.
- Finally, we provide a consensus protocol based on Virtual ASICs by generalizing existing protocols for proof-of-stake consensus.

1 Introduction

Nakamoto's blockchain protocol [25] crucially relies on a *proof-of-work (PoW)* component to secure the chain. In order to make the system secure against double spending attacks, honest miners are encouraged to join the system via high valued block rewards. The competitive nature of mining quickly led miners to use specialized hardware for the mining process. Proof-of-work based mining nowadays uses Application Specific Integrated Circuits (ASIC) to perform the required computations. Since manufacturing and operating ASICs requires resources such as electricity to power and cool the ASICs, Bitcoin's mining exacts a high toll on the world's resources [9,26] and is a major contributor to carbon footprint [21]. Since the economics of mining suggests that miners should purchase more machines as long as rewards outweigh costs, more efficient mining equipment still wastes just as many resources at equilibrium [30]. For the same reason, other variants of proof-of-work, e.g. those that require more memory such as Ethash [14] or even processor down time or ownership [24], lead to waste at a similar large scale. The wasteful nature of PoW led to the exploration of alternative consensus mechanisms. *Proof-of-stake consensus protocols (PoS)* provide guarantees similar to PoW assuming that a majority of the *wealth* in the system is controlled by honest participants (as opposed to a majority of the *computing power* being honest). The rationale is that users who have a significant *stake* in the system have an incentive to keep the system running. Otherwise, they risk a devaluation of their holdings. Starting from the initial idea of proof-of-stake in an online Bitcoin forum [27], there have been a series of candidates for such PoS protocols [3,4,20]. More recently, there have been works on formal models for proof-of-stake and constructions with provable security guarantees [1,5,11,17,19].

In this paper we argue that the design space of PoS-like protocols can be expanded and that further improvements are possible. We start by discussing some advantages and disadvantages of PoW and PoS and show how the best of both worlds can be combined with a system based on *virtual ASICs*. Virtual ASICs are tokenized representations of mining power that mimic many of the properties of their physical counterparts but do not waste any physical resources. Their properties can be fine-tuned to further adjust the incentives of miners in ways that improve the stability, well-being, and decentralization of the system.

1.1   Our Contributions

We present the following technical contributions:

On-Chain Auctions for ASICs. We show how to bootstrap our virtual ASIC blockchain system by constructing a mechanism for acquiring ASICs on the blockchain. Towards this, we construct a sealed-bid auction that, in addition to bid confidentiality, independence and verifiability, provides *censorship resilience*, that is, parties cannot be prevented from bidding on ASICs even by other miners, and unretractability, that is, the winner of the auction cannot retract their bid in the decision stage of the auction. In constructing our auction protocol, we first construct a building block that we call an *all-or-nothing broadcast*.

All-or-Nothing Broadcast Channel. At a high level, an all-or-nothing broadcast channel allows parties to broadcast a message with delay or, in other words, to "encrypt it to the future". In the first phase, parties can input messages, but no party can retrieve them. After the delay time has elapsed, parties can retrieve all the messages in the second phase. The guarantee is that an adversary can (at most) prevent the delivery of all messages, but the delivery of any specific message cannot be prevented. We use this channel to construct an ASIC auction and also to allow miners to commit in advance to powering their ASICs. We believe all-or-nothing broadcast on the blockchain could be of independent interest for other applications. We use an ad hoc threshold encryption scheme to construct our channel, and then discuss how to use rewards to disincentivize aborts, thus achieving a delay broadcast which guarantees output delivery.

Consensus Based on Virtual ASICs. Finally, we generalize an existing proof-of-stake protocol (e.g. Ouroboros Praos (OP) [11]) to implement a consensus protocol that is based on a leader election lottery, where the probability that a party is elected as a leader in a given slot is proportional to the party's mining rate of the virtual ASICs in the system. While we do this for OP for the sake of concreteness, the idea of replacing stake with virtual ASIC power in a lottery could be generalized to other proof-of-stake protocols.

1.2   The Advantages and Disadvantages of Physical ASICs vs. PoS

On top of their infamously high resource consumption, ASICs introduce further problems compared to PoS systems. Specifically, they have side-effects that lead to more centralization in the system, and to miner behavior that causes mining power to oscillate between different cryptocurrencies based on profitability.

ASICs as a Centralizing Force. ASIC based PoW systems are particularly efficient in mining relative to general computing platforms such as CPUs, GPUs or even FPGAs. When they first appeared, ASICs were seen as a potential threat to the decentralization of Bitcoin: They conferred substantial advantages to the few miners that possessed them. These miners could then easily push others below the threshold of profitability, and essentially control the cryptocurrency. Similar concerns were raised with respect to the manufacturing of ASICs that had a high barrier of entry and is thus controlled by even fewer parties. Another such barrier is represented by patents on hardware designs and methods that allow for even more efficient mining. One such example is ASIC Boost, a technique for running SHA256 hashes more efficiently in hardware. When ASIC Boost appeared, it was feared that patent protections would be used to restrict the profitability of competing miners and again allow only a single entity to mine profitably. ASIC-resistant mining schemes were explored in an attempt to alleviate these issues, but were also met with objections. Arguably, ASIC resistance raises the barrier to create an efficient mining machine, which implies that once that barrier is breached, it will be in even fewer hands. For example, Ethereum purposefully chose a PoW system based on intensive memory access [14], claiming that memory available on the market is already extremely efficient, and it is unlikely that some single ASIC manufacturer would deploy an ASIC that is substantially better than other miners. Nonetheless, ASICs for Ethereum did eventually appear (although their mining efficiency is not as far from conventional miners as was the case in Bitcoin). Finally, the operation of ASICs often leads to centralization via an effect of "Economies of Scale". Large miners are able to obtain ASICs, electricity, and other resources at far lower prices. Their large size often confers a discount on operating costs. This again translates to higher profits than small miner. Needless to say, PoS systems as well as our Virtual ASICs do not suffer from any of these disadvantages; they work just as efficiently for small miners, and are available to all at the same price.

The Advantage of ASICs. One often cited advantage of ASICs is the very fact that they are, as the acronym ASIC suggests, application specific. The owners of ASICs are in this way invested heavily in the cryptocurrency—their ASICs are useless for any other purpose. This is a major advantage for cryptocurrency security because any miner that holds a large amount of ASICs would refrain from using them to attack the protocol, due to the fear of lost future earnings that the ASICs would have otherwise provided, coupled with the inability to sell or re-purpose the ASICs. Other general mining equipment such as GPUs have in the past been repurposed and resold when, e.g. the exchange rate of Ethereum plummeted (In 2017 GPUs were sold back into the second hand parts market mainly to gamers causing record losses for GPU manufacturers on the following year) [8]. We note that the existence of other cryptocurrencies that utilize the same PoW mechanisms offers some possibility to repurpose mining equipment (to mine on these alternative cryptocurrencies). Such is the case with many of the Bitcoin forks such as "Bitcoin Cash". Since our Virtual ASICs are held "on chain", they cannot be used to mine other cryptocurrencies. They thus represent an idealized form of ASIC that is truly useless outside the confines of the system. They therefore achieve the same effect, tying the future rewards of miners to the success of the system.

Borrowing Money and Rental Attacks—The Weakness of PoS. Proof-of-Stake systems seem to offer the right incentives: those holding many tokens are also those that have the most to lose: if the system is crippled by an attack, one could argue that the value of their tokens will be lost. While this seems on the surface to align incentives of miners with the good of the system, it is not necessarily the case. The primary reason is that in any well functioning economic system, it is possible to borrow money. Thus, an attacker that borrows money for the period of one year, could use these funds as stake and attack the system. At the end of the year, the stake can be returned, and thus the attacker is left unaffected by any loss of value of the tokens (this attacker is essentially also shorting[1] the currency he is attacking, which offsets any loss due to devaluation).

A similar observation was made in the ASIC market: if rental of large amounts of ASICs is possible, the cost to attackers is just the cost of renting equipment [6]. Arguably, this is the reason why miners would never loan out large amounts of equipment for potential use by attackers. While mining contracts can be drawn up to provide someone slices of the mining profits, the owner of miners typically retains control of their operation and thus ensures they are not used for attacks.

Our proposal for Virtual ASICs separates the mining tokens from the currency. We thus achieve an effect similar to that of ASICs: transferring a Virtual ASIC to another party allows it to attack the system, and therefore miners ought to refuse to loan out mining equipment (selling it for its full market price is okay). A market for loans in the currency token of the system can still exist, including the ability to short the currency.

1.3   Related Work

Time-Elapsed Cryptography. Our notion of the all-or-nothing broadcast channel is reminiscent of Time-lapse cryptography [28]. In [28] too, the goal is to send a message to the future so that it can be decrypted after a specified amount of time has elapsed. However, the service that is built in the work of [28] requires a distributed key generation process among the participants. In our setting, it is prohibitive to have to know the set of participants in advance. In addition, we would like the key generation to be a local ad hoc process that does not involve communication. In our construction, parties just publish one message as a public key component and at release time, publish a private key. Our construction also exploits the ledger property of the blockchain in order to achieve broadcast with all or nothing property such that all the messages sent to the channel are revealed after a specific amount of time has elapsed, or none of them are. Time-lock puzzles, introduced in [29] allow one to encrypt messages for the future, by generating a puzzle together with a solution that remains hidden until the specified time has elapsed. However, the hardness parameter needs to be set conservatively large so as to avoid the secrets becoming public sooner than desired. Fine-tuning the parameterization of a time-lock puzzle in practice requires estimating adversarial time. Thus, the parameter of the puzzle must, by design, be large (to accommodate for an adversary willing to devote computational power) thus making the release phase inefficient, since in the worst case honest parties have to compute the puzzle of all corrupt parties. The work of [23]

---

[1] Shorting means investing such that one profits if the value of the asset falls.

constructs homomorphic time-lock puzzles with application to sealed-bid auctions on the blockchain. Each bidder time-locks their bid and the highest bidder is computed homomorphically over the puzzles. However, the resulting protocol requires fully-homomorphic time-lock puzzles and is not efficient in practice. A construction with similar guarantees as our all-or-nothing broadcast in the synchronous setting is given in [18]. In [18], the authors construct a broadcast in the adaptive threshold adversary setting that utilizes verifiable secret sharing techniques, and can be seen as an analogue of our channel in the synchronous setting.

On-Chain Auctions. In HAWK [22], smart contracts are employed to run auctions on top of a blockchain. However, the existence of a trusted party is assumed to run the auction contract. This manager of the bidding contract is trusted with the bidders' inputs. In our setting, we do not have a trusted party since we need the auction to sell ASICs used in the consensus protocol of the blockchain. In [13], the authors propose a protocol to run an auction over a blockchain in the context of constructing a minting mechanism based on waiting-time first-price auctions. They use time-lock puzzles to deter parties from refusing to open their bids.

2   Model

We defer cryptographic preliminaries to the full version [15].

Time and Network. In our setting, we consider time as divided into discrete *slots*. An *epoch* consists of k slots. Parties have clocks that indicate the current slot. We assume a network with bounded delay, which is parameterized by an upper bound Δ on the network delivery time. It allows parties to multicast messages. That is, any message sent by an honest party in round r is guaranteed to arrive at all honest parties until round $r + \Delta$. The actual delay of messages (per message and party) can be set by the adversary (within Δ). The delay Δ is *not* known to the honest parties.

Virtual ASICs. In our consensus protocol parties use virtual ASICs to win the right to create new blocks. The probability of being selected as block creator is proportional to the ASIC's mining rate of the total rate of all powered ASICs.

Definition 1. *A* virtual ASIC *is a tuple* $(\mathsf{id}, \mathsf{vk}, \mathsf{pk}, \mathsf{initMR}, j_0)$ *where* id *is the identifier,* vk *is the signature public key of the owner,* pk *is the ASIC's verifiable random function (VRF) public key (cf. [11]),* $\mathsf{initMR} \in [0, 1]$ *is the initial mining rate, and* j_0 *is the spawn epoch, i.e., the first epoch in which the ASIC can be used.*

We use the notation $\mathsf{ASIC}.x$ to refer to property x of ASIC. In an epoch, a virtual ASIC is either *powered* or *unpowered*. To power an ASIC in epoch j, the owner buys power on the blockchain before the previous epoch. The function $\mathsf{ispowered}$ (parametrized by the blockchain) takes as input an ASIC, and an epoch j and returns true if the ASIC is powered in epoch j. We will simply write, ASIC.ispowered$_j$ to denote this output.

ASICs degrade over time. The *degradation* is discrete and occurs at the end of each epoch. The degradation rate in epoch j may depend on whether the ASIC is powered in that epoch or not. The degradation is formally captured by the degradation function **g** which takes as input the mining rate for epoch j, and a bit indicating whether the ASIC was powered in epoch j or not. The output is the mining rate for epoch $j + 1$. We denote by ASIC.MR$_j$ the mining rate of ASIC in epoch j. The *actual mining rate* of an ASIC in epoch i is its mining rate if powered or 0 otherwise, i.e., MR$_j \cdot$ ispowered$_j$. All the above information is assumed to be extractable from the blockchain. In particular, the actual mining rate of an ASIC is public.

Buying ASICs. In the most simple case, parties could buy new ASICs (e.g. with a fixed initial mining) by sending money to a specific payment address. It is important that parties are not censored from buying ASICs. We describe an auction protocol for ASIC in Sect. 4 that is resilient to censorship and allows for more complex economic models as described in the full version [15].

Buying Power for ASICs. Parties need to buy power in order to use their ASIC to create blocks in an epoch. The price of power will depend on the economic model used. See the full version [15] for more details on power pricing. For the consensus protocol described in Sect. 3.2 parties must buy power for epoch j before the start of epoch $j - 1$. Otherwise, parties could buy power after learning the actual winning chances of their ASICs in epoch j.

The technical solution to buying power is simple. To buy power a party sends the necessary amount to a special "power" address. The transaction contains the ID of the ASIC and the epoch in which the ASIC shall be powered. Power transactions can be subject to censorship as well, and to prevent this, one could use a similar solution as for auctions as discussed in Sect. 4.2. The idea is that parties first pay the money to the power address using shielded transactions, which hide source, destination, and the amount (see e.g. ZCash [2]), and then use the all-or-nothing broadcast to announce which ASIC they want to power. The money sent to the payment and/or power address can be either burned or used later for block rewards. A potentially simpler solution to prevent censorship is to reveal the shielded transaction when a new block is created. However, with this solution the total mining power is not known at the beginning of the epoch. Thus the lottery difficulty must be set using estimates on the total mining power from previous epoch. Note that in our consensus protocol in Sect. 3.2 we assume that the total mining power is known.

3 Consensus Based on Virtual ASICs

At a high level, a lottery-based consensus works by implementing a publicly verifiable "lottery" mechanism that elects a committee or a leader who is allowed to produce the next block of the blockchain. The probability that a party wins the lottery is proportional to the amount of some "scarce resource" that the party owns. This scarce resource is computing power in the case of proof-of-work, and the amount of coins the party owns in the system in the case of proof-of-stake. Roughly, the scarce resource cannot be replicated to increase the probability of winning by mounting a Sybil attack. Together with the assumption that the majority of this resource is in the hands of honest parties, one gets the guarantees necessary to build consensus.

Ledger Properties. Given a protocol that derives the ledger from a data structure in the form of a blockchain, it is known that persistence and liveness can be inferred from the following three properties [16].

Common-Prefix: With parameter $k \in \mathbb{N}$. The chains C_1, C_2 possessed by two honest parties at the onset of the slots $sl_1 < sl_2$ are such that $C_1^{\lceil k} \leq C_2$, where $C_1^{\lceil k}$ denotes the chain obtained by removing the last k blocks from C_1, and $\leq$ denotes the prefix relation.

Chain-Quality: With parameters $\mu \in (0,1]$ and $k \in \mathbb{N}$. Consider any portion of length of at least k of the chain possessed by an honest party at the onset of a round; the ratio of blocks originating from the adversary is at most $1 - \mu$. We call μ the chain quality coefficient.

Chain-Growth: With parameters $\tau \in (0,1], s \in N$. Consider the C_1, C_2 possessed by two honest parties at the onset of two slots $sl_1 < sl_2$ with sl_2 at least s slots ahead of sl_1. Then it holds that $len(C_2) - len(C_1) \geq \tau \cdot s$. We call τ the speed coefficient.

3.1   From Proof of Stake to Virtual ASICs

Our consensus is essentially a transformation that takes a proof-of-stake protocol and converts it into a protocol for consensus based on virtual ASICs. At a high level, the idea is as follows: A proof-of-stake protocol works via lottery that parties participate in, and winners of the lottery are assigned roles (for example, leader, committee member etc.). The security guarantee of the protocol is that the properties like chain quality, growth and consistency are achieved if enough stake is in the control of honest parties. The transformed protocol runs the same steps as the underlying protocol by replacing the stake by virtual ASICs, that is, by defining the stake pool by powered ASICs. Let us begin by considering the static case first. In the static case, the stake distribution is static and known to all participants. In this case, the stake distribution is defined by the powered ASIC distribution in the transformed protocol, and the same security guarantees follow assuming enough virtual ASICs are in honest control. When the static assumption does not hold, that is, stake is moving and the distribution is dynamic, proof-of-stake protocols like Ouroboros make the assumption that stake does not change too quickly, that is, the distribution stays the same for a certain number of epochs. Then the consensus protocol can be analysed for dynamic stake distribution and similar properties can be shown to hold. In the transformed protocol with virtual ASICs, we can enforce this in the system by having auctions at certain intervals and forcing the ASICs to be powered an epoch in advance, that is, only ASICs powered in the previous epoch can be used as lottery tickets in the current epoch. Thus, conducting auctions for virtual ASICs on the same blockchain is safe by the guarantees of consensus in the dynamic stake setting. Now, we show an instantiation of such a consensus protocol that is obtained from Ouroboros Praos.

Remark 1. Note that, in our system, the miners maintain the very blockchain on which they perform the virtual ASIC auction. This might seem to admit other attack vectors where the parties may have incentives to discard the results of an auction by discarding the blocks where this auction was performed. However, this is similar to the underlying proof of stake system as well where parties have incentive to discard blocks where stake was transferred.

3.2 Example: Nakamoto Style Consensus Protocol

As an example of the above transformation we present a Nakamoto style consensus protocol using virtual ASICs. Our starting point is Ouroboros Praos (OP) [11], a popular proof-of-stake protocol. In OP, time is divided into slots and for each slot a VRF-based lottery is held. The winning probability is proportional to the stake held by a party. Lottery winners create a block for that slot that extends their longest chain.

Blocks and Blocktree. A block is given by a tuple that indicates the slot, the data, a pointer to the previous block, a block proof and a signature of the entire block content under the signing key of ASIC that won the slot lottery. The block proof $(\mathsf{ASIC.id}, y, \pi)$ consists of the ASIC ID, and the necessary values to check the VRF evaluation. A block is valid if it has the right format, contains valid data, and the creator of the block actually won the slot lottery. This condition can be verified publicly. Every party locally stores a *blocktree*. Initially, the blocktree consists of the genesis block. During the consensus protocol the party will extend the blocktree by all valid blocks it receives. In the consensus protocol honest parties will try to extend their *longest chain*. Roughly, the length of a chain is a weighted sum of its blocks where the weight of a block is the difficulty of its slot lottery. Therefore, for constant difficulty the length of a chain is exactly the number of blocks.

The Static Case. We begin by first describing how to transform the static stake OP protocol into a protocol with a static ASIC distribution. The idea is to replace parties by ASICs and stake by the mining rate of (powered) ASICs. That is, the initial stake distribution (cf. Definition 1 in [11]) is replaced by an initial ASIC distribution of the form $\big(\mathsf{ASIC}_j = (\mathsf{id}_j, \mathsf{vk}_j, \mathsf{pk}_j, \mathsf{initMR}_j, 0)\big)$ where initMR is the initial mining rate, vk is a signature verification key and pk is VRF public key. We assume that all initial ASICs are, by definition, powered. The total mining rate is defined as $\mathsf{totalMR} = \sum_{\mathsf{ASIC}} \mathsf{ASIC.initMR}$.

An ASIC ASIC wins lottery for slot sl if $y < 2^\ell \cdot (1 - (1 - f)^{\mathsf{rp}})$ where $\mathsf{rp} = \frac{\mathsf{MR}_j}{\mathsf{totalMR}_j}$, $(y, \pi) = \mathsf{VRF}(\mathsf{ASIC.sk}, \mathsf{sl})$, $\mathsf{MR} = \mathsf{ASIC.initMR}$, $\ell = |y|$, and f is the difficulty of the lottery. A party can locally check if one if its ASICs won using the VRF evaluation keys. If the party won with ASIC ASIC in sl it will include $(\mathsf{ASIC.id}, y, \pi)$ in the newly created block. This allows anyone to verify the winning condition.

The following is a description of the consensus protocol from the view of party P.

Protocol ConsensusProtocol

The party P stores a blocktree $\mathcal{T}$ which initially consists of the genesis block which contains the ASIC distribution. In slot sl P does the following:

1. Add all new valid blocks to the block tree $\mathcal{T}$.
2. For all owned ASICs check if they won the lottery for sl.
3. If an ASIC won the lottery create a new block that extends the currently longest chain in $\mathcal{T}$.

Lemma 1. *If a majority of* totalMR *is controlled by honest parties, the above protocol achieves common-prefix, chain-growth, and chain-quality.*

Proof. Observe that the static distribution of actual mining rate corresponds to the static stake distribution of OP. This allows us to use the analysis given in Sect. 4 of [11]. We get common-prefix (Theorem 5 [11]), chain-growth (Theorem 6 [11]), and chain-quality (Theorem 7 [11]) as long as a strict[2] majority of the mining rate is controlled by honest parties. ☐

The Dynamic Case. Now, we turn towards constructing a protocol for the dynamic case, where the distribution of powered virtual ASICs changes as the protocol is executed. As in Ouroboros Praos, we divide protocol execution into a number of independent epochs during which the stake distribution used for electing slot leaders remains unchanged. The strategy used to bootstrap the static protocol into a protocol for the dynamic case is the same as OP.

For each epoch the distribution of ASICs and their actual mining rate is fixed one epoch in advance and can be computed from the longest chain in the blocktree. This also requires that the initial ASICs as defined in the genesis block are, by definition, powered for the first two epochs. The total mining rate in epoch j is defined as $\mathsf{totalMR}_j = \sum_{\mathsf{ASIC}} \mathsf{ASIC.ispowered}_j \cdot \mathsf{ASIC.MR}_j$. An ASIC ASIC wins the lottery for slot sl of epoch j if $y < 2^\ell \cdot (1 - (1 - f)^{\mathsf{rp}})$ where $\mathsf{rp} = \frac{\mathsf{MR}_j}{\mathsf{totalMR}_j}$, $(y, \pi) = \mathsf{VRF}(\mathsf{ASIC.sk}, \mathsf{sl}\|\mathsf{nonce}_j)$, $\mathsf{MR}_j = \mathsf{ASIC.ispowered}_j \cdot \mathsf{ASIC.MR}_j$, and f is the difficulty of the lottery. The epoch nonce nonce_j is used to make the lottery unpredictable for the far future. Without such a nonce, parties could selectively power the ASICs in epochs where they have an above average chance of winning.

---

[2] The exact amount depends on the network delay.

Epoch nonces can be generated using randomness extracted from blocks of the previous epoch, following the approach in Sects. 5.1 and 5.2 [11].

The protocol for any fixed epoch corresponds to the protocol with a static ASIC distribution as described above.

Lemma 2. *If a majority[3] of* totalMR *is controlled by honest parties and the ASIC distribution does not change too[4] fast, the dynamic consensus protocol achieves common-prefix, chain-growth, and chain-quality.*

Proof. We can again follow the analysis in [11] as our transformation simply replaces stake by powered ASICs. In particular, the ASIC distribution of epoch i is agreed upon on using the consensus in epoch $i - 2$ (or genesis block if $i < 3$). By following the analysis in Sects. 5.1 and 5.2 [11], we can see that the claim follows from Theorem 9 and Corollary 3 in [11].   □

Remark 2. To achieve security in the dynamic case, we need to limit the amount of change of the ASIC distribution over time as expressed by parameter σ in the conditions of Lemma 2. In practice, one can do so by regulating the ASIC auction and limiting the decay rate of ASICs.

4   Auction Protocol for Virtual ASICs

In a system using consensus based on virtual ASICs, we need to allow new miners a chance to join the system. We therefore need new ASICs in the system. We propose conducting auctions on-chain for such newly created virtual ASICs. Consider the following, simplistic way of implementing ASICs auctions: all parties commit to their bids on the blockchain and then, after some agreed deadline, they open the bids. This is not a satisfactory auction since it allows bids to be selectively revealed i.e., an adversary might wait for some of the other bids to be opened before choosing whether to open its own bids or not. Moreover, as the blockchain is an imperfect bulletin board, a malicious miner could prevent the bids of an honest party from appearing on the blockchain, effectively *censoring* the bids of the honest parties. Therefore, we need to design an auction mechanism which is resilient to censorship. In this way honest parties will not be prevented from acquiring, and therefore owning, ASICs. We achieve this by designing a novel mechanism that might be of independent interest, which achieves an *all-or-nothing property* meaning that either all bids will be revealed or none will. Thanks to this tool we can effectively design an *all-or-nothing broadcast channel*, which in turn can be used to construct an auction protocol.

Two-Stage Sealed-Bid Auction. A sealed-bid auction consists of a bidding phase and a decision phase, and the bids are kept secret during the bidding

---

[3] The exact condition is $\alpha_H (1 - f)^{\Delta} \geq \frac{1+\epsilon}{2} + \sigma$ where α_H is a lower bound on ratio of honest mining rate, Δ an upper bound on the network delay, ϵ a security parameter, and σ an upper bound on the mining power shift during a single epoch.

[4] As expressed by the upper bound σ on the stake shift per epoch in Theorem 9 [11].

phase. In the bidding phase, parties can submit their bids to the auction. In the decision phase, the winner(s) and the winning price is determined. We consider a $(k+1)$-st price auction used to sell k ASICs, where the $(k+1)$-st highest bid is the winning price, and parties who bid higher than the winning price are declared winners. A $(k+1)$-st price is equivalent to the Vickrey auction for $k = 1$. In our application, we do not want more than k parties winning, since the number of goods is fixed (giving out more ASICs interferes with the total mining rate in the system) and hence, in the decision phase, k bidders are declared winners (after breaking ties). We want the auction protocol to satisfy the following properties:

Bid confidentiality. No information about the bid and the bidder's identity is revealed during the bidding stage.

Bid independence. A bidder cannot create a bid depending on a submitted honest bid.

Public verifiability. The outcome of the auction can be verified publicly.

Censorship-resilience. No party is prevented from submitting a bid in the auction.

Binding (unretractability). A winning bidder cannot retract the bid in the decision stage or abort the auction.

We do not consider other auction designs in this work, and leave exploring other economic models and auctions to future work.

4.1 All-or-Nothing Broadcast

Towards implementing an auction mechanism on chain for ASICs, we define and construct a building block that allows "encryption to the future on the blockchain". At a high level, this building block immediately gives a way to create an all-or-nothing broadcast channel. Such a broadcast channel has two phases. In the first phase, parties can input messages, but no one can retrieve them. After some delay, parties can retrieve all the messages in the second phase. The adversary can abort the delivery of all messages, but it cannot prevent the delivery of a specific message.

Functionality $\mathcal{F}_{\text{AON-BC}}$

The all-or-nothing broadcast parametrized by times τ_1, τ_2, τ_3.
The function maintains a buffer B which initially is empty.

Phase 1: Input

- This phase starts at time τ_1 and ends at time τ_2.
- During this phase parties can input messages which are then stored in buffer B.

Phase 2: Output

- At time τ_3 the functionality outputs the content of buffer B to the adversary.
- The functionality then asks the adversary if the content of B should be released to the honest parties.
- If the adversary released the contents the honest parties can now query the functionality for the content of buffer B.

Adversarial Access

The adversary can at any point in time query the size of the buffer B (but not its content before Phase 2).

We use this property of the AON broadcast channel in Sect. 4.2 to create a simple auction. In the first part, parties input their bids into the broadcast and in the second phase we use the now revealed bids to determine the winner of the auction. We believe all-or-nothing broadcast and encryption to the future on the blockchain could be of independent interest and useful for other applications.

All-or-Nothing Broadcast on the Blockchain. The following protocol uses the encryption-to-the-future idea to construct an all-or-nothing broadcast based on an ad-hoc threshold encryption (ATE) scheme (see e.g. [12]). It runs in three phases which are described below. We assume that parties have access to a (t, n) ad hoc threshold-encryption scheme parametrized by the number of key-shares n of which t are required to decrypt.

Protocol All − or − nothingbroadcast

The protocol is parametrized by the threshold encryption parameters (t, n) and delays d_1, d_2, d_3.

Phase 0: Key Generation

- This phase lasts until n blocks have been created.
- If a miner creates a block, they use KeyGen to generate key shares and add the public-key share to the block.
- After n blocks have been created, any party can obtain the set of all public keys $\mathsf{PK} = \{\mathsf{pk}_i\}$.
- The miners have to keep the secret keys secret until the Decryption Phase.

Phase 1: Encryption

- This phase starts right after the key-generation phase and lasts until d_1 blocks have been created.
- To encrypt a message m to the future, a party encrypts m under PK using Enc and posts the resulting ciphertext c on the blockchain.

Phase 2: Decryption

- This phase starts d_2 blocks after the encryption phase and lasts d_3 blocks.
- Any miners that created a block in the key-generation phase publish their secret key (on the blockchain).
- Once $t+1$ secret keys have been published, all messages can be decrypted (publicly) using Dec.

Lemma 3. *Assume that in any* n *consecutive blocks at most* t *blocks were created by dishonest parties. Let* d_1 *be so large, that at least one block in any* d_1 *consecutive blocks was created by an honest party. Then, the above protocol achieves the all-or-nothing broadcast* $\mathcal{F}_{\mathsf{AON\text{-}BC}}$.

Proof. By the assumption on n and t, at most t blocks in Phase 0 are created by dishonest parties. Thus the adversary knows at most t keys and can therefore not decrypt messages which have been put on the blockchain before the honest parties release their keys in Phase 2. This means that the adversary can only see the number of messages, i.e. the size of buffer B. The adversary can also not prevent honest parties from inputting messages, as we assume that in Phase 1 at least one honest block is created which could contain all honest inputs. In Phase 2, the honest parties from Phase 0 will all release their generated keys. This allows the adversary to read all messages that were input, i.e. the contents of B. Now, if the adversary also releases enough of its keys, the honest parties can read all the input messages. The time τ_1 corresponds to the time it takes to create n blocks, time τ_2 is the time it takes to create $n + d_1$ blocks, and τ_3 is the time it takes to create $n + d_1 + d_2$ blocks. □

Lemma 4. *Assuming an honest majority of Virtual ASICs, there exist parameters* n, t, *and* d_1 *such that the above protocol achieves* $\mathcal{F}_{\mathsf{AON\text{-}BC}}$ *on the virtual ASICs blockchain.*

Proof. The honest majority implies that the virtual ASIC blockchain satisfies the chain-quality property (see Lemma 2), i.e., we have that for any n (large enough), there is a bound $\nu < n$ on the number of dishonest blocks within n consecutive blocks. We can set $t = \nu$. Furthermore, chain-quality also guarantees that for d_1 large enough there must be at least one honest block within d_1 consecutive blocks. The statement follows by Lemma 3. □

The bound on the number of dishonest blocks within n consecutive blocks in the above proof depends on the size of n and the fraction of honest ASICs. If we assume a strong honest majority, i.e. at least $\frac{2}{3}$ honest ASICs, then $\nu < \frac{n}{2}$ holds even for smaller n. In this case, the protocol achieves the stronger delay broadcast $\mathcal{F}_{\mathsf{D\text{-}BC}}$. This broadcast has the same functionality as $\mathcal{F}_{\mathsf{AON\text{-}BC}}$ except that the adversary can no longer abort, that is, we have guaranteed output delivery.

Lemma 5. *If $\frac{2}{3}$ of all virtual ASICs are under honest control, then for large enough n the above protocol achieves $\mathcal{F}_{\text{D-BC}}$ on the virtual ASICs blockchain for $t = n/2$.*

Proof. A large honest majority of virtual ASICs (e.g. $\frac{2}{3}$) ensures that there exists n such that less than $t := \frac{n}{2}$ of n consecutive blocks are dishonest. There also exists d_1 (resp. d_3) such that any d_1 (resp. d_3) consecutive blocks contain at least one honest block. By Lemma 3 we get the properties of $\mathcal{F}_{\text{AON-BC}}$. Furthermore, in Phase 2 all honest parties will release their keys which is enough to decrypt all inputs. The adversary cannot prevent that key release as there will be at least one honest block in Phase 2. Thus the adversary cannot abort the channel. □

Remark 3. Using the virtual ASICs blockchain for AON broadcast does not lead to a bootstrap paradox as blockchain protocol uses an initial ASIC distribution allowing it to start without the use of an auction.

On Disincentivizing Aborts. The above protocol might only achieve $\mathcal{F}_{\text{AON-BC}}$ (that is, not achieve guaranteed output delivery) either due to high corruption or choice of parameters (e.g. choosing $t > \frac{n}{2}$ which allows for smaller n, where n is the parameter such that in any n consecutive blocks at most t blocks are created by dishonest parties). In this case the dishonest parties can abort the channel. We can use financial rewards to disincentivize aborts, and achieve stronger properties of the delay broadcast. One option is that block rewards are only paid out if miners release their key shares within the decryption phase. To prevent early-release, if someone posts the key share of a miner before the decryption phase they get a fraction (e.g. $\frac{1}{10}$) of the miners block reward while the miner gets nothing. If the key-share is released too late, no one gets a reward. Note that this solution still requires d_1 large enough to prevent input censorship. See the full version [15] for more details.

4.2   The Auction Protocol

We now show how to implement a censorship-resilient ASIC auction using the broadcast functionality from the previous section. We assume a system that supports *shielded transactions*; transactions that provide privacy of the sender, receiver and the amount being transferred. A $(k + 1)$-st price auction protocol is described below where k ASICs are won. In the case that there are less than k bids in an auction, we assume there is a reserve price paid by the winner(s).

To ensure that the auction is binding, parties are required to prepay their bidding amount onto an escrow account. A bid is a tuple (vk, amount, π, pk) consisting of bidders' signature verification key vk, the bidding amount, the proof of payment π, and a VRF public-key pk. The bid is signed under by the bidder. The proof of payment shows that the bidder prepaid amount to the escrow account. It is essentially the secrets that open the shielded transaction, together with reference to the payment transaction. The VRF key pk will be used to create a new ASIC in the event that the bidder wins.

Protocol ASICAuction

Bidding Phase To submit a bid a party P does the following.

1. The party P generates a fresh VRF key pair, $(\mathsf{sk}, \mathsf{pk}) \leftarrow \mathsf{KeyGen}$.
2. The party makes a shielded transaction of the bid amount to a pre-specified escrow address. The transaction includes a return address.
3. Finally, the party P inputs their signed bid $(\mathsf{vk}, \mathsf{amount}, \pi, \mathsf{pk})$ into the broadcast channel.

Decision Phase

1. All bids are read from the broadcast channel.
2. Invalid bids (e.g. that are not accompanied by a valid proof of payment) are discarded.
3. The valid bids are sorted in decreasing order of bid value into a list. The first k valid bids (after breaking ties) are announced as winners. The $(k + 1)$ valid bid amount is announced as the auction price.
4. Each winning bid defines a new ASIC $(\mathsf{id}, \mathsf{vk}, \mathsf{pk}, \mathsf{initMR}, j_0)$ where vk, pk are the signature verification key and the VRF public key of the bid. The $\mathsf{id}, \mathsf{initMR}, j_0$ are determined by the auction itself, vk, pk by the winning party's input to the broadcast channel.
5. A transaction is made from the auction address to each winning return address containing the difference amount between the bid made and the amount paid, and the ASIC attributes. Transactions returning the bid amounts are made for all other non-winning participants.
6. If the auction fails, participants reveal their bid transactions. The bid amount is returned to the return addresses for all auction participants.

Remark 4. The IDs of the newly created ASICs could for example be $i.j$ where i is the number of the auction, and j is a number between 1 and k. The initial mining rate of the ASICs will depend on the economic model used. The spawn epoch of the ASICs must be at least the epoch after the auction's epoch.

Remark 5. For security reasons, the escrow account should be a "virtual" account without account keys. Deposit works as with any other account. Payouts can be triggered by publicly verifiable conditions, e.g. a bidder revealing their bid on-chain. Such a virtual account can for example be created using smart contracts. See the full version [15] on how to hide payments to the escrow account in a system without full-fledged shielded addresses.

Lemma 6. *The protocol* ASICAuction *achieves the desired properties when the broadcast channel is delay broadcast* $\mathcal{F}_{\text{D-BC}}$.

Proof. Bid confidentiality: The shielded transaction to the escrow address does not reveal the amount nor the bidder's identity. The properties of the broadcast channel ensure that the actual bid cannot be extracted before the decision phase. *Bid independence:* This also follows directly from the properties of shielded transactions and the broadcast. *Public verifiability.* A bid contains all information necessary to verify its validity. In particular, the proof of payment allows to check that the bidder paid the right amount to the escrow. The consistency of the blockchain and the broadcast imply that all parties will agree on the set of (valid) bids. *Censorship-resilience.* The use of shielded transactions prevents the adversary from censoring honest payments to the escrow account. The adversary cannot prevent parties from input to the broadcast nor prevent the overall output of the broadcast. *Binding (unretractability).* First note that the adversary cannot prevent bids from being revealed by broadcast. Furthermore, any bid which is deemed valid in the decision phase is linked to a valid payment to the escrow account. This winner of the auction therefore already paid for their ASICs. □

Corollary 1. *Assuming $\frac{2}{3}$ of all virtual ASICs are under honest control, the protocol* ASICAuction *using the protocol from Sect. 4.1 to emulate broadcast achieves desired properties.*

This follows directly from Lemmata 5 and 6. If we only use the all-or-nothing broadcast for our auction protocol, the adversary can publicly abort the auction. That is, the adversary can look at the bids and then decide to abort by not releasing them from the broadcast channel.

Lemma 7. *The protocol* ASICAuction *achieves auction with abort when broadcast channel is* $\mathcal{F}_{\text{AON-BC}}$. *All other desired properties still hold.*

Corollary 2. *Given an honest majority of virtual ASICs the* ASICAuction *protocol achieves auction with abort when using the protocol from Sect. 4.1 to emulate broadcast.*

Assuming rational parties, we have the means to deal with aborts and punish the adversary for doing so (see Sect. 4.1). Thus an auction with abort is fine.

Other Uses for Encryption to the Future. The encrypt to future functionality can be extremely useful for other interactions on the blockchain. One example of this is as a solution to the front-running problem which is often experienced in Ethereum [10]. Allowing traders to commit to trades simultaneously via our AON broadcast functionality and then executing all trades together in a batch would solve the problem. We note that similar suggestions have been raised with respect to conventional trading in the stock exchange [7], where flash trades appear to also hinder exchanges.

References

1. Badertscher, C., Gaži, P., Kiayias, A., Russell, A., Zikas, V.: Ouroboros genesis: composable proof-of-stake blockchains with dynamic availability. Cryptology ePrint Archive, Report 2018/378 (2018). https://eprint.iacr.org/2018/378

2. Ben-Sasson, E.: Zerocash: decentralized anonymous payments from bitcoin. In: 2014 IEEE Symposium on Security and Privacy, pp. 459–474. IEEE Computer Society Press, May 2014

3. Bentov, I., Gabizon, A., Mizrahi, A.: Cryptocurrencies without proof of work. In: Clark, J., Meiklejohn, S., Ryan, P.Y.A., Wallach, D., Brenner, M., Rohloff, K. (eds.) FC 2016. LNCS, vol. 9604, pp. 142–157. Springer, Heidelberg (2016). https://doi.org/10.1007/978-3-662-53357-4_10

4. Bentov, I., Lee, C., Mizrahi, A., Rosenfeld, M.: Proof of activity: extending bitcoin's proof of work via proof of stake [extended abstract]. ACM SIGMETRICS Perform. Eval. Rev. **42**(3), 34–37 (2014)

5. Bentov, I., Pass, R., Shi, E.: Snow white: provably secure proofs of stake. Cryptology ePrint Archive, Report 2016/919 (2016). http://eprint.iacr.org/2016/919

6. Bonneau, J.: Why buy when you can rent? In: Clark, J., Meiklejohn, S., Ryan, P.Y.A., Wallach, D., Brenner, M., Rohloff, K. (eds.) FC 2016. LNCS, vol. 9604, pp. 19–26. Springer, Heidelberg (2016). https://doi.org/10.1007/978-3-662-53357-4_2

7. Budish, E., Cramton, P., Shim, J.: The high-frequency trading arms race: frequent batch auctions as a market design response. Q. J. Econ. **130**(4), 1547–1621 (2015)

8. Campbell, M.: Used GPUs flood the market as Ethereum's price crashes below $150. Overclock 3D (2017)

9. Croman, K., et al.: On scaling decentralized blockchains. In: Clark, J., Meiklejohn, S., Ryan, P.Y.A., Wallach, D., Brenner, M., Rohloff, K. (eds.) FC 2016. LNCS, vol. 9604, pp. 106–125. Springer, Heidelberg (2016). https://doi.org/10.1007/978-3-662-53357-4_8

10. Daian, P.: Flash boys 2.0: frontrunning, transaction reordering, and consensus instability in decentralized exchanges. arXiv preprint arXiv:1904.05234 (2019)

11. David, B., Gaži, P., Kiayias, A., Russell, A.: Ouroboros praos: an adaptively-secure, semi-synchronous proof-of-stake blockchain. In: Nielsen, J.B., Rijmen, V. (eds.) EUROCRYPT 2018. LNCS, vol. 10821, pp. 66–98. Springer, Cham (2018). https://doi.org/10.1007/978-3-319-78375-8_3

12. Daza, V., Herranz, J., Morillo, P., Ràfols, C.: CCA2-secure threshold broadcast encryption with shorter ciphertexts. In: Susilo, W., Liu, J.K., Yi, M. (eds.) ProvSec 2007: 1st International Conference on Provable Security. Lecture Notes in Computer Science, vol. 4784, pp. 35–50. Springer, Heidelberg (2007)

13. Deuber, D., Döttling, N., Magri, B., Malavolta, G., Thyagarajan, S.A.K.: Minting mechanisms for blockchain - or - moving from cryptoassets to cryptocurrencies. Cryptology ePrint Archive, Report 2018/1110 (2018). https://eprint.iacr.org/2018/1110

14. Ethash. https://eth.wiki/en/concepts/ethash/ethash

15. Ganesh, C., Orlandi, C., Tschudi, D., Zohar, A.: Virtual ASICs: generalized proof-of-stake mining in cryptocurrencies. Cryptology ePrint Archive, Report 2020/791 (2020). https://ia.cr/2020/791

16. Garay, J., Kiayias, A., Leonardos, N.: The bitcoin backbone protocol: analysis and applications. In: Oswald, E., Fischlin, M. (eds.) EUROCRYPT 2015. LNCS, vol. 9057, pp. 281–310. Springer, Heidelberg (2015). https://doi.org/10.1007/978-3-662-46803-6_10

17. Gilad, Y., Hemo, R., Micali, S., Vlachos, G., Zeldovich, N.: Algorand: scaling byzantine agreements for cryptocurrencies. Cryptology ePrint Archive, Report 2017/454 (2017). http://eprint.iacr.org/2017/454

18. Hirt, M., Zikas, V.: Adaptively secure broadcast. In: Gilbert, H. (ed.) EURO-CRYPT 2010. LNCS, vol. 6110, pp. 466–485. Springer, Heidelberg (2010). https://doi.org/10.1007/978-3-642-13190-5_24

19. Kiayias, A., Russell, A., David, B., Oliynykov, R.: Ouroboros: a provably secure proof-of-stake blockchain protocol. In: Katz, J., Shacham, H. (eds.) CRYPTO 2017. LNCS, vol. 10401, pp. 357–388. Springer, Cham (2017). https://doi.org/10.1007/978-3-319-63688-7_12

20. King, S., Nadal, S.: PPCoin: peer-to-peer crypto-currency with proof-of-stake. Technical report, Peercoin (2012)

21. Köhler, S., Pizzol, M.: Life cycle assessment of bitcoin mining. Environ. Sci. Technol. **53**(23), 13598–13606 (2019)

22. Kosba, A.E., Miller, A., Shi, E., Wen, Z., Papamanthou, C.: Hawk: the blockchain model of cryptography and privacy-preserving smart contracts. In: 2016 IEEE Symposium on Security and Privacy, pp. 839–858. IEEE Computer Society Press, May 2016

23. Malavolta, G., Thyagarajan, S.A.K.: Homomorphic time-lock puzzles and applications. In: Boldyreva, A., Micciancio, D. (eds.) CRYPTO 2019. LNCS, vol. 11692, pp. 620–649. Springer, Cham (2019). https://doi.org/10.1007/978-3-030-26948-7_22

24. Milutinovic, M., He, W., Wu, H., Kanwal, M.: Proof of luck: an efficient blockchain consensus protocol. In: Proceedings of the 1st Workshop on System Software for Trusted Execution, pp. 1–6 (2016)

25. Nakamoto, S.: Bitcoin: a peer-to-peer electronic cash system. Working Paper (2008). https://bitcoin.org/bitcoin.pdf

26. O'Dwyer, K.J., Malone, D.: Bitcoin mining and its energy footprint. In: 25th IET Irish Signals Systems Conference 2014 and 2014 China-Ireland International Conference on Information and Communications Technologies (ISSC 2014/CIICT 2014), pp. 280–285 (2014)

27. QuantumMechanic: Proof of stake instead of proof of work, July 2011. https://bitcointalk.org/index.php?topic=27787.0

28. Rabin, M.O., Thorpe, C.: Time-lapse cryptography. Technical report, Harvard Computer Science Group (2006)

29. Rivest, R.L., Shamir, A., Wagner, D.A.: Time-lock puzzles and timed-release crypto. Technical report, Massachusetts Institute of Technology (1996)

30. Tsabary, I., Spiegelman, A., Eyal, I.: Just enough security: reducing proof-of-work ecological footprint. arXiv preprint arXiv:1911.04124 (2019)

Asymmetric Asynchronous Byzantine Consensus

Christian Cachin$^{(\boxtimes)}$ and Luca Zanolini$^{(\boxtimes)}$

Institute of Computer Science, University of Bern, Bern, Switzerland
{cachin,luca.zanolini}@inf.unibe.ch

Abstract. An important element of every blockchain network is its protocol for reaching consensus. In traditional, permissioned consensus protocols, all involved processes adhere to a global, *symmetric* failure model, typically only defined by bounds on the number of faulty processes. More flexible trust assumptions have recently been considered, especially in connection with blockchains. With *asymmetric trust*, in particular, a process is free to choose which other processes it trusts and which ones might collude against it.

Cachin and Tackmann (OPODIS 2019) introduced *asymmetric quorum systems* as a generalization of *Byzantine quorum systems*, which are the key abstraction for realizing consensus in a system with symmetric trust. This paper shows how to realize randomized signature-free asynchronous Byzantine consensus with asymmetric quorums. This results in an optimal consensus protocol with subjective, asymmetric trust and constant expected running time, which is suitable for applications in blockchain networks.

1 Introduction

Consensus represents a fundamental abstraction in distributed systems. It captures the problem of reaching agreement among multiple processes on a common value, despite unreliable communication and the presence of faulty processes. Most protocols for consensus operate under the assumption that the *number* of faulty processes is limited. Moreover, all processes in the system share this common *trust assumption*. Traditionally, the trust assumption has been *symmetric* in this sense: all processes adhere to the global assumption about the number of faulty processes and properties of protocols are guaranteed for all correct processes, but not for the faulty ones. Since the advent of blockchains systems, however, more flexible trust models have been introduced. The Ripple (www.ripple.com) and Stellar (www.stellar.org) blockchains have pioneered practical models that let each process express its *own set* of trusted processes and assumptions can be more flexible than bounding only the number of faulty processes. Motivated by this desire to make trust assumptions more flexible, Cachin and Tackmann [5] introduced *asymmetric Byzantine quorum systems* as a generalization of Byzantine quorum systems. Originally defined by Malkhi and Reiter [17], Byzantine quorum systems capture one global, but arbitrarily

© Springer Nature Switzerland AG 2022
J. Garcia-Alfaro et al. (Eds.): DPM 2021/CBT 2021, LNCS 13140, pp. 192–207, 2022.
https://doi.org/10.1007/978-3-030-93944-1_13

complex trust relation through a so-called fail-prone system. This permits protocols in which processes can be differentiated from each other and in which not only the number of faults is bounded. Since Byzantine quorum systems provide a widely used abstraction for realizing consensus for blockchain networks and other distributed systems, asymmetric quorum systems open up the possibility to implement consensus with subjective trust. However, no consensus algorithms with asymmetric trust have been formulated so far.

In this paper, we present the first asynchronous Byzantine consensus protocol with asymmetric trust. It uses randomization, provided by an asymmetric common-coin protocol, to circumvent the impossibility of (purely) asynchronous consensus. Our protocol takes up the randomized and signature-free implementation of consensus by Mostéfaoui et al. [20]. This represents a landmark result because it has been praised for its simplicity, was the first to achieve optimal complexity, that is, expected quadratic cost in the number of processes, and does not use digital signatures. Their protocol has been extended later and taken up in practical systems, such as "Honey Badger BFT" [19]. Our protocol shows how to realize asynchronous consensus with asymmetric trust and maintains the simplicity of the original approach of Mostéfaoui et al. [20].

Asymmetric quorum systems go back to the notion of asymmetric trust introduced by Damgård et al. [9]. Every process in the system subjectively selects its own fail-prone system. Depending on the choice that a correct process makes about who it trusts and who not, and considering the processes that are actually faulty during an execution, two different situations may arise. A correct process may either make a "wrong" trust assumption, for example, by trusting too many processes that turn out to be faulty or by tolerating too few faults; such a process is called *naïve*. Alternatively, when the correct process makes the "right" trust assumption, it is called *wise*. Protocols with asymmetric trust do not guarantee the same properties for naïve processes as for wise ones.

As an additional contribution, we extend our knowledge about the relation between naïve and wise processes in protocols with asymmetric trust. We show that, under certain conditions, guarantees can only be given by assuming the existence of a subset of the wise processes called *guild*. The existence of a guild is necessary for a protocol execution with asymmetric trust to terminate.

The remainder of this work is structured as follows. In Sect. 2 we discuss related work. We present our system model together with preliminaries on Byzantine quorums in Sect. 3. In Sect. 4 we recall and extend the theory behind asymmetric quorums. We define and implement asymmetric strong Byzantine consensus in Sect. 5 by extending and improving on the randomized consensus algorithm by Mostéfaoui et al. [20]. Moreover, we build a common coin based on secret sharing that works in our randomized protocol with asymmetric trust. All the proofs can be found in the full version [6].

2   Related Work

Flexible trust structures have recently received a lot of attention [5, 9, 10, 15, 16, 18], primarily motivated by consensus protocols for blockchains, as introduced by

Ripple (www.ripple.com) and Stellar (www.stellar.org). According to the general idea behind these models, processes are free to express individual, *subjective* trust choices about other processes, instead of adopting a common, global view of trust.

Damgård *et al.* [9] define the basics of *asymmetric trust* for secure computation protocols. This model is strictly more powerful than the standard model with symmetric trust and abandons the traditional global failure assumption in the system. Moreover, they present several variations of their asymmetric-trust model and sketch synchronous protocols for broadcast, verifiable secret sharing, and general multi-party computation.

Mazières [18] introduces a new model for consensus called *federated Byzantine agreement* (FBA) and uses it to construct the *Stellar consensus protocol* [14]. In FBA, every process declares *quorums slices*—a collection of trusted sets of processes sufficient to convince the particular process of agreement. These slices are subsets of a *quorum*, which is a set of processes sufficient to reach agreement. More precisely, a quorum is defined as a set of processes that contains one slice for each member, and all quorums constitute a *federated Byzantine quorum system* (FBQS).

Byzantine quorum systems have originally been formalized by Malkhi and Reiter [17] and exist in several forms; they generalize the classical quorum systems aimed at tolerating crashes to algorithms with Byzantine failures. Byzantine quorum systems assume one global shared fail-prone system.

A link between FBQS and Byzantine quorums system has been built by García-Pérez and Gotsman [10], who implement Byzantine reliable broadcast on an FBQS. They prove that a FBQS *induces* a Byzantine quorum system.

Asymmetric Byzantine quorum systems have been introduced by Cachin and Tackmann [5] and generalize Byzantine quorum systems [17] to the model with asymmetric trust. This work also explores properties of asymmetric Byzantine quorum systems and differences to the model with symmetric trust. In particular, Cachin and Tackmann [5] distinguish between different classes of correct processes, depending on whether their failure assumptions in an execution are correct. The standard properties of protocols are guaranteed only to so-called *wise* processes, i.e., those that made the "right" trust choices. Protocols with asymmetric quorums are shown for Byzantine consistent broadcast, reliable broadcast, and emulations of shared memory. In contrast to FBQS, asymmetric quorum systems appear to be a natural extension of symmetric quorum systems.

Recently, Losa *et al.* [15] have formulated an abstraction of the consensus mechanism in the Stellar network by introducing *personal Byzantine quorum systems* (PBQS). In contrast to traditional notions of "quorums", their definition does not require a global intersection among quorums. This may lead to several separate *consensus clusters* such that each one satisfies agreement and liveness on its own.

Another generalized approach for designing Byzantine fault-tolerant (BFT) consensus protocols has been introduced by Malkhi *et al.* [16], namely *Flexible BFT*. This notion guarantees higher resilience by introducing a new *alive-but-*

corrupt fault type, which denotes processes that attack safety but not liveness. Malkhi *et al.* [16] also define *flexible Byzantine quorums* that allow processes in the system to have different faults models.

Mostéfaoui *et al.* [20] present a randomized, signature-free, and round-based asynchronous consensus algorithm for binary values. It achieves optimal resilience and takes $O(n^2)$ constant-sized messages. Randomization is achieved through a common coin as defined by Rabin [23]. Their binary consensus algorithm has been taken up for constructing the "Honey Badger BFT" protocol by Miller *et al.* [19], for instance. One important contribution of Mostéfaoui *et al.* [20] is a new binary validated broadcast primitive with a non-deterministic termination property; it has also found applications in other protocols [8].

3   System Model and Preliminaries

Processes. We consider a system of n *processes* $\mathcal{P} = \{p_1, \ldots, p_n\}$ that communicate with each other. The processes interact by exchanging messages over reliable point-to-point links, specified below.

A protocol for $\mathcal{P}$ consists of a collection of programs with instructions for all processes. Protocols are presented in a modular way using the event-based notation of Cachin *et al.* [3].

Failures. A process that follows its protocol during an execution is called *correct*. On the other hand, a *faulty* process may crash or deviate arbitrarily from its specification, e.g., when *corrupted* by an adversary; such processes are also called *Byzantine*. We consider only Byzantine faults here and assume for simplicity that the faulty processes fail right at the start of an execution.

Functionalities and Modularity. A *functionality* is an abstraction of a distributed computation, either used as a primitive available to the processes or defining a service that a protocol run by the processes will provide. Functionalities may be composed in a modular way. Every functionality in the system is specified through its *interface*, containing the *events* that it exposes to applications that may call it, and through a number of *properties* that define its behavior. There are two kinds of events in an interface: *input events* that the functionality receives from other abstractions, typically from an application that invokes its services, and *output events*, through which the functionality delivers information or signals a condition.

Multiple functionalities may be composed together modularly. In a modular protocol implementation, in particular, every process executes the program instructions of the protocol implementations for all functionalities in which it participates.

Links. We assume there is a low-level functionality for sending messages over point-to-point links between each pair of processes. In a protocol, this functionality is accessed through the events of "sending a message" and "receiving a message." Point-to-point messages are authenticated and delivered reliably among correct processes.

Moreover, we assume FIFO ordering on the reliable point-to-point links for every pair of processes. This means that if a correct process has "sent" a message m_1 and subsequently "sent" a message m_2, then every correct process does not "receive" m_2 unless it has earlier also "received" m_1. FIFO-ordered links are actually a very common assumption. Protocols that guarantee FIFO order on top of (unordered) reliable point-to-point links are well-known and simple to implement [3,11]. We remark that there is only one FIFO-ordered reliable point-to-point link functionality in the model; hence, FIFO order holds among the messages exchanged by the implementations for all functionalities used by a protocol.

Time and Randomization. In this work we consider an asynchronous system, where processes have no access to any kind of physical clock, and there is no bound on processing or communication delays. The randomized consensus algorithm delegates probabilistic choices to a *common coin* abstraction [23]; this is a functionality that delivers the same sequence of random binary values to each process, where each binary value has the value 0 or 1 with probability $\frac{1}{2}$.

3.1 Byzantine Quorum Systems

Let us recall Byzantine quorums as originally introduced [17]. We refer to them as *symmetric* Byzantine quorums.

Definition 1 (Fail-prone system). *Let $\mathcal{P}$ be a set of processes. A fail-prone system $\mathcal{F}$ is a collection of subsets of $\mathcal{P}$, none of which is contained in another, such that some $F \in \mathcal{F}$ with $F \subseteq \mathcal{P}$ is called a* fail-prone set *and contains all processes that may at most fail together in some execution.*

Definition 2 (Symmetric Byzantine quorum system). *Let $\mathcal{P}$ be a set of processes and let $\mathcal{F} \subseteq 2^{\mathcal{P}}$ be a fail-prone system. A symmetric Byzantine quorum system for $\mathcal{F}$ is a collection of sets of processes $\mathcal{Q} \subseteq 2^{\mathcal{P}}$, where each $Q \in \mathcal{Q}$ is called a* quorum, *such that*

Consistency:
$$\forall Q_1, Q_2 \in \mathcal{Q}, \forall F \in \mathcal{F} : Q_1 \cap Q_2 \not\subseteq F.$$

Availability:
$$\forall F \in \mathcal{F} : \exists Q \in \mathcal{Q} : F \cap Q = \emptyset.$$

For example, under the common threshold failure model, the quorums are all sets of at least $\lceil \frac{n+f+1}{2} \rceil$ processes, where f is the number of processes that may fail. In particular, if $n = 3f + 1$, quorums have $2f + 1$ or more processes.

Malkhi and Reiter [17] refer to the above definition as *Byzantine dissemination quorum system*. They also define other variants of Byzantine quorum systems.

Note that in our notion of a quorum system, one quorum can be contained in another.

We say that a set system $\mathcal{T}$ *dominates* another set system $\mathcal{S}$ if for each $S \in \mathcal{S}$ there is some $T \in \mathcal{T}$ such that $S \subseteq T$. In this sense, a quorum system for $\mathcal{F}$ is *minimal* whenever it does not dominate any other quorum system for $\mathcal{F}$.

Definition 3. (Q^3-condition [12,17]). *Let $\mathcal{F}$ be a fail-prone system. We say that $\mathcal{F}$ satisfies the Q^3-condition, abbreviated as $Q^3(\mathcal{F})$, if it holds*

$$\forall F_1, F_2, F_3 \in \mathcal{F} : \mathcal{P} \not\subseteq F_1 \cup F_2 \cup F_3.$$

This is the generalization of the threshold condition $n > 3f$ for Byzantine quorum systems. Let $\overline{\mathcal{S}} = \{\mathcal{P} \setminus S | S \in \mathcal{S}\}$ be the *bijective complement* of a set $\mathcal{S} \subseteq 2^{\mathcal{P}}$.

Lemma 1. (Quorum system existence [17]). *Let $\mathcal{F}$ be a fail-prone system. A Byzantine quorum system for $\mathcal{F}$ exists if and only if $Q^3(\mathcal{F})$. In particular, if $Q^3(\mathcal{F})$ holds, then $\overline{\mathcal{F}}$, the bijective complement of $\mathcal{F}$, is a Byzantine quorum system called* canonical quorum system *of $\mathcal{F}$.*

Note that the canonical quorum system is not always minimal. The canonical quorum system will play a role in Sect. 5 for implementing a common-coin functionality with asymmetric quorums.

Given a symmetric Byzantine quorum system $\mathcal{Q}$, we define a *kernel* K as a set of processes that overlaps with every quorum. A kernel generalizes the notion of a *core set* [13].

Definition 4 (Kernel system). *A set $K \subseteq \mathcal{P}$ is a* kernel *of a quorum system $\mathcal{Q}$ whenever it holds*

$$\forall Q \in \mathcal{Q} : K \cap Q \neq \emptyset.$$

This can be viewed as a consistency *property.*

We also define the kernel system $\mathcal{K}$ of $\mathcal{Q}$ to be the set of all kernels of $\mathcal{Q}$. Given this, the minimal kernel system *is a kernel system for which every kernel K satisfies*

$$\forall K' \subsetneq K, \exists\, Q \in \mathcal{Q} : K' \cap Q = \emptyset.$$

For example, under a threshold failure assumption where any f processes may fail, every set of $\lfloor \frac{n-f+1}{2} \rfloor$ processes is a kernel. In particular, $n = 3f + 1$ if and only if every kernel has $f + 1$ processes.

Lemma 2. *For every $F \in \mathcal{F}$ and for every quorum $Q \in \mathcal{Q}$ there exists a kernel $K \in \mathcal{K}$ such that $K \subseteq Q$.*

4   Asymmetric Trust

In this section, we review and extend the model of asymmetric trust, as introduced by Damgård *et al.* [9] and by Cachin and Tackmann [5]. We first recall asymmetric quorums. Then we focus on a *maximal guild*, which is needed for ensuring liveness and consistency in protocols, and we prove that the maximal guild is unique. We also characterize it in relation to *wise* processes, which are those correct processes whose a failure assumption turns out to be right.

In the asymmetric-trust model, every process is free to make its own trust assumption, expressing it through a subjective fail-prone system.

Definition 5 (Asymmetric fail-prone system). *An asymmetric fail-prone system* $\mathbb{F} = [\mathcal{F}_1, \dots, \mathcal{F}_n]$ *consists of an array of fail-prone systems, where* $\mathcal{F}_i \subseteq 2^{\mathcal{P}}$ *denotes the trust assumption of* p_i.

One often assumes that $\forall F \in \mathcal{F}_i : p_i \notin F$ for practical reasons, but this is not necessary. For a system $\mathcal{A} \subseteq 2^{\mathcal{P}}$, let $\mathcal{A}^* = \{A' | A' \subseteq A, A \in \mathcal{A}\}$ denote the collection of all subsets of the sets in $\mathcal{A}$.

Definition 6 (Asymmetric Byzantine quorum system). *Let* $\mathbb{F} = [\mathcal{F}_1, \dots, \mathcal{F}_n]$ *be an asymmetric fail-prone system. An asymmetric Byzantine quorum system for* $\mathbb{F}$ *is an array of collections of sets* $\mathbb{Q} = [\mathcal{Q}_1, \dots, \mathcal{Q}_n]$, *where* $\mathcal{Q}_i \subseteq 2^{\mathcal{P}}$ *for* $i \in [1, n]$. *The set* $\mathcal{Q}_i \subseteq 2^{\mathcal{P}}$ *is called the* quorum system of p_i *and any set* $Q_i \in \mathcal{Q}_i$ *is called a* quorum (set) *for* p_i *whenever the following conditions hold:*

Consistency: $\forall i, j \in [1, n]$

$$\forall Q_i \in \mathcal{Q}_i, \forall Q_j \in \mathcal{Q}_j, \forall F_{ij} \in \mathcal{F}_i^* \cap \mathcal{F}_j^* : Q_i \cap Q_j \not\subseteq F_{ij}.$$

Availability: $\forall i \in [1, n]$

$$\forall F_i \in \mathcal{F}_i : \exists\, Q_i \in \mathcal{Q}_i : F_i \cap Q_i = \emptyset.$$

In other words, the intersection of two quorums for any two processes contains at least one process for which neither process assumes that it may fail. Furthermore, for all fail-prone sets of every process, there exists a disjoint quorum for this process.

The following property generalizes the Q^3-condition from Definition 3 to the asymmetric-trust model.

Definition 7 (B^3-condition [5,9]). *Let* $\mathbb{F}$ *be an asymmetric fail-prone system. We say that* $\mathbb{F}$ *satisfies the* B^3*-condition, abbreviated as* $B^3(\mathbb{F})$, *whenever it holds for all* $i, j \in [1, n]$ *that*

$$\forall F_i \in \mathcal{F}_i, \forall F_j \in \mathcal{F}_j, \forall F_{ij} \in \mathcal{F}_i^* \cap \mathcal{F}_j^* : \mathcal{P} \not\subseteq F_i \cup F_j \cup F_{ij}.$$

An asymmetric fail-prone system satisfying the B^3-condition is sufficient for the existence of a corresponding asymmetric quorum system [5].

Theorem 1 (Asymmetric quorum system existence [5]). *An asymmetric fail-prone system* $\mathbb{F}$ *satisfies* $B^3(\mathbb{F})$ *if and only if there exists an asymmetric quorum system for* $\mathbb{F}$.

For implementing consensus, we also need the notion of an asymmetric kernel system.

Definition 8 (Asymmetric kernel system). *Let* $\mathbb{Q} = [\mathcal{Q}_1, \ldots, \mathcal{Q}_n]$ *be an asymmetric quorum system. An asymmetric kernel system* $\mathbb{K}$ *is an array of collections of sets* $[\mathcal{K}_1, \ldots, \mathcal{K}_n]$ *such that each* $\mathcal{K}_i$ *is a kernel system of* $\mathcal{Q}_i$. *We call a set* $K_i \in \mathcal{K}_i$ *a kernel for* p_i.

In traditional Byzantine quorum systems, under a symmetric-trust assumption, every process in the system adheres to a global fail-prone system $\mathcal{F}$ and the set F of faults or corruptions occurring in a protocol execution is in $\mathcal{F}$. Given this common trust assumption, properties of a protocol are guaranteed at each correct process, while they are not guaranteed for faulty ones. With asymmetric quorums, there is a distinction among correct processes with respect to F, namely the correct processes that consider F in their trust assumption and those who do not. Given a protocol execution, the processes are classified in three different types:

Faulty: A process $p_i \in F$ is *faulty*.
Naïve: A correct process p_i for which $F \notin \mathcal{F}_i^*$ is called *naïve*.
Wise: A correct process p_i for which $F \in \mathcal{F}_i^*$ is called *wise*.

Recall that all processes are wise under a symmetric-trust assumption. Protocols for asymmetric quorums cannot guarantee the same properties for naïve processes as for wise ones.

A useful notion for ensuring liveness and consistency for protocols is that of a *guild*. This is a set of wise processes that contains at least one quorum for each member.

Definition 9 (Guild). *Given a fail-prone system* $\mathbb{F}$, *an asymmetric quorum system* $\mathbb{Q}$ *for* $\mathbb{F}$, *and a protocol execution with faulty processes* F, *a guild* $\mathcal{G}$ *for* F *satisfies two properties:*

Wisdom: $\mathcal{G}$ *consists of wise processes,*

$$\forall p_i \in \mathcal{G} : F \in \mathcal{F}_i^*.$$

Closure: $\mathcal{G}$ *contains a quorum for each of its members,*

$$\forall p_i \in \mathcal{G}, \exists\, Q_i \in \mathcal{Q}_i : Q_i \subseteq \mathcal{G}.$$

The following lemma shows that every two guilds intersect.

Lemma 3. *In any execution with a guild* $\mathcal{G}$, *there cannot exist two disjoint guilds.*

Observe that the union of two guilds is again a guild. It follows that every execution with a guild contains a unique *maximal guild* $\mathcal{G}_{\max}$. Analogously to the other asymmetric notions, for a given asymmetric fail-prone system, we call the list of canonical quorum systems of all processes an *asymmetric canonical quorum system*.

The following lemma shows that if a guild exists, then there cannot be a quorum for any process p_j containing only faulty processes.

Lemma 4. *Let $\mathcal{G}_{max}$ be the maximal guild for a given execution and let $\mathbb{Q}$ be the canonical asymmetric quorum system. Then, there cannot be a quorum $Q_j \in \mathcal{Q}_j$ for any process p_j consisting only of faulty processes.*

Lemma 5. *Let $\mathcal{G}_{max}$ be the maximal guild for a given execution and let p_i be any correct process. Then, every quorum for p_i contains at least one process from the maximal guild.*

Finally, we show with an example that it is possible for a wise process to be outside the maximal guild.

Example 1. Let us consider a seven-process asymmetric quorum system $\mathbb{Q}$, defined through its fail-prone system $\mathbb{F}$. The notation $\Theta_k^n(\mathcal{S})$ for a set $\mathcal{S}$ with n elements denotes the *threshold* combination operator and enumerates all subsets of $\mathcal{S}$ of cardinality k. The diagram below shows fail-prone sets as shaded areas and the notation $\frac{n}{k}$ in front of a fail-prone set stands for k out of the n processes in the set. The operator $*$ for two sets satisfies $\mathcal{A} * \mathcal{B} = \{A \cup B : A \in \mathcal{A}, B \in \mathcal{B}\}$.

$$\mathbb{F}: \quad \begin{aligned} \mathcal{F}_1 &= \Theta_2^3(\{p_2, p_4, p_5\}) * \{p_6\} * \{p_7\} \\ \mathcal{F}_2 &= \Theta_2^3(\{p_3, p_4, p_5\}) * \{p_6\} * \{p_7\} \\ \mathcal{F}_3 &= \Theta_2^3(\{p_1, p_4, p_5\}) * \{p_6\} * \{p_7\} \\ \mathcal{F}_4 &= \Theta_1^4(\{p_1, p_2, p_3, p_5\}) * \{p_6\} * \{p_7\} \\ \mathcal{F}_5 &= \Theta_1^4(\{p_1, p_2, p_3, p_4\}) * \{p_6\} * \{p_7\} \\ \mathcal{F}_6 &= \Theta_3^3(\{p_1, p_3, p_7\}) \\ \mathcal{F}_7 &= \Theta_3^3(\{p_3, p_4, p_5\}) \end{aligned}$$

One can verify that $B^3(\mathbb{F})$ holds. Let $\mathbb{Q}$ be the canonical quorum system for $\mathbb{F}$. With $F = \{p_4, p_5\}$, for instance, processes p_1, p_2, p_3 and p_7 are wise, p_6 is naïve, and the maximal guild is $\mathcal{G}_{\max} = \{p_1, p_2, p_3\}$. It follows that process p_7 is wise but outside the guild $\mathcal{G}_{\max}$, because quorum $Q_7 \in \mathcal{Q}_7$ contains the naïve process p_6.

On the Importance of a Guild in a Protocol. Lemma 5 reveals an interesting result, i.e., that every quorum of every correct process contains at least a process inside the maximal guild. This means that $\mathcal{G}_{\max}$ is a kernel for every correct process. The maximal guild $\mathcal{G}_{\max}$ plays then a fundamental role in protocols with kernels by allowing correct processes (wise and naïve) to not halt during an execution and, especially, by helping wise processes outside the guild to reach termination. This means that whenever the processes in $\mathcal{G}_{\max}$ act, this has an influence on every correct process. The guild can then be intended as the mathematical formalization of "sufficiently many wise processes such that it is possible to reach termination". Assume, for example, to have only one wise process p_i in an execution. This means that all of its quorums contain at least a naïve process. This may not be sufficient to conclude that every quorum of every naïve process contains p_i. However, by assuming the existence of $\mathcal{G}_{\max}$, there would exist at least a quorum made by only wise processes.

A notion parallel to a guild is considered in Stellar consensus, called *consensus cluster* [15], within which it is possible to reach consensus among correct processes. However, in contrast to our result, consensus clusters can be disjoint and an unique consensus cannot be reached among processes in disjoint consensus clusters.

5   Asymmetric Randomized Byzantine Consensus

In this section we define asymmetric Byzantine consensus. Then we implement it by a randomized algorithm, which is based on the protocol of Mostéfaoui *et al.* [20].

Our notion of Byzantine consensus uses strong validity in the asymmetric model. Furthermore, it restricts the safety properties of consensus from all correct ones to *wise* processes. For implementing asynchronous consensus, we use a system enriched with randomization. In the asymmetric model, the corresponding probabilistic termination property is guaranteed only for wise processes.

Definition 10 (Asymmetric strong Byzantine consensus). *A protocol for asynchronous asymmetric strong Byzantine consensus satisfies:*

Probabilistic termination: *In all executions with a guild, every wise process decides with probability 1, in the sense that*

$$\lim_{r \to +\infty} (\mathrm{P}[a \text{ wise process } p_i \text{ decides by round } r]) = 1.$$

Strong validity: *In all executions with a guild, a wise process only decides a value that has been proposed by some processes in the maximal guild.*
Integrity: *No correct process decides twice.*
Agreement: *No two wise processes decide differently.*

Common Coin. Our randomized consensus algorithm delegates its probabilistic choices to a *common coin* abstraction [3,23]. We define this in the asymmetric-trust model.

Definition 11 (Asymmetric common coin). *A protocol for asymmetric common coin satisfies the following properties:*

Termination: *In all executions with a guild, every process in the maximal guild eventually outputs a coin value.*

Unpredictability: *Unless at least one correct process has released the coin, no process has any information about the coin output by a wise process.*

Matching: *In all executions with a guild, with probability 1 every process in the maximal guild outputs the same coin value.*

No bias: *The distribution of the coin is uniform over $\mathcal{B}$.*

An asymmetric common coin has an output domain $\mathcal{B}$. Here we consider binary consensus and $\mathcal{B} = \{0, 1\}$. The *termination* property guarantees that every process in the maximal guild eventually output a coin value that is ensured to be the same for each of them by the *matching* property. The *unpredictability* property ensures that the coin value is kept secret until a correct process releases the coin. Finally, the *no bias* property specifies the probability distribution of the coin output. The bias and matching properties may be weakened using well-known methods.

Implementing an Asymmetric Common Coin. Our implementation of asymmetric common coin relies on the scheme of Benaloh and Leichter [1] and is shown in Algorithm 1. Furthermore, following the approach started by Rabin [23], we assume that coins are *predistributed* by an ideal dealer using secret sharing, in a way that for every round r there is exactly one coin with value $s \in \{0, 1\}$. Specifically, given an asymmetric quorum system $\mathbb{Q}$, the dealer creates random shares $s_{i_1}, \ldots, s_{i_{m-1}}$ for one random coin value $s \in \{0, 1\}$ per round and for each $Q_i = \{p_{i_1}, \ldots, p_{i_m}\} \in \mathcal{Q}_i$ of $\mathbb{Q}$ with $|Q_i| = m$. Then the dealer sets $s_{i_m} = s + \sum_{j=1}^{m-1} s_{i_j} \mod 2$ and gives the shares to every process in Q_i. This ensures that any quorum can reconstruct the secret by computing the sum modulo 2 of the shares. This procedure is done for each quorum in every quorum system of $\mathbb{Q}$. Furthermore, the dealer authenticates the shares, preventing Byzantine processes to send inconsistent bits to other processes in the quorum (omitted from Algorithm 1). Correctness of this protocol follows easily. Given a quorum of correct processes, every wise process can thus reconstruct the secret and all of them will output the same coin value. On the other hand, in every execution with a guild, Byzantine processes cannot recover the secret without receiving at least one share from a correct process by Lemma 4.

Algorithm 1 is expensive because the number of shares for one particular coin held by a process p_i is equal to the number of quorums in which p_i is contained. In practical systems, one may also implement an asymmetric coin "from scratch" according to the direction taken by Canetti and Rabin [7] or recently by Patra *et al.* [22]. Alternatively, distributed cryptographic implementations appear to be possible, for example, as introduced by Cachin *et al.* [4].

5.1   Asymmetric Binary Validated Broadcast

The *binary validated broadcast* primitive has been introduced by Mostéfaoui *et al.* [20] under the name *binary-value broadcast*.[1]

---

[1] Compared to their work, we adjusted some conditions to standard terminology and chose to call the primitive "binary *validated* broadcast" to better emphasize its aspect of validating that a delivered value was broadcast by a correct process.

Algorithm 1. Asymmetric common coin for round *round* (code for p_i)

1: **State**
2:        $coin[k] \leftarrow [\bot]^n$: for $k \in [1, |\mathcal{Q}_i|]$, $coin[k][j]$ holds the share received from p_j
3:                                for quorum $Q_{i,k}$ of p_i
4:
5: **upon event** *release-coin* **do**
6:        **for all** $p_j \in \mathcal{P}$ **do**   // send all shares to all process p_j
7:              **for all** $Q_{j,k} \in \mathcal{Q}_j$ **do**
8:                    **if** $p_i \in Q_{j,k}$ **then**
9:                          send message $[\text{COIN}, s_i, Q_{j,k}, r]$ to p_j
10:                         // s_i is share of p_i for $Q_{j,k}$ of p_j
11:
12: **upon** receiving a message $[\text{COIN}, s_j, Q_{i,k}, r]$ from p_j **such that**
13:        $r = round \wedge Q_{i,k} \in \mathcal{Q}_i \wedge p_j \in Q_{i,k}$ **do**
14:     **if** $coin[k][j] = \bot$ **then**
15:          $coin[k][j] \leftarrow s_j$
16:
17: **upon exists** k **such that**
18:        $Q_i^* = \{p_j \in \mathcal{P} |\ coin[k][j] \neq \bot\} \in \mathcal{Q}_i$ **do**   // a quorum for p_i
19:     $s \leftarrow \sum_{p_j \in Q_i^*} coin[k][j]$
20:     **output** *output-coin(s)*

We generalize it to the asymmetric-trust model. All safety properties are restricted to wise processes, and a guild is required for validity and integrity properties. Liveness property is restricted to wise processes too. Observe that every process may broadcast a binary value $b \in \{0, 1\}$ by invoking *abv-broadcast(b)*. The broadcast primitive outputs at least one value b and possibly also both binary values through an *abv-deliver(b)* event, according to the following notion.

Definition 12 (Asymmetric binary validated broadcast). *A protocol for* asymmetric binary validated broadcast *satisfies the following properties:*

Validity: *In all executions with a guild, let K_i be a kernel for a process p_i in the maximal guild. If every process in K_i is correct and has abv-broadcast the same value $b \in \{0, 1\}$, then every wise process eventually abv-delivers b.*

Integrity: *In all executions with a guild, if a wise process abv-delivers some b, then b has been abv-broadcast by some process in the maximal guild.*

Agreement: *If a wise process abv-delivers some value b, then every wise process eventually abv-delivers b.*

Termination: *Every wise process eventually abv-delivers some value.*

Note that it guarantees properties only for processes that are wise or even in the maximal guild. Liveness properties also assume there exists a guild.

When a correct process p_i invokes *abv-broadcast(b)* for $b \in \{0, 1\}$, it sends a VALUE message containing b to all processes. Afterwards, whenever a correct process p_i receives VALUE messages containing b from kernel K_i for itself and has

---

Algorithm 2. Asymmetric binary validated broadcast (code for p_i)

1: **State**
2:      $sentvalue \leftarrow [\text{FALSE}]^2$: $sentvalue[b]$ indicates whether p_i has sent $[\text{VALUE}, b]$
3:      $values \leftarrow [\emptyset]^n$: list of sets of received binary values
4:
5: **upon event** $abv\text{-}broadcast(b)$ **do**
6:      $sentvalue[b] \leftarrow \text{TRUE}$
7:      send message $[\text{VALUE}, b]$ to all $p_j \in \mathcal{P}$
8:
9: **upon** receiving a message $[\text{VALUE}, b]$ from p_j **do**
10:      **if** $b \notin values[j]$ **then**
11:           $values[j] \leftarrow values[j] \cup \{b\}$
12:
13: **upon exists** $b \in \{0, 1\}$ **such that** $\{p_j \in \mathcal{P}\mid b \in \ values[j]\} \in \mathcal{K}_i$
14:           **and** $\neg sentvalue[b]$ **do**   // a kernel for p_i
15:      $sentvalue[b] \leftarrow \text{TRUE}$
16:      send message $[\text{VALUE}, b]$ to all $p_j \in \mathcal{P}$
17:
18: **upon exists** $b \in \{0, 1\}$ **such that**
19:           $\{p_j \in \mathcal{P}\mid b \in \ values[j]\} \in \mathcal{Q}_i$ **do**   // a quorum for p_i
20:      **output** $abv\text{-}deliver(b)$

---

not itself sent a VALUE message containing b, then it sends such message to every process. Finally, once a correct process p_i receives VALUE messages containing b from a quorum Q_i for itself, it delivers b through $abv\text{-}deliver(b)$. Notice that a process may $abv\text{-}deliver$ up to two values.

Theorem 2. *Algorithm 2 implements asymmetric binary validated broadcast.*

5.2   Asymmetric Randomized Consensus

In the following primitive, a correct process may *propose* a binary value b by invoking $arbc\text{-}propose(b)$; the consensus abstraction *decides* for b through an $arbc\text{-}decide(b)$ event.

Algorithm 3 proceeds in rounds, and in each round an instance of $abv\text{-}broadcast$ is invoked. A correct process p_i executes $abv\text{-}broadcast$ and waits for a value b identified by a tag characterizing the current round. Once received, p_i adds b to *values*, broadcasts b into a AUX message to all other processes and all of them add b to *aux*. When p_i has received a set $B \subseteq values$ of values carried by AUX messages from all processes in a quorum Q_i for itself, then p_i releases its coin with tag r. Then process p_i waits for *output-coin* with tag r and the common coin value s. Observe that Algorithm 3 allows the set B to change while reconstructing the common coin (line 35).

Subsequently, p_i checks if there is a single value b in B. If so, and if $b = s$, then it becomes ready to decide b and it does so by broadcasting a DECIDE

Algorithm 3. Asymmetric randomized binary consensus (code for p_i).

1: **State**
2:     $round \leftarrow 0$: current round
3:     $values \leftarrow \{\}$: set of abv-$delivered$ binary values for the round
4:     $aux \leftarrow [\{\}]^n$: sets of values received in AUX messages in the round
5:     $decided \leftarrow []^n$: binary values reported as decided by other processes
6:     $sentdecide \leftarrow$ FALSE: indicates whether p_i has sent a DECIDE message
7:
8: **upon event** $arbc$-$propose(b)$ **do**
9:     **invoke** abv-$broadcast(b)$ with tag $round$
10:
11: **upon** abv-$deliver(b)$ with tag r **such that** $r = round$ **do**
12:     $values \leftarrow values \cup \{b\}$
13:     send message [AUX, $round, b$] to all $p_j \in \mathcal{P}$
14:
15: **upon** receiving a message [AUX, r, b] from p_j **such that** $r = round$ **do**
16:     $aux[j] \leftarrow aux[j] \cup \{b\}$
17:
18: **upon** receiving a message [DECIDE, b] from p_j **such that** $decided[j] = \perp$ **do**
19:     $decided[j] = b$
20:
21: **upon exists** $b \neq \perp$ **such that**
22:         $\{p_j \in \mathcal{P} \mid decided[j] = b\} \in \mathcal{K}_i$ **do**   // a kernel for p_i
23:     **if** $\neg sentdecide$ **then**
24:         send message [DECIDE, b] to all $p_j \in \mathcal{P}$
25:         $sentdecide \leftarrow$ TRUE
26:
27: **upon exists** $b \neq \perp$ **such that**
28:         $\{p_j \in \mathcal{P} \mid decided[j] - b\} \subset \mathcal{Q}_i$ **do**   // a quorum for p_i
29:     $arbc$-$decide(b)$
30:     **halt**
31:
32: **upon exist** $\{p_j \in \mathcal{P} \mid aux[j] \subseteq values\} \in \mathcal{Q}_i$ **do**   // a quorum for p_i
33:     $release$-$coin$ with tag $round$
34:
35: **upon event** $output$-$coin(s)$ with tag $round$ **and exists** $B \neq \{\}$ **such that**
36:         $\forall p_j \in Q_i, B = aux[j]$ **do**
37:     $round \leftarrow round + 1$
38:     **if exists** b **such that** $|B| = 1 \wedge B = \{b\}$ **then**
39:         **if** $b = s \wedge \neg sentdecide$ **then**
40:             send message [DECIDE, b] to all $p_j \in \mathcal{P}$
41:             $sentdecide \leftarrow$ TRUE
42:         **invoke** abv-$broadcast(b)$ with tag $round$ // propose b for the next round
43:     **else**
44:         **invoke** abv-$broadcast(s)$ with tag $round$ // propose s for the next round
45:     $values \leftarrow [\perp]^n$
46:     $aux \leftarrow [\{\}]^n$

---

message with value b to every process. If there is more than one value in B, then p_i changes its proposal to s. In any case, the process starts another round and invokes a new instance of abv-$broadcast$ with its proposal.

In parallel, the protocol potentially disseminates DECIDE messages and may terminate. When p_i receives a DECIDE message from a kernel of processes for itself containing the same value b, then it broadcasts a DECIDE message itself containing b to every processes, unless it has already done so. Once p_i receives a DECIDE message from a quorum of processes for itself with the same value b, it arbc-decides(b) and halts. This "amplification" step is reminiscent of Bracha's reliable broadcast protocol [2]. Hence, the protocol does not execute rounds forever, in contrast to the original formulation of Mostéfaoui et al. [21].

Lemma 6. *If a wise process p_i outputs the coin with $B = \{0, 1\}$, then every other wise process that outputs the coin has also $B = \{0, 1\}$.*

Theorem 3. *Algorithm 3 implements asymmetric strong Byzantine consensus.*

Acknowledgments. The authors thank Orestis Alpos, Vincent Gramoli, Giorgia Azzurra Marson, Achour Mostéfaoui, and anonymous reviewers for interesting discussions and helpful feedback.

This work has been funded by the Swiss National Science Foundation (SNSF) under grant agreement Nr. 200021_188443 (Advanced Consensus Protocols).

References

1. Benaloh, J., Leichter, J.: Generalized secret sharing and monotone functions. In: Goldwasser, S. (ed.) CRYPTO 1988. LNCS, vol. 403, pp. 27–35. Springer, New York (1990). https://doi.org/10.1007/0-387-34799-2_3
2. Bracha, G.: Asynchronous byzantine agreement protocols. Inf. Comput. **75**(2), 130–143 (1987)
3. Cachin, C., Guerraoui, R., Rodrigues, L.E.T.: Introduction to Reliable and Secure Distributed Programming, 2 edn. Springer, Heidelberg (2011)
4. Cachin, C., Kursawe, K., Shoup, V.: Random oracles in constantinople: practical asynchronous byzantine agreement using cryptography. J. Cryptol. **18**(3), 219–246 (2005)
5. Cachin, C., Tackmann, B.: Asymmetric distributed trust. In: Proceedings of the OPODIS. LIPIcs, vol. 153, pp. 7:1–7:16 (2019)
6. Cachin, C., Zanolini, L.: From symmetric to asymmetric asynchronous byzantine consensus. e-print, arXiv:2005.08795 [cs.DC] (2020)
7. Canetti, R., Rabin, T.: Fast asynchronous byzantine agreement with optimal resilience. In: Proceedings of the STOC, pp. 42–51 (1993)
8. Crain, T., Gramoli, V., Larrea, M., Raynal, M.: DBFT: efficient leaderless byzantine consensus and its application to blockchains. In: Proceedings of the NCA, pp. 1–8 (2018)
9. Damgård, I., Desmedt, Y., Fitzi, M., Nielsen, J.B.: Secure protocols with asymmetric trust. In: Kurosawa, K. (ed.) ASIACRYPT 2007. LNCS, vol. 4833, pp. 357–375. Springer, Heidelberg (2007). https://doi.org/10.1007/978-3-540-76900-2_22
10. García-Pérez, Á., Gotsman, A.: Federated byzantine quorum systems. In: Proceedings of the OPODIS. LIPIcs, vol. 125, pp. 17:1–17:16 (2018)
11. Hadzilacos, V., Toueg, S.: Fault-tolerant broadcasts and related problems. In: Mullender, S.J. (ed.) Distributed Systems (2nd ed.), pp. 97–145. ACM Press (1993)

12. Hirt, M., Maurer, U.M.: Player simulation and general adversary structures in perfect multiparty computation. J. Cryptol. **13**(1), 31–60 (2000)
13. Junqueira, F.P., Marzullo, K.: Synchronous consensus for dependent process failure. In: Proceedings of the ICDCS, pp. 274–283 (2003)
14. Lokhava, M., et al.: Fast and secure global payments with stellar. In: Proceedings of the SOSP, pp. 80–96 (2019)
15. Losa, G., Gafni, E., Mazières, D.: Stellar consensus by instantiation. In: Proceedings of the DISC. LIPIcs, vol. 146, pp. 27:1–27:15 (2019)
16. Malkhi, D., Nayak, K., Ren, L.: Flexible byzantine fault tolerance. In: Proceedings of the ACM CCS, pp. 1041–1053 (2019)
17. Malkhi, D., Reiter, M.K.: Byzantine quorum systems. Distrib. Comput. **11**(4), 203–213 (1998)
18. Mazières, D.: The Stellar consensus protocol: a federated model for Internet-level consensus. Stellar, available online (2016). https://www.stellar.org/papers/stellar-consensus-protocol.pdf
19. Miller, A., Xia, Y., Croman, K., Shi, E., Song, D.: The honey badger of BFT protocols. In: Proceedings of the ACM CCS, pp. 31–42 (2016)
20. Mostéfaoui, A., Hamouma, M., Raynal, M.: Signature-free asynchronous byzantine consensus with t $2<n/3$ and $o(n^2)$ messages. In: Proceedings of the PODC, pp. 2–9 (2014)
21. Mostéfaoui, A., Moumen, H., Raynal, M.: Signature-free asynchronous binary byzantine consensus with t $<$ n/3, o(n2) messages, and O(1) expected time. J. ACM **62**(4), 31:1–31:21 (2015)
22. Patra, A., Choudhury, A., Rangan, C.P.: Asynchronous byzantine agreement with optimal resilience. Distrib. Comput. **27**(2), 111–146 (2014)
23. Rabin, M.O.: Randomized byzantine generals. In: Proceedings of the FOCS, pp. 403–409 (1983)

Using Degree Centrality to Identify Market Manipulation on Bitcoin

Daiane M. Pereira$^{(\boxtimes)}$ and Rodrigo S. Couto

Universidade Federal do Rio de Janeiro - PEE/COPPE/GTA,
Rio de Janeiro, RJ, Brazil
{daiane,rodrigo}@gta.ufrj.br
http://www.gta.ufrj.br

Abstract. In 2014, the Mt.Gox Bitcoin exchange had its internal dataset hacked and leaked. After that, some studies employ this dataset to evaluate if Mt.Gox was doing market manipulation on Bitcoin. Also, they identify patterns of this manipulation. Based on these studies, this paper analyzes the Bitcoin blockchain in the period where Mt.Gox was active. We model the transactions in the blockchain as a graph and evaluate the degree centrality of each node. We thus analyze how the ranking of nodes with the highest centrality values changes over time. Our conclusions indicate that top nodes are stable, but there is a period where it changes. To better understand this behavior, we simulate the insertion of transactions in the network and verify how the ranking changes. As a result, we provide indications that we can use ranking changes to detect malicious activities. We also show a case study using this ranking to predict abnormal behavior in the network.

Keywords: Bitcoin · Mt.Gox · Complex networks

1 Introduction

A Bitcoin exchange is a place where people can store, buy, or sell Bitcoins using fiat currencies or other cryptocurrencies (i.e., altcoins). Despite their importance, the interaction with these companies can represent a risk factor for Bitcoin holders. It is true since storing fiat or cryptocurrencies in accounts at these companies can be seen as a type of centralization, that is, a single point of failure. Also, the lack of Bitcoin regulation makes it difficult to recover money in fraud cases on an exchange platform. Between 2010 and 2013, 45% of the exchange were closed, and 45% of these platforms did not compensate their customers for their losses [19]. Another problem raised by some companies is the

This study was financed in part by the Coordenação de Aperfeiçoamento de Pessoal de Nível Superior - Brasil (CAPES) - Finance Code 001. It was also supported by CNPq, FAPERJ Grants E-26/203.211/2017 and E-26/211.144/2019, and FAPESP Grant 15/24494-8.

J. Garcia-Alfaro et al. (Eds.): DPM 2021/CBT 2021, LNCS 13140, pp. 208–223, 2022.
https://doi.org/10.1007/978-3-030-93944-1_14

suspicion that they perform market manipulation and their activity artificially increases the USD-BTC price [5].

In 2014, the major Bitcoin exchange, called Mt.Gox, was filed for bankruptcy and had its trade history leaked. This leakage allows researchers to analyze more closely the behavior of this exchange since not all trading in an exchange appears in the blockchain [2]. It happens because some users store their bitcoins in the exchange wallet. As the exchange controls these wallets, their transactions are not added to the blockchain. In this case, the exchange keeps the Bitcoin in its address and uses internal data to controls the users' amount. The users do not have Bitcoins, as they do not have a pair of keys to prove their ownership. The same occurs when two users of the same exchange transfer values between them. In these two cases, these transactions are called off-chain transactions. A different scenario occurs when a user buys Bitcoin in an exchange and transfer the Bitcoins to his wallet (i.e., any wallet that this user has the pair of keys). In this case, a transaction must be added to the blockchain. It is called on-chain transactions.

The leaked data from Mt. Gox is analyzed in papers that try to find evidence of market manipulation. They find transaction patterns in the leaked data that support the hypothesis that Mt.Gox was making market manipulation [2,5]. Based on the analysis of [2,5], this work performs a graph analysis of the blockchain, focusing on the same period used in these papers. We hypothesize that the market manipulation made by Mt.Gox changes the expected behavior of blockchain nodes, generating instability in it. To investigate this hypothesis, we are interested in knowing how the top-ranked users change over time and examining if these changes can be related to the Mt.Gox malicious activity and the increase in the Bitcoin price.

Our primary contribution is analyzing how the top-ranked nodes change in the blockchain to identify malicious activity in the network. We show how these changes occurred during the Mt.Gox activity period and how the network's behavior was different from the others. Also, we provide a forecast model to predict this unstable behavior.

This work is organized as follows. Section 2 describes related work. Section 3 presents information about data acquisition and graph construction, including also a preliminary analysis. Next, Sect. 4 presents the stability analysis and discusses our main findings. Section 5 presents the case study, while Sect. 6 concludes the paper.

2   Related Work

Different papers analyze aspects of the Bitcoin network. One important aspect is its decentralization, addressed in [3,8]. These works show that few entities control most of the computing power used for Bitcoin mining.

Anonymity is another aspect addressed in Bitcoin literature. The studies about this aspect show that Bitcoin is not entirely anonymous. Fleder *et al.* were able to link Bitcoin addresses to real user identities [4], using data from

Internet forums. Other approaches also break user anonymity, such as linking Bitcoin addresses to IP addresses [11]. The work in [12] provides a survey covering aspects of Bitcoin anonymity [12].

Extracting complex network characteristics from the Bitcoin environment is also an interesting research topic. For example, the studies conducted in [14] and [16] identifies that the degree distribution of Bitcoin nodes follows a power law. Another fact about the Bitcoin network is that it has characteristics of the small-world phenomenon but with a high diameter [15,17]. The authors also studied the outliers in the in-degree and out-degree distributions. Maesa *et al.* consider as outliers the nodes with the in-degree or out-degree with at least one order of magnitude higher than the average degree. Both behaviors are associated with the presence of artificial transactions in the network [16,18]. One example of an artificial transaction is a transference where one node transfers the exact amount 0.00001 BTC to 101 other nodes.

Another topic of interest in the Bitcoin network is the analysis of frauds and market manipulation. In [5], the Mt. Gox leaked data is used to verify if this exchange made market manipulation. The authors find out suspicious trade activity in accounts listed in the leaked data. These accounts were called Willy and Markus bots. The article shows evidence that the increase in the Bitcoin price is related to these bots' activity. In 2017, during a trial in Japan, the Mt. GOX CEO confirmed that the company was responsible for the Willy activity [24].

Chen *et al.* also analyze market manipulation by Mt.Gox [2]. They perform this investigation in the Bitcoin network through graph analysis. The authors use the Mt.Gox leaked data to make a graph analysis to find malicious trade evidence. They classify the accounts of the dataset into three categories (i.e., extremely high, extremely low, and normal) based on the amount that each account paid for the Bitcoins and the daily price reference. They consider that the extremely high account and the extremely low account are abnormal accounts and verify that they have different characteristics when compared with the normal ones. After that, they analyze the dataset looking for patterns in the transactions made by the abnormal accounts. They find out the existence of many self-loops, unidirectional transactions, triangles, and other structures and conclude that these patterns are strong evidence of price manipulation. Most of these abnormal transactions occurred during the last 12 months of Mt.Gox operations, with a more relevant presence in the last six months of 2013.

Although the investigations of [5] and [2] give essential contributions to the studies about market manipulation in the exchanges, they focus the analysis on the Mt. Gox leaked data. As details about internal transactions in other exchanges are not available (i.e., transactions that occur in the exchange and do not appear in the blockchain), their analysis is not extensible to other periods where the Bitcoin price had a high increase. Our work contributes to the literature showing that the abnormal transaction patterns identified in [2] change blockchain's graph behavior. This analysis can be a base to design mechanisms to identify malicious activities, regardless of leaked data.

3   Base Methodology and Preliminary Analysis

In this section, we present the methodology applied in our analysis, together with preliminary results. We start with the details of our dataset. Then we show the graph definitions used in this work. We also conduct the first part of our graph analysis to analyze if there is a relationship between the top user ranking and the Bitcoin price.

3.1   Data Acquisition

To receive an amount of money in the Bitcoin network, a user needs to create a wallet with at least one pair of public/private keys. The public key is used to create the Bitcoin address, used as an input or an output in the transaction. The private key proves the ownership of this address. If a user has Bitcoins in one address and wants to send these Bitcoins to other users, he/she has to prove the ownership of this address. It means that only the user who has the private key can transfer the Bitcoins of the corresponding Bitcoin address.

When a transaction occurs, it is broadcasted to the other nodes in the network. The miners get this transaction, groups with others, and create a block. The transaction is only complete when included in a block in the blockchain. The blockchain contains blocks with all the transactions that have ever happened in the network since its creation. The entire Bitcoin transaction history (i.e., blockchain transactions) is available for download using a Bitcoin client, such as Bitcoin Core [21].

We use the ELTE Bitcoin project dataset, available in[1]. This dataset has pre-processed blockchain data, organized into spreadsheet format. Using this data, instead of downloading and processing more than 270 GB of data (i.e., the corresponding size of the Bitcoin blockchain), we have to deal with less than 40 GB (the size of the ELTE dataset) of data. Also, we choose the dataset to avoid dealing with the script code format of the blockchain.

An additional pre-processing is necessary to remove inconsistent data from the dataset, such as the mining rewards, represented in the dataset as transactions without input addresses. We also aggregate the Bitcoin addresses that belong to the same entity. However, as we are interested in transactions between the same exchange, we choose to use the well-known aggregate heuristic rule noted in [20]. Using this heuristic, if a transaction has multiple input addresses, we consider all these addresses belonging to the same entity. This assumption is reasonable since the entity that creates the transaction must have all input addresses' private keys to prove its ownership.

The final dataset used in this work has all the transactions up to 02-2018. However, we select the interval between 06-2012 up to 05-2015 to analyze. This period is selected because we are interested in the blockchain's behavior during the reported malicious activities of Mt.Gox, which occurs in the year 2013. We select an interval before and after this year to compare the behavior. For each month in this interval, we create a graph and perform our analysis.

---

[1] https://senseable2015-6.mit.edu/bitcoin/.

3.2 Graph Definition

We model our data as an undirected weighted graph, $G_m(V_m, E_m, w)$ where V_m is the set of nodes representing users that made transactions during the month m. E_m is the set of edges representing the transactions between users that occur in m, and w is a weight associated with each edge. If two users have at least one transaction between them during the month m, there is an edge connecting these nodes. This edge's weight is the total number of transactions made between them in m.

We make our analysis using degree centrality, which measures a node's importance based on its number of edges. Equation 1 shows how to evaluate the degree centrality. In this equation, $N - 1$ is the maximum number of edges that a node can have in month m, and e_{ij} is one if there is a link between node i and node j in month m. If a node has $N - 1$ edges, it has one edge with all other nodes.

$$C_D = \frac{\sum_{i=1}^{N} e_{ij}}{(N - 1)}. \tag{1}$$

3.3 Rank Analysis

We start our analysis by creating one graph G_m for each month between 06-2012 ($m = 1$) and 05-2015 ($m = 36$). Figure 1 shows the number of nodes and edges of each G_m. As explained in Sect. 3.1, we use an aggregate rule to group Bitcoin addresses. It means that the total number of nodes for each G_m is less than the total number of Bitcoin addresses used as input and output each month.

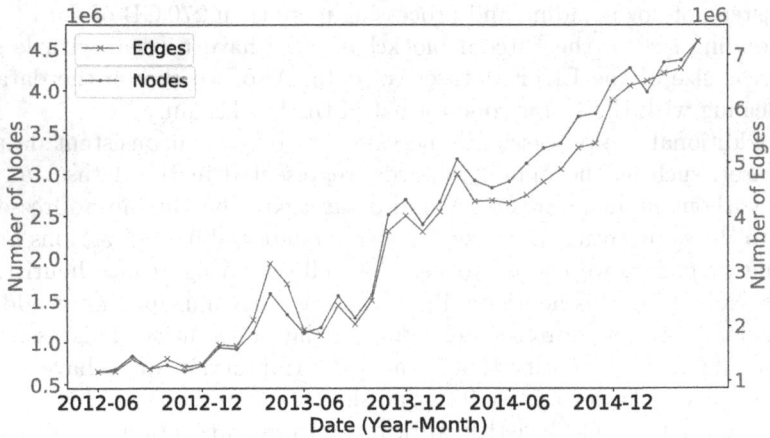

Fig. 1. Total number of nodes and edges in each G_m

After the graph creation, we evaluate the degree centrality of Eq. 1 for all nodes V_m, for each G_m. We then list the k nodes with the highest degree centrality in each month m. We use this top-k nodes to build the set $\mathcal{N}_m^k$. This set has the top-k nodes. We evaluate different values for k, and we use the number of transactions these nodes have made to uphold our decision. The top-10 nodes are responsible for almost 20% of transactions. For the top-100, we get precisely 33%. For the top-150, we have 34%. As we increase k to top-1000, we have approximately 40%, and for the top-2000, we have 44%. We choose to use k = 100 to simplify our analysis. Also, because these few nodes are responsible for an expressive number of transactions.

After selecting the top-k nodes, we analyze how this ranking changes over time. To this end, we compare the nodes of each set $\mathcal{N}_m^k$ with the set $\mathcal{N}_{m-1}^k$ of the month before. In this analysis, we are interested in finding out the number of repeated nodes. It means that we are interested in the cardinality of the intersection between $\mathcal{N}_m^k$ and $\mathcal{N}_{m-1}^k$. We call this number User Repetition, and Eq. 2 formalizes it.

$$UserRepetition = |\mathcal{N}_m^k \cap \mathcal{N}_{m-1}^k|. \tag{2}$$

Figure 2 shows how User Repetition changes over time[2]. This figure also includes the Bitcoin price difference during this period by comparing the bitcoin price in the month m with the month $m-1$. We use the bitcoin historical market price, available in [1]. We can note that, in the period between 2013-02 and 2013-12, User Repetition has its lowest values. It means that we have fewer nodes repeated in the top-100 ranking list. This behavior is different from the previous and the next months, where we have a higher User Repetition. These higher values in the other months show that the 100 top-ranked nodes change little, indicating stability in this ranking's behavior. An exception occurs between 2014-12 and 2015-05. Although, in this case, User Repetition remains low for a short period, it could indicate that external factors (e.g., political scandals, terrorist attacks, government decisions, etc.) can influence the metric. This analysis is not covered in this paper and will be studied in future work.

We also calculate the average User Repetition in each six-month interval of the considered period, shown in Table 1. We use the interval names of this table in the rest of this paper. The six intervals were called A0, A1, A2, B1, B2, and C1. The intervals A1 and A2 represent the period where the evidence points out that the exchange Mt.Gox made most of its suspicious transactions [2]. A1 and A2 are also intervals with the lowest User Repetition. In the interval A0, we already had Mt.GOX activity, but based on the leaked data analysis, the number of suspicious transactions was inferior to the number presented in A1 and A2. We can also see that the interval A2 (i.e., between 06-01-2013 and 11-30-2013) has the lowest average, as expected based on Fig. 2. This paper focuses on understanding network behavior during interval A2 because of its low average User Repetition, its high exchange market price, and the reported malicious activity [2,5].

The results of Fig. 2 and Table 1 lead to a hypothesis that there is a relationship between the User Repetition metric and the market manipulation made by Mt.Gox, noted by the relationship between our metric and the Bitcoin price.

---

[2] To evaluate User Repetition in the first month (i.e.,$m = 1$), we use the set $\mathcal{N}_1^{100}$ and the set $\mathcal{N}_0^{100}$, where $m = 0$ indicates the month 2012-05.

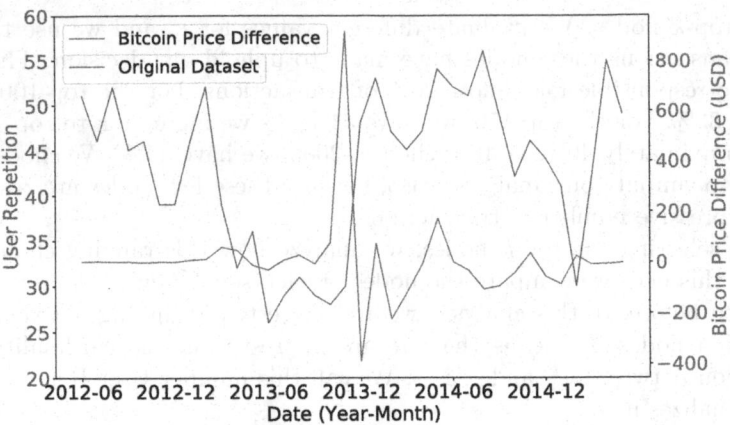

Fig. 2. Bitcoin market price and user repetition per month

Table 1. Average rank difference

Date Range (From~To)	Interval name	Average rank difference
06-01-2012~11-30-2012	A0	46.5
12-01-2012~05-31-2013	A1	40.6
06-01-2013~11-30-2013	A2	28.8
12-01-2013~05-31-2014	B1	49.0
06-01-2014~11-30-2014	B2	49.3
12-01-2014~05-31-2015	C1	43.5

In Sect. 4.2, we investigate if this hypothesis holds, analyzing the behavior of the User Repetition metric in G_m. In a nutshell, we analyze how a node enters the top-k ranking. It gives us information about how many transactions a node needs to perform and how it needs to behave to enter in this ranking.

4 Stability Analysis

As explained in Sect. 2, there is evidence of fraudulent behavior of Mt.Gox during the months before its filing for bankruptcy. The leaked data analysis shows evidence of artificial trades, mostly during its last months of operations, which correspond to our interval A2 and part of interval A1 of Table 1. Based on our analysis of Sect. 3.3, where we observe low values in User Repetition, we want to verify how the insertion of new transactions affects our User Repetition metric. To this end, we perform a stability analysis. In this section, we first describe the employed methodology and then present its results.

4.1 Methodology

To perform the analysis, we select a six-month interval to insert the new trans-actions. For each month in this interval, we create the graph G_m and we use a uniform distribution to choose a subset S_m with $k = 100$ nodes from V_m. The nodes in S_m are responsible for the input of the new transactions. We choose each transaction's output from V_m or S_m, depending on the methodology that we are applying.

As Mt.Gox suspended all trading in 02-2014, we insert the new transaction in the interval B2 (06-01-2014~11-30-2014) to make sure we are making our analysis without the influence of this exchange. Hence, in the rest of this section, the variable m refers to the months included in the interval B2, $m \in B2$. In other words, it means that our m values range from 25 to 30. The amount of new transactions inserted in each month m is based on a percentage of the total number of transactions that occurred in it.

The percentage of the total number of transactions that we choose goes from 2% up to 16% of the total number of transactions that occurred in the month, increasing 2% at each step. It means that, at each step, we generate a new graph $G'_m(V'_m, E'_m, w')$, where V'_m, E'_m, and w' are the set of nodes, edges and weights updated with the new transactions included. We calculate the degree centrality, select the top-100 nodes, and calculate User Repetition for each step, repeating the same procedure in all months $m \in B2$.

We employ three different methods to add new transactions. Our objective is to analyze how organized the transactions must be to change the ranking. In Method 1, we want to investigate our metric's behavior when we increase the network transactions, but with a high number of nodes responsible for making them. In Method 2, we also analyze our metric's behavior when we increase the network transactions, but this with fewer nodes being responsible for making them. In Method 3, we stably insert new transactions keeping the same nodes during all months.

Our goal with Method 1 is to analyze the impact of random transactions in User Repetition. It means that we want to verify User Repetition's behavior when random users made many new transactions. We assume that random transactions are not organized and controlled by an entity. It represents nodes that increase their number of transactions without any control of the network's major players.

In Method 1, for each percentage, we make the following procedures. First, we randomly choose the subset S_m (i.e., a subset with 100 nodes) used in the transaction generation. We remove these nodes from V_m. After that, we generate new transactions using uniform distribution to select an input node from S_m. We randomly choose the output node from V_m (i.e., a subset with all nodes that make transactions during the month m) or S_m. At each transaction, we use one of the sets in the output. The selection from S_m increases the number of self-loops and triangles, as this group has fewer nodes than V_m. When we select from V_m, we increase the chance that this transaction will create a new edge. It happens because, as this set has a higher number of nodes, we have less chance of selecting a node that already has an edge with the input. Next, we create G'_m and evaluate C_D, using Eq. 1. Then, we select the top-k nodes and evaluate User Repetition, using Eq. 2.

Method 2 and Method 3 have many similarities with Method 1. Because of that, we explain next only the differences between these methods and Method 1. The difference is in how we choose S_m.

In Method 2, we select only one subset S_m, for each m, and this subset is responsible for creating all-new transactions in G_m. This process is different from Method 1, where we select one subset for each percentage. The behavior simulated in Method 2 is the insertion of a high number of transactions made by the same group of nodes. The consequence is that few users control the transaction. Thus, these users make a considerable amount of interactions (from 2% up to 16% of all transactions in the network).

In Method 3, instead of selecting S_m from each G_m, we create a graph $G(V, E, w)$, using the entire B2 dataset and select the S_m from this graph. It means that all months use the same subset S_m. In other words, an edge exists between two nodes if they have a transaction in any month of the B2 dataset. In the same way as Method 2, in Method 3, the subset S_m is responsible for the input of all new transactions for each m. If in a month m the node selected in S_m is not in G_m, we add this node to the graph. Our goal in this method is to analyze the stability of the original top-k changes, as we force nodes to be inserted and repeated each month. It gives us information about the behavior in the periods with high User Repetition (e.g., A0, A1, B1, and B2).

4.2   Results

We apply the three methods described in Sect. 4.1 to the employed dataset. The figures below show the average values of User Repetition and the confidence intervals, evaluated with a confidence level of 95%. It is difficult to visualize the confidence intervals in our curves because our results have a narrow confidence interval.

Figure 3 shows User Repetition after applying Method 1. The mark by a shaded area in the graph shows the B2 interval. As described before, this method changes S_m for each percentage. There is a difference in User Repetition between the original dataset curve and the curve for 2%. However, as we keep adding transactions, this difference does not have a considerable change, even when inserting 16% of new transactions. This happens because the subset S_m changes constantly, and we select $|S_m| = 100$ new nodes in the entire G_m. Even without any rules forbidding a node to be selected again, the probability that it happens is small. It implies that a node's chance to make more than 2% of new transactions is small.

Method 1 gives us information about the concentration of transactions in the network. With 2% of transactions created by random users, we decrease User Repetition by 15 positions. As User Repetition represents the number of repeated nodes in the top-100 rank, this decrease means that we insert 15 new nodes in the top-100 by just creating 2% of new transactions. Figure 3 shows this decrease as the maximum difference between the original dataset curve and the curve for 2%.

As we insert further transactions, the other curves (i.e., 4%,8%, and 16%) do not change significantly. It happens because of the randomness and frequency in selecting the subset S_m. We change the nodes in this subset frequently (i.e., at each percentage of new transactions). Hence, at each change, a different set of new nodes enter the top-k rank and keeps User Repetition with this decrease by almost 15 nodes.

Before the insertion of new transactions, our top-100 nodes were responsible for almost 30% of the total number of transactions each month. Based on that, the fact that we can change 15 positions in this rank with 2% of new transactions indicates a higher concentration of transactions in the first ranking positions, showing that the addition of random transactions can change the subset of top-100 nodes, but not the major part of these nodes.

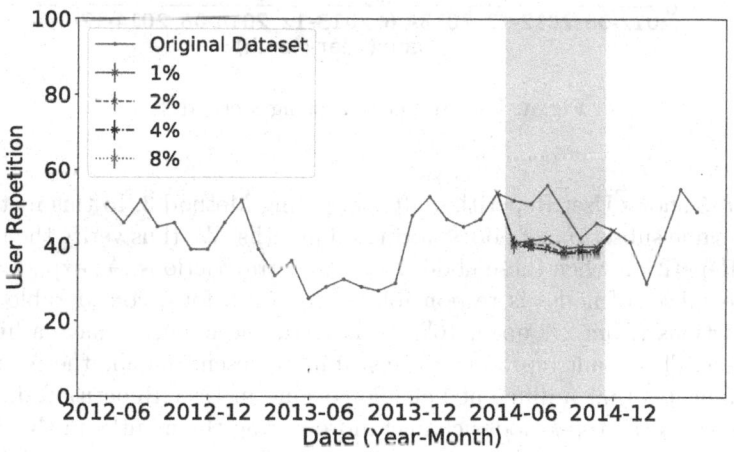

Fig. 3. User Repetition using method 1

Figure 4 shows User Repetition after applying Method 2. In this method, we do not change the subset S_m for each percentage (i.e., as in Method 1). Instead, we change it only once each month. For example, in a given month, to evaluate User Repetition for 16% of new transactions, we use the same subset S_m employed for 8%, and so on. Figure 4 shows that, for 4% of new transactions, we include almost 35 new nodes in the top-k ranking (i.e., the maximum decrease in User Repetition). Furthermore, with 16% of new transactions, User Repetition is low. It means that at each month in B2, we insert most of S_m nodes in the top-k list. As this list changes once per month, User Repetition keeps low values because fewer nodes are repeated. The behavior of User Repetition in Method 2 looks more similar to the one of the A2 interval (i.e., the period where Bitcoin prices have increased due to market manipulation). It reinforces our initial hypothesis that the decrease in User Repetition is related to the activity of Mt. Gox.

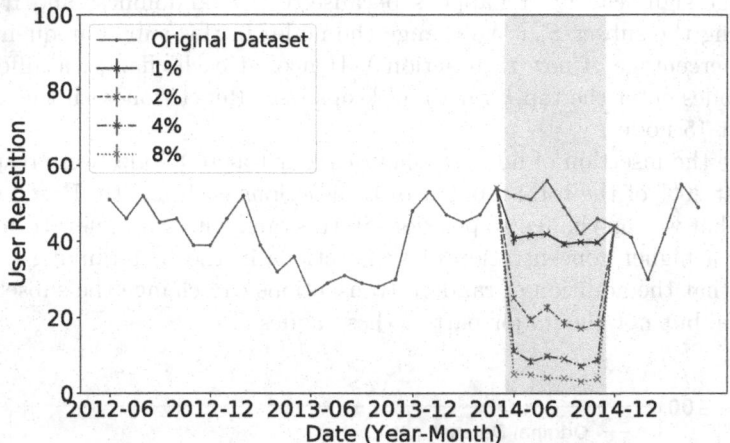

Fig. 4. User Repetition using method 2

Figure 5 shows User Repetition after applying Method 3. In this method, we keep the same subset S_m of nodes during all months. We thus verify the behavior of User Repetition when these nodes insert new transactions. As expected, when the same subset of nodes is responsible each month for a considerable number of transactions (from 2% up to 16% of new transactions), we have a high User Repetition. This result reproduces the stability present outside the A2 interval. It also indicates that a different behavior occurs in User Repetition during the A2 interval, as the top-k nodes change more during the months in this interval.

This section showed User Repetition's behavior after applying the three methods described in Sect. 4.1. Method 1 showed us that an arbitrary transaction insertion is not able to decrease User Repetition considerably. This result reinforces that the decrease during the A2 interval is not a natural behavior in the network. Method 2 showed that to reproduce the behavior present during the A2 interval, we need to insert the random transactions in a more organized way. Method 3 reproduced the natural behavior during the intervals outside A2, where we have stability in the top-k rank. These results reinforce our initial intuition that the low values during the interval A2 are related to the fraudulent behavior of Mt.Gox.

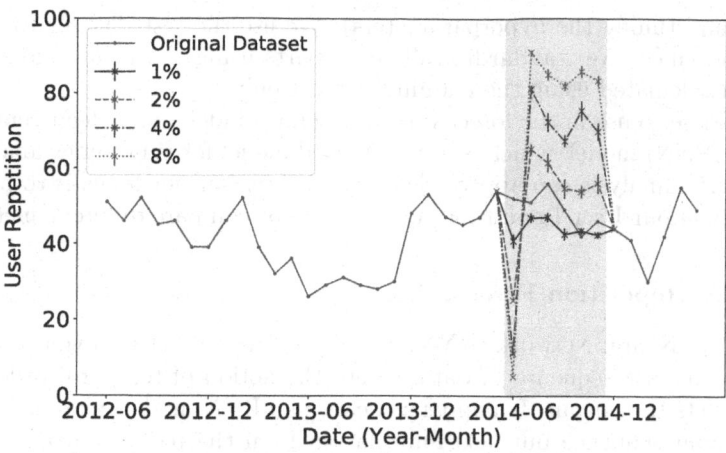

Fig. 5. User Repetition using method 3

5   Case Study

This section provides a case study using a time-series model to forecast the User Repetition metric. This model allows an online behavior estimation of the best-ranked nodes and, together with the previous analysis, can indicate malicious activity in the network. Next, we first detail the data pre-processing steps. After that, we explain the forecast model and show an example of its execution.

5.1   Data Pre-processing

As mentioned before, the previous sections perform a per-month analysis. The forecast model uses the User Repetition metrics per hour since this case study can be a base to an online mechanism. Hence, it is more helpful for this mechanism to have malicious activity clues in a shorter period.

In the first part of our data-preprocessing step, we repeat the graph analysis of Sect. 4, evaluating the User Repetition metric. Different from Sect. 4, we have one graph per hour instead of one graph per month. Hence, our dataset has the information of User Repetition in a one-hour interval. We employ a fixed-size sliding-window approach. It means that we break our dataset into sequences with the same length. We choose to use the last 24 h to predict the User Repetition metric in the next hour. Consequently, we use the windows with a length of 25 (i.e., 24 for the input and 1 for the target). We also use the same approach to forecast for two hours in the future, based on the last 48 h. Consequently, we use the windows with a length of 50 in this case.

Next, we split our dataset into three parts, with the data grouped into windows. One for training, with 80% of the data. Another for validation, with 10% of the data. And the last one for the test, with the remaining 10% of the data. We use the training dataset and the validation dataset to build the model (i.e., training and tuning the hyperparameters). We use the test dataset to evaluate the performance. We standardize all three parts using the mean and standard deviation calculated using the training dataset only.

We choose to use in the forecasting a baseline model and a Recurrent Neural Network (RNN) model, which is a widely used model for time-series analysis [9]. A time-series analysis can apply other approaches, but our focus is to present a case study of our User Repetition metric and not compare different methods.

5.2   User Repetition Forecasting

A Recurrent Neural Network (RNN) is a type of neural network that can recognize patterns in a sequence of data, where the notion of temporal order in the inputs affects the output. It happens because an RNN model takes as input the current input sequence but also information from the past. It means that the decision made at a time step t is affected by the decision made at a time step $t - 1$.

Figure 6 shows an example of a model using a single RNN neuron. It is an unrolled through time representation [6]. In this figure, $x(t)$ is the input, $\hat{y}(t)$ the prediction, $h(t)$ is the transferred state, and the target is the correct value that we are trying to predict. This example shows that this model predicts one value of $x(t)$ in the future (i.e., $x(t + 1)$). We can also note that we use the transferred state $h(t)$ as an input in the next time step. As $h(t)$ is a function of the current input $x(t)$ and the previous state $h(t - 1)$, it illustrates the idea of memory in an RNN, as the state transferred to the next time step depends on the current value of the input and the previous state.

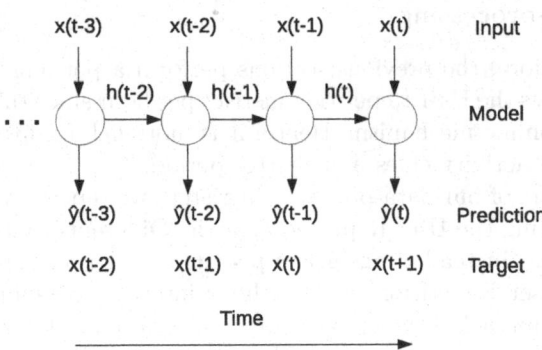

Fig. 6. Simple recurrent neural network model

RNNs are common in speech recognition, language modeling, stock price prediction, and other tasks based on time-series data [7]. The RNNs models have problems modeling long-term dependency, which means that they are not able to remember information for long periods [7]. One alternative is to use LSTM (Long Short-Term Memory) networks [22]. LSTM is a special type of RNN that can learn long-term dependency. To be able to do that, an LSTM cell has its internal states split into two, $h_{(t)}$ and $c_{(t)}$. We can consider the first one as a short-term state and the second one as a long-term state. The long-term state allows the LSTM to remember information for long periods. At each timestep, the LSTM updates the $c_{(t)}$ by forgetting unnecessary information and adding new ones.

Given the above discussion, we use an LSTM model in our case study. We implement this model using Keras and TensorFlow libraries[3]. Our architecture has two hidden layers and 128 neurons each. We use the TANH (Hyperbolic Tangent) activation function [23] in both layers and a dense layer in the output. We choose to use the ADAM optimization algorithm [13]. The model is trained during 300 epochs, using the infrastructure of Google Colaboratory[4].

Figure 7 shows a one-window example of our prediction during the test. This window is used to predict one hour in the future. At each time step in this window, we plot the input (i.e., the 24 consecutive User Repetitions), the correct value of our target (i.e., 24 target values), and the predictions made by our model (i.e., 24 predictions). We can see that our model gets close to the Target value in most of the points.

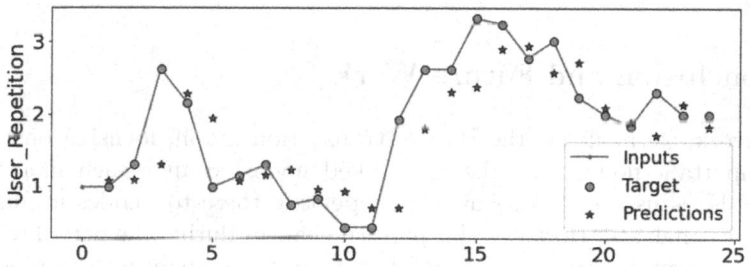

Fig. 7. User Repetition forecasting (1 h)

This case study also uses a trivial baseline solution adopted in the literature [10]. As mentioned before, our focus is to show a case study of the User Repetition metric and not investigate the best forecasting method. As we are dealing with a time-series, we choose to use as a baseline an approach where we consider the forecast at time $t + 1$ to be equal to the value at time t. It means that $y(t + 1) = y(t)$. For the two hour prediction, we use $y(t + 2) = y(t + 1) = y(t)$. We evaluate the RNN model's performance and the baseline using the MAE (Mean Absolute Error) and the RMSE (Root Mean-Square Error). MAE computes the absolute average distance between the real value and the predicted value. RMSE evaluates the root squared difference between the real value and the predicted value.

---

[3] https://www.tensorflow.org/.
[4] http://colab.research.google.com.

Table 2 shows the performance of both models, considering our test set. In this table, we also provide the error for the forecast 2 h in the future. We can see that the RNN model performs slightly better than the baseline model in both cases.

Table 2. Model evaluation

Metric	1 h		2 h	
	RNN	Baseline	RNN	Baseline
MAE	0.3650	0.3722	0.3990	0.4239
RMSE	0.4781	0.4998	0.5228	0.5646

In this section, we provided a case study using two approaches to forecast User Repetition. This analysis, together with the one made in Sect. 4, makes it possible for us to identify periods of suspicious activities by forecasting the User Repetition metric. For example, if the difference between our predicted and current User Repetition is high, we can consider that the network is in a suspicious state. If so, we can trigger a more detailed analysis to detect anomalous behavior.

6   Conclusion and Future Work

In this work, we analyzed the Bitcoin transaction graph, focusing on how the most important nodes (i.e., the top-ranked nodes) change each month. This analysis shows us a stable behavior in repeating these top nodes in almost all the months analyzed. However, this pattern changes during the period when Mt. Gox made its major number of fraudulent trades. We analyze the period where this pattern was changed by simulating new transactions in the network. This analysis gives us evidence that this change can be the consequence of market manipulation.

We also use an RNN model, together with a simples baseline one, to forecast User Repetition. As the results show, the RNN model was able to predict the behavior of our metric. With further analysis, the idea is that this prediction model can be extended to build an online model to identify periods of abnormal behavior.

As future work, we want to investigate the behavior of our metric in the entire blockchain to measure its ability to detect malicious activity. This analysis will also allow us to understand how facts not related to Bitcoin can influence our metrics. We also plan to perform the same analysis for other centrality metrics, such as Eigenvector Centrality and Closeness Centrality.

References

1. Blockchain.info: Bitcoin market price. https://blockchain.info/charts/market-price?timespan=all&format=json. Accessed March 2021

2. Chen, W., Wu, J., Zheng, Z., Chen, C., Zhou, Y.: Market manipulation of bitcoin: evidence from mining the Mt. Gox transaction network. In: IEEE Conference on Computer Communications (INFOCOM), pp. 964–972 (2019)
3. Cong, L.W., He, Z., Li, J.: Decentralized mining in centralized pools. Technical report, National Bureau of Economic Research (2019)
4. Fleder, M., Kester, M.S., Pillai, S.: Bitcoin transaction graph analysis. arXiv preprint arXiv:1502.01657 (2015)
5. Gandal, N., Hamrick, J., Moore, T., Oberman, T.: Price manipulation in the bitcoin ecosystem. J. Monet. Econ. **95**, 86–96 (2018)
6. Géron, A.: Neural networks and deep learning. O'Reilly (2018)
7. Géron, A.: Hands-on machine learning with scikit-learn, keras, and tensorflow: concepts, tools, and techniques to build intelligent systems. O'Reilly Media (2019)
8. Gervais, A., Karame, G.O., Capkun, V., Capkun, S.: Is bitcoin a decentralized currency? IEEE Secur. Priv. **12**(3), 54–60 (2014)
9. Hewamalage, H., Bergmeir, C., Bandara, K.: Recurrent neural networks for time series forecasting: current status and future directions. Int. J. Forecast. (2020)
10. Hyndman, R.J., Athanasopoulos, G.: Forecasting: Principles and Practice. OTexts (2018)
11. Juhász, P.L., Stéger, J., Kondor, D., Vattay, G.: A Bayesian approach to identify Bitcoin users. PloS one **13**(12) (2018)
12. Khalilov, M.C.K., Levi, A.: A survey on anonymity and privacy in bitcoin-like digital cash systems. IEEE Commun. Surv. Tutor. **20**(3), 2543–2585 (2018)
13. Kingma, D.P., Ba, J.: Adam: A method for stochastic optimization. arXiv preprint arXiv:1412.6980 (2014)
14. Kondor, D., Pósfai, M., Csabai, I., Vattay, G.: Do the rich get richer? An empirical analysis of the bitcoin transaction network. PloS one **9**(2) (2014)
15. Lischke, M., Fabian, B.: Analyzing the Bitcoin network: the first four years. Future Internet **8**(1), 7 (2016)
16. Maesa, D.D.F., Marino, A., Ricci, L.: An analysis of the bitcoin users graph: inferring unusual behaviours. In: International Workshop on Complex Networks and their Applications, pp. 749–760 (2016)
17. Maesa, D.D.F., Marino, A., Ricci, L.: Uncovering the Bitcoin blockchain: an analysis of the full users graph. In: 2016 IEEE International Conference on Data Science and Advanced Analytics (DSAA), pp. 537–546 (2016)
18. Maesa, D.D.F., Marino, A., Ricci, L.: Detecting artificial behaviours in the bitcoin users graph. Online Soc. Netw. Media **3**, 63–74 (2017)
19. Moore, T., Christin, N.: Beware the middleman: empirical analysis of bitcoin-exchange risk. In: International Conference on Financial Cryptography and Data Security, pp. 25–33 (2013)
20. Nakamoto, S.: Bitcoin: a peer-to-peer electronic cash system. Technical report, Manubot (2019)
21. Project, B.: Bitcoin core. https://bitcoin.org/en/bitcoin-core. Accessed March 2021
22. Quinn, J., McEachen, J., Fullan, M., Gardner, M., Drummy, M.: Dive Into Deep Learning: Tools for Engagement. Corwin Press, Thousand Oaks (2019)
23. Sharma, S.: Activation functions in neural networks. Towards Data Sci. **6** (2017)
24. Suberg, W.: Mt. Gox trial update: Karpeles admits willy bot existence. https://cointelegraph.com/news/mt-gox-trial-update-karpeles-admits-willy-bot-existence. Accessed March 2021

CBT Workshop: Smart Contracts and Anonymity

Augmenting MetaMask to Support TLS-endorsed Smart Contracts

Ulrich Gallersdörfer$^{(\boxtimes)}$ ⓘ, Jonas Ebel, and Florian Matthes

Technical University of Munich, Arcisstrasse 21, Munich, Germany
{ulrich.gallersdoerfer,jonas.ebel,matthes}@tum.de

Abstract. Users in blockchain systems are exposed to address replacement attacks due to the weak binding between websites and smart contracts, as they have no way to verify the authenticity of obtained addresses. Prior research introduced TLS-endorsed Smart Contracts (TeSC) that equip Smart Contracts with authentication information, proving the relation to the domain name of the respective website. For an efficient and user-friendly approach, this technology needs to be integrated with wallets. Based on the analysis of browser warnings regarding TLS-certificates, we augment MetaMask with the ability to detect TeSC and warn users if attack scenarios are detected. To evaluate our work, we conduct a study with 40 participants to show the effectiveness of TeSC to prevent address-replacement attacks and ensure the safe interaction of users and addresses.

Keywords: Ethereum · TLS · DNS · TeSC · PKI · MetaMask · Wallet

1 Introduction

Users face a highly hostile environment within blockchain-based systems. Many beginners are prone to deception, fraud, or other criminal activity, aiming to steal the user's funds. One type of attack that deals damage to a multitude of users is a so-called *address replacement attack*. These types of attacks try to convince the user to use a malicious address as the recipient of a transaction, resulting in loss of funds. One example of such attacks was the Coindash ICO.

Coindash launched an Initial Coin Offering, collecting funds to develop and extend their platform. Many users invested as they expected returns on this investment. Users sent their funds to the contract displayed on the webpage. Unfortunately, attackers replaced the address of the intended recipient with their own, leading to the loss of over 7 million USD worth of Ether [29]. There is no way to authenticate an address within a blockchain system or prove its connection to a Web 2.0 entity. As websites are often the starting point for blockchain interactions, the lack of authentication information is fatal.

Often, problems like this are mitigated by information redundance, e.g., publishing the correct address multiple times (e.g., in a newsletter and the website), leaving the responsibility to manually verify the correctness of the address to the

© Springer Nature Switzerland AG 2022
J. Garcia-Alfaro et al. (Eds.): DPM 2021/CBT 2021, LNCS 13140, pp. 227–244, 2022.
https://doi.org/10.1007/978-3-030-93944-1_15

user. In previous research, we solved the issue of loose coupling between Web 2.0 addresses and addresses within blockchain systems and proposed TLS-endorsed Smart Contracts [16]. We equip smart contracts with additional information that allows software (e.g., a wallet) to verify that a smart contract indeed belongs to a specific domain, eliminating the need for cross-verifying addresses. Even if the webserver is hacked or a second TLS-certificate for the same domain is obtained, attacks can be detected and mitigated. Our system currently aims at Ethereum, but the theoretical foundations can be applied to any blockchain that supports smart contracts. A more detailed introduction to the system is given in Sect. 2.

In this paper, we extend our previous work and propose a wallet implementation supporting this system. As our approach is based on TLS broadly adopted in browsers, we analyze security warnings in the most popular browsers, Firefox, Chrome, and Edge. We fork MetaMask, a well-known browser wallet, and augment it to support the validation of TLS-endorsed smart contracts. We evaluate our approach by conducting an experiment with 40 participants to understand whether the process helps in reducing the chance a user falls for an address replacement attack.

Our paper is structured as follows. In Sect. 2, we outline the technology introduced in previous work [16]. We discuss our analysis of browsers regarding TLS and other certificate warnings in Sect. 3. The design and implementation of our MetaMask augmentation is described in Sect. 4. We evaluate or prototype in Sect. 5 and conclude in Sect. 7.

2   Background

We discuss the usage of TLS-certificates in blockchain networks as outlined in [16]. We give an overview of the components of using TLS certificates in the context of blockchain, discuss the usage of endorsed smart contracts and elaborate on security concerns.

2.1   Components of the System

Endorsement. To use TLS certificates in the context of blockchains, it has to be understood how these certificates are applied. TLS certificates are used every time a client (e.g., a web browser) contacts a web server via HTTPS in a WWW context. The web server responds with a message signed with the private key belonging to the respective certificate. In the context of blockchains, we also need a form of signature. Together with the plaintext, we refer to the signature of the respective certificate's private key as **endorsement**.

An endorsement states that the certificate's owner intends that an address is acting on behalf or in his name. As the address in the signature also relates to cryptographic material (e.g., a private key belongs to the address), endorsements can be seen as *sub-certificates* directly aimed at addresses for blockchain networks. It is stored within the respective smart contract. For that, the endorsement contains the to-be endorsed address, the fully-qualified domain name, an expiry date, flags and a signature created by the private key of the respective certificate over the above mentioned fields. Flags allow for advanced settings, e.g., if subendorsements are allowed.

Verifier. The verifier is a software application that retrieves the endorsement from the contract and verifies its authenticity. For that, it considers three distinct properties. First, it obtains the certificate that signed the endorsement, verifies it, and if the certificate path is valid as well as it trusts the root certificate. Second, it verifies if the endorsement was created with the respective certificate and belongs to the address from which it was obtained. Third, it verifies if other properties are correct, such as the expiry date has not been passed. It applies further checks as we describe in Sect. 2.3.

Endorsement Registry. The endorsement registry stores an overview of smart contracts endorsed by domains. As the verifier relies on the registry for the detection of specific attack types (see Sect. 2.3), properties like integrity, authenticity, and availability must hold. For that reason, the registry is deployed as a separate smart contract in the blockchain in which the owner of the respective contract adds TLS-endorsed smart contracts. A logically centralized smart contract from which information cannot be deleted holds these properties mentioned above. Nonetheless, other system designs are also conceivable.

2.2   Usage of TLS-endorsed Smart Contracts

Most of the interactions of regular end-users start at a website. The user intends to use a decentralized application, for example, a decentralized exchange, and either uses the web app directly with a Web3.js-interface or copies the address displayed on the webpage directly into a wallet. The website itself can be targeted for attacks, and relevant addresses can be replaced without anyone noticing, leading to the so-called *address replacement attack*. The augmented wallet and the context of the webpage allows a simple verification if the respective address can be authenticated and belongs to the respective website.

2.3   Security Considerations

In our use case, there are two main ways to undermine the security of TLS-endorsed smart contracts. The first scenario is the result of a downgrade attack, e.g., the verifier does not know that there is a smart contract endorsed by the respective domain. The second scenario describes an attacker being able to obtain not only access to the website, but also to the private key of a certificate belonging to the domain. The discussion of further security questions can be found in previous work [16].

Downgrade Attack. If an attacker obtains access to the website and wants to replace an address, he would not link to a smart contract with an invalid endorsement but rather include no endorsement at all. For that, the verifier needs to know whether endorsed smart contracts exist for a given domain. Because of the existence of the registry that keeps track of all endorsed smart contracts, the verifier can check if previously endorsed smart contracts exist and warn the user. It can be assumed that if an owner of a website endorses one smart contract, all other smart contracts the domain is referencing should be endorsed, too. Therefore warning the user can prevent a successful downgrade attack.

Website Ownership Impersonation. An attacker could try either to get direct access to the private keys on the server (e.g., through privilege escalation) or generate a new valid certificate through means such as the Automatic Certificate Management Environment (ACME) [8] or Certificate Signing Requests (CSR) [18][1]. While there is no way to prevent the attacker to impersonate the ownership of the website, as the verifier cannot differentiate between a maliciously issued and a regularly issued certificate, the attack can be detected by the owner of the domain. It is possible to monitor for new smart contracts being created and endorsed by a respective domain. The domain owner (or a trusted third party) is able to look out for such new contracts and warn the respective owner that a new valid endorsed contract was deployed on the blockchain. The domain owner can then react to this incident and take the necessary steps to reverse the effects of the attack.

3   Analysis

This section we analyze the warning indications in browsers. Our prototype adopts several aspects of their concepts. Then, we evaluate which errors can occur during the authentication algorithm of TeSC.

3.1   Browser Warnings and Security Indicator Designs

We evaluate Mozilla Firefox, Google Chrome, and Microsoft Edge, three out of the four most used desktop browsers to date [3]. To analyze the browser during different states, we need to induce different certificate validation states. A description of potential certificate or protocol errors can be found in the related GitHub repository [15]. The Chromium project provides a testing page at *badssl.com* that triggers several browser errors [17]. Additionally, we generate certificates manually with OpenSSL [21] for each state that is not covered by the web page.

Positive Indication in Browsers. According to RFC 8446 [25], the browser can trust the server's certificate after a successful HTTPS message exchange. Otherwise, an error would have occurred. The browser indicates this secure state to the user.

When the connection is secure, all three browsers show a lock icon next to the web address. The design does not show many differences between Firefox,

---

[1] These systems usually require a proof of control for the respective domain, e.g., being able to place files in specific paths.

Edge, and Chrome. The ancillary shield icon in Firefox provides a privacy utility unrelated to HTTPS and X.509 certificates. All browsers choose different
approaches to highlight sub-parts of the URL.

The user can click on the lock symbol, and a popup shows up for all three
browsers. The popups state with a green text that the connection is secure. In
Chrome and Edge, the user can inspect the certificate in a system-specific tool
when s/he clicks on the popup's certificate entry, in Firefox a second page allows
to further inspect the certificate.

3.2 Negative Indication in Browsers

Firefox. We identify two different types of error pages in Firefox. We define the
first type as an overridable error page. This type has two stages: The first stage
informs about a potential security risk. If the user accesses the second stage
with the *advanced* button, an explanation of the root cause of the error becomes
available. Depending on the error, the user can resolve some of the errors that
are causing this page to show up. If that is the case, the second stage displays
an explanatory sentence. The user can always ignore the error and continue to
the page. A yellow frame highlights the warning visually on both stages.

Firefox displays the second error type on critical failures. This type of screen
has no yellow border and only one stage. The user cannot resolve or ignore this
issue. Thus, the explanation of a root cause is reduced to one sentence with
a remark that s/he may contact the website owner for resolution. The most
apparent difference to the overridable error is the missing yellow frame. Other
differences become apparent when we compare the conceptual models.

To understand the user interface concept on an abstract level, we develop
conceptual models following the framework for interactive systems by Parush [23]
for Firefox, Chrome and our augmented MetaMask model. We display the model
of Parush's iterative process halted at the configuration level. For brevity reasons,
we include all modes in the related GitHub repository [15].

Negative Indication in Chrome & Edge. The browsers Google Chrome and
Microsoft Edge are both based on the open-source project Chromium. Thus, the
general behavior is very much alike. Therefore, all referrals to Chrome's user
interface also apply to Edge unless stated otherwise.

Chrome has one general design concept for all certificate-caused errors. The
page has two stages. The first one warns the user that the connection is not
private and what the attackers can do. It displays the error code, has a button
to show the second stage, and a button to get back to the previous secure page.
The content of the second stage is dependent on the current error code and
explains the technical reason for the error in more detail. Depending on the
error code, the user might proceed visiting the respective website.

The conceptual model of chrome's error page is comparable to Firefox's overridable error page. The two-stages mode is present, and the error can only be
ignored on the second stage, while the user can always go back to a secure
page on both stages. Additionally, both browsers have a conceptual separation

between a general-purpose warning on the first stage and a more detailed technical explanation on the second stage.

3.3   Indication of a Protocol Downgrade

A protocol downgrade means that the browser is unable to establish HTTPS. In that case, a plain HTTP connection transports the information in an unsafe and unauthenticated manner. However, because the adoption of HTTPS is not high enough to block the older HTTP protocol entirely, the browsers show only a passive negative indication. In Firefox, the lock symbol, which would indicate a positive security state, is crossed out with a red line. Both Chrome and Edge display the same warning symbol as in an error case but without any colors.

3.4   Authentication Error Scenarios for TLS-endorsed Smart Contracts

Authentication errors within the newly proposed system can be attributed to two different causes: 1) Protocol errors that are newly introduced solely because of the design of TLS-endorsed Smart Contracts and 2) Errors that stem from the certificate, standardized in RFC 5280 [9].

Protocol Errors. Analyzing our protocol yields different forms of errors. We assume that the analyzed smart contract is compliant to the protocol. First, we evaluate errors that are the result of faulty data stored in the endorsement: The address of the contract and the endorsement could deviate. The endorsement could be expired. The signature could be corrupt or not signed by the respective domain. Flags set in the endorsement could result in an error.

Second, we analyze errors that could result from the interaction of the verifier with other entities: The verifier retrieves the certificate from the respective domain. If this certificate is not available, the protocol cannot continue.

Third, we analyze errors that could result from the verifier's internal processes: The public key in the certificate and the signature in the endorsement allow verifying that the endorsement's claims are legit and that the certificate's owner has signed and thus created the endorsement. If this verification fails, TeSC cannot establish the receiver's authenticity.

Fourth, there are errors in which the global state of endorsed smart contracts needs to be considered: To help the user understand downgrade errors of the protocol, we specify a protocol downgrade algorithm. The algorithm decides whether MetaMask should interrupt the user actively or only show a passive negative indication. It assumes that in most cases, the user manually retrieves the receiver's address from a website, or a decentralized web application triggers the transaction programmatically. Hence, most transactions in MetaMask originate from the context of a current webpage, where the owner of the website controls the information about the receiving address and a mismatch between website domain and endorsement indicates a higher risk. These errors need to be displayed to the user accordingly.

The algorithm also considers the known TeSC registration of the website's domain. This aspect allows assessing the threat level more exhaustively. The algorithm only perceives an address mismatch as dangerous if the website's domain is already bound to an Ethereum address. The receiver seems to be unfitting if the website is known to endorse a different Ethereum address than the transaction receiver. However, if the domain's endorsement behavior is unknown, MetaMask cannot determine whether a different Ethereum address would be more plausible in the current context. In that case, MetaMask should only indicate the downgraded security to the user with a passive indication.

The algorithm results in three different error states:

A Downgrade Attack. happens if the website's domain is bound to a different Ethereum address. It is not relevant whether another domain endorses the receiving address or it is not TeSC compliant. **An Address Mismatch** happens if the receiver's address is TeSC compliant, but the domain of the current website, which is not listed in the TeSC registry, does not endorse it. Finally, if the website is not listed in the TeSC registry and the receiver's address is not TeSC compliant, the algorithm resolves to a **Downgrade Warning**.

Certificate Errors. The verification process also evaluates the certificate of the domain on its internal validity. Trusted authorities must sign it, and the endorsed domain must match the subject of the certificate. During this process, many different errors may occur. These are discussed in detail in RFC 5280 [9]. To complement this set of errors, we also consider error states defined in RFC 8446 [25], which describes TLS v1.3. For brevity, we outline errors in the associated GitHub repository [15].

4   Design and Implementation

In this section, we discuss the design concept in MetaMask we propose to communicate the authentication state to the user. Then, we describe the integration of TeSC in MetaMask.

4.1   Design Concept for TLS-endorsed Smart Contracts in MetaMask

For any new to-be signed transaction, MetaMask shows a confirmation screen to the user before it signs and submits the transaction to the Ethereum network. The user cannot edit the transaction on this confirmation screen but may reject it or return to the previous pages. After MetaMask has evaluated the transaction parameters, it shows this confirmation page. We augment this confirmation screen with an indicator to communicate the TLS-dependent validation state. We replace the confirmation screen with a warning page if the protocol throws any errors.

For communicating the protocol state to the user, we define a positive state indication, a passive warning indicator in case of a protocol downgrade, and a conceptual model for interrupting the user in a potentially dangerous situation.

The best-case scenario from a user's perspective is a successful authentication of the receiving address. The protocol established the correct binding between the current browser page and the receiver's Ethereum address. Thus, this binding shall be made visible by placing the domain name and the address next to each other. Such a close placement supports the user in considering whether s/he expects this binding to exist for the current transaction. We follow the passive positive indication known from the browsers when we place a green tick next to the addresses. The browsers use a lock symbol to indicate a connection, which HTTPS protects in terms of confidentiality, message integrity, and end-point authentication. However, our protocol does not provide the features of a protected communication channel. Thus, we choose a tick instead. If the user hovers over the symbol, a popup confirms the identification of the receiver. The current confirmation screen of MetaMask already displays the receiver's address on its top.

If the receiver's address does not abide by the TLS-endorsed smart contract interface, MetaMask cannot perform the authentication. In that case, the transaction is in an insecure but not necessarily dangerous state. The user must manually verify whether the receiving address can be trusted. To indicate the negative state, we show a yellow warning indicator next to the receiver's address instead of the tick symbol. MetaMask also uses the symbol in other warning messages. If s/he hovers over the symbol, a message explains that the user has to verify whether this is the correct receiving address. Figure 1 shows both the upper half of the confirmation screen and the yellow warning sign for the erroneous case.

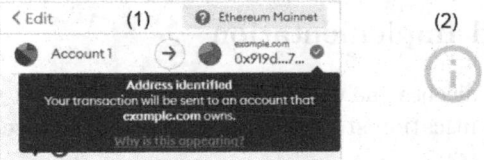

Fig. 1. Positive (1) and warning state (2) indication in MetaMask's confirm screen

Any other error is communicated with an active interruption of the user. If such an error occurs, the transaction is in a potentially dangerous state. We design a general page and base it on a conceptual model from the previous browser analysis. The model has a two-stages approach. First, it stops the user during a dangerous transaction. A general warning message is displayed, and the user may access an additional informational page. On the second stage, the user reads more about the technical cause of the error and gets informed what s/he can do about it. The user may always "go back to safety", i.e., cancel the transaction on both stages. However, to ignore the transaction, s/he has to be on the second stage. The conceptual model is closely related to both Firefox's and Chrome's HTTPS error pages.

We explain the instantiation of the conceptual model using the example of an *expired endorsement error* displayed in Fig. 2. At the bottom of the error screen are always two buttons available: "show/hide advanced" opens and closes the second stage; "cancel" aborts the transaction. Similar to Chromium-based browsers, we highlight the cancel button as the main action. This action is the safest option the user can choose.

Between the buttons and the information about the transaction, an area is reserved for the two stages. The first stage summarizes the current situation. The stage shows the error code, and a link forwards to a general information page. This page informs about TeSC in general and each error code in detail. The warning's design is inspired by Chrome's error pages due to its comprehensive error design. The second stage explains the error. A bold text highlights the main reason for the error. If the error is overridable, the text ends with a link that allows ignoring the error and continuing to the confirmation screen. If the user proceeds, MetaMask shows only a passive warning indicator on the subsequent confirmation screen. The content of the second stage depends on the error type of the TeSC validation. The reference implementation adds an overview for all texts of the second stage based on their error type [15]. It also defines whether a user may override an error or not.

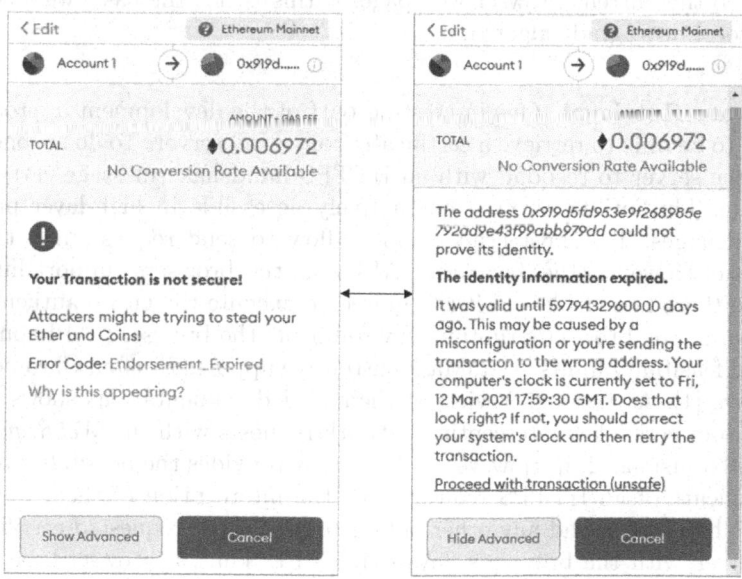

Fig. 2. Error page in MetaMask if a TeSC endorsement has expired

4.2   Integration of TeSC in MetaMask

To evaluate our previous design concept and scrutinize the technical feasibility of authenticating Ethereum accounts with our protocol, we extend the existing MetaMask application with our verification logic. At the time of this work, MetaMask's current version was 9.0.3 [14]. In this section, we discuss the verification flow and some technical details. As not all technical details are relevant, we highlight some insights that arised during development.

The Verification Flow. The metadata of an unapproved transaction must be added to MetaMask's state management before it shows the confirmation screen, where the user may accept or cancel the transaction. Based on our previous work, we develop the verification logic [15]. The algorithm expects the receiving address as input and the current web page serving as the point of reference. The algorithm determines whether a smart contract exists at the given Ethereum address that abides by the TeSC interface. If that is not the case, the protocol downgrade algorithm defined in Sect. 3.4 determines a suitable warning message for the user. If the address implements the interface, MetaMask retrieves the claims of the endorsement. The method evaluates the expiry date and some additional flag. The algorithm requests a valid TLS certificate from the domain that the receiver's address claims to be endorsed by. Given a certificate is available and trusted, the signature of the endorsement is evaluated. If all steps are successful, the endorsement is generally valid. Finally, we assert that the endorsing domain is equal to the current browser web page. If this is not the case, we forward to the protocol downgrade algorithm.

Certificate Retrieval. One interesting part of the development approach was the goal to be able to retrieve a certificate from a webserver. To do so, one has to trigger the server to respond with an HTTPS handshake message carrying the certificate. This utility is often not natively accessible in high-layer programming languages. The JavaScript engines allow to send requests and trigger a handshake. However, the JavaScript API that the browsers support limits the access to these handshakes. If it is required to execute the entire authentication algorithm in the browser's runtime environment, the browser's API constitutes technical feasibility limits. MetaMask currently supports Firefox, Chrome, Edge, and Brave [1]. A thorough review of their API documentations shows that all of these browsers allow intercepting network requests with the *WebRequest* API for WebExtensions [2,4]. However, only Firefox provides the possibility to access the certificate of an HTTPS request with the interception of the WebRequest API. We have not found any other option to access the requested certificates of a webserver with the browser's JavaScript API. Thus, a browser-based implementation of the certificate retrieval is only feasible with Firefox. Other browsers do not support the method *getSecurityInfo*. Therefore, it is not possible in the Chromium-based browsers to access a certificate. Thus, an alternative would be a server-based approach where MetaMasks forwards the request to a suitable server that handles certificate retrieval for the given domain. As this increases complexity and promote centralization, we do not further discuss this approach and recognize this as limitiation in our work.

5   Evaluation

After developing our prototype, we need to evaluate if our proposition improves the user's security within Ethereum. For this, we evaluate our prototype with a user study of 40 participants. Each participant is required to interact with MetaMask and our prototype. In this study, the user enters the address manually (usually copy/paste) from the website into MetaMask. While the user is repeating the transaction several times, we induce a Downgrade Attack. We choose this type of error because it could be detectable without using TeSC: the deviating address should alert the participant. Additionally, we suspect that this error would have shown during the Coindash attack, which we describe in the introduction.

5.1   Test Setup

Test users connect from their own devices, using RDP to our Windows server instance. On the desktop, we store three PDF documents containing instructions. Two of them contain a link to an imaginary enterprise called *greatcoin.io*, which simulates an initial coin offering. We augment the server and the Firefox instances with Nginx and self-signed certificates, such that the respective websites work as intended.

The Windows server has installed two different Firefox instances: the regular one and the Firefox Developer Edition, one for each version of MetaMask. Both MetaMask instances connect to a private test chain that we run on an additional server instance. We configure each MetaMask with the same Ethereum account, which owns two ether for each test run.

The test chain contains three contracts, one TeSC-compliant, one registry contract and one attacker contract. The TeSC-compliant contract is endorsed by certificate of GreatCoin.io. The smart contract addresses are randomly chosen, there is no overlap of beginning or ending characters [15]. Users comparing the addresses should have no difficulty to spot that they are different.

5.2   Test Procedure

To determine the efficiency of our prototype, we use an A/B-testing design. Thus, we compare the participant's ability to detect an attack if s/he uses the original MetaMask or our augmented prototype. Each participant receives both treatments during the experiment: the original MetaMask and the prototype. Therefore, the measurement is within-subjects. To control biasing the user's response based on the treatments' order, we randomly assign the order to each participant. The tasks for the participants is independent of the order of treatments.

We ensure that all participants have at least an elementary understanding of the technology. Thus, the experiment starts with an informational document that explains the basics of Ethereum and MetaMask. After the participant has read this information, we show where to find MetaMask in the browser and how to access it.

Then, we describe with an additional text a scenario during which the participants shall execute a transaction. In this text we have to make sure that s/he is still aware of the possibility of losing funds if something goes wrong. Therefore, the text of the scenario establishes a trusted friend named Alice. The document highlights that the participant is willing to invest his/her ether in high-risk ventures. Alice recommends an investment in a cryptocurrency that is called "GreatCoin". The text ends with a mail that Alice sends. The e-mail contains a link to the enterprise's homepage and the Ethereum address of Great-Coin's smart contract. Alice also states that the participant is bearing the risk all by him/herself.

With this background information, the experimenters ask the participants to project themselves in this situation and start interacting with the system. Eventually, they open the link in the mail to investigate the proposed investment. While the page provides some information about the coin, secondary sources of information, such as Etherscan or blog posts, are not available. If the participant asks for such information, the experiment's conductors tell them that they should assume to find compelling information about the enterprise in general. We do not answer any questions about our assessment of the situation: e.g., "Is this secure?" should be answered by asking the participant to decide this as s/he would in a real-life situation.

After the successful transaction, the participants read a second text, which further extends the scenario. It states that the first investment proves to be profitable. It also contains a new mail, which Alice sends a couple of days later. Alice suggests an additional offer that the enterprise extends to its early investors. The mail contains a new link for this offer. We also include the previous mail, which contains the Ethereum address of the previous investment.

When the participants open the provided link, the website is similar to the previous one with differences: The text highlights that this is a special offer for GreatCoin's early investors and the displayed Ethereum address is different. This Ethereum address points to the malicious contract that is not associated with GreatCoin in any way. If the participants transact their ether to this address, they lose their funds. Depending on the current treatment, i.e. the MetaMask instance, a transaction to this address is interrupted with a TeSC error. We measure the conversion rate, whether the user will confirm the transaction or is reluctant to do so.

After this second transaction, we request the participants to answer the first half of a survey. We ask about the participant's experience with blockchain and his/her perception of any errors that might have happened. After that, the participant repeats the entire scenario with both transactions while s/he is unknowingly exposed to a different MetaMask instance. After this second treatment, we ask the participants to finish the survey. Then, we wrap up the experiment and answer any questions the participants might have.

5.3   Result Analysis

As a result of the experiment, we collect two different data sets. The experimenters observe whether the participant recognizes the attack with the TeSC MetaMask and with the original MetaMask. Additionally, they note open text observations about significant events. A questionnaire serves as a complementary source of data. It asks the participants about demographic factors, their previous knowledge of blockchain, and the attendants' understanding of the TeSC errors. For that reason, there are three questions: whether the user noticed an error, what s/he believes was the cause of the error, and why s/he canceled the transaction or ignored the error.

Sample Demographics. Overall we test 40 participants. We recruit them from various places. We ask students of a course about blockchain at **blinded university** to participate. Other respondents are associated with the **blinded blockchain-focused association**. Additionally, the authors approach personal networks to include participants without a technical background in the sample. This inclusion facilitates a broad knowledge pool in the sample. We assume that prior experience with blockchain correlates with the ability to recognize a fraudulent Ethereum address.

Our sample overrepresents the age group of people between 20 and 30, potentially limiting the applicability of our results for older generations. More than 75% of the participants have either a Bachelor's or a Master's degree, and everyone has attended high school or an advanced degree. Regarding prior knowledge about blockchain, the group with previous experience and the group that never worked with the technology are almost the same size. From the subset with previous experience, three participants state that they were developing a blockchain themselves. Five explain they developed applications, which use a blockchain platform. The rest of the subset has interacted with one.

Security Performance of the TeSC Warning. We compare the security of the original MetaMask with our prototype. We are interested in the ability of the participants to notice a dangerous transaction. Thus, we measure the task conversion rate for both MetaMask instances. The task is to detect that the transaction is dangerous and cancel it. Table 1 shows the contingency table of the user behavior during the fraudulent transaction on both applications. Twenty-nine users cancel the dangerous transaction with TeSC but execute the transaction with the original MetaMask. Simultaneously, no one recognizes the error without TeSC but transacts to the fraudulent address when MetaMask shows a TeSC error. We see four participants who do not transact to this address with either one of the MetaMask instances. Finally, seven participants send the transaction in the original MetaMask and if the wallet shows a TeSC error. Thus, these participants would have lost their funds using the augmented wallet.

To determine whether the different behavior between both applications is significant, we use a McNemar test statistic to determine the p-value. As there

is no participant recognizing the error without TeSC but with TeSC s/he transacts to the address, the calculation for the p-value of the exact McNemar test:
$p(0) = \frac{29!}{0!(29-0)!}0.5^0(1 - 0.5)^{(29-0)} = 1.862645e^{-9}$. Thus we can reject the null
hypothesis that the proportion between the two discordant pairs is 0.5 with a
significance level beyond $\alpha = 0.001$. Thus, the communication of the TeSC state
helps significantly to increase the security of users that attackers try tricking
into transacting to a fraudulent Ethereum address.

To further analyze the performance, we estimate the probability that users
will abide by a downgrade attack warning that MetaMask displays. We present
two confidence intervals because there are two groups of participants: one starts
the experiment by working with the original MetaMask instance, the other begins
with the prototype of this thesis. Both have exposure to the augmented Meta-
Mask instance, but the random order of treatments requires this separation.

We estimate the confidence intervals with the help of the adjusted Wald methods by Agresti and Coull [6]. The significance level is at alpha = 0.05. Table 2
shows the values of the confidence intervals. As one can see, both intervals spread
over an area of 32.5% respectively 34.7%. A study with more participants could
decrease the interval's width. In general, the results show that most participants
are not willing to send a transaction on a TeSC error as the lower bound is
above 50%. The upper bounds are 92.5% respectively 95.6%. The data does not
suggest that we should dismiss the concept, but it is ambiguous whether the
proposed solution enhances the user's security sufficiently or whether additional
measures need to supplement it. It is certainly interesting to investigate this
question further.

The experiment uncovers a particular user behavior. We identify two particular elements which we deemed to be not an obvious choice, besides the two-stages
warning page.

If the user hovers over the TeSC indicator, a popup provides some additional
information on the current evaluation state. We consider this a *hidden feature*
because the indicator's design does not reveal the popup's existence. Thus, the
user must discover the popup merely by accident. The data in the figure confirms
its invisibility. In total, only nine participants look at the popup. We expected
such low attention for the UI element. Thus, the popup does not provide information that is not already available on the warning page.

Table 1. Paired behaviour when participants encounter a fraudulent transaction.

	Cancel in MetaMask with TeSC	Confirm in MetaMask with TeSC
Cancel in MetaMask v9.0.3	4	0
Confirm in MetaMask v9.0.3	29	7

Table 2. Confidence intervals of probability that users adhere to the TeSC warning

	Lower bound	Upper bound
Starting with TeSC	57.8 %	92.5 %
Starting without TeSC	63.1 %	95.6 %

While the popup affirms our assumption to be a feature that is seldomly noted, the explanation page attracts more interest from the participants than we assumed. Overall, 27 users open the external informational site. The page provides a general explanation of TeSC and discusses technical details about the cause of each error. Its design is not yet optimized for usability, which also some participants remark. A production-grade implementation of TeSC authentication should reiterate this page.

We also observe that only eleven participants do neither use the explanation page nor the popup. These participants gain enough information from the two-stages warning sites to decide whether they want to continue with the transaction. We cannot identify one approach to be significantly better to hinder the user from transacting to the fraudulent address. Two participants confirm the transaction considering only MetaMask's warning. Additionally, two participants, who access the popup, and two participants opening the explanation page ignore the warning. One participant transacts to the fraudulent address after looking at the popup and the explanation page.

6 Related Work

The design concept in this work is heavily influenced by the security indicator designs found in the browser. Hence, we provide an overview of different seminal papers that contribute insights on design principles and uncover ineffective concepts of browser designs.

Early research efforts rely on controlled group experiments. The results show in general an ineffective security design. The users are unable to identify fraudulent pages based on the browser's indication [12]. They do not notice passive indicators [26]. Research also shows that some users cannot comprehend the warning situation and cannot make an informed decision [10,11]. Additionally, a high false-positive rate of active warning messages due to the low adoption of HTTPS leads to the users' habituation and eventually ignorance of actual errors [19,22].

Later research efforts leveraging field studies find an improved adherence to browser warnings [7]. The researchers emphasize that the warnings should be more context-specific and provide a classification of causes for browser warnings [5,24].

Part of the discussion is the usage of passive warnings. Thompson et al. emphasize that the browser should display an active negative warning in case of certificate errors, as the passive warnings are often ignored by the users. [28]

Jelovčan et al. review literature on security indicators and show that researchers agree that passive indicators are not effective means to stop users from interacting with fraudulent pages. However, there are findings that these indicators can be an efficient part of a greater security design concept [20].

Another issue is the warning's comprehensibility. Researchers identify a gap between novice and advanced user's behavior as the advanced users are able to comprehend these warnings, while novice users cannot [10]. Researchers show that Chrome's error messages are not understandable for most users because the terms are too technical. [27,30] Felt et al. improve the warning adherence with a text that is "simple, non-technical, brief and specific" [13].

We concluded from these findings to focus on active negative warnings with understandable explanations, interrupting the user if a valid error scenario occurs. We include a passive indication in the security concept to support the warning purpose further. With this passive indication we thrive to control effects of habituation to high-frequent warnings due to the low adoption of TeSC.

7   Conclusion

In this paper, we describe our approach to augment the Ethereum-based wallet MetaMask to support TLS-endorsed Smart Contracts to prevent *address-replacement attacks*. These attacks trick the user into sending their coins to addresses they do not intend to. We first analyze the behavior of popular browsers such as Mozilla Firefox, Google Chrome, and Microsoft Edge how they behave in case of certificate or protocol errors in X.509 and TLS protocols. We then outline how we design and implement positive and negative indicators and warnings in MetaMask and discuss implementation-specific details. We analyze our prototype by conducting a user study with 40 participants that receive treatments with and without our augmentation in a scenario in which an address-replacement attack occurs.

Our work shows that users are vulnerable to address replacement attacks and that our approach helps reducing the damage resulting from such attacks. We further provide the first prototype to include such verification in a browser-based wallet. The augmented prototype is limited to Firefox only; due to other browsers' inability to access HTTPS certificates, a third-party service is required for other browsers to retrieve certificates.

Future works can aim at different perspectives: Certificate retrieval and trustworthy third parties that allow browser wallets to access respective information can help mitigate the limitations mentioned above, allowing the usage of the system in other browsers. Certificate Transparency (CT) also has potential ways to access issued certificates and use them for evaluating the state of a TLS-endorsed Smart Contract. Due to the Merkle-tree structure, direct search and access of certificates is still a problem. Final, other systems such as the Ethereum Name Service (ENS) map human-readable names to Ethereum addresses. Combining these approaches could yield more trustworthy on-chain identities.

References

1. MetaMask. https://metamask.io/download.html
2. chrome.webrequest   (2021).   https://developer.chrome.com/docs/extensions/reference/webRequest/
3. Desktop browser market share worldwide (2021). https://gs.statcounter.com/browser-market-share/desktop/worldwide. Accessed 28 July 2021
4. Webextensions api (2021). https://developer.mozilla.org/en-US/docs/Mozilla/Add-ons/WebExtensions/API/webRequest
5. Acer, M.E., et al.: Where the wild warnings are. In: Thuraisingham, B. (ed.) Proceedings of the 2017 ACM SIGSAC Conference on Computer and Communications Security, pp. 1407–1420. Association for Computing Machinery (2017). https://doi.org/10.1145/3133956.3134007
6. Agresti, A., Coull, B.A.: Approximate is better than exact for interval estimation of binomial proportions. Am. Stat. **52**(2), 119 (1998). https://doi.org/10.2307/2685469
7. Akhawe, D., Felt, A.P.: Alice in warningland: a large-scale field study of browser security warning effectiveness. In: King, S. (ed.) 22nd USENIX Security Symposium, pp. 257–272. Usenix Association (2013). cited By :164 Export Date: 15 October 2020 Conference Paper
8. Barnes, R., Hoffman-Andrews, J., Kasten, J.: Automatic certificate management environment (acme). Internet-Draft draft-ietf-acme-acme-09, IETF Secretariat (2017)
9. Boeyen, S., Santesson, S., Polk, T., Housley, R., Farrell, S., Cooper, D.: Internet X.509 Public Key Infrastructure Certificate and Certificate Revocation List (CRL) Profile. RFC 5280 (May 2008). https://doi.org/10.17487/RFC5280, https://rfc-editor.org/rfc/rfc5280.txt
10. Bravo-Lillo, C., Cranor, L.F., Downs, J., Komanduri, S.: Bridging the gap in computer security warnings: a mental model approach. IEEE Secur. Priv. Mag. **9**(2), 18–26 (2011). https://doi.org/10.1109/MSP.2010.198
11. Bravo-Lillo, C., Cranor, L.F., Downs, J., Komanduri, S., Sleeper, M.: Improving computer security dialogs. In: Campos, P., Graham, N., Jorge, J., Nunes, N., Palanque, P., Winckler, M. (eds.) INTERACT 2011. LNCS, vol. 6949, pp. 18–35. Springer, Heidelberg (2011). https://doi.org/10.1007/978-3-642-23768-3_2
12. Dhamija, R., Tygar, J.D., Hearst, M.: Why phishing works. In: Grinter, R. (ed.) Proceedings of the SIGCHI Conference on Human Factors in Computing Systems, p. 581. ACM Special Interest Group on Computer-Human Interaction, ACM (2006). https://doi.org/10.1145/1124772.1124861
13. Felt, A.P., et al.: Improving ssl warnings. In: Kim, J. (ed.) Proceedings of the 33rd Annual CHI Conference on Human Factors in Computing Systems, pp. 2893–2902. ACM (2015). https://doi.org/10.1145/2702123.2702442
14. Finlay, D., et al.: MetaMask-extension (2020). https://github.com/MetaMask/metamask-extension
15. Gallersdörfer, U., Ebel, J., Matthes, F.: Additional material to paper augmenting metamask to support tls-endorsed smart contracts (2021). https://github.com/UliGall/paper-tesc-metamask. Accessed 2 Aug 2021
16. Gallersdörfer, U., Matthes, F.: TeSC: TLS/SSL-certificate endorsed smart contracts. In: 2021 IEEE International Conference on Decentralized Applications and Infrastructures (DAPPS), pp. 95–100 (2021). https://doi.org/10.1109/DAPPS52256.2021.00016

17. Garron, L., et al.: badssl.com (2020). https://github.com/chromium/badssl.com
18. Grajek, G., Moore, S., Lambiase, M.: Method and system for generating digital certificates and certificate signing requests (Jun 3 2010). uS Patent App. 12/326,002
19. Holz, R., Braun, L., Kammenhuber, N., Carle, G.: The ssl landscape. In: Thiran, P. (ed.) Proceedings of the 2011 ACM SIGCOMM Conference on Internet Measurement Conference, p. 427. ACM Special Interest Group on Measurement and Evaluation, ACM (2011). https://doi.org/10.1145/2068816.2068856
20. Jelovčan, L., Vrhovec, S., Mihelič, A.: A literature survey of security indicators in web browsers. Elektrotehniški vestnik **87**(1–2), 31–38 (2020). export Date: 7 October 2020 Review CODEN: ELVEA Correspondence Address: Mihelič, A.; University of Maribor, Faculty of Criminal Justice and Security, Kotnikova 8, Slovenia; email: anze.mihelic@um.si
21. Kaduk, B., et al.: Openssl (2021). https://www.openssl.org/
22. Maurer, M.-E., De Luca, A., Stockinger, T.: Shining chrome: using web browser personas to enhance SSL certificate visualization. In: Campos, P., Graham, N., Jorge, J., Nunes, N., Palanque, P., Winckler, M. (eds.) INTERACT 2011. LNCS, vol. 6949, pp. 44–51. Springer, Heidelberg (2011). https://doi.org/10.1007/978-3-642-23768-3_4
23. Parush, A.: Conceptual Design for Interactive Systems, first edn. Morgan Kaufmann, Burlington (2015)
24. Reeder, R.W., Felt, A.P., Consolvo, S., Malkin, N., Thompson, C., Egelman, S.: An experience sampling study of user reactions to browser warnings in the field. In: Mandryk, R., Hancock, M. (eds.) Engage with CHI, pp. 1–13. The Association for Computing Machinery (2018). https://doi.org/10.1145/3173574.3174086
25. Rescorla, E.: The Transport Layer Security (TLS) Protocol Version 1.3. RFC 8446 (August 2018). https://doi.org/10.17487/RFC8446, https://rfc-editor.org/rfc/rfc8446.txt
26. Sobey, J., Biddle, R., van Oorschot, P.C., Patrick, A.S.: Exploring user reactions to new browser cues for extended validation certificates. In: Jajodia, S., Lopez, J. (eds.) ESORICS 2008. LNCS, vol. 5283, pp. 411–427. Springer, Heidelberg (2008). https://doi.org/10.1007/978-3-540-88313-5_27
27. Stojmenović, M., Oyelowo, T., Tkaczyk, A., Biddle, R.: Building website certificate mental models. In: Ham, J., Karapanos, E., Morita, P.P., Burns, C.M. (eds.) PERSUASIVE 2018. LNCS, vol. 10809, pp. 242–254. Springer, Cham (2018). https://doi.org/10.1007/978-3-319-78978-1_20
28. Thompson, C., Shelton, M., Stark, E., Walker, M., Schechter, E., Porter Felt, A.: The web's identity crisis: understanding the effectiveness of website identity indicators. In: Proceedings of 28th USENIX, pp. 1715–1732 (2019)
29. Wieczner, J.: Ethereum: CoinDash ICO Hacked, $7 Million in Ether Stolen | Fortune (2017). https://fortune.com/2017/07/18/ethereum-coindash-ico-hack/
30. Yi, C.L.X., Zaaba, Z.F., Aminuddin, M.A.I.M.: Appraisal on user's comprehension in security warning dialogs: browsers usability perspective. In: Anbar, M., Abdullah, N., Manickam, S. (eds.) ACeS 2019. CCIS, vol. 1132, pp. 320–334. Springer, Singapore (2020). https://doi.org/10.1007/978-981-15-2693-0_23

Smart Contracts for Incentivized Outsourcing of Computation

Alptekin Küpçü[1]([✉]) and Reihaneh Safavi-Naini[2]

[1] Koç University, İstanbul, Turkey
kupcu@acm.org
[2] University of Calgary, Calgary, Alberta, Canada

Abstract. Outsourcing computation allows a resource limited client to expand its computational capabilities by outsourcing computation to other computing nodes or clouds. A basic requirement of outsourcing is providing assurance that the computation result is correct. We consider a smart contract based outsourcing system that achieves assurance by replicating the computation on two servers, and accepts the computation result if the two responses match. Correct computation result is obtained by using incentivization to instigate correct behaviour in servers. We show that all previous replication based incentivized outsourcing protocols with proven correctness fail when automated by a smart contract, because of the copy attack where a contractor simply copies the submitted response of the other contractor. We then design an incentivization mechanism that uses two lightweight challenge-response protocols that are used when the submitted results are compared, and employs monetary rewards, fines, and bounties to incentivize correct computation. We use game theory to model and analyze our mechanism, and prove that with appropriate choices of the mechanism parameters, there is a single Nash equilibrium corresponding to the contractors' strategy of correctly computing the result. Our work provides a foundation for replicated incentivized computation in smart contract setting, and opens new research directions.

Keywords: Incentivized computation · Outsourced computation · Smart contract · Game theory · Mechanism design

1 Introduction

Outsourcing computation enables a client to expand its computational capability by using computational power of cloud providers such as Microsoft Azure and Amazon Web Services. Outsourcing computation has increasingly been used to distribute large computations among computing nodes by breaking the computation into smaller pieces that are outsourced to volunteer nodes, that are

Full version available on IACR ePrint Archive, Report 2021/174.

driven by altruistic causes or are incentivized to participate in the computation. One of the earliest examples of such a distributed computation system is SETI@home project [24] that had the goal of finding extraterrestrial intelligence. More recently the approach has been used during pandemic for projects such as finding COVID vaccine [18].

Belenkiy et al. [4] formalized the basic *rational adversary* setting when a *Problem Giver* hires two *rational Contractor(s)* (minimum number of replicas) for the computation, and used game theoretic analysis to prove that by choosing the monetary values of *reward*, *fine*, and *bounty* (extra reward in certain defined cases), the contractors can be incentivized to correctly perform their respective computations. That is, they proved that their game of incentivized computation has a single Nash equilibrium that corresponds to the contractors being *Diligent* (honest). In their system, the *Problem Giver* simply compares the received responses and accepts if they match. If the results do not match, extra assumptions are made on the system; for example, with high probability one of the two servers is diligent, or the outsourcing is repeated with two new servers [17].

Smart Contracts for Outsourcing. A blockchain-based smart contract (SC) is a public program that resides on the blockchain, and runs on the underlying consensus based computation platform that ensures *trusted execution* of the program. Smart contracts offer an attractive approach to constructing an outsourcing computation service based on replication, using the trusted SC to manage outsourcing and result comparison, as well as payments and fund transfers natively. An attractive way of building an SC-based outsourced computation system would be to base it on a protocol with provable correctness, such as Belenkiy et al. [4]: (i) *Problem Giver* sends the computation description to the SC, (ii) SC chooses two contractors to perform the computation; (ii) if the submitted results match, SC accepts and rewards the contractors, else, it uses followup procedures, such as running the protocol with another set of two contractors, to obtain the result. Using monetary compensations will ensure with a high probability that the protocol will produce correct results, according to Belenkiy et al. (We omit details such as registration fees).

Our main observation is that this SC-managed system that is based on a protocol with provable correctness will completely fail because of the *copy attack*, in which a contractor will wait for the other contractor to send its response, and copy and submit the same response. This attack is inevitable because SC cannot hold any private randomness and so *its communication and computation will be transparent*. Copy attack perfectly matches the rationality assumption, as it minimizes the computation of the copying contractor, and is possible because of (i) the delay due to the communication with the blockchain and the consensus algorithm, and (ii) the transparency of SC. The attack effectively incentivizes computing nodes *not* to perform the correct computation, and undermines the independence of the two computations, which is the basis of computation correctness by replication.

An Overview of Our Results. We define the game of incentivized computation outsourcing to two independent *rational contractors* using an SC, define strategies of the contractors, and design two challenge-response protocols that are used by the SC to detect deviating contractors that, together with the monetary incentives, will provably result in the correct computation result. Our proof is game theoretic and uses Nash equilibrium as the solution concept, and provides a foundation for incentivized verifiable computation in SC setting.

Defining the Game. Copy attack can create a "waiting deadlock" which could leave the parties waiting indefinitely: each contractor waits to see the result of the other contractor. Rational contractors however can avoid this deadlock by using randomized submission time. The SC will use time limits (that can be implemented, for example, by requiring certain number of blocks added to the blockchain) to ensure timely completion of the results, and challenge-response protocols together with the payments to influence the behaviour of the players. The game is between two contractors, each wanting to maximize their utility.

Strategies. We start with the two basic strategies that were introduced in [4]: *Diligent (D)* strategy where the contractor follows the protocol, and *Lazy (L)* where the contractor uses a shortcut algorithm that produces the correct result with probability $q < 1$. Note that the Lazy strategy is general and includes any maliciously-constructed computation that has less cost (fewer computation steps) than the original computation. We assume that the same algorithm is used by all Lazy contractors.[1] This is effectively the worst case in the sense that two Lazy contractor will have matching results and in Belenkiy et al. protocol, they both will receive the reward (and SC will accept the matching result). In the SC setting, however, we show that the contractors will have four new attractive strategies: a third basic strategy, *Guess (G)*, where the computation result is simply guessed, and three types of copy strategies where the contractor starts with the aim of copying but uses one of the three basic strategies as a backup strategy when its copy attempt fails. In more details, a Copy attacker will choose a random time (within a well-defined interval) to copy; however, if there is no published result by the other contractor, it will use its backup strategy, which is one of the three basic types (D, L, G).

Our Protocol. Each contractor will submit a *response* that is a pair (y, z) where y is the computation result and z is a commitment to the execution trace of its computation. The commitment is constructed by forming a Merkle tree on the sequence of computation states of the contractor as it computes the function. The presented responses will match if the contractors both use Diligent, Lazy, or Copy strategies, where the latter two cases correspond to incorrect and untrusted results. Thus, matching responses will *not* guarantee correct result, and SC must use extra checking protocols. We introduce two challenge-response cryptographic subprotocols between the SC and the contractors, to assist the SC in distinguishing strategies of deviating contractors. The first subprotocol is the Match Check, protocol, which is a single-round challenge-response protocol and is used when the two responses match. The protocol allows the SC to decide if (y, z) is obtained through a computation or, it is copied or simply guessed (using

---

[1] The same assumption as [4,17].

G strategy). (We note that the responses will match if one contractor simply guesses its response, and the second contractor copies it.) The second subprotocol is called the Mismatch Check protocol, and is used when the two responses do not match. The subprotocol is an efficient multi-round challenge-response bisection protocol that allows the SC to correctly decide the correct one between a response pair (D, L) by performing a single computation step on the blockchain. These subprotocols, however, cannot distinguish (L, L) from (D, D), and (L, G) from (D, G), leading to rewarding non-diligent servers. That is, the Match Check protocol will accept the responses of two contractors corresponding to (L, L), and Mismatch Check protocol, when used for non-matching responses of contractors with strategy pair (L, G), will accept the contractor with strategy L. Proving correctness of computation result is by showing that with the above protocols and correct choices of incentive values, the game has a single Nash Equilibrium that corresponds to the strategy pair (D, D). Using reasonable assumptions on the system parameters (Sect. 5), we prove that our solution achieves correctness of the computation result (Theorem 2).

Contributions: Copy attack is the *rushing* behaviour of a rational contractor in the SC setting. Our work shows that copy attack has a devastating effect on the correctness of SC managed outsourcing services that are based on known incentivized replicated computation systems with provable correctness [4,17,19]. Game modelling in SC setting requires a wider set of strategies because of blockchain and SC environment. Our analysis lays the foundation of incentivized outsourcing to multiple rational contractors in this setting.

2 Related Work

Malicious Adversary Model. An essential requirement of outsourcing computation is the guarantee that the computed result is correct. Verifying computation results dates back the work of Babai [2] on proof systems that show NP hardness of a class of group theory problems, leading to a large body of influential works in cryptography and theoretical computer science [3,12,15], and more recently to *verifiable computation* systems [7,10,11,30] (see a survey [30] for more). These verifiable computation systems are cryptographic; they use a single computing server to provide security guarantee against a *malicious* cloud that can arbitrarily deviate from the computation. The systems are elegant and attractive theoretically, but have limited applications in practice because of high computation and communication cost, rigidity of parameters, and the challenge of correct implementation of complex cryptographic algorithms [14,29].

A natural way of obtaining confidence in the computation result is to *replicate the computation on multiple computing nodes*, with the smallest number of replicas being *two*. To obtain correct result with two possibly malicious servers, one must assume that at least one server is honest and computes correctly; otherwise, there can be no correct result in the system to guarantee correctness. Canetti et al. [5,6] showed that in this minimum setting *with the assumption of one honest server*, one can use an efficient interactive protocol based on refereed computation model of Feige et al. [9], to always identify the malicious server and obtain correct computation result. This assumption, however, cannot be made in real-life outsourcing scenarios where a client simply chooses two servers from a pool of bidding ones.[2] Avizheh et al. [1] showed that [5] is vulnerable to copy attack in the SC setting. [5] requires secure channels and cannot be used in SC setting.

Using replicated computation for integrity checking has been used in works such as [23,28]. These works do not provide formal cryptographic or game theoretic modelling and analysis of their systems.

Rational Adversary Model. Outsourcing computation to multiple independent rational entities has been popularized by projects such as SETI@Home [24] and Rosetta@Home [21] where idle CPU time of the users were employed for computing on scientific data.

The focus of this paper is on designing an *efficient mechanism that can be used by a smart contract*, with two rational contractors, both of which can deviate from the correct computation. This is similar to the settings in [8,13,16,23,25, 26], with the key addition of SC that automates (takes the role of) the referee (judge) protocol to decide on the correct computation result.

Incentivized outsourcing systems remove the assumption of a trusted server and allow that both servers to deviate from the computation, however assume they are *rational* and have well-defined utilities, which is reducing their computing costs. The model captures deviating behaviour of clouds, whose goal is to cut their cost and receive the reward with minimum amount of work and has been used to analyze deployed outsourcing systems such as Truebit [27] that uses a smart contract and replicated computation to provide correctness guarantee for outsourced computation.

Belenkiy et al. [4] were the first to define Diligent and Lazy strategies, when outsourcing to *two* rational contractors simply comparing the returned responses. They argued the need to use *fines* in addition to *reward*, to achieve correctness. They further showed that using *bounty* for a contractor who performed Diligently against a Lazy contractor will lead to a single Nash equilibrium corresponding to correct results.

Küpçü [17] extended the framework of [4] to multiple contractors, and added altruistic and malicious contractors to the framework in addition to the rational ones. The protocol uses the results of potentially multiple rounds of outsourcing to arrive at a correct decision.

Copy Attack in Related Works. Avizheh et al. [1] showed that copy attack will break security of [5] in the malicious adversary model (that assumes one honest contractor) when used in the SC setting. Avizheh et al. showed the attack can be prevented by adding a single challenge-response step when the two responses match. The protocol, however, does not provide full security proof in blockchain

---

[2] In fact, if the client was able to know one of the clouds is honest, then with high likelihood can determine which of the two is the trustworthy one.

environment. Our game model for incentivized outsourcing in SC setting is an overhaul of the mechanism in [4] and we prove correctness of our mechanism with respect to the desired outcome.

All above works in the rational setting assume that the *Problem Giver* directly interacts with the contractors, and communication channels can be secured (e.g., using TLS). Thus, in that setting, copy attack need not be considered. *All these works are vulnerable to copy attack in the SC setting* considered here.

3   Preliminaries

Smart Contracts. A smart contract is a trusted program that runs on a distributed ledger system (e.g., Ethereum), and its computation, communication, and stored values are transparent. More details can be found in [22].

Strategic Games. A strategic game is a model of interactive decision making where players choose their actions simultaneously and independently. A player's *utility* is their received payments minus their costs. We consider two-player games that can be described by a table, with rows and columns labelled by possible strategies (actions) of players 1 and 2, respectively. Each cell of the table contains a pair of real numbers corresponding to the utilities of players 1 and 2, respectively. The goal of a player is to maximize their utility. Nash equilibrium corresponds to a cell of the table where every player's strategy is the best response, given the other player's strategies. Therefore, no single rational player would deviate from the equilibrium. In the computational setting, negligible differences in the utilities may be ignored, and players should be implementable in probabilistic polynomial time. For details, refer to [20].

Incentivizing Correct Computation. Belenkiy et al. proposed an incentive mechanism [4] including (i) reward, the money paid to a contractor that correctly performs the computation, (ii) fine, the money charged to a contractor that is detected to have produced an incorrect result, and (iii) bounty, which is the money that is paid to a contractor that correctly performs the computation while the other contractor is detected to return an incorrect result. The two contractors use two strategies D or L. Using game theoretic analysis, Belenkiy et al. proved that the game of incentivized computation has a single Nash equilibrium, which corresponds to both contractors performing the computation correctly.

Merkle Hash Tree is a binary tree that is constructed over a sequence of data elements $D = (d_1, \cdots, d_n)$ using a *collision-resistant* hash function. The leaves of the tree are the hash values of elements of D, and an internal node is the hash of the concatenation of its two child nodes. A Merkle tree construction starts from the leaves and moves to the root that is denoted by $z = MH_{root}(D)$. The *proof of consistency* for the element d_i with respect to the root z, called *Merkle proof*, is denoted by $p_i = MH_{proof}(D, d_i)$, and consists of the hash values of the siblings of nodes along the path from $H(d_i)$ to the root. Given a Merkle proof p_i for the element d_i and the root z for the data sequence D, the

$VerifyMHProof(z, i, d_i, p_i)$ function verifies consistency of d_i, with respect to the Merkle tree with root z using the proof p_i.

Computation Trace. The response of a contractor consists of a claimed calculated value, and a commitment to the computation trace. We express the computation by a Turing machine (TM) with an input tape that initially stores the input. A computation state corresponds to a *TM configuration* $(state, head, tape)$ and can be stored as a **reduced configuration** defined by [5]:

$$(state, head, tape[head]; MH_{root}(tape))$$

where $tape[head]$ denotes the tape content at the location of the *head*, and MH_{root} denotes the root of a Merkle Hash tree over the *tape*. A contractor uses the sequence of execution states to express the computation trace.

4 Model

We consider a setting with three types of entities: (i) a *Problem Giver* who wants to outsource the computation of a *deterministic* function[3] $f()$ on an input x, (ii) a set of *Contractors* who are incentized to perform the computation, and (iii) a *Smart Contract (SC)* that interacts with the parties.

The SC receives deposits from the participants, and after receiving responses from the contractors, executes a *Judge* protocol that decides on the computation result based on the received responses, and possibly additional interactions with the contractors, and performs money transfers to/from contractors' accounts as specified by the protocol. The *Problem Giver* makes the required deposit to the SC in advance, and expects to obtain the correct computation result. A *Contractor* is *rational* and wants to maximize its utility that is expressed as the net reward. *The SC* is a transparent trusted program that runs on the blockchain consensus computer and executes the prescribed protocol. The SC can be created by the *Problem Giver*, or by an established service provider.

Outsourced Computation. The *Problem Giver* wants the value of a function $f()$ on an input x. The function is expressed by a Turing Machine (TM) for the computation of $f()$ on the input tape that contains x. The **response** of a contractor is a pair (y, z) where y is the computation **result** (if correct, $y = f(x)$), and z is the root of a Merkle hash tree that is constructed on the sequence of reduced configurations of the TM's computation. SC randomly chooses two contractors, from a pool of available contractors. The pool is large enough that we can assume the two chosen contractors are independent.

Goals of Incentivized Outsourced Computation are the following:

1. With overwhelming probability the *Problem Giver* receives correct result.

---

[3] A randomized algorithm can be outsourced after de-randomization using a pseudo-random generator.

2. Contractors are incentivized to participate and correctly perform the computation.
3. The computation and communication of the SC is minimal.

An implied goal of the system is that a contractor that has correctly performed the computation is always rewarded.

Strategies. There are two basic strategies, (i) **Diligent** (*D*) that correctly executes $f(x)$, and (ii) **Lazy** (*L*), where the contractor deviates from correct calculation to reduce its computation cost. A lazy algorithm is referred to as a *q*-algorithm, and generates the correct *result* (not the correct *response*) with a non-negligible chance *q* (generating the correct *response* has negligible probability ϵ). A *q*-algorithm can be *any* maliciously constructed algorithm that performs fewer computation steps and produces an acceptable value for the computation. It can simply skip some steps of the original computation; but in all cases the contractor has a computation trace that matches its committed root of execution tree. We assume all *all Lazy contractors use the same algorithm* and so their computation results match. Thus, without additional measures, they will receive the reward. Belenkiy et al. [4] made the same assumption, inspired by the case that the same SETI@Home [24] fake clients were downloaded by multiple participants (see [4]). A maliciously constructed program can be made available to rational contractors, who will be attracted to the reduced computation and the possibility of not being caught.

New Strategies. We consider a new basic **Guess** (*G*) strategy, where a contractor guesses the value of $f(x)$. The strategy has negligible cost and because of copy attack, can lead to matching results. The main difference between *G* and *L* strategies is that a (*G, G*) strategy pair will not lead to matching responses (negligible chance), while an (*L, L*) pair will output matching responses. By requiring the Merkle hash of the computation to be included in the contractor's response, the probability that two submitted guessed responses match will be negligible even when the computation result itself ($f(x)$) is from a small domain.

Copy strategy allows a contractor to completely skip the computation. A Copy contractor waits for the "other" contractor to submit its response to the SC and copies and submits that response as its own. This strategy is possible because of (i) SC's transparency of computation and communication, and (ii) the time interval between submitting a transaction to the blockchain network, and having it published on the blockchain. Copy strategy is very attractive because it allows a contractor to produce a matching result, and receive the reward with negligible work. However, since both contractors can use this strategy, both contractors may end up waiting indefinitely. To overcome this deadlock, a contractor will use a random time that is chosen from an appropriate range $[T_1, T_2]$, and copies the published response if exists; else, it resorts to one of the basic strategies. This leads to *Copy-Diligent (CD)*, *Copy-Lazy (CL)*, and *Copy-Guess(CG)* strategies. Thus we obtain a total of six strategies (including D, L, G) as below:

- **Diligent** (*D*): Computes using the original algorithm. The response will always be accepted and rewarded. The cost is $cost(1)$.

- **Lazy** (L): Computes using a q-algorithm that is assumed common for all Lazy contractors. The *result* will be correct with probability q, and the cost will be $cost(q)$.
- **Guess** (G): Creates a random bit string that matches the format of the submission to the SC. The response will be correct with probability ϵ, and the cost is $cost(\epsilon)$.
- **Copy:** The contractor chooses a random time from a time period; if the "other" contractor has sent its response, it copies the response; else the contractor continues with one of the original strategies: D, L, and G. There are three variations: *Copy-Diligent* (CD), *Copy-Lazy* (CL), and *Copy-Guess* (CG). The cost of successful copying is $cost(\epsilon)$.

Towards a Sound *Judge* Protocol in the SC Setting. A first attempt to construct a *Judge* protocol is to base it on the Belenkiy et al. [4] protocol with proved correctness: (i) if the two responses match, the *Judge* protocol outputs the result rewarding the contractors, (ii) else (when the responses differ) the *Judge* uses additional steps to identify the correct result and the contractor that is Diligent (if any). The following theorem proves that in the SC setting this *Judge* protocol cannot produce correct result for the *Problem Giver* using reward, bounty (extra reward that is paid to a contractor who helps catch a cheating contractor), and fine as incentive.

Theorem 1. *The incentivized computation protocol, with the possible contractor strategies D, L, CG and the* Judge *protocol above (based on [4, 17, 19]) in the smart contract setting, has a single Nash equilibrium that corresponds to the (CG, CG) strategy pair, leading to incorrect computation result for the* Problem Giver. *Proof is in the full version.*

The proof of this theorem (formally given in the full version) is based on the idea that copying is better than being Lazy since it has a lower cost, and CG is the best response against D again because of having a lower cost. Indeed, the Copy attacker gets the reward without getting caught when matched against a Diligent contractor, and its cost is minimal. When two Copy-Guess contractors get matched, one of them will copy the other, resulting in neither being caught, and therefore both getting the reward.

5   A *Judge* Protocol with Guaranteed Correctness

We first introduce notations that are used to express the working of the system, and then give reasonable assumptions that will be used in the game analysis.

Notations

- y, z: The *response* of a contractor, which includes the result y of the computation, together with the Merkle root z of the computation trace.

- r: The reward of a contractor in two cases, (i) when the SC receives two matching responses, and (ii) when the SC receives two conflicting responses, but the contractor succeeds in the Mismatch Check protocol.
- f: The fine charged to a contractor when their response is detected as incorrect. The fine can be enforced by requiring the contractor s to make a deposit at the start of the protocol.
- $cost(1)$: The cost of the original algorithm, run by the Diligent contractors.
- $cost(q)$: The cost of a q-algorithm, run by the Lazy contractors.
- $cost(\epsilon)$: The cost of guessing and copying both. ϵ is a negligible value.
- τ_D, τ_L: Time to compute the function using D and L strategies.
- τ_N: Network delay between a contractor and the SC.
- τ_{SC}: Smart Contract deadline for receiving computation results.
- q_S: The probability that the copying is successful for a Copy contractor, when the other contractor also uses Copy strategy. (Interestingly, our results turn out to be nicely independent of the actual value of this probability.)
- C refers to a Copy contractor (CD, CL, or CG) who could successfully copy.

System Parameters and Assumptions

1. $r > cost(1)$. That is, the reward of performing the computation correctly exceeds the cost of the computation. Otherwise, a rational contractor will not join the system.
2. When a Lazy contractor is matched against a Diligent contractor, the probability that their responses (y, z) match, is negligible. This is because the Lazy and Diligent algorithms are different in at least one step, and so their corresponding execution trace on the same input x and their associated Merkle roots, will be different with overwhelming probability. Similarly, when a Guessing contractor gets matched against a non-copy contractor, the probability that they return the same response is negligible. The probability of guessing a response that matches the response of another G, L, or D amounts to correct guessing of binary strings that are at least 128 or 160 bits (Merkle root), and so is negligible.[4]
3. The cost of a q-algorithm is $cost(q)$, and $cost(1) > cost(q)$. (Otherwise there is no need to employ a q-algorithm.)
4. $cost(q) > cost(\epsilon)$. Thus, guessing and copying constitute the least costly actions.
5. Once a computation result is produced, it will be submitted to the SC. That is, a contractor will not add additional delay to the computation.
6. A contractor knows a good estimate of the computation time of different strategies, as well as network delay. That is, in particular, it knows upper bounds on $\tau_D > \tau_L$ and τ_N.

---

[4] Recall that the difference between G and L strategies is that the response submitted by two L contractors will match, whereas the response submitted by two G contractors will *not* match, except with negligible probability. Thus, the Lazy contractor paradigm is enough to model submitting matching guesses (e.g., using the same pseudorandom seed).

7. The interval $[T_1, T_2]$ that is used by the Copy contractors is $[\tau_D + \tau_N, \tau_{SC} - \tau_N]$. That is, a copying contractor waits for a non-copy contractor to produce and submit its response.
8. The probability that two Copy contractors pick very close random times such that neither have the opportunity to copy from the other is negligible. This can happen if the first contractor cannot copy because no result is published, and the second contractor's time is too close to the first contractor to receive its published value. Note that the random time can always be selected at coarser intervals (e.g., at multiples of τ_N). We assume the probability of selecting the exact same (coarse) time is negligible.
9. The computation deadline, τ_{SC}, is set by the smart contract and is public. This time satisfies $\tau_{SC} > \tau_D + \tau_N$ so that a Diligent strategy can succeed.
10. The interval $[T_1, T_2]$ that is used by the Copy contractors is $[\tau_D + \tau_N, \tau_{SC} - \tau_N - T]$ where T is τ_D if the contractor is Copy-Diligent, τ_L if the contractor is Copy-Lazy, negligible if the contractor is Copy-Guess.
11. $\tau_{SC} \gg 2\tau_D + 2\tau_N$ such that Copy-Diligent is a viable strategy (a CD contractor can wait for a D contractor to finish, and if there is still no submitted response, can still execute its own Diligent computation).

Assumptions (5), (6) and (7) imply that the copy strategy C will be used after the contractor that uses D, L, or G strategy has completed and submitted its computation, and the result can be seen by the copying contractor. This implies a Copy contractor always succeeds copying the response of a non-copy contractor. Assumption (8) implies that when two Copy contractors play against each other, one of them will succeed in copying (i.e., q_0 is negligible). We show in the full version that our results turn out to be independent of this assumption and we only use it for simplicity of the presentation and analysis.

5.1 The New *Judge* Protocol

Let the two contractors, denoted by $P_i, i = 1, 2$, send the response pairs $(y_i, z_i), i = 1, 2$ to the SC. For D strategy $y_i = f(x)$. For other basic strategies $y_i = f(x)$ with be with probabilities q and ϵ for L and G, respectively. Upon the receipt of both responses, the SC runs the following *Judge* protocol:

– If $(y_1, z_1) = (y_2, z_2)$, run the *Match Check* protocol (Algorithm 1).
– Else, $(y_1, z_1) \neq (y_2, z_2)$, run the *Mismatch Check* protocol (Algorithm 2).

Checking Matching Submissions. Matching responses occur in all variations of Copy, and also for strategy pairs (L, L) and (D, D) and so does not correspond to guaranteed correctness. Without this check for matching submissions, it is not possible to prevent copy attack. We prove this in the full version by showing that the equilibrium remains at (CG, CG) when only Mismatch Check subprotocol (Algorithm 2) is used, and matching responses are simply accepted. This is true even with the use of bounties. The subprotocols employ an algorithm $VerifyCommittedReducedStep()$ that first checks consistency of two consecutive computation state (TM configuration) against the submitted Merkle root

---

Algorithm 1. Match Check

Let $n_i, i = 1, 2$ denote the lengths of $RC^i, i = 1, 2$.
Judge generates two PRNs, $rand_1$ and $rand_2$.
Judge $\rightarrow P_i : rand_i, i = 1, 2$
$P_i \rightarrow Judge : (rc^i_{rand_i}, rc^i_{rand_i+1}, MHProof(RC^i, rc^i_{rand_i}),$
$\qquad\qquad MHProof(RC^i, rc^i_{rand_i+1}), p^i_{rand_i}), i = 1, 2.$
Judge uses $VerifyComittedReducedStep()$ on the submitted response.
The result of a contractor who passes the verification will be accepted.

Algorithm 2. Mismatch Check Protocol

$n' = \min\{n_1, n_2\}$, where n_i is the length of the sequence of reduced configurations
of P_i.
$z^i = MHroot(RC^i), i = 1, 2$
Perform Committed Binary-Search given $z^i = MHroot(RC^i), i = 1, 2$, with the two
contractors to find the smallest j, where $rc^1_j = rc^2_j$ and $rc^1_{j+1} \neq rc^2_{j+1}$.
Judge $\rightarrow P_i : j$, i=1,2.
$P_i \rightarrow Judge :$
$(rc^i_j, MHProof(rc^i_j, RC^i), rc^i_{j+1}, MHProof(rc^i_{j+1}, RC^i), p^i_j)$
Judge verifies using $VerifyCommittedReducedStep()$.
Result of P_i is accepted if the output is True.

---

by verifying their corresponding submitted paths to the root, and then runs that single step of computation *on the SC* starting from the earlier state and verifies the resulting state against the latter one. Details are in the full version.

Note That The Strategy Pair (L, L) *Will Be Rewarded with a Probability.* This is because this pair will result in matching responses, that leads to Match Check protocol be run. The challenged steps, however, will be responded consistently with the committed roots, because there is a (good) probability (assuming the worst-case) that the Match Check protocol chooses a computation step that is the same in the q-algorithm and the original computation. This leaves the Lazy approach undetected. Similarly, for (L, C) strategy pair, the challenged step of the q-algorithm can be the same as the correct algorithm and so L strategy will mistakenly be identified as D, whereas C strategy will be detected and penalized, since it cannot respond to the challenge as it did not perform any computation. With the new Match Check protocol, copying is bad because it cannot respond to the *Judge* challenges.

Despite these incorrect detections, using fines, rewards, and bounties will result in the desired (Diligent) equilibrium.

Checking Mismatching Submissions. When the submitted responses do not match, the SC needs to decide which one to accept (if any). The goal is to distinguish a D strategy against L or G strategies, as well as variations of copy strategy that result in similar strategy pairs. The Committed Binary-Search protocol is a challenge-response bisection protocol that starts with comparing the state of the two submitted execution traces at the mid-point, and depending

Table 1. *Judge* protocol results. The worst-case for the *Problem Giver* is assumed. There is no ordering of the contractors since the result would be symmetric (e.g., D, C and C, D are the same in this representation). $+$ indicates being rewarded, $-$ indicates being fined.

Strategies	Match Check Result		Strategies	Mismatch Check Result	
D, D	$D+$	$D+$	D, L	$D+$	$L-$
D, C	$D+$	$C-$	D, G	$D+$	$G-$
L, L	$L+$	$L+$	L, G	$L+$	$G-$
L, C	$L+$	$C-$	G, G	$G-$	$G-$
G, C	$G-$	$C-$			

on the match or mismatch, chooses mid point of the right or left half of the trace and this is repeated until the first step where the two computation traces of the contractors differ is found. Then, SC finds the correct execution using $VerifyCommittedReducedStep()$. Details are in the full version.

Judge Protocol. Table 1 visualizes the *Judge* protocol results. Observe that when two Copy contractors get matched, the cases boil down to one of the cases in the table: (CD, CD) boils down to (D, C) since one (either P_1 or P_2) copies and the other executes the computation Diligently, and similarly (CL, CL) boils down to (L, C) and (CG, CG) boils down to (G, C). The *Judge* protocol identifies a Diligent contractor (if any) and always rewards them (never fines Diligent contractors). But, the *Judge* protocol may also incorrectly reward non-diligent contractors with incorrect responses.

Remark. We note that neither the Mismatch Check and Match Check protocols, nor the bounty usage alone, can lead to an equilibrium that corresponds to the correct result. However, with a well designed combination of them, we achieve the desired mechanism. This is an innovative aspect of our work.

5.2 Game Analysis

Our *Judge* protocol design results in Table 2. Below, we detail the utilities in the table (we follow the row order):

- The utility of D against another D is $u_D = r - cost(1)$: The results match, the contractor will receive the reward, and pays the cost of the computation.
- The utility of D against others is $r - cost(1) + b(1 - \epsilon)$: The *Judge* protocol will identify the diligent versus others, except with negligible probability, as discussed. The Diligent contractor will obtain the reward and the bounty. We approximate this utility as $r - cost(1) + b(1 - \epsilon) \approx r - cost(1) + b$ and denote as u_{DB}.

Table 2. Utility table, *with copy protection*. The utilities in the table represent a symmetric game (not a symmetric matrix), thus unnecessary cells are omitted.

P_1, P_2	D	L	G	CD	CL	CG
D	u_D, u_D	u_{DB}, u_-	u_{DB}, u_-	u_{DB}, u_-	u_{DB}, u_-	u_{DB}, u_-
L	–	u_L, u_L	u_{LB}, u_-	u_{LB}, u_-	u_{LB}, u_-	u_{LB}, u_-
G	–	–	u_-, u_-	u_-, u_-	u_-, u_-	u_-, u_-
CD	–	–	–	u_{CDB}, u_{CDB}	u_{CDB}, u_{CLB}	u_{CDB}, u_-
CL	–	–	–	–	u_{CLB}, u_{CLB}	u_{CLB}, u_-
CG	–	–	–	–	–	u_-, u_-

- The utility of the others against the D strategy is $r\epsilon - f(1-\epsilon) - cost(q) < 0$: The *Judge* protocol will catch them against Diligent. We approximate this as $r\epsilon - f(1-\epsilon) - cost(q) \approx -f - cost(q)$ which is negative, and denote it in the table with u_-.
- The utility of strategy L, against another L is $u_L = r - cost(q)$: They both return the same response, will be able to pass the *Judge* protocol (since we assume the worst-case q-algorithm), hence they both get the reward. In any case, they pay the cost of the q-algorithm.
- The utility of the L strategy against other non-Diligent strategy (G, CD, CL, CG) is $r - cost(q) + b(1-\epsilon)$: The *Judge* protocol may (mistakenly) reward the L strategy and provide extra bounty, while fining the others. We approximate this utility as $r - cost(q) + b(1-\epsilon) \approx r - cost(q) + b$ and denote it as u_{LB}.
- The utility of the G strategy against any strategy, and the utility of copy variants (CD, CL, CG) against any non-copy strategy are all u_-. This is because they cannot respond properly to the challenges of *Judge* (guessing cannot respond to Mismatch Check and *successful copying* cannot respond to Match Check), and will be fined. This also applies to CG against CG, since in that case one of them will act like G in practice and the other will successfully copy.
- The utility of a CD contractor against any other Copy contractor is $u_{CDB} = q_S u_- + (1 - q_S)u_{DB}$: When it can successfully copy, which happens with probability q_S, it will be caught by the new *Judge* protocol, thereby getting fined and obtaining negative utility. But, when it cannot copy, which happens with probability $(1 - q_S)$, it will act Diligently, and will help catch the other contractor, obtaining u_{DB}.
- The utility of a CL contractor against any other Copy contractor is $u_{CLB} = q_S u_- + (1 - q_S)u_{LB}$: When it can successfully copy, which happens with probability q_S, it will be caught by the new *Judge* protocol, thereby getting fined and obtaining negative utility. But, when it cannot copy, which happens with probability $(1 - q_S)$, it will act Lazily, but will not be caught by the *Judge* protocol. Instead, it will be seen as helping to catch the other contractor, thereby obtaining u_{LB}.

Theorem 2. *Under the reasonable assumptions stated in Sect. 5, and if $b >$ $cost(1)$, then the pair of strategies (D, D) gives the only computational Nash equilibrium of the strategic game in Table 2.*

Intuitively, Guess or Copy-Guess strategies will fail with our Match Check protocol, since they will be caught and fined. Moreover, being completely Diligent is better than being Copy-Diligent, since the latter will be caught and fined when it successfully copies. Similarly, being Lazy is better than being Copy-Lazy. Using bounties with our *Judge* protocol with two checking protocols Mismatch Check and Match Check results in an all-Diligent equilibrium.

Proof. G and CG strategies always get u_-. Thus, we focus on D, L, CD, CL. We have $u_{DB} > u_{CDB}$ and $u_{LB} > u_{CLB}$ since $q_S > 0$. We also have $u_{LB} > u_{DB}$ $(r - cost(q) + b > r - cost(1) + b)$, which holds because $cost(q) < cost(1)$. Hence, L is the best response against CL and CD. We further have $u_{DB} > u_L$ $(r - cost(1) + b > r - cost(q))$ which holds as long as $b > cost(1) - cost(q)$ (or $b > cost(1)$) as stated in the theorem. This means, while L is the best response against all Copy strategies, if a contractor should choose L, then the other contractor is better of being D.

Lastly, D is the best response against D since $u_D > u_-$. In plain words, when the other contractor is Diligent, we should be Diligent as well, as all other options get negative utility. Therefore, no contractor has incentive to deviate from this (D, D) equilibrium. (More details are in the full version.)   □

Corollary. *The (D, D) strategy pair results in correct computation result for the* Problem Giver. *Together with bounties, our* Judge *protocol, which is an efficient verification mechanism run with every pair of submissions, disincentivizes free riding and incentivizes Diligent behavior.*

An interesting property of the bounties in our setting is that while using them partly help change the equilibrium, they will *not* be used when all contractors are rational and hence act Diligently. Thus, bounty should not be seen as an extra expense for the *Problem Giver*.

6 Concluding Remarks

Our work is motivated by the rise of the blockchain and smart contracts, and the possibility of automating outsourcing and using cryptocurrency for implementing incentives. Replicated computation has minimum cryptographic computation overhead for the *Problem Giver* and the contractors. Surprisingly, however, because of the Copy attack, none of the incentivized replicated computation systems with provable game-theoretic correctness can provide correctness in this setting. We proposed an SC based incentivization mechanism with two checking protocols that guarantees correctness of the results. One of the challenges of our work has been to model the smart contract environment and behaviour of rational parties that realistically captures the effect of the Copy attack. This includes the random waiting times to avoid infinite waiting loops, and identifying attractive strategies. Our final *Judge* protocol is the first outsourcing protocol with guaranteed correct computation result, and lays the foundation for the more general case of multiple contractors. Several potential extensions of our work include a full implementation using SC and measuring concrete efficiency of the storage of the computation trace, properly estimating the deadline τ_{SC}, and potentially considering a malicious *Problem Giver* (e.g., performing resource exhaustion attacks on contractors and SC).

Acknowledgements. Alptekin Küpçü acknowledges support from TÜBİTAK, the Scientific and Technological Research Council of Turkey, under project number 119E088. The work of Reihaneh Safavi-Naini has been in part supported by Natural Sciences and Engineering Research Council of Canada Discovery Grant Program.

References

1. Avizheh, S., Nabi, M., Safavi-Naini, R., Venkateswarlu, K.M.: Verifiable computation using smart contracts. In: ACM CCSW (2019)
2. Babai, L.: Trading group theory for randomness. In: ACM STOC (1985)
3. Babai, L., Moran, S.: Arthur-Merlin games: a randomized proof system, and a hierarchy of complexity classes. J. Comput. Syst. Sci. **36**(2), 254–276 (1988)
4. Belenkiy, M., Chase, M., Erway, C., Jannotti, J., Küpçü, A., Lysyanskaya, A.: Incentivizing outsourced computation. In: NetEcon (2008)
5. Canetti, R., Riva, B., Rothblum, G.N.: Practical delegation of computation using multiple servers. In: ACM CCS (2011)
6. Canetti, R., Riva, B., Rothblum, G.N.: Two protocols for delegation of computation. In: Smith, A. (ed.) ICITS 2012. LNCS, vol. 7412, pp. 37–61. Springer, Heidelberg (2012). https://doi.org/10.1007/978-3-642-32284-6_3
7. Chung, K.-M., Kalai, Y., Vadhan, S.: Improved delegation of computation using fully homomorphic encryption. In: Rabin, T. (ed.) CRYPTO 2010. LNCS, vol. 6223, pp. 483–501. Springer, Heidelberg (2010). https://doi.org/10.1007/978-3-642-14623-7_26
8. Du, W., Murugesan, M., Jia, J.: Uncheatable grid computing. In: Algorithms and Theory of Computation Handbook. Chapman & Hall/CRC (2010)
9. Feige, U., Kilian, J.: Making games short. In: ACM STOC (1997)
10. Gennaro, R., Gentry, C., Parno, B.: Non-interactive verifiable computing: outsourcing computation to untrusted workers. In: Rabin, T. (ed.) CRYPTO 2010. LNCS, vol. 6223, pp. 465–482. Springer, Heidelberg (2010). https://doi.org/10.1007/978-3-642-14623-7_25
11. Goldwasser, S., Kalai, Y.T., Rothblum, G.N.: Delegating computation: interactive proofs for muggles. J. ACM **62**(4), 27:1–27:64 (2015)
12. Goldwasser, S., Micali, S., Rackoff, C.: The knowledge complexity of interactive proof systems. SIAM J. Comput. **18**(1), 186–208 (1989)
13. Golle, P., Mironov, I.: Uncheatable distributed computations. In: Naccache, D. (ed.) CT-RSA 2001. LNCS, vol. 2020, pp. 425–440. Springer, Heidelberg (2001). https://doi.org/10.1007/3-540-45353-9_31
14. Halevi, S.: Advanced cryptography: promise and challenges (2018). https://shaih.github.io/pubs/Advanced-Cryptorgaphy.pdf

15. Kilian, J.: A note on efficient zero-knowledge proofs and arguments. In: ACM STOC (1992)
16. Kong, Y., Peikert, C., Schoenebeck, G., Tao, B.: Outsourcing computation: the minimal refereed mechanism. In: Caragiannis, I., Mirrokni, V., Nikolova, E. (eds.) WINE 2019. LNCS, vol. 11920, pp. 256–270. Springer, Cham (2019). https://doi.org/10.1007/978-3-030-35389-6_19
17. Küpçü, A.: Incentivized outsourced computation resistant to malicious contractors. IEEE Trans. Dependable Secure Comput. **14**(6), 633–649 (2017)
18. Patrizio, A.: The coronavirus pandemic turned Folding@Home into an exaFLOP supercomputer, April 2020
19. Pham, V., Khouzani, M.H.R., Cid, C.: Optimal contracts for outsourced computation. In: Poovendran, R., Saad, W. (eds.) GameSec 2014. LNCS, vol. 8840, pp. 79–98. Springer, Cham (2014). https://doi.org/10.1007/978-3-319-12601-2_5
20. Rapoport, A.: Prisoner's dilemma - recollections and observations. In: Rapoport, A. (ed.) Game Theory as a Theory of a Conflict Resolution. TDLU, vol. 2, pp. 17–37. Springer, Dordrecht (1974). https://doi.org/10.1007/978-94-010-2161-6_2
21. Rosetta@home. http://boinc.bakerlab.org/rosetta
22. Ruoti, S., Kaiser, B., Yerukhimovich, A., Clark, J., Cunningham, R.: SoK: blockchain technology and ts potential use cases. arXiv:1909.12454 (2019)
23. Sarmenta, L.F.: Sabotage-tolerance mechanisms for volunteer computing systems. Future Gener. Comput. Syst. **18**(4), 561–572 (2002)
24. Seti@home. http://setiathome.berkeley.edu
25. Szajda, D., Lawson, B., Owen, J.: Hardening functions for large scale distributed computations. In: IEEE Security and Privacy (2003)
26. Szajda, D., Lawson, B., Owen, J.: Toward an optimal redundancy strategy for distributed computations. In: IEEE Cluster Computing (2005)
27. Teutsch, J., Reitwießner, C.: A scalable verification solution for blockchains. arXiv:1908.04756 (2019)
28. Ulusoy, H., Kantarcioglu, M., Pattuk, E.: TrustMR: computation integrity assurance system for MapReduce. In: IEEE Big Data (2015)
29. van Dijk, M., Juels, A.: On the impossibility of cryptography alone for privacy-preserving cloud computing. In: USENIX HotSec (2010)
30. Walfish, M., Blumberg, A.J.: Verifying computations without reexecuting them. Commun. ACM **58**(2), 74–84 (2015)

Anonymous Sidechains

Foteini Baldimtsi[1]($\boxtimes$), Ian Miers[2], and Xinyuan Zhang[1]

[1] George Mason University, Fairfax, USA
{foteini,xzhang44}@gmu.edu
[2] University of Maryland, College Park, USA
imiers@umd.edu

Abstract. Sidechains allow two or more blockchains to communicate with each other by transferring coins (or other ledger assets) from one to the other. Their functionalities set sidechains as one of the most prominent solutions towards blockchain scalability and interoperability.

A number of sidechain constructions have already been proposed on the literature presenting ways to securely move assets between blockchains for different types of underlying consensus mechanisms (PoW and PoS). In this work we study the problem of sidechains in the *anonymous* setting by demonstrating how multiple anonymous blockchains can interact with each other. We present the first formal definition for an anonymous sidechain and provide a first construction for privacy-preserving Zerocash [5] cross-ledger transactions.

1 Introduction

After the introduction of Bitcoin [23], there has been an extreme interest on decentralized digital currencies and their underlying blockchain mechanisms. As a result, hundreds of different cryptocurrencies have been deployed and a large amount of users participate in cryptocurrency trading. This creates a crucial need for blockchain *interoperability*, i.e. mechanisms that allow users to transfer assets from one blockchain to another. Currently, the most commonly used mechanism for asset transfer is that of centralized exchanges. However, relying on trusted parties is far from ideal in the blockchain world and the need for interoperability mechanisms that do not rely on intermediaries is critical.

Sidechains [3,12,18] is one of the most prominent approaches for blockchain interoperability without intermediaries. Essentially, sidechains allow for cross-chain transactions that transfer assets from a blockchain L to another blockchain L'. When assets are transferred from L to L', they actually disappear from L (i.e. the supply of L gets reduced) and they appear as newly minted assets in L'. Sidechains can be defined for various relations between L and L'. A *one-way peg* is if assets can be transferred from L to L' but not back to L, while a *two-way peg* allows transfers back to L. The main security property of sidechains is that of *balance* (or "firewall" as defined in [12]) that states that no more assets can ever return from a sidechain, than the amount of assets that was moved into it. Beyond blockchain interoperability without intermediaries, sidechains can

© Springer Nature Switzerland AG 2022
J. Garcia-Alfaro et al. (Eds.): DPM 2021/CBT 2021, LNCS 13140, pp. 262–277, 2022.
https://doi.org/10.1007/978-3-030-93944-1_17

also positively affect the issues of scalability and upgradability on blockchain. Namely, sidechains can allow the creation of multiple blockchains that interact with each other while "sharing" the work of transaction validation and storage which boosts scalability. Additionally, sidechains allow an easier adoption of new features since specialized sidechains can be created to explore such features while still smoothly interacting with the main chain.

While concrete sidechains constructions have been given for blockchains operating under the most popular consensus mechanisms (further discussed in the Related Work Sect. 1.2), the question of how to operate sidechains in the *anonymous setting* has not been studied. Privacy has been an important challenge in the blockchain world given the possibility of tracking movements of funds in non-private systems [2,7,26]. The community has reacted by designing private cryptocurrencies [5,22,28] or "mixing" mechanisms that work on top of existing non-private cryptocurrencies [8,14,19,20,27]. While existing sidechain designs might work well with mixing mechanisms (as mixed transactions end up as regular-looking transactions), employing sidechains for standalone private cryptocurrencies such as Zerocash [5] is an open problem.

1.1 Our Contributions

In this work we define and build *anonymous sidechains*. We start by providing a definitional framework (API) for sidechains and then define security and privacy properties. In a high level we set the following privacy goals for cross-ledger transactions between two private ledgers L and L':

1. Every transaction should hide the amount, the sender and the receiver.
2. By looking at the public information posted on both blockchains, an adversary should not be able to distinguish between cross-ledger transactions and "regular" on-chain transactions.
3. If more than two blockchains exist, a user cannot tell whether a particular cross-ledger transaction is between which ledgers (i.e. a user should not be able to tell if a transaction is in the direction of $L1 \leftrightarrow L2$ or $L3 \leftrightarrow L2$).

We also provide a sample construction by extending the private cryptocurrency Zerocash [5] to allow for cross-ledger transactions. The main idea is to have a uni-directional cross-ledger transaction scheme that can be easily extended to a two-way pegged system. We divide the transactions into *types*, include the type as a commitment into the coin structure, and include a proof of each type in the resulting transaction depending on whether it is on-chain or not. We preserve the Zerocash anonymity level for "regular" on-chain payments. Plus, since the type is hidden in the commitment just like the public keys and coin values, an observer looking at the public transaction history cannot tell whether a transaction is on a single chain or between two chains.

1.2 Related Work

Blockchain Interoperability Without Intermediaries. A number of existing efforts aim at designing protocols that enable such cross-ledger payments.

Atomic swaps [16] allow the exchange of coins between chains without using a third party. An atomic swap is usually arranged between two peers and involves time-lock functionalities to guarantee that the exchange either does not take place at all or goes through for both parties. When an atomic swap takes place, the supply on both chains remains the same (only assets change hands). This is a main technical difference from sidechains where supply actually changes when assets gets moved. Additionally, sidechains are trustless and there is no need to match with a peer to facilitate the transaction. Some recent atomic-swap advancements [1,15] suggest adding reserves to eliminate the need of finding a trading partner but this still requires a level of trust.

Sidechains were first introduced in [3] but without any formalization of construction. The first sidechain construction was given in [18] for Proof-of-work (PoW) sidechains. The scheme of [18] utilizes smart-contracts and is based on a primitive called "Non-interactive Proofs of Proof-of-work" (NIPoPoW) [17]. The first formal security definitions for sidechains were given in [12]. In the same work, a Proof-of-Stake sidechain construction was proposed. To our best knowledge, none of the sidechain related works consider privacy towards transaction values or sender-recipient addresses.

Blockchain Privacy. Many existing works address the privacy issues on the blockchain space but for a single blockchain and a particular asset. One popular method is mixing, which ensures k-anonymity through combining the transactions of a group to fit in one block. A mixing protocol [19,27] removes the link between coin senders and output receivers by hiding in this group of k members, but usually requires the same denomination for all transactions and has limited scalability. Therefore, some protocols add an intermediary [8,14,20] to facilitate the mixing. This third party can be partially trusted or even trustless. An alternative to mixing approach are standalone private blockchains [5,22,28]. Our construction utilizes the Zerocash [5] private cryptocurrency and extends its functionality to a cross-ledger scheme.

Blockchain Interoperability with Privacy. Some recent works add a privacy layer to mechanisms for blockchain interoperability. ZEXE [9] was recently proposed as a decentralized anonymous exchange which aims to preserve user anonymity during an asset exchange. Another recent work called MANTA [10] tries to realize this functionality by leveraging the anonymity level of Zerocash to design an asset swap scheme. Their work is based on automated market maker, while ours uses sidechains. Finally, [11] proposed anonymous atomic-swaps. Sidechains have fundamental differences from both atomic-swaps and exchanges as explained above.

2   Preliminaries

Notation: Throughout this work, L denotes a mainchain and L' denotes a sidechain. We let pp_L, $pp_{L'}$ denote public parameters on the respective chains and let $pp_{L \to L'}$ denote cross-ledger public parameters that define transactions from L to L'. By λ we denote the security parameter. We use c to denote coins and v to denote coin values.

2.1 Cryptographic Building Blocks

We recall the descriptions of the following cryptographic primitives: commitment schemes, Merkle Trees, and zk-SNARKs.

Cryptographic Commitments. A non-interactive commitment [24,25] takes as input public parameters *params*, a message m and randomness r and outputs value $\mathsf{cm} \leftarrow \mathsf{COMM}_r(m)^1$ such that, on one hand, reveals no information about the message (*hiding* property) but, on the other hand, it is hard to find (m', r') such that $\mathsf{COMM}_r(m) = \mathsf{COMM}_{r'}(m')$, when $m' \neq m$ (*binding* property).

Merkle Trees. A Merkle tree [21] is a binary tree that uses cryptographic hash functions to derive a path from a leaf to the root, rt, as a proof of membership. Each leaf represents one or many attributes, and each leaf derives a hash digest of its own attributes concatenated with its children's digests.

Zero-Knowledge Proofs and zk-SNARKs. A zero-knowledge (ZK) proof is a two-party protocol between a prover P, holding some private data (or else *witness*) w for a public instance x, and a verifier V. The goal of the prover P is to convince a verifier V that some property of w is true i.e. $R(x, w) = 1$, for an NP-relation R, without V learning anything more.

zk-SNARK stands for "Zero-Knowledge Succinct Non-Interactive Argument of Knowledge" [6,13], and refers to a zero-knowledge proof that is "succinct", which means that it has the smallest proof size and can be verified within a few milliseconds. zk-SNARKs are fundamental tools for Zerocash, and also our scheme, to provide transaction privacy while keeping the proof short enough to be verified and published on the blockchain.

2.2 Zerocash

Zerocash [5] is a cryptographic protocol for decentralized anonymous payment on a blockchain. It was originally proposed as an extension to Bitcoin [23], using the same proof of work consensus mechanism. However, unlike Bitcoin, Zerocash transactions are cryptographically opaque.

Concretely, a typical transaction recorded on the Bitcoin blockchain consists of the receiver's address, the amount of funds, and a pointer to the source of the funds (i.e., a previous transaction). All these attributes are publicly revealed since the blockchain and the history of all transactions can be viewed by anyone. Even though the randomly generated wallet address in payments is intended to replace people's real-life identity, this "pseudonymity" suffers from various attacks [2,7,26] that deanonymize people through observing the transaction patterns or network interactions.

In Zerocash, a typical transaction is called a "Pour" operation, which provides a privacy preserving analog of a Bitcoin transaction. Transaction state (e.g., source, destination, amount) is stored inside a coin commitment cm that is opaque. In addition to standard (committed) transaction data, Zerocash blocks

---

[1] To simplify notation we consider *params* an implicit input and we omit it.

contain a Merkle Tree over all of the coin commitments that have ever been recorded up to that point. Any user can therefore demonstrate ownership of a coin commitment (and thus the money stored on chain) by showing they know the path to the coin c in a Merkle Tree with root rt and the opening of the commitment cm. To preserve privacy, this is done using a zk-SNARK proof π. To prevent double spending, the "Pour" transaction then burns the old coins and creates a new coin by revealing a serial number sn associated with the coin. Thus, a Zerocash transaction consists of a zero-knowledge proof that there exists money owed by the sender, a serial number to prevent double spending, and one or more new coin commitments that pay the recipients.

3   Anonymous Sidechains Definition

As discussed in the Introduction, while a number of sidechain constructions already exist in the literature [3,12,18] (all for the non-anonymous setting), none of them provides a comprehensive definitional framework. The only relevant formalization so far has been done by Gazi et al. [12] who provide a formal security definition for the so called "firewall" property, which ensures that the overall incoming values to the mainchain never exceed the outgoing amounts. In this section we describe a definitional framework for cross-chain transactions and define security and anonymity properties.

Before describing our framework we list a set of assumptions we make throughout this work. For simplicity, but without loss of generality, we assume that the mainchain L and the sidechain L' are created and initialized upon pegging. L and L' are therefore guaranteed to be identical and share the same type of assets, consensus algorithms, transaction models, security parameters etc. We also assume that correctness, security, and consensus hold for the individual chains.

Our definitions are on the UTXO transaction model. Namely, users create pairs of secret and public keys (or addresses) $(addr^{pk}, addr^{sk})$ which carry some value v. Values are sent to public addresses, and are spent by using the secret key that corresponds to an address.

Definition 1 (Cross-ledger Transaction Scheme). *A Cross-ledger transaction scheme Π_{CL} for two transaction ledgers L, L' is a tuple of polynomial-time algorithms (Pegging, Transaction, Cross-ledger Transaction, Verify Transaction).*[2]

Pegging. *The algorithm Pegging generates two ledgers and the public parameters for cross-ledger transactions:*

$$\begin{cases} input:\ security\ parameter\ \lambda \\ output:\ mainchain\ L,\ sidechain\ L',\ cross\text{-}ledger\ public\ parameter\ pp_{L \to L'} \end{cases}$$

---

[2] Our definition is stated for the case of cross-chain transactions between two ledgers, but it can be generalized to multiple ledgers by employing pair-wise peggings.

The output ledgers L, L' additionally have their own public parameters $pp_L, pp_{L'}$ which we assume are embedded in the description of L, L'. The established pegging is uni-directional (one-way peg), which means users can from now on make cross-ledger transactions only from L (which we consider to be the mainchain) to L' (aka the sidechain). We could extend our definition to bi-directional by including an additional output parameter $pp_{L' \to L}$.

Transaction. *The algorithm Transaction performs a regular payment within a single ledger:*

$\begin{cases} \text{input: mainchain } L, \text{ sidechain } L', \text{ old address secret key } addr_{old}^{sk}, \text{ old coin } c_{old}, \\ \text{new value } v_{new}, \text{ destination address public key } addr_{new}^{pk}, \text{ transaction fee } v_{pub} \\ \text{output: transaction } tx \end{cases}$

This algorithm creates a transaction tx of value v_{new} which is sent to address $addr_{new}^{pk}$ in L.

Cross-Ledger Transaction. *The algorithm Cross-ledger Transaction performs a cross-ledger payment from mainchain L to sidechain L':*

$\begin{cases} \text{input: cross-ledger public parameter } pp_{L \to L'}, \text{ mainchain } L, \text{ sidechain } L', \text{ secret} \\ \text{address } addr_L^{sk} \text{ to spend coin on } L \text{ and } addr_{L'}^{sk} \text{ to spend coin on } L', \text{ old coin } c_{old}, \\ \text{new value } v_{new}, \text{ destination address on } L' \, addr_{L'}^{pk}, \text{ transaction fee } v_{pub}, v_{pub'} \\ \text{output: transaction pairs } tx \text{ (in } L), \, tx' \text{ (in } L') \end{cases}$

This algorithm creates a transaction tx that "burns" assets of value $v_{new} + v_{pub}$ in L and creates assets of value v_{new} in L' which belong address $addr_{L'}^{pk}$.

Verify Transaction. *The algorithm Verify Transaction takes as input a transaction tx and outputs a bit determining whether this transaction is valid:*

$\begin{cases} \text{input: cross-ledger public parameter } pp_{L \to L'}, \text{ mainchain } L, \text{ sidechain } L', \text{ transaction } tx \\ \text{output: bit } b, \text{ equals 1 } iff \text{ the transaction is valid} \end{cases}$

This algorithm verifies whether a transaction tx is valid in ledger L. (The algorithm would be defined in exactly the same manner for L'.)

Note that, for simplicity, we omit the mechanism by which new money is created in the system. In particular, we omit both the mechanism by which the monetary supply grows and the actual means by which new monetary value is put into coins (i.e. minting). These choices are orthogonal to our construction.

Correctness. Correctness should guarantee that unspent coins can be spent. As discussed above, we assume that correctness holds for the underlying ledgers L, L', thus correctness for "regular" on-chain transactions should hold. Additionally, we require correctness for the cross-chain transactions.

Informally, we require that if $(tx, tx') =$ Cross-ledger Transaction between L, L', then tx must happen before tx' and if $tx \in L$, tx' must be includable in L'. By includable, we mean tx' is valid according to the consensus algorithm of L' and is compatible with the transaction model of L'. Additionally, we require that $v_{tx}^{old} = v_{tx'}^{new} + v_{pub} \le v_{max}$ where v_{max} is a system parameter that defines the maximum transaction value allowed on the system.

3.1 Security

The security of distributed, ledger-based payment systems is typically defined by *transaction malleability* and *balance*. Transaction malleability (when just dealing with a single ledger), implies that no bounded adversary A can alter any of the data stored within a valid transaction tx, *before* the transaction is added to the ledger. Balance guarantees that no bounded adversary A can own more money than what they minted or received via payments from others.

As with correctness, we assume that such properties hold for on-chain transactions within L and L'. However, we need an additional balance guarantee for the case of cross-chain transactions which states that the incoming amount in L' cannot be more than the outgoing amount of L and reverse.

Oracles. To describe our security definitions we first need to introduce an oracle. O^{CL} stands for a cross-ledger oracle that the adversary interacts with during the security games. The oracle provides an interface for executing Transaction and Verify Transaction algorithms for honest parties. To elicit behavior from honest parties, the adversary passes a query q to the Challenger which executes the corresponding operation for the honest user. Whenever the adversary makes a query for an honest party to execute a transaction, the adversary learns the resulting transaction, but not any of the secrets or trapdoors involved in producing that transaction. The oracle also provides an additional function "Insert" to the adversary, which allows it to insert arbitrary within-chain or cross-ledger transactions directly into any ledger. We finally note that access to the oracle implies view access to the two ledgers L and L'.

For simplicity but without loss of generality, we assume the security games start with "empty" chains L and L' that are initialized upon pegging (consistent to our definition).

Cross-ledger Balance guarantees that the total coin values coming into the sidechain should never exceed the total coin values going out from the mainchain. The security game is characterized by an experiment BAL (described in Fig. 1), which involves a polynomial-time adversary A attempting to break balance of a given Π_{CL} scheme. q denotes a query to O^{CL}. A query can be either a regular or cross-ledger transaction or an "Insert" transaction (supported by the oracle). a denotes the answer received from O^{CL} for a particular query. $v_{L \to L'}^{in}$, denotes the total sum of all transaction values coming into the sidechain L' and $v_{L \to L'}^{out}$ is the total sum of all transaction values going out from mainchain L. Σv_{pub} is the sum of transaction fees v_{pub} for all cross-chain transactions in queries q.

Definition 2 (Cross-ledger Balance). *A Π_{CL} scheme maintains cross-ledger balance if for every PPT adversary A there exists a negligible function negl and sufficiently large λ such that:*

$$Adv_{\Pi,A}^{\mathsf{BAL}}(\lambda) := Pr[\mathsf{BAL}(\Pi_{CL}, A, \lambda) = 1] < negl(\lambda)$$

The adversary submits a set of queried transactions q, and receives a set of transaction outputs a. The adversary wins if the total outgoing coin values from

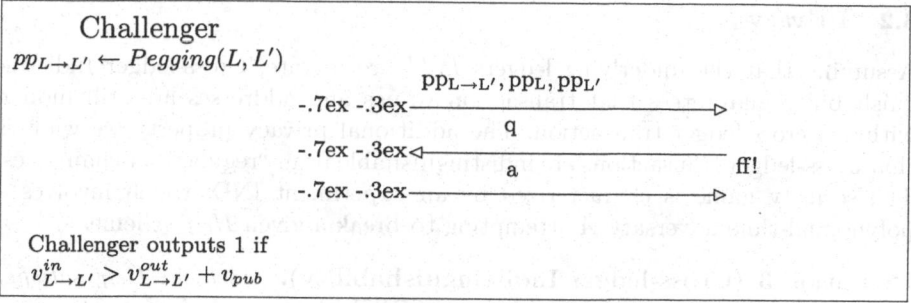

Fig. 1. The balance experiment: BAL

the mainchain is less than the total value of incoming coin values to the sidechain. The challenger can check the equation since it controls all honest users and has all adversarial secret values (since they are submitted by the adversary at the end of the game). The challenger can therefore check whether the information the adversary outputs matches the information of honest users and can also count all values transferred. The items of the equation can be calculated as the following:

- $v^{in}_{L \to L'}$, the total value of payments sent from L' to L. To compute this value, the challenger first deduces all coins that belong to an address in L and are generated by a cross-ledger transaction. $v^{in}_{L \to L'}$ equals the sum of the values of coins in this set.
- $v^{out}_{L \to L'}$, the total value of payments sent from L to L'. To compute this value, the challenger looks up all cross-ledger transactions placed on L and sums up the coin values.
- v_{pub}, the total value of transaction fees for a cross-ledger transaction from L to L' on the ledger. To compute this value, the challenger looks up all cross-ledger transactions placed on L by and sums up the corresponding v_{pub} values

An adversary can always submit a transaction on L that transfers value from L to L', but then not confirm on L'; thus, making the coins end up in "limbo". However, this does not contradict our security requirement as we only restrict that incoming coins to L' cannot exceed outgoing coins from L to prevent one-sided failures. In [12], they defined a "firewall" property similar to our definition for balance. The "firewall" property however considers a bi-directional scenario where users can make transactions between L and L'. Therefore, the "firewall" property states that the incoming value to the mainchain L cannot exceed what has been going out from itself and it compares the balance of this single chain before and after asset transfers. Our definition is for the uni-directional case and needs to check the balance of both chains. We note that our "balance" property can be extended to the bi-directional case as well by having the uni-directional requirement on both the mainchain and sidechain.

3.2 Privacy

Assuming that the underlying ledgers L, L' are private, Cross-ledger Indistinguishability guarantees that transaction values and addresses are still hidden within a cross-ledger transaction. The additional privacy property we want is that cross-ledger transactions are indistinguishable from "regular" on-chain ones. The security game is characterized by an experiment IND, which involves a polynomial-time adversary A attempting to break a given Π_{CL} scheme.

Definition 3 (Cross-ledger Indistinguishability). *A scheme Π_{CL} satisfies cross-ledger indistinguishability if for every PPT adversary A there exists a negligible function negl and sufficiently large λ such that:*

$$Adv_{\Pi,A}^{\mathsf{IND}}(\lambda) := Pr[\mathsf{IND}(\Pi, A, \lambda) = 1] - \frac{1}{2} < negl(\lambda)$$

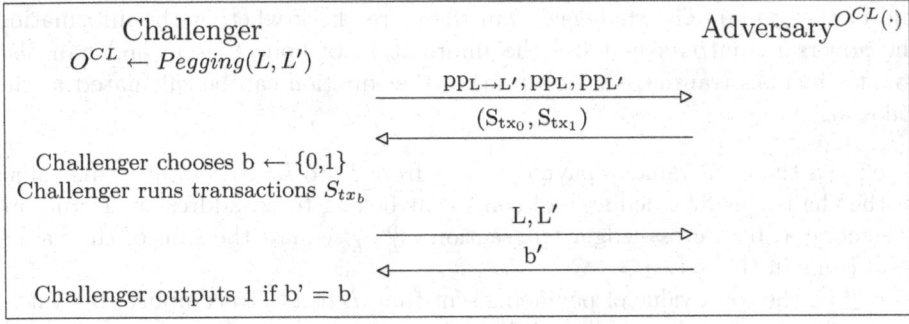

Fig. 2. The indistinguishability experiment: IND

The adversary starts by submitting two sets of transactions to the challenger S_{tx_0} and S_{tx_1}, where one of the sets only contains regular payments within a single chain and the other set contains only cross-ledger transactions from L to L'. All transactions in the sets will be in pairs. For example, suppose S_{tx_0} contains only on-chain payments, and (tx_0, tx_1) is one of the transaction pairs within the set. Then, tx_0 will be a single payment on L, while tx_1 a single payment on L'. In the all cross-ledger set S_{tx_1}, a pair (tx_0, tx_1) would mean a particular cross-ledger payment such that tx_0 is published on L and tx_1 is then confirmed on L'. Challenger then chooses a bit b and runs the transactions described in set S_{tx_b}. The adversary wins if b can be guessed correctly with probability larger than $\frac{1}{2}$ upon observing the returned ledgers. In other words, the adversary should not be able to distinguish between the two, and therefore not able to distinguish between an on-chain payment and a cross-ledger payment (Fig. 2).

Timing attacks are excluded from our particular definition. The pairwise transactions guarantee that the number of transactions included in both sets are the same. Since each transaction in a pair corresponds to either L or L', the number of transactions published on both ledgers are the same as well. Therefore, a timing attack that tries to distinguish on-chain from cross-ledger by observing the number of transactions posted in each ledger will not work. In practice, we expect this problem to be overcomed by high enough transaction volume. We discuss this in more details in Sect. 4.1.

4   Anonymous Sidechain Construction

We now describe an anonymous sidechain construction for the Zerocash [5] cryptocurrency. Our design preserves the security and anonymity properties of Zerocash and provides a mechanism to allow for cross-ledger Zerocash transfers.

Recall, that a transaction in Zerocash typically consists of the following values: $tx = (rt, sn_{old}, cm_{new}, v_{pub}, \pi)$ where rt is the Merkle Tree root that stores all coin commitments posted on the ledger, sn_{old} is the serial number of the old coin, cm_{new} is the commitment of the new coin, v_{pub} is the transaction fee and π is the ZK-SNARK for proving coin ownership (i.e. the spending user owns c_{old}, a commitment for c_{old} appears on the ledger and the user knows the merkle tree path to it, the revealed sn_{old} corresponds to c_{old} and transaction balance is maintained). We note that a regular Zerocash transaction includes some additional information (marked by $*$ when describing transactions in [5]) that encrypts the randomness used for the commitments and ties the sender's secret key with the coin in an unlikable way. This information remains the same in our construction and we omit it in our descriptions below to simplify notation.

The main difference between our transaction algorithm and regular transactions in Zerocash, is that each coin now also include the $type$: "on-L" or "to-L'". This "type" will be encoded within cm_{new} and will be checked to match the destination chain along with value, secret key, serial number etc. In other words, when spending a transaction in a chain, the spender needs to prove in ZK that the type of the transaction is "on-L", otherwise the coin is considered "burned".

Below we describe our construction which builds on top of Zerocash. Note that the Pegging and Cross-ledger Transaction algorithms do not exist in Zerocash, while the Transaction and Verify Transaction algorithms have been updated to support the special type attribute we include in the coins. For notation simplicity, we present all our algorithms for the simple case where each transaction spends a single old coin into a new coin. We do not discuss Zerocash algorithms that are orthogonal to our construction (i.e. Mint). The challenge of our design is to maintain Zerocash privacy but additionally offer cross-ledger indistinguishability.

In our full version [4] we also include an alternative, simpler and more efficient construction for Zerocash cross-chain transactions, which only offers a weaker version of privacy, i.e. does not offer cross-ledger indistinguishability.

Our Construction. We assume two Zerocash ledgers: the mainchain L and the sidechain L'. Our construction works as follows.

1. Pegging
   - inputs: security parameter λ
   - output: ledgers L, L', cross-ledger public parameters $pp_{L \to L'}$

   (a) The local public parameters for each ledger pp_L and $pp_{L'}$ are implied in L and L' respectively. pp_L and $pp_{L'}$ include signature, encryption parameters, and Merkle Tree roots for each chain.
   (b) Each ledger is labeled L or L' respectively.
   (c) $pp_{L \to L'}$ gives L' access to the Merkle Tree root of L by having a pointer to it (given that a Merkle root is a dynamic value).

2. Cross-ledger Transaction[3]
   - inputs: mainchain L and its Merkle Tree root rt, sidechain L' and its Merkle Tree root rt', cross-ledger public parameters $pp_{L \to L'}$, old coin c_{old} on L, secret address $addr_L^{sk}$ from which the coin is spent on L, secret address $addr_{L'}^{sk}$ from which the coin is spent on L', authentication path $path$ from commitment cm_{old} to root rt, new value v_{new}, destination address $addr_{L'}^{pk}$ on L', transaction fee v_{pub}, $v_{pub'}$
   - outputs: new coins c_{new} on L and $c_{new'}$ on L', transaction pairs tx (in L), tx' (in L')

   The idea here is that the coin c_{new} on L will not be spendable on L. We will ensure that by setting its type to "to-L'" which basically denotes a "burned" coin. The user first makes a deposit to L (similar to a "regular" transaction), but with a public key on L'.

   Concretely, the user that wants to do a cross-ledger transaction from L to L' takes the following steps:

   Actions on L: Parses the old (or else to be spent) coin $c_{old} = ($type $=$ "on-L", $addr_L^{pk}$, v_{old}, ρ_{old}, r_{old}, s_{old}, $cm_{old})^{[4]}$. Then, the sender who should also know $addr_L^{sk}$ computes:

   - $sn_{old} := \mathsf{PRF}_{addr_L^{sk}}(\rho_{old})$
   - Sample ρ_{new} and r_{new}, s_{new}.
   - $cm_{new} := \mathsf{COMM}_{s_{new}}($type $=$ "to-L'" $||v_{new}||k)$ where for k it holds that $k := \mathsf{COMM}_{r_{new}}(addr_{L'}^{pk}||\rho_{new})$. The value cm_{new} is added to merkle tree with root rt.
   - Set $c_{new} = ($type $=$ "to-L'", $addr_{L'}^{pk}$, v_{new}, ρ_{new}, r_{new}, s_{new}, $cm_{new})$.
   - The transaction will be recorded publicly on ledger L as:
     $tx := (rt, sn_{old}, cm_{new}, v_{pub}, \pi)$

   The statement for the proof π is tx, rt and it proves that:

   - sn_{old}, cm_{old} and cm_{new} are well formed.
   - The type in c_{old} and cm_{old} is equal to "on-L".

---

[3] This is a new algorithm introduced to allow cross-ledger transactions.
[4] ρ denotes serial number randomness and r, s commitment randomness.

- cm_{old} that corresponds to c_{old}, appears on L (i.e. the input path is the authentication that cm_{old} is under the root rt).
- The secret key address $addr_L^{sk}$ corresponds to $addr_L^{pk}$.
- Balance is preserved, i.e. $v_{old} = v_{new} + v_{pub}$.

Actions on L': The sender from L then mints a coin on L' by confirming that cm_{new} with type = "to-L'" is a leaf of rt. We now describe the specific steps. It first parses $c_{new} = $ (type, $addr_{L'}^{pk}$, v_{new}, ρ, r, s, cm_{new}). Then, the sender who should also know $addr_{L'}^{sk}$ (we assume that the sender moves the funds to an address that it knows in L') computes:

- $sn_{new} := \mathsf{PRF}_{addr_{L'}^{sk}}(\rho_{new})$
- Sample $\rho_{new'}$ and $r_{new'}, s_{new'}$.
- $cm_{new'} := \mathsf{COMM}_{s_{new'}}(\text{type} = \text{"on-}L'\text{"} \,||v_{new'}||k')$ where for k' it holds that $k' := \mathsf{COMM}_{r_{new'}}(addr_{L'}^{pk}||\rho_{new'})$. The value $cm_{new'}$ is added to merkle tree with root rt'.
- Set $c_{new'} = $ (type = "on-L'", $addr_{L'}^{pk}$, $v_{new'}$, $\rho_{new'}$, $r_{new'}$, $s_{new'}$, $cm_{new'}$).
- The transaction will be recorded publicly on ledger L' as:
  $tx' := (rt', sn_{new}, cm_{new'}, v_{pub'}, \pi')$

The statement for the proof π' is tx', rt, rt' and it proves that:

- sn_{new}, cm_{new} and $cm_{new'}$ are well formed.
- The type in $c_{new'}$ and $cm_{new'}$ is equal to "on-L'".
- cm_{new} that corresponds to c_{new}, appears on L and has type "to-L'" so that it is ensured to have been "burned" on L. To prove that it appears on L it shows that the input path is the authentication that cm_{new} is under the root rt.
- The secret key address $addr_{L'}^{sk}$ corresponds to $addr_{L'}^{pk}$.
- Balance is preserved, i.e. $v_{new} = v_{new'} + v_{pub'}$.

Converting π to an OR Proof: If our proofs π, π' are computed as stated above, then a verifier could distinguish between transactions within L (or withing L') and cross-ledger transactions to L' since the statements in π, π' differ.

To overcome this issue, the proof π included in a transaction, will instead be a disjunctive proof that includes tx, rt, rt' in the statement. The proof will prove that either (a) the old coin c_{old} to be spent, is on L (i.e., its commitment is in rt) and has type "on-L" OR (b) the old coin c_{old} is on L and has type "to-L'" and the new coin c_{new} is on L' (its commitment is in rt') has type "on-L'".

3. Transaction

- inputs: mainchain L (includes parameters and Merkle tree root rt), sidechain L' (includes parameters and Merkle tree root rt'), old coin c_{old}, old address secret key $addr_{old}^{sk}$, authentication path $path$ from commitment cm_{old} to root rt, new value v_{new}, destination address public key $addr_{new}^{pk}$, transaction fee v_{pub}
- outputs: new coin c_{new}, transaction tx

Transaction performs "Regular" transactions on a single ledger (here described for L) following the Zerocash "Pour" mechanism. The spender performs the exact same operations as those detailed on the "Actions on L" part of cross-ledger transaction algorithm above. The only difference is that for an on-chain transaction the type of the generated coin $c_{new'}$ will be "on-L". To ensure indistinguishability, the ZK proof π will be computed as on OR proof as detailed above.

4. Verify Transaction

- input: cross-ledger public parameters $pp_{L \to L'}$, ledger L, L' transaction tx
- output: bit b, equals 1 iff the transaction is valid

This algorithm verifies a transaction before it is included in the current ledger. It works in the same way for both L and L'. It first parses tx to $(rt, sn_{old}, cm_{new}, v_{pub}, \pi)$. Then:

- If sn_{old} already appears in L then output 0.
- If rt does not appear in L then output 0.
- If π verifies then output 1 else output 0.

Miners are required to honestly submit the current chain status and block header of L to L' with a certificate.

Relation to Zerocash. The Cross-ledger Transaction does not exist in Zerocash and is a new algorithm that supports anonymous cross-chain transactions that move assets between chains and changes the coin balance on both chains. Besides the new "type" attribute introduced in our construction, all algorithms require both ledgers as inputs due to our cross-ledger indistinguishability property.

Efficiency Discussion. The Zerocash construction stores the list of all serial numbers and all coin commitments in two separate Merkle Trees. In addition to the regular Zerocash storage requirement, a ledger in our construction requires a pointer to the Merkle Tree root of each chain that it is pegged with in order to perform cross-ledger transactions. In terms of computation, proving time is slightly increased since the underlying SNARK circuit requires additional statements on the coin type and an OR proof, while verification needs to take as input merkle tree roots from both chains.

4.1 Security Analysis

In Sect. 3 we defined the correctness, security and privacy guarantees for anonymous sidechains. Our protocols rely on consistency and liveness of the underlying consensus of L and L', binding and hiding properties of the commitment scheme and the Merkle tree, soundness and ZK of zk-SNARKs and security of Zerocash. Below we informally argue how our design satisfies all the required properties.

Correctness. Our construction satisfies the correctness guarantees by preserving the security and correctness of all "regular" Zerocash on-chain activities. Therefore, properties such as "unspent coins can be spent" and "tx is includable in L" are fulfilled with the underlying consensus of each chain. We only require an additional cross-ledger correctness requirement such that tx is guaranteed to happen before tx'. This is fulfilled as spending the coin to get tx' requires checking for the serial number in tx. Plus, the value of cross-ledger transaction needs to be checked to match (i.e. $v_{tx}^{old} = v_{tx'}^{new} + v_{pub}$) to successfully spend on L' the coin burned in L.

Security. For security, we first want that a transaction announced on L cannot be modified in any way before confirming. In other words, we want to prevent an on-chain transaction to be double spent into a cross-ledger transaction. This requirement is satisfied by the standard non-malleability property on each Zerocash chain, which we assume to hold. We argue that mix and match attacks do not work either. Suppose we run 2 cross-chain transactions and two valid resulting pairs $(tx_1, tx_{1'})$ and $(tx_2, tx_{2'})$ are generated, where tx_1 and tx_2 are transactions published on L and $tx_{1'}$ and $tx_{2'}$ are on L'. $(tx_1, tx_{2'})$ and $(tx_2, tx_{1'})$ can never become valid pairs. First, standard malleability says that no adversary can alter any of the data stored within a valid transaction. Second, tx_1 specifies the receiving address in $tx_{1'}$ and $tx_{1'}$ can only be valid if the address in tx_1 matches. Third, the coin commitment is strictly hiding because of hiding property of the commitment scheme and the serial numbers cannot repeat because of collision resistant in Merkle Tree. Thus, a mix and match attack is impossible.

For the balance guarantee that protects total value of incoming coins to the sidechain to never exceed all outgoing coins from the mainchain, we rely on the balance property of Zerocash. As we are no different from how their coin commitments are stored in the Merkle Tree, it is impossible to find another valid authenticated path from a leaf to the root for proof of membership. So it is impossible to have coins not in the Merkle Tree to be validated for a transaction from sidechain to mainchain. We can also add timelock functionalities to cross-ledger transactions to prevent aborts. So coins not deposited after a certain period of time will go back to the payer's public key address.

Privacy. We rely on the indistinguishability property in Zerocash transactions, and our construction is different in two ways. First, our newly introduced "type" attribute is never revealed during checks and confirmations due to the zk-SNARK used in Zerocash. Since the only visible public information for a coin is its commitment. Its type (L or L'), value, and associated public keys cannot be inferred from the commitment and all coin commitments are indistinguishable from each other. Second, our OR proof design for the proof π included in transactions, guarantees that the proof does not reveal the flow of a coin while correctly verifies a transaction. The coin to be spent and the coin generated will either be both on the same ledger or the coin to be spent is marked as a cross-ledger one and the corresponding new coin indeed ends up on the different ledger. We force the proof to look at both ledgers so that the coin source and destination will not be trivially revealed. Similarly, we take both ledgers as inputs for all our algorithms.

We have argued in Sect. 3.2 that "timing attacks" that attempt to deduce the "type" by observing the number of transactions on each ledger are excluded under our Cross-ledger Indistinguishability definition. In practice, we assume that in an actual implementation, there are enough incoming transactions to L' so that L' is growing with L when a new on-chain transaction is performed on L. On-chain transactions keep happening on both ledgers and the traffic makes pairing transactions on L and L' to be confused with a cross-ledger transaction pair possible in reality. For instance, we note that Zerocash has an average of 7 transactions per block. One can also make dummy transactions with zero value to the sidechain when making a transaction on the mainchain with a transaction fee to achieve perfect indistinguishability. Therefore, timing attack is not a concern in reality and an observer cannot easily tell a regular "Transaction" operation from a "Cross-ledger Transaction" due to regular real-time coin flow.

Acknowledgments. We thank the anonymous reviewers for all their useful constructive comments and editorial suggestions. Foteini Baldimtsi is supported by NSF Grant CNS-01717067, by NSA Grant 204761 (under a CMU Subcontract No. 1990713-40018), by an IBM faculty award and by a Facebook faculty award.

References

1. Commonwealth crypto. https://www.commonwealthcrypto.com
2. Androulaki, E., Karame, G.O., Roeschlin, M., Scherer, T., Capkun, S.: Evaluating user privacy in bitcoin. In: Sadeghi, A.-R. (ed.) FC 2013. LNCS, vol. 7859, pp. 34–51. Springer, Heidelberg (2013). https://doi.org/10.1007/978-3-642-39884-1_4
3. Back, S.A., et al.: Enabling blockchain innovations with pegged (2014)
4. Baldimtsi, F., Ian Miers, X.Z.: Anonymous sidechains. In: Garcia-Alfaro, J., et al. (eds.) DPM 2021/CBT 2021. LNCS, vol. 13140, pp. 262–277. Springer, Cham (2022)
5. Ben-Sasson, E., et al.: Zerocash: decentralized anonymous payments from bitcoin. In: 2014 IEEE Symposium on Security and Privacy, pp. 459–474. IEEE Computer Society Press, May 2014. https://doi.org/10.1109/SP.2014.36
6. Ben-Sasson, E., Chiesa, A., Tromer, E., Virza, M.: Succinct non-interactive zero knowledge for a von Neumann architecture. In: Fu, K., Jung, J. (eds.) USENIX Security 2014, pp. 781–796. USENIX Association, August 2014
7. Biryukov, A., Khovratovich, D., Pustogarov, I.: Deanonymisation of clients in Bitcoin P2P network. CoRR abs/1405.7418 (2014)
8. Bonneau, J., Narayanan, A., Miller, A., Clark, J., Kroll, J.A., Felten, E.W.: Mixcoin: anonymity for bitcoin with accountable mixes. In: Christin, N., Safavi-Naini, R. (eds.) FC 2014. LNCS, vol. 8437, pp. 486–504. Springer, Heidelberg (2014). https://doi.org/10.1007/978-3-662-45472-5_31
9. Bowe, S., Chiesa, A., Green, M., Miers, I., Mishra, P., Wu, H.: ZEXE: enabling decentralized private computation. In: 2020 IEEE Symposium on Security and Privacy, pp. 947–964. IEEE Computer Society Press, May 2020. https://doi.org/10.1109/SP40000.2020.00050
10. Chu, S., Xia, Q., Zhang, Z.: Manta: privacy preserving decentralized exchange. Cryptology ePrint Archive, report 2020/1607 (2020)
11. Deshpande, A., Herlihy, M.: Privacy-preserving cross-chain atomic swaps. In: Bernhard, M., et al. (eds.) FC 2020. LNCS, vol. 12063, pp. 540–549. Springer, Cham (2020). https://doi.org/10.1007/978-3-030-54455-3_38

12. Gazi, P., Kiayias, A., Zindros, D.: Proof-of-stake sidechains. In: 2019 IEEE Symposium on Security and Privacy, pp. 139–156. IEEE Computer Society Press, May 2019. https://doi.org/10.1109/SP.2019.00040

13. Groth, J.: Short pairing-based non-interactive zero-knowledge arguments. In: Abe, M. (ed.) ASIACRYPT 2010. LNCS, vol. 6477, pp. 321–340. Springer, Heidelberg (2010). https://doi.org/10.1007/978-3-642-17373-8_19

14. Heilman, E., Alshenibr, L., Baldimtsi, F., Scafuro, A., Goldberg, S.: TumbleBit: an untrusted bitcoin-compatible anonymous payment hub. In: NDSS 2017. The Internet Society, February/March 2017

15. Heilman, E., Lipmann, S., Goldberg, S.: The arwen trading protocols. In: Bonneau, J., Heninger, N. (eds.) FC 2020. LNCS, vol. 12059, pp. 156–173. Springer, Cham (2020). https://doi.org/10.1007/978-3-030-51280-4_10

16. Herlihy, M.: Atomic cross-chain swaps. In: PODC (2018)

17. Kiayias, A., Miller, A., Zindros, D.: Non-interactive proofs of proof-of-work. In: Bonneau, J., Heninger, N. (eds.) FC 2020. LNCS, vol. 12059, pp. 505–522. Springer, Cham (2020). https://doi.org/10.1007/978-3-030-51280-4_27

18. Kiayias, A., Zindros, D.: Proof-of-work sidechains. In: Bracciali, A., Clark, J., Pintore, F., Rønne, P.B., Sala, M. (eds.) FC 2019. LNCS, vol. 11599, pp. 21–34. Springer, Cham (2020). https://doi.org/10.1007/978-3-030-43725-1_3

19. Maxwell, G.: CoinJoin: bitcoin privacy for the real world (2013). https://bitcointalk.org/index.php?topic=279249.0

20. Maxwell, G.: CoinSwap: transaction graph disjoint trustless trading (2013). https://bitcointalk.org/index.php?topic=321228.0

21. Merkle, R.C.: A digital signature based on a conventional encryption function. In: Pomerance, C. (ed.) CRYPTO 1987. LNCS, vol. 293, pp. 369–378. Springer, Heidelberg (1988). https://doi.org/10.1007/3-540-48184-2_32

22. Miers, I., Garman, C., Green, M., Rubin, A.D.: Zerocoin: anonymous distributed E-cash from bitcoin. In: 2013 IEEE Symposium on Security and Privacy, pp. 397–411. IEEE Computer Society Press, May 2013. https://doi.org/10.1109/SP.2013.34

23. Nakamoto, S.: Bitcoin: a peer-to-peer electronic cash system (2009). http://www.bitcoin.org/bitcoin.pdf

24. Naor, M.: Bit commitment using pseudo-randomness. In: Brassard, G. (ed.) CRYPTO 1989. LNCS, vol. 435, pp. 128–136. Springer, New York (1990). https://doi.org/10.1007/0-387-34805-0_13

25. Pedersen, T.P.: Non-interactive and information-theoretic secure verifiable secret sharing. In: Feigenbaum, J. (ed.) CRYPTO 1991. LNCS, vol. 576, pp. 129–140. Springer, Heidelberg (1992). https://doi.org/10.1007/3-540-46766-1_9

26. Reid, F., Harrigan, M.: An analysis of anonymity in the bitcoin system. In: 2011 IEEE Third International Conference on Privacy, Security, Risk and Trust and 2011 IEEE Third International Conference on Social Computing, pp. 1318–1326 (2011). https://doi.org/10.1109/PASSAT/SocialCom.2011.79

27. Ruffing, T., Moreno-Sanchez, P., Kate, A.: CoinShuffle: practical decentralized coin mixing for bitcoin. In: Kutyłowski, M., Vaidya, J. (eds.) ESORICS 2014. LNCS, vol. 8713, pp. 345–364. Springer, Cham (2014). https://doi.org/10.1007/978-3-319-11212-1_20

28. van Saberhagen, N.: Cryptonote v 2.0 (2013). https://bytecoin.org/old/whitepaper.pdf

CBT Workshop: Short Papers

Filling the Tax Gap via Programmable Money

Dimitris Karakostas[1]([✉]) and Aggelos Kiayias[1,2]

[1] University of Edinburgh, Edinburgh, Scotland
dimitris.karakostas@ed.ac.uk, akiayias@inf.ed.ac.uk
[2] IOHK, Edinburgh, Scotland

Abstract. We discuss the problem of facilitating tax auditing assuming "programmable money", i.e., digital monetary instruments that are managed by an underlying distributed ledger. We explore how a taxation authority can verify the declared returns of its citizens and create a counter-incentive to tax evasion by two distinct mechanisms. First, we describe a design which enables auditing it as a built-in feature with minimal changes on the underlying ledger's consensus protocol. Second, we offer an application-layer extension, which requires no modification in the underlying ledger's design. Both solutions provide a high level of privacy, ensuring that, apart from specific limited data given to the taxation authority, no additional information—beyond the information already published on the underlying ledger—is leaked.

1 Introduction

A tax gap [8] is a difference between the reported and the real tax revenue, for a given jurisdiction and period of time. Research estimated that the tax gap in the USA was 16.4% of revenue owed [11] between 2008–2010, the total loss throughout the EU due to the tax gap to €151.5 billion in 2015 [12], while $\frac{1}{3}$ of taxpayers in the UK under-report their earnings [1] (albeit half of UK's lost taxes are product of a small, wealthy fraction of misbehaving taxpayers). Therefore, reducing the tax gaps can significantly enhance the efforts of tax-collecting authorities.

Central bank digital currencies (CBDC) have also come to prominence in recent years. In the past decade, distributed ledger-based financial systems, which were kick-started with the creation of Bitcoin [13], were accompanied by the increasing digitalization of payments [4]. CBDCs are the culmination of these trends, enabling fast, cheap, and safe transactions in fiat assets. Crucially though, although still mostly on a research stage,[1] CBDCs have caused great concerns on citizens regarding transaction privacy [7].

Our work offers two mechanisms that facilitate tax auditing and the identification of tax gaps in distributed ledger-based currency systems. The first is a

---

[1] https://cbdctracker.org [July 2021].

© Springer Nature Switzerland AG 2022
J. Garcia-Alfaro et al. (Eds.): DPM 2021/CBT 2021, LNCS 13140, pp. 281–288, 2022.
https://doi.org/10.1007/978-3-030-93944-1_18

wrapper around a generic distributed ledger, which enables taxpayers to declare their assets directly to the authorities, while undeclared assets are frozen. The second is a proof mechanism that enables the sender of some assets to prove, in a privacy-preserving manner, whether the transferred assets have been taxed. Both mechanisms are examples of programmable money (also referred to as smart money [3]), where currency is programmed to be transferable under a suitable set of circumstances or its transfer has specific implications.

1.1 Desiderata

In distributed ledger-based currency systems, a user $\mathcal{U}$ manages their assets via addresses. Each address α is associated with a key pair (sk, vk), such that the private key sk is used to claim ownership of the assets, e.g., by signing special messages; typically $\alpha = \mathsf{H}(vk)$ for some hash function H. Each address α is associated with a (public) balance $\mathsf{bal}(\alpha)$ so, given a list $[\alpha_1, \ldots, \alpha_n]$ of all addresses that $\mathcal{U}$ controls, $\mathcal{U}$'s total assets are $\Theta = \sum_{i=1}^{n} \mathsf{bal}(\alpha_i)$. Our goal will be to retain as much privacy as possible, so Θ should be the only information leaked to tax authority $\mathcal{T}$, without de-anonymization of specific transaction data.

To showcase the limitations of current systems, consider the following example. Assume that Alice tax evades, i.e., creates a secret, undeclared address α and controls some assets θ in it. Given the pseudonymous nature of the ledger, α cannot be correlated with Alice, until she uses it. Following, Alice issues a transaction τ which sends θ assets from α to Bob. If Bob suspects that Alice evaded taxation for these θ assets, they might want to report her to the authorities for inspection. However, the complaint should be accompanied by a proof that α is controlled by Alice, i.e., a proof that Alice knows the private key associated with α. This is necessary as $\mathcal{T}$ needs to distinguish between two scenarios: i) Alice controls α and tax evades; ii) Bob is lying about Alice owning α. In the first scenario, Bob *does* know that α is controlled by Alice, but τ is not sufficient to prove it. Instead, Bob needs a proof which can only be supplied by Alice, e.g., a signature from Alice which acknowledges τ or α. However, if Alice tax evades, naturally she would not create such incriminating proof.

It is important that we retain as many good features of existing ledger systems as possible. The most notable such feature is transaction privacy, thus our work considers pseudonymous, Bitcoin-like levels of privacy, and minimizes the information leaked to the authorities during a tax auditing. Another important aspect is the mechanism's performance. A fundamental ingredient of payment systems is the seamless transaction experience, so it is important to allow users to transact at all times, while also avoiding significant strain during taxation periods. Finally, our mechanisms aim to minimize the amount of (additional) published data, since storage in distributed ledgers is particularly costly.

In summary, the desiderata of our mechanisms are as follows:

- *Tax gap identification and counterincentive*: Tax evasion, i.e., failure of a user $\mathcal{U}$ to declare the amount of assets they own, should be either detectable by a tax authority $\mathcal{T}$, with access to the ledger, or render the assets unusable.

- *High level of privacy*: T should—at most—learn the total amount of assets owned by each taxpayer at the end of a fiscal year; this information should be leaked only to T and no additional information should be leaked to any other party, apart from the information already published on the ledger.
- *Unobstructed operation*: The introduction of a taxation mechanism should not result in any period during which the—tax compliant—users are prohibited from transacting.
- *Low performance overhead*: The taxation mechanism should not introduce a major performance overhead, in terms of computation and storage requirements from the users and the taxation authority.
- *Balanced load*: The computation and storage overhead of taxation should be spread over a period of time, rather than introduce performance spikes.

1.2 Related Work

Literature offers various works on auditing of distributed ledger-based assets. A holistic approach is taken in zkLedger [14], which combines a permissioned ledger with zero-knowledge proofs to create a tamper-resistant, verifiable ledger of transactions. PRCash [18] also employs a permissioned ledger and offers a regulation mechanism that restricts the total amount of assets a user can receive anonymously for a period of time. Also Garman *et al.* [10] propose an anonymous ledger, which can enforce specific transaction policies. In our paper, Sect. 2 aims at offering a simpler design, which can be more easily integrated in existing pseudonymous distributed ledgers, compared to the aforementioned works. Another interesting research thread considers proofs of solvency. The first such scheme for Bitcoin exchanges, proposed by Maxwell [17], leaks the total amount of both assets and liabilities of the exchange; more importantly, it enables an attack that allows the exchange to hide assets, as detailed by in Zeroledge [6], which also proposed a privacy-preserving system that allows exchanges to prove properties about their holdings. Provisions [5] is a zero-knowledge proof of solvency mechanism for Bitcoin exchanges, based on Sigma protocols i.e., without the need to reveal the addresses or the amount of assets that an exchange controls. Similarly, Agrawal *et al.* [2] describe a proof of solvency which achieves better performance compared to Provisions, although assuming a trusted setup. The mechanism of Sect. 3 extends Provisions and is also applicable to [2].

2   Tax Auditable Distributed Ledger

In this section we describe a ledger with a built-in tax auditing mechanism. Our design is generic, such that existing ledgers can incorporate it with minimal changes in the underlying consensus protocol. An *auditable ledger* enforces a user U to declare the amount of assets they own to a taxation authority T, with failure to do so rendering the assets unusable. We achieve this while leaking to T only the total amount of assets that U owns at a specific point in time, e.g., the end of a fiscal year. We note that we consider only pseudonymous ledgers, so potentially de-anonymizable data may be published on the ledger, e.g., addresses which may be linked to the user who controls them.

We assume that $\mathcal{T}$ holds a list of all taxpayers and is identified by a key $(sk_\mathcal{T}, vk_\mathcal{T})$. Also there exist taxation periods, which last for a pre-specified amount of time d. For example, a taxation period may last 1 calendar year, at the end of which taxpayers need to declare their assets to the authorities.

The core idea is that assets unaccounted for, at the end of the taxation period, are frozen, until their owners declare them to the authority. Specifically, at the end of a taxation period, all assets are frozen. To unfreeze an asset, a taxpayer $\mathcal{U}$ declares it to $\mathcal{T}$ as follows.

First, $\mathcal{U}$ creates a new key pair $(sk_\mathcal{U}, vk_\mathcal{U})$ and the corresponding address $\alpha_\mathcal{U}$ and sends $\alpha_\mathcal{U}$ to $\mathcal{T}$ as part of a KYC process. Next, $\mathcal{T}$ certifies $\alpha_\mathcal{U}$ by issuing the signature $\sigma = \mathsf{Sign}(\alpha_\mathcal{U}, sk_\mathcal{T})$, which it gives to $\mathcal{U}$. The tuple $\alpha_\mathcal{U}^t = \langle \alpha_\mathcal{U}, \sigma \rangle$ is the *certified address*, which is used by the user to transact with frozen assets. $\mathcal{T}$ maintains a mapping of taxpayers and certified addresses, i.e., for every taxpayer $\mathcal{U}$ it holds a list $A_\mathcal{U}$ of all certified taxation addresses that $\mathcal{U}$ requested.

A transaction $\tau = \langle \alpha_s, \alpha_d, \Theta \rangle$, which moves Θ frozen assets from an address α_s, is valid only if $\alpha_d = \langle \alpha, \sigma \rangle \wedge \mathsf{Verify}(\alpha, \sigma, vk_\mathcal{T}) = 1$. Consequently, miners accept transactions that unfreeze assets only as long as said assets are transferred to a certified address. Therefore, $\mathcal{T}$ can compute the amount of $\mathcal{U}$'s assets as $\Theta_\mathcal{U} := \sum_{i=1}^n \mathsf{bal}(\alpha_\mathcal{U}[i])$, n being the total number of $\mathcal{U}$'s certified addresses.

We note that the system can accommodate multiple taxation authorities from different countries. In that case, $\mathcal{T}$ is a federation of authorities, each identified by a single key. Each authority's key is published on the ledger and a taxpayer can certify their addresses and declare their assets to the respective authorities.

Naturally, this mechanism introduces some challenges. Although standard pay-to-public-key-hash addresses are 25 bytes, certified addresses may be significantly larger, due to the certification signature of $\mathcal{T}$. For instance, ECDSA signatures in the DER format result in 72 additional bytes, thus making certified addresses 99 bytes long. Nevertheless, certified addresses are expected to be used only once, to declare the assets, thus the overall storage cost should not be significant. Another important consideration regards to the private state of the taxation authority; given the statute of limitations, $\mathcal{T}$ might need to maintain its taxation private key and the mapping of certified addresses for a significant period, possibly resulting in significant maintenance costs.

We showcase our design via an auditable variation of Bitcoin ledger, denoted as $\mathcal{L}^t$. $\mathcal{L}^t$ is initially parameterized by the public key of the authority $(sk_\mathcal{T}, vk_\mathcal{T})$, which is part of the ledger's genesis block. During the execution, $\mathcal{T}$ can update its key by simply signing a new key $vk_\mathcal{T}'$ with $sk_\mathcal{T}$ and publishing it on the ledger. A taxation period lasts 52560 blocks, i.e., roughly 1 calendar year, so block 52560 and its multiples are "tax-auditing" blocks. When a tax-auditing block is issued, all assets on $\mathcal{L}^t$ which are controlled by non-certified addresses are frozen. To transact with assets from a frozen address, a user sends them to a certified address, as described above.

Freezing complicates the system in a number of ways. First, the liveness of a transaction [9] may be affected. For instance, a transaction which spends from a non-certified address will be rejected, if it is created before but published after a tax-auditing block. We sidestep this issue by enabling users to use certified addresses before the freezing period, hence the liveness guarantees of the ledger apply unconditionally on certified addresses. Second, it is possible that multiple competing tax-auditing blocks are created, e.g., multiple blocks which extend the tax-auditing block. Therefore, $\mathcal{T}$ needs to pick one and certify it. Afterwards, this certified block cannot be reverted and acts as a "checkpoint".

We note that $\mathcal{L}^t$ covers the desiderata proposed in Sect. 1.1. Regarding privacy, although $\mathcal{T}$ can de-anonymize the set of $\mathcal{L}^t$ users at a specific point in time, i.e., when the assets freeze, the users can employ standard Bitcoin addresses and transactions outwith this period. Additionally, as with standard Bitcoin addresses, third parties cannot obtain information regarding the identity of a certified address's owner (as long as the signature itself does not leak it). In terms of performance, a user can transact with their assets effortlessly, as long as they use certified addresses to receive or unfreeze assets around the taxation period. Importantly, users can certify their addresses ahead of the freezing time, thus the additional load can be spread over a period of a few days or weeks.

3   A Tax-Auditing Extension for Provisions

We now build a tax auditing mechanism for existing ledgers based on Provisions [5]. The goal of this mechanism is to enable all payment recipients to verify whether the assets used by a sender $\mathcal{E}$ in a transaction have been properly declared to the authority $\mathcal{T}$. This is achieved in two stages, first with an asset declaration stage that involves $\mathcal{T}$ and second with a payer address auditing protocol, which is created in tandem with the transaction that pays a recipient, and after $\mathcal{E}$ commits to owning the assets. If $\mathcal{E}$ fails to provide such proof, the implication is that $\mathcal{E}$ performs tax evasion. To build this mechanism we rely on Provisions [5], particularly its *proof of assets*. Our scheme comprises of two simple protocols, which $\mathcal{E}$ runs with the taxation authority and their counter-party respectively. As we show, our protocols retain Provisions' privacy guarantees.

Provisions is a privacy-preserving auditing mechanism for Bitcoin exchanges. Using Provisions a party can verify that a (cooperating) Bitcoin exchange is solvent, i.e., possesses enough assets to cover the liabilities towards its users. In order to achieve this, Provisions defines three protocols: i) proof of assets, ii) proof of liabilities, and iii) proof of solvency. Our work is only concerned in the assets owned by the exchange, thus we focus on the proof of assets. All proofs are considered under a group G of prime order q with fixed public generators g, h. The proof of assets considers the following:

- $\text{PK} = \{y_1, \ldots, y_n\}$: the total (anonymity) set of public keys;
- s_i: a bit such that, if the exchange controls y_i, i.e., if it possesses the private key of y_i, then $s_i = 1$, otherwise $s_i = 0$;
- $\text{bal}(y_i)$: the amount of assets that the address corresponding to y_i controls;

- $\Theta = \sum_{i=1}^{n} s_i \cdot \mathsf{bal}(y_i)$: the amount of assets that the exchange controls;
- $b_i = g^{\mathsf{bal}(y_i)}$: a binding (but not hiding) commitment to the balance of y_i.

The exchange publishes the Pedersen commitments [15] for each $s_i \cdot \mathsf{bal}(y_i), s_i$:

$$p_i = b_i^{s_i} \cdot h^{v_i} = g^{\mathsf{bal}(y_i) \cdot s_i} \cdot h^{v_i} \tag{1}$$

$$l_i = y_i^{s_i} h^{t_i} = g^{\hat{x}_i} h^{t_i} \tag{2}$$

where $v_i, t_i \in \mathbb{Z}_q$ are chosen at random, x_i is the private key for y_i, and $\hat{x}_i = x_i \cdot s_i$.

Asset Declaration. $\mathcal{E}$ declares the total amount of assets it controls, i.e., the value Θ, to $\mathcal{T}$ who verifies that $\mathcal{E}$'s commitments correspond to Θ. We obtain the condition $Z_\Theta = \prod_{i=1}^{n} p_i = g^\Theta \cdot h^v$, where $v = \sum_{i=1}^{n} v_i$, is a (publicly computable) Pedersen commitment to $\mathcal{E}$'s assets. Given that $\mathcal{T}$ knows Θ, $\mathcal{E}$ needs only to prove knowledge of a value v, such that this condition is satisfied. This is done via the Schnorr protocol [16] of Fig. 1, which guarantees privacy (cf. Lemma 1).

Asset Declaration Protocol $\mathcal{P}_{asset}$

Public data: $g, h, Z_\Theta = \prod_{i=1}^{n} p_i$
Verifier's input from prover: Θ
Prover's input: $v = \sum_{i=1}^{n} v_i$

1. The prover ($\mathcal{E}$) chooses $r \xleftarrow{\$} \mathbb{Z}_q$ and sends $\lambda = h^r$ to the verifier ($\mathcal{T}$).
2. The verifier replies with a challenge $c \xleftarrow{\$} \mathbb{Z}_q$.
3. The prover responds with $\theta = r + c \cdot v$.
4. The verifier accepts if $h^\theta \overset{?}{=} \lambda \cdot (Z_\Theta \cdot g^{-\Theta})^c$.

Fig. 1. Tax-auditing between $\mathcal{E}$ (prover) and $\mathcal{T}$ (verifier).

Lemma 1. *For public values g, h and Z_Θ, the protocol $\mathcal{P}_{asset}$ is an honest-verifier zero-knowledge argument of knowledge of quantity v satisfying $Z_\Theta = \prod_{i=1}^{n} p_i = g^\Theta \cdot h^v$ for $i \in [1, n]$.*

Payer Address Auditing. The second part of our taxation proof enables the auditing of a specific address of a payer $\mathcal{E}$, when a payment is made to another user $\mathcal{U}$. $\mathcal{E}$ will prove two conditions to $\mathcal{U}$: i) for some $i \in [1, n]$, the public key y_i (which is published as part of the Provisions scheme) corresponds to the address from which $\mathcal{U}$ receives their assets; ii) the corresponding bit s_i for y_i in the commitment condition (2) is $s_i = 1$. The first condition can be easily proven by providing $\mathcal{U}$ with an index i, such that $\mathcal{U}$ confirms that the address in question is equal to the hash of y_i. To prove the second condition, we observe that, for $s_i = 1$, $p_i = g^{\mathsf{bal}(y_i)} h^{v_i}$ and $l_i = y_i h^{t_i}$. Therefore, $\mathcal{E}$ needs only to prove knowledge of t_i and v_i, such that this statement is satisfied, which can be achieved via the Schnorr protocol of Fig. 2, its privacy properties formalized in Lemma 2.

Address Verification Protocol $\mathcal{P}_{address}$

Public data: h, (y_i, l_i), $\mathsf{bal}(y_i)$ for $i \in [1, n]$
Verifier's input from prover: i
Prover's input: t_i

1. The prover ($\mathcal{E}$) chooses $r_1, r_2 \xleftarrow{\$} \mathbb{Z}_q$ and sends $\lambda_1 = h^{r_1}, \lambda_2 = h^{r_2}$ to the verifier.
2. The verifier replies with a challenge $c \xleftarrow{\$} \mathbb{Z}_q$.
3. The prover responds with $\theta_1 = r_1 + c \cdot t_i$, $\theta_2 = r_2 + c \cdot v_i$.
4. The verifier accepts if $h^{\theta_1} \overset{?}{=} \lambda_1 \cdot (l_i \cdot y_i^{-1})^c$ and $h^{\theta_2} \overset{?}{=} \lambda_2 \cdot (p_i \cdot g^{-\mathsf{bal}(y_i)})^c$.

Fig. 2. Address verification between $\mathcal{E}$ (prover) and a user $\mathcal{U}$ (verifier).

Lemma 2. *For public values g, h and $y_i, l_i, p_i, \mathsf{bal}(y_i)$, the protocol $\mathcal{P}_{address}$ is an honest-verifier zero-knowledge argument of knowledge of quantities t_i, v_i satisfying $l_i = y_i h^{t_i}$ and $p_i = g^{\mathsf{bal}(y_i)} h^{v_i}$ respectively.*

4   Conclusion

Our work offers a programmable money approach for authorities to audit the citizens' tax returns and create a tax-gap counter-incentive: undeclared fund transfers are programmed to be frozen in the ledger. We identify a number of limitations and desiderata and present two basic designs, which can act as a stepping stone for more concrete solutions. Our mechanisms can be employed by different tax authorities and be applied on different ledger designs. Naturally, to efficiently utilize it on a global scale for decentralized systems, like Bitcoin, tax authorities of all countries would need to collaborate, an assumption which seems infeasible in our current fragmented landscape. Nevertheless, a single country's sovereign could deploy it as a feature of, for example, a central bank digital currency. Particular points of interest for future work are the effect of freezing on user experience, as well as the storage overhead. Additionally, our scheme considers pseudonymous systems; future work could explore fully anonymous applications, which utilize zero-knowledge schemes to achieve cryptographic-grade transaction anonymity. Finally, an interesting direction is the design of incentive schemes that motivate the system's adoption and reduce the dependence on enforcement by the authorities.

References

1. Advani, A.: Who does and doesn't pay taxes? Fiscal Studies (2020)
2. Agrawal, S., Ganesh, C., Mohassel, P.: Non-interactive zero-knowledge proofs for composite statements. In: Shacham, H., Boldyreva, A. (eds.) CRYPTO 2018. LNCS, vol. 10993, pp. 643–673. Springer, Cham (2018). https://doi.org/10.1007/978-3-319-96878-0_22

3. Avital, M., Hedman, J., Albinsson, L.: Smart money: blockchain-based customizable payments system. Dagstuhl Rep. **7**(3), 104–106 (2017)
4. Boar, C., Szemere, R.: Payments go (even more) digital* (2011). https://www.bis.org/statistics/payment_stats/commentary2011.htm
5. Dagher, G.G., Bünz, B., Bonneau, J., Clark, J., Boneh, D.: Provisions: privacy-preserving proofs of solvency for bitcoin exchanges. In: Ray, I., Li, N., Kruegel, C. (eds.) ACM CCS 2015: 22nd Conference on Computer and Communications Security, pp. 720–731. ACM Press, Denver, 12–16 October 2015. https://doi.org/10.1145/2810103.2813674
6. Doerner, J., Shelat, A., Evans, D.: Zeroledge: proving solvency with privacy
7. ECB: Eurosystem report on the public consultation on a digital euro (2021). https://www.ecb.europa.eu/pub/pdf/other/Eurosystem_report_on_the_public_consultation_on_a_digital_euro~539fa8cd8d.en.pdf
8. FISCALIS, T.G.P.G.: The concept of tax gaps. report ii: Corporate income tax gap estimation methodologies (2018). https://op.europa.eu/en/publication-detail/-/publication/a5da4716-e7c1-11e8-b690-01aa75ed71a1
9. Garay, J., Kiayias, A., Leonardos, N.: The bitcoin backbone protocol: analysis and applications. In: Oswald, E., Fischlin, M. (eds.) EUROCRYPT 2015. LNCS, vol. 9057, pp. 281–310. Springer, Heidelberg (2015). https://doi.org/10.1007/978-3-662-46803-6_10
10. Garman, C., Green, M., Miers, I.: Accountable privacy for decentralized anonymous payments. In: Grossklags, J., Preneel, B. (eds.) FC 2016. LNCS, vol. 9603, pp. 81–98. Springer, Heidelberg (2017). https://doi.org/10.1007/978-3-662-54970-4_5
11. IRS: Federal tax compliance research: tax gap estimates for tax years 2008–2010 (2016)
12. Murphy, R., Guter-Sandu, A.: Resources allocated to tackling the tax gap: a comparative EU study. Working Pap. Combating Financ. Fraud Empowering Regul. (COFFERS) Horiz. 2020 Proj. November(A) (2018)
13. Nakamoto, S.: Bitcoin: a peer-to-peer electronic cash system (2008)
14. Narula, N., Vasquez, W., Virza, M.: zkledger: privacy-preserving auditing for distributed ledgers. In: 15th {USENIX} Symposium on Networked Systems Design and Implementation ({NSDI} 18), pp. 65–80 (2018)
15. Pedersen, T.P.: Non-interactive and information-theoretic secure verifiable secret sharing. In: Feigenbaum, J. (ed.) CRYPTO 1991. LNCS, vol. 576, pp. 129–140. Springer, Heidelberg (1992). https://doi.org/10.1007/3-540-46766-1_9
16. Schnorr, C.P.: Efficient identification and signatures for smart cards. In: Brassard, G. (ed.) CRYPTO 1989. LNCS, vol. 435, pp. 239–252. Springer, New York (1990). https://doi.org/10.1007/0-387-34805-0_22
17. Wilcox, Z.: Proving your bitcoin reserves (2014)
18. Wüst, K., Kostiainen, K., Capkun, V., Capkun, S.: PRCash: centrally-issued digital currency with privacy and regulation. Cryptology ePrint Archive, Report 2018/412 (2018). https://eprint.iacr.org/2018/412

Impact of Delay Classes on the Data Structure in IOTA

Andreas Penzkofer$^{(\boxtimes)}$, Olivia Saa, and Daria Dziubałtowska

IOTA Foundation, Berlin, Germany
`andreas.penzkofer@iota.org`

Abstract. In distributed ledger technologies (DLTs) with a directed acyclic graph (DAG) data structure, a message-issuing node can decide where to append that message and, consequently, how to grow the DAG. This DAG data structure can typically be decomposed into two pools of messages: referenced messages and unreferenced messages (tips). The selection of the parent messages to which a node appends the messages it issues, depends on which messages it considers as tips. However, the exact time that a message enters the tip pool of a node depends on the delay of that message. In previous works, it was considered that messages have the same or similar delay; however, this generally may not be the case. We introduce the concept of classes of delays, where messages belonging to a certain class have a specific delay, and where these classes coexist in the DAG. We provide a general model that predicts the tip pool size for any finite number of different classes.

This categorisation and model is applied to the first iteration of the IOTA 2.0 protocol (a.k.a. Coordicide), where two distinct classes, namely value and data messages, coexist. We show that the tip pool size depends strongly on the dominating class that is present. Finally, we provide a methodology for controlling the tip pool size by dynamically adjusting the number of references a message creates.

1 Introduction

Distributed Ledger Technologies (DLTs) have gained much attention as a means to process and confirm data and transactions in a decentralised fashion. A fundamental component is the underlying data structure, which records messages either totally or partially ordered. Many DLTs, such as Bitcoin [1], employ a blockchain structure, in which transactions are accumulated in blocks. These blocks are appended to each other creating a totally-ordered child-parent relationship, which makes the fate of the child block dependent on the parent. Certain DLTs such as IOTA, Nano, or Avalanche employ a more complex, partially-ordered Directed Acyclic Graph structure (DAG) [2–4], in which a message (or block) appends to several parent messages (or blocks), see Fig. 1a.

Typically, it is assumed that messages require similar time for propagation, processing and creation, which can be summarized by a generic *delay* [5]. While

© Springer Nature Switzerland AG 2022
J. Garcia-Alfaro et al. (Eds.): DPM 2021/CBT 2021, LNCS 13140, pp. 289–300, 2022.
https://doi.org/10.1007/978-3-030-93944-1_19

this may be reasonably precise when messages have the same content and similar size, this assumption may not hold in scenarios where different types of messages exist or even when messages have similar content but different sizes; first, messages can have different roles and content—such as utility messages, value transactions, or only generic data—, which can lead to differences in the processing time. For example, a value transaction will have to pass additional checks compared to generic data, since a value transfer affects the token ownership in the ledger. Second, the propagation time may also depend on other factors, such as message size or prioritization of messages on the communication layer (as an example, in Bitcoin, the propagation time of a block depends on the byte size of the content [6]). Which Third, for rate control purposes, messages may have to be created with a proof of consumption of a scarce resource. Typically, the proofs of consumption used are Proof of Work (PoW) or Verifiable Delay Functions (VDFs) which, due to the computation time, add a delay. If several types of devices are present in the network, or messages require different difficulty levels for the PoW/VDF, the times for the message creation may differ significantly.

Figure 1b) illustrates how the introduction of a new class of (yellow) messages with larger delay can extend the time until first reference, alter the DAG structure and the size of the tip pool—i.e., the pool of messages that were not referenced yet. Specifically, the yellow class of messages will be added to the tip pool at a much later time compared to their issuance time, thus, effectively contributing to the DAG much later than the original class of messages. Moreover, the delay in the addition of this message *to* the tip pool implies a delay in the removal of its parents *from* the tip pool (messages are removed from the tip pool during inclusion of messages referencing them). Thus, a second message with a smaller delay can also reference those same parents. Since this second message can be effectively added to the DAG before the old (and delayed) first message, the delayed message might not contribute to the tip pool removal at all. Generally, the larger the delay of a message in comparison to other messages, the smaller the contribution it has to the removal of tips from the tip pool. These alterations in the DAG growth dynamics can lead to a significant change in some variables of interest, such as the number of tips or the width of the DAG. Since these attributes can have a major impact on the performance of the DLT, their accurate prediction and control are of vital importance.

Overview of the Paper. In Sects. 2 and 3, we will focus on the first iteration of the IOTA 2.0 protocol [7] (a.k.a. Coordicide), and describe how it introduces two specific classes of messages with distinct delay times. Since the Coordicide is still an ongoing research project, progressing through several iterative development stages, it is worth noting that the substance of the delay classes may be significantly altered in subsequent protocol implementations. However, the implementation details described in this paper are aligned with the initially proposed protocol [7]. Due to the generic dependency on the delay of messages, the derived results can be readily transferred to other scenarios and DLTs, where messages with differing delay times are present.

In general, there can be several classes of messages with different delay times, which are introduced in Sect. 4. We provide a generic model for n different classes, that accurately predicts the tip pool size, and validate it against simulation and experimental results. Finally, in Sect. 5 we apply the model by describing a mechanism that enables the control of the tip pool size.

2 Types of Messages and Their Processing

In the IOTA 2.0 protocol,[1] two different classes of messages coexist: data messages and value messages. The first type consists of messages containing a payload with only data (called data payload), whereas the second one may also contain information about the transfer of funds and its associated unlock data, such as signatures. A payload containing this additional information is called a value payload. Value messages are required to pass additional checks, which expose them to a voting mechanism if double-spends are attempted [8,9]. In this section, we briefly explain how these messages get handled and why transactions have to pass an additional voting filter. This will lead to Sect. 3, where the introduction of an additional delay time for value messages is explained.

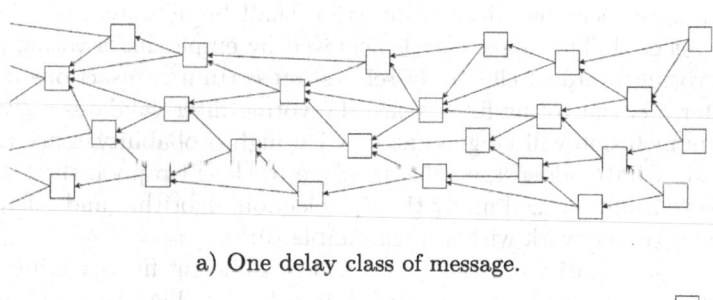

a) One delay class of message.

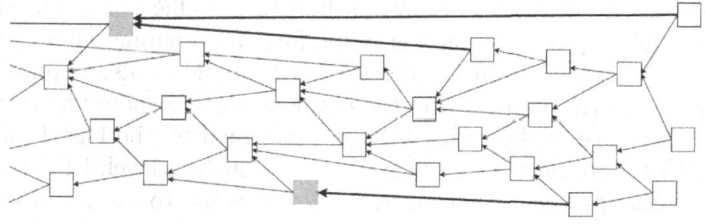

b) Two delay classes of messages.

Fig. 1. The illustrations show a DAG data structure, where messages are displayed as blocks, and child-parent relationships are displayed as arrows. Messages are sorted from left to right by their time of issuance. In **a)** all messages have a similar delay, while in **b)** a new class of message is introduced (marked in yellow) with noticeably increased delay, thus extending the typical time difference between parent and child. (Color figure online)

---

[1] https://github.com/iotaledger/IOTA-2.0-Research-Specifications.

Inclusion of Messages into the Ledger. For messages to be considered final, a mechanism to ensure the permanent addition to the ledger is required. If the majority of nodes processes the same (or similar) parts of the DAG, this requirement will be satisfied whenever a proportion θ of messages in the tip pool directly or indirectly references the message (since honest nodes would keep growing this same part of the DAG). We call this the inclusion criterion.

In this paper, we assume there are no restrictions for the addition of data messages to the ledger. Thus, data messages can be considered final once the inclusion criteria is satisfied. For value messages, the situation is more complicated, as we will see in the following section and Sect. 3.2.

Voting Filter. In IOTA 2.0, the transfer and allocation of funds are handled through an unspent transaction output (UTXO) model, which implies that an unspent output can only be spent once in the ledger, being considered thereafter as consumed. In an honest setting and without the existence of errors, we could apply the same as for data messages and assume that the inclusion criteria could be sufficient to consider transactions as final. However, due to user errors or in the presence of a malicious actor, it is possible that there are multiple transactions that attempt to spend the same output. These types of conflicting messages are called double-spends, and their occurrence requires the network to come to agreement on which transaction shall be accepted, or whether all should be rejected. This agreement is achieved by employing a voting protocol. Since the voting protocol effectively selects out certain transactions it forms a type of filter, i.e. the voting filter. Once the voting filter validates a given value message, its inclusion will be guaranteed with high probability: since the nodes in the network have added the value message to their tip pool, the transaction should be eventually picked up by the tip selection algorithm and referenced by a majority of the network within a reasonable time.

For the vast majority of situations, this is a sufficient finality criterion when dealing with double-spendings. However, it may be possible that a node may have an agreement failure on a transaction, thus, forming a wrong opinion about its inclusion into the ledger [9]. It is, therefore, reasonable to also require that the message inclusion criteria defined in the previous section should be satisfied.

In IOTA, the role of the voting filter is performed by the Fast Probabilistic Consensus (FPC) protocol [8,9]. On a more fundamental level, FPC constitutes the pre-consensus protocol, that allows nodes to come to an initial agreement on the state of a bit, by querying a random subset of nodes. With very high probability (see [8]), after a finite number of rounds, the FPC will finalize on a boolean value, which is utilized for the decision on accepting or rejecting the transaction.

A message that is rejected by the voting filter cannot enter the tip pool and must become orphaned, which means it should not be accounted for in the ledger. Note that any message that references the rejected transaction should not be included to the normal tip pool. Without any rescue mechanism for the referencing messages, such as re-attachments, these would also become orphaned.

This orphanage issue can be avoided to a large extent by introducing a quarantine time on value messages, which is discussed in the following section.

3   Delay Time for Value Messages

Messages are subject to several delay vectors before they can enter the tip pool of a node. First, the broadcast in the network does not happen instantly, but rather is dominated by a natural network delay that depends on several factors, such as geographical distance and distance in the P2P virtual network [10]. Second, messages also need to be processed locally, are members in a waiting pool before being processed, or depend on messages that have not yet arrived. All of this adds together to a delay time, which results in an average delay time h.

In this section, we introduce and reason for an additional delay (or quarantine time) d_Q for value messages, which effectively extends the delay time h to $d = h + d_Q$. Specifically, in Sect. 3.1, we provide the setup of synchronicity assumptions that shape the requirements for the quarantine, whereas in Sect. 3.2, we describe some implementation details for the quarantine procedure.

3.1   Synchronicity Assumptions

For simplicity, we require in this paper that messages are delivered within a bound $d_Q/2$. Thus, in this paper, we do not treat the case where the network is partitioned for a time window larger than $d_Q/2$. We set d_Q such that it is much larger than the average network delay and processing time of messages h. In more realistic conditions, this situation is more complicated, since packet losses may occur or faulty nodes might be present. However, due to the interconnection and dependencies of messages, which are mapped by the DAG structure, nodes can identify missing messages and request them to their peers. This decreases the likelihood that a given node does not receive a message before $d_Q/2$.

For the dependencies on FPC, it is sufficient for a super-majority of messages to arrive within $d_Q/2$ to maintain the integrity of the initial opinion. Moreover, for the FPC opinion exchange—which is not part of the normal gossiping of messages—, the protocol will correctly finalize even if a part of those messages are lost. Thus, for the opinion exchange, it is sufficient to assume a probabilistic synchronous model, where we require that a large majority of opinion exchanges arrive within some bound time $t < d_Q/2$. The probabilistic character of this type of synchronicity assumption is given by the requirement that the large majority of communication occurs within this window, w.h.p. [9]. If the synchronicity assumption is not met (e.g. if a node did not receive a minimum required number of FPC responses), the node may ignore a voting round. In this sense, the security of the consensus protocol is ensured, while the liveness is temporarily halted.

3.2   Quarantine Procedure

The protocol component that is tasked with quarantining a transaction also oversees the initial opinion setting, and delegates whether the message is immediately added to the tip pool, if it first must pass the voting filter, or if it is rejected even before being processed by the voting filter. In theory one could also forward all transactions to the voting filter instead of employing a quarantine time. However, since the communication overhead for the voting protocol could become excessive, this option is not feasible if there are many transactions issued. Furthermore, even non-double spending transactions would have to pass the voting filter, which would impose an excessive delay time, i.e. much larger than d_Q.

Initial Opinion Setting. The output that the voting filter provides on a given transaction is given in the form of a boolean value, *liked* (for accepting the transaction) or *disliked* (for rejecting the transaction). We can further decrease the probability for agreement failures by introducing an initial time window of length $d_Q/2$, during which a transaction's like-status is *unknown*. The transaction is set to *liked*, only if no other double-spending transaction arrives within $d_Q/2$. This ensures that, if there are double-spending transactions, at most one of them can be *liked* by a large proportion of the nodes. We apply the following rules:

1. A transaction is *liked* after $d_Q/2$ if no other double-spending transaction arrives within $d_Q/2$, and *disliked* otherwise.
2. A transaction is *disliked* on arrival if there is already a transaction that is spending the same output.

Tip Inclusion and Voting Filter Activation. We enforce a quarantine time d_Q on an arriving transaction, during which the voting is not yet enabled and the transaction is not included to the tip pool yet. Once the quarantine time has elapsed, the transaction has to pass a tip inclusion check, which either will immediately pass the transaction to the tip pool or will initiate the voting filter instead. The outcome of the filter then determines whether the transaction is finally included into the tip pool. We apply the following rules:

1. If no double spend transaction arrives within d_Q, the transaction passes a tip inclusion check and is added to the tip pool.
2. If a double spend transaction arrives within d_Q, it fails the tip inclusion check, and it is only added to the tip pool if it is *liked* by the voting filter.

Note that the time between setting the *like* status and performing the tip inclusion check is $d_Q/2$, which satisfies the requirements for the probabilistic synchronicity. Due to this window, a node that applies rule number 1) can be certain that the nodes that applied 2)—instead of 1)—will eventually *like* the transaction, since it was already *liked* by a super-majority of nodes that applied 1). Thus, FPC guarantees that the initially *liked* transaction will become the winning transaction w.h.p. The combined approach of rules 1) and 2) must be required, since value transactions must not enter the tip pool pre-maturely and get *disliked* retrospectively. Contrarily, assume a transaction enters the tip pool and is approved by the node, but the transaction is later *disliked*, then the transaction (as well as its referencing message) must be orphaned, i.e. fail to be included into the ledger.

4   Delay Classes and Tip Pool Model

In the previous sections we showed, using the example of the IOTA 2.0 protocol, how the existence of different types of messages can result in differing delay times for them. In this section, we describe an analytical model of the tip pool size for the case where n different classes are present. Furthermore, we investigate the case for $n = 2$, which applies to the previous sections, in more detail.

The dynamics and message relationships within the DAG data structure affect several metrics that have an impact on the performance of the DLT. For example, the time and order in which messages arrive affect the number of references that they obtain. Generally speaking, nodes do not share a global view and, as a consequence, if a certain node considers a certain message as unreferenced, this may not be the case from the point of view of another node. The underlying cause of this is the existence of delays until a message is processed, which also differs from node to node. Furthermore, the tip pool size is also correlated to the time until first reference and, ultimately, the time until finalization of messages. In this paper, we will focus on the tip pool size. We introduce *delay classes* C_i, where the messages with this classification have a specific delay time d_i. The introduction of delay classes creates a more complex scenario, where not always the first message to select a tip will be the message to remove this message from the tip pool. Since the delay introduced by the quarantine time of the value messages is order of magnitudes larger than the network and other processing-related delays, we can introduce—in the case described in the previous section—two delay classes C_{value} and C_{data}, i.e. value and data messages, with strongly distinct and constant delay times. This can lead to the situation that, if a fraction p_{value} of the issued messages are value messages (which have an extended delay), the probability of a tip being removed from the tip pool by a value message can be significantly smaller than p_{value}. This affects the tip pool size and the time until the first reference of messages.

4.1   General Model for the Tip Pool Size

Let $\mathcal{C} = \{C_i\}_{i=1,\ldots,n}$ be the family of classes of messages. For each class C_i, we define the following variables:

- d_i: delay of a message of class C_i (w.l.g., we assume $d_i \leq d_{i+1}$)
- k_i: number of referenced messages, (i.e. parents), of each message of class C_i
- p_i: fraction of messages of class C_i (thus, $\sum_{i=1}^{n} p_i = 1$)

To issue a message, a node must select a certain number of messages k_i as parents for it. The relation created through these parent-child references forms the DAG structure. We now proceed to calculate the average tip pool size L. We model the different classes of messages' arrival as independent Poisson processes of rates $p_i \lambda$, for $i = 1, \ldots, n$. Thus, assuming that the size of the tip pool does not excessively deviate from the average value L, each new message of class C_i will have a probability k_i / L of referencing a given message in the tip pool (here, we

implicitly assume that $L \gg k_i$, so that the probability of a tip being referenced
by two or more references of the same incoming message is low). Thus, a tip sees
the incoming references as independent Poisson processes of rates $\mu_i := p_i \lambda k_i / L$
(for $i = 1, \ldots, n$). Generally, the number of references (i.e., children) a message
receives can vary; however, since we are only interested in the tip status of a
message, we are also only interested in the reference that removes the message
from the tip pool. Now, let S_1^i be the time until the first event of the Poisson
process describing the reference arrival of class C_i (from the point of view of a
single tip). Then, the time T until the removal of this tip from the tip pool will
be given by the minimum between $d_i + S_1^i$ for $i = 1, \ldots, n$. Thus, we have

$$F_T(x) = 1 - \prod_{i=1}^{n} \left[1 - F_{d_i + S_1^i}(x) \right] \tag{1}$$

where

$$F_{d_i + S_1^i}(x) = [1 - \exp(-\mu_i(x - d_i))] \, \mathbb{1}_{(x > d_i)} \tag{2}$$

By Eqs. (1) and (2) and letting $a_i = \sum_{j=1}^{i} \mu_j$ and $b_i = \sum_{j=1}^{i} \mu_j d_j$:

$$F_T(x) = \sum_{i=1}^{n-1} [1 - \exp(-a_i x + b_i)] \, \mathbb{1}_{(d_i < x \leq d_{i+1})} + [1 - \exp(-a_n x + b_n)] \, \mathbb{1}_{(d_n < x)}$$

Finally, the expected value of T will be given by

$$E(T) = \int_{\mathbb{R}^+} x f_T(x) dx = d_1 + \frac{1}{a_1} - \sum_{i=2}^{n} \exp(-d_i a_{i-1} + b_{i-1}) \left(\frac{1}{a_{i-1}} - \frac{1}{a_i} \right)$$

By Little's Law, we have $L = E(T)\lambda$, implying the following implicit equation:

$$L \left(1 - \frac{1}{p_1 k_1} \right) = d_1 \lambda - \sum_{i=2}^{n} e^{-\frac{\lambda}{L} \sum_{j=1}^{i-1} p_j k_j (d_i - d_j)} \left(\frac{L}{\sum_{j=1}^{i-1} p_j k_j} - \frac{L}{\sum_{j=1}^{i} p_j k_j} \right) \tag{3}$$

4.2   Experimental and Simulation Validation

In the case of the IOTA 2.0 protocol, a total of $n = 2$ different delay classes
with constant number of parents k are observed. Applying the model developed
in the last section to this specific case, we have the following implicit equation
for the expected tip pool size L (where $p := p_{\text{value}}$):

$$L = h\lambda + \frac{L}{k(1-p)} \left[1 - p \exp\left(-\frac{(1-p)\lambda k d_Q}{L} \right) \right] \tag{4}$$

We proceed by finding the critical value p^*, that divides the domain in two
regions $[0, p^*)$ and $[p^*, 1]$ with different dominating classes of delays. We begin

by linearising the solution of (4) around $p = 0$ which gives us an approximate value of L close to this point of

$$L \approx \frac{\lambda hk}{k-1} + p\frac{\lambda hk}{(k-1)^2}\left[1 - \exp\left(-\frac{d_Q(k-1)}{h}\right)\right] \approx \frac{k}{k-1}\lambda h = L^- \quad (5)$$

Analogously to the case above, if p is large enough the tip pool size is increasingly controlled by value messages. As p increases it becomes more likely that a given message is removed by a value message rather than a data message. More specifically, for large values of p, we have

$$L \approx L^+ = \frac{k\lambda}{k-1}(h + pd_Q) - \frac{k\lambda d_Q^2}{2(d_Q + h)}(1 - p) \quad (6)$$

The intersection of the curves for Eqs. (5) and (6) provides the approximate proportion of value messages p^*, for which the value messages start to have a noticeable impact on the tip pool size. Taking $L^-(p^*) = L^+(p^*)$, we have:

$$p^* = \frac{d_Q(k-1)}{(2h + (k+1)d_Q)} \quad (7)$$

In order to validate the analytical derived equations above (specifically, 4), we compare them against experimental as well as simulation results. We run simulations for the Tangle for the 2-class message model, where one class has a fixed lower delay of h, and the second class has a fixed higher delay of d. Messages arrive randomly through a Poisson process. For each parameter set, we run the simulations for 1,000,000 message arrivals.

Experimental values are obtained by measuring the tip pool of a node connected to a network that operates with the prototype implementation *GoShimmer* of the IOTA 2.0 protocol[2]. *GoShimmer* is a full node software, that is developed to test and validate the IOTA 2.0 solution for a fully decentralized DLT. For each parameter set, we issue messages at a combined rate for value and data of 200 messages per second (Mps). We remove the data obtained for the ramp-up and down phase, which underestimates the tip pool size, since the data is not obtained from the stable phase, where the tip pool size stays constant.

Figure 2 shows the tip pool size as a function of the proportion of value messages p, comparing the analytical, simulated (2a), and experimental (2b) results. The total rate of incoming messages λ is measured in Mps. A good agreement between analytical prediction, experimental results, and simulation results can be observed. From the figure and by referring to Eq. (4) we can see that the tip pool size has a small and roughly constant slope close to $p = 0$, i.e. the tip pools size is strongly dominated by the data messages in this region. Analogously, if p is large enough the tip pool size is increasingly controlled by value messages. As p increases it becomes more likely that a given message is removed by a value message rather than a data message. Furthermore, when k is increased the tip pool can be kept stable for an increased proportion of value messages.

---

[2] https://github.com/iotaledger/goshimmer.

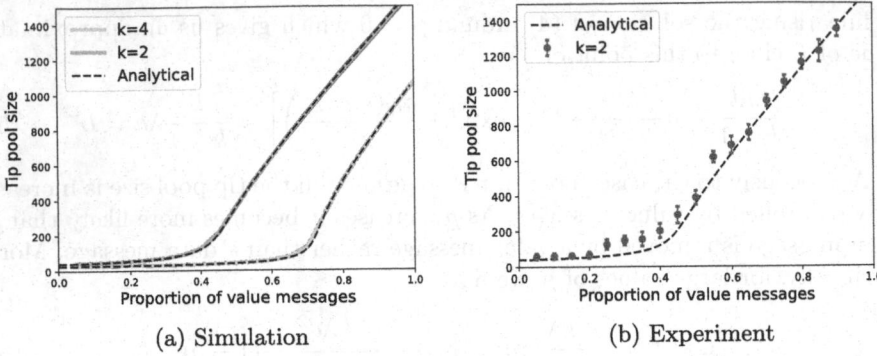

(a) Simulation   (b) Experiment

Fig. 2. Tip pool size as a function of the proportion of value messages. We show data from simulations (a), experiments (b), as well as analytical results for the parameters $\lambda = 200\,\mathrm{Mps}$, $h = 0.1\,\mathrm{s}$ and $d_Q = 40\,\mathrm{h}$. In figure a) we provide values for two different numbers of referenced messages k. The standard deviation is $<3\%$ for the simulation. In figure b) results are marked along with their error for a confidence level of 95%.

5   Controlling the Tip Pool Size

As we show in the previous section, the tip pool can vary significantly depending on the dominant class of messages. However, the tip pool size affects some important performance metrics in the DAG. For example, with an increased tip pool size, the width of the DAG increases, which, in turn, affects the time until the inclusion criterion is fulfilled. Therefore, it is desirable to keep the tip pool small. This must be ensured even in the presence of fluctuations of incoming data and value messages, which can change which class of message is dominant.

Applying this to the results of the previous section, we can observe that for a fixed number of parents k, p can exceed the critical value p^* occasionally. During such periods of excess of value messages, the tip pool size and the time until first reference could, therefore, increase substantially, if the parent number is fixed.

From (7) we can see that for $h \ll d_Q$ the value for p^* is independent of h, d_Q and the absolute values of the transaction rates. By measuring a moving average of the value and data message rates, and calculating the moving average of the proportion of value messages $\bar{p}$, a node can locally adapt k—up to a predefined maximum value k_{max}—in its tip selection algorithm, such that $p^*(k) > \bar{p}$. Algorithm 1 shows the pseudo code that should be called before selecting the parents.

Note that increasing k may increase the message size, since the parents have to explicitly be mentioned. Furthermore, increasing k may also increase the processing time of the data messages and thus effectively increase h. However, this increase is negligible, since h is typically dominated by other factors, such as the propagation time of the message through the network. If the majority of nodes in the network adopt this strategy, the tip pool sizes and the time for inclusion can be kept low in exchange for a minimally increased parent number.

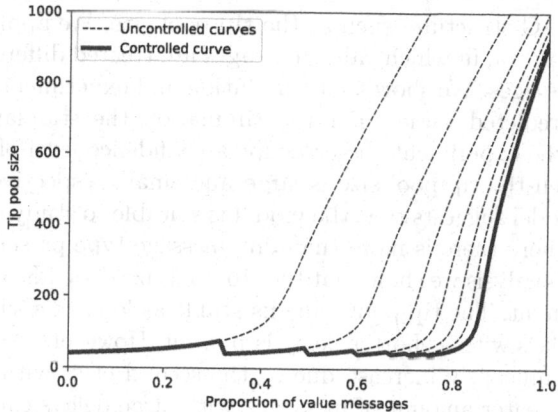

Fig. 3. Tip pool size as a function of the proportion of value messages, when the number of parents is adapted and controlled (blue). The tip pool size is also indicated for the cases where the parent number is fixed (dashed). $\lambda = 200\,\mathrm{Mps}$, $h = 0.1\,\mathrm{s}$ and $d_Q = 40\,\mathrm{h}$. (Color figure online)

Algorithm 1: Adaptive parent number control

---

1 Input: $\bar{p}$
2 k=2
3 **while** $p^*(k) < \bar{p}$ *AND* $k < k_{max}$ **do**
4   ⌊ k ++
5 return k

Figure 3 shows how the tip pool size would vary with the proportion of value messages, if the parent number can be variably controlled up to a maximum number of parents of $k_{max} = 8$. For reference, the curves representing a fixed number of parents are also indicated. We show that using this procedure the tip pool can be kept stable at a small size for a much larger proportion of value messages.

6 Conclusion

Messages in DAG-based DLTs are appended to each other through parent-child relations. Certain aspects of the DAG structure created through this append process—such as the width of the DAG and the pool of non-referenced messages—, depend on the delay of these messages. Since messages can have different purposes, such as transfer of value, utility, or generic data transfer, the processing time and delivery may create distinct classes in terms of perceived delay.

In order to model the effects of the delay classes, we develop an analytical model for the generic case of n distinct classes that can accurately predict certain metrics of the DAG structure, such as the tip pool size. We apply the model to the IOTA 2.0 protocol, in which value messages are treated differently compared to plain data messages. We show that simulation and experimental results agree well with the predicted values. For the simulation the standard deviation is <3%, while for the experiment the error for a confidence level of 95% is <3.3% and <28.9% when the tip pool size is large and small, respectively. The shown validity of the model suggests that the model is suitable to study also other DAG scenarios, and where there is more than one message type present.

Through the analysis we show that the tip pool size depends on which class of message is dominant. The tip pool remains stable as long as a sufficient amount of the message class with a shorter delay is present. However, at some point, the tip pool may significantly increase due to the second class with a larger delay. Furthermore, a greater amount of messages with large delays can be supported, if the parent number is increased. This can be done statically, or dynamically through an adaptive mechanism.

References

1. Nakamoto, S.: Bitcoin: a peer-to-peer electronic cash system (2008)
2. Pervez, H., Muneeb, M., Irfan, M.U., Haq, I.U.: A comparative analysis of DAG-based blockchain architectures. In: 2018 12th International Conference on Open Source Systems and Technologies (ICOSST), pp. 27–34 (2018)
3. Benčić, F.M., Podnar Žarko, I.: Distributed ledger technology: blockchain compared to directed acyclic graph, pp. 1569–1570 (2018)
4. Boyen, X., Carr, C., Haines, T.: Blockchain-free cryptocurrencies: a framework for truly decentralised fast transactions. Cryptology ePrint Archive, Report 2016/871 (2016)
5. Popov, S.: The tangle (2015)
6. Decker, C., Wattenhofer, R.: Information propagation in the bitcoin network. In: IEEE P2P 2013 Proceedings, pp. 1–10 (2013)
7. Popov, S., et al.: The coordicide (2020)
8. Popov, S., Buchanan, W.J.: FPC-BI: fast probabilistic consensus within byzantine infrastructures. J. Parallel Distrib. Comput. **147**, 77–86 (2021)
9. Capossele, A., Müller, S., Penzkofer, A.: Robustness and efficiency of voting consensus protocols within byzantine infrastructures. Blockchain Res. Appl. **2**(1), 100007 (2021)
10. Mao, Y., Deb, S., Venkatakrishnan, S.B., Kannan, S., Srinivasan, K.: Perigee: efficient peer-to-peer network design for blockchains. In: Proceedings of the 39th Symposium on Principles of Distributed Computing, pp. 428–437 (2020)

Secure Static Content Delivery for CDN Using Blockchain Technology

Mauro Conti[1], P. Vinod[2], and Pier Paolo Tricomi[1]([✉])

[1] University of Padua, Padua, Italy
{conti,tricomi}@math.unipd.it
[2] Cochin University of Science and Technology, Kochi, Kerala, India
vinod.p@cusat.ac.in

Abstract. A Content Distribution Network (CDN) is a new kind of network to distribute services and content spatially relative to end-users, providing high availability and high performance. The Origin server uses several replicas to reach this goal, but trust issues are present between them and between servers and clients.

In this work, we present a proof-of-concept for secure static content delivery (e.g., documents, images) by using Blockchain, a technology with the capability to ensure reliability and trust without a central authority. To test our proposal's feasibility, we developed a system prototype on the Ethereum private network. The test shows the system's goodness and the ability to create a new content distribution model over the Internet.

Keywords: Blockchain · CDN · Client server · Secure content delivery

1 Introduction

Content distribution is an important aspect of the Internet, and Content Distribution Networks (CDNs) were born to improve it. CDNs provide high availability and performance because many replicas (Edge servers) of the Origin server are spatially distributed to fulfill requests faster. Services like Cloudflare CDN [4] allows to create a CDN starting from an Origin server, replicating and distributing content to end-users from the best server, usually the geographically nearest. In this scenario, three new trust issues arise. First, an attacker could modify the content sent from the Origin server to the Edge server. If such Edge server inadvertently serves that modified content, it will be labeled a misbehaving replica. Second, if the Origin server owner does not directly manage an Edge server, the Edge server can serve different content, such as stale or outright modified content, e.g., adding ads. Third, in this architecture, the Origin server is a single point of failure. If the Origin server is compromised, all the servers misbehave.

This work's main contribution is two-fold: first, we suggest a new architecture to overcome trust issues between servers, maintaining the CDN properties. Second, we present a novel content integrity verification system that solves trust

J. Garcia-Alfaro et al. (Eds.): DPM 2021/CBT 2021, LNCS 13140, pp. 301–309, 2022.
https://doi.org/10.1007/978-3-030-93944-1_20

issues between servers and clients. Both solutions rely on Blockchain, and as a proof-of-concept, we implemented a prototype to test their feasibility.

The paper is structured as following: Sect. 2 presents related works. Section 3 and Sect. 4 provides system design and experiments respectively. Discussion are presented in Sect. 5 and Sect. 6 concludes the paper.

2   Related Works

Checking the integrity of data retrieved from untrusted servers is a crucial problem. The SSL protocol provides primitives to digitally sign data. However, by always requiring a connection to the Origin server, CDNs' functionality and distribution are negated. Merkle tree authentication [3] and digital rights management schemes [1] can be used, but both are useless if the server is compromised.

In peer-to-peer (p2p) CDNs, these problems are accentuated because clients can serve content too. LOCKSS [10] uses a voting system for content integrity. Rx [13] and Vigilante [5] repeat the server execution to detect misbehavior. These approaches imply significant overhead on the client side. In Pioneer [14] the verify effort is on a trusted platform, but it is not suitable for large-scale systems. Finally, in Repeat and Compare [12], clients ask for the content to multiple replicas and compare the results to detect misbehaving edge servers. However, the process has significant overhead. Thus, only partial content is verified.

In this work, we rely on Blockchain technology. Kishigami et al. [7] propose a video sharing system using a Blockchain, but implementation details are not provided. Vu et al. [16] proposes a blockchain-based content delivery network architecture, but the authors do not address the problem of edge servers delivering tampered content. Similarly, [2] presents a CDN based on blockchain technology, but the focus is on the routing strategy and high latency. A blockchain-based CDN has been developed for Information-Centric Networking [8].

3   System Design

We now present the system to distribute and check content integrity, focusing on the attack scenario, system overview, typical usage, benefits and drawbacks.

3.1   Attack Scenario

The system wants to resolve trust issues between Origin and Edge servers and between servers and clients. In particular, we identify three malicious scenarios:

1. the attacker modifies the content sent from Origin server to Edge server;
2. the Edge server is compromised and serves altered content to the clients;
3. the Origin server is compromised, and so all the replicas misbehave.

All these scenarios can negatively impact both the CDN owner and users. If 1. occurs, the Edge server serving the altered content will be considered a misbehaving server, even if it was not compromised, and the owner would do (useless) checks on that server to find the non-existent problem. In case an Edge server is compromised, as in 2., it is clear that clients will face a negative experience impacting the content provider's reputation. Lastly, if all replicas trust the Origin server, if it is attacked as in 3., the whole CDN would be compromised.

3.2 Overview

In our system, we use two private Blockchains based on Proof Of Authority (PoA) [9] consensus. Transactions and blocks are validated by approved accounts (validators), authorizing and authenticating data in a cheap and efficient way.

Content Blockchain. We build the CDN on the *Content Blockchain*. Each Edge server is a node of this Blockchain wherein content will be stored. The Origin server is unnecessary since every authorized node (Edge server) can add content. The content will automatically be distributed on each server thanks to Blockchain technology. To authorize the upload of content, PoA and an access control system is used (see Sect. 4). Clients seeking the content have no access to this Blockchain. They download the servers' content using regular ways (e.g., HTTP requests) and check the integrity afterward using the *Check Blockchain*.

Check Blockchain. The *Check Blockchain* is used to check received objects integrity. Using hash functions, checking message integrity is simple [15]. When uploading content to the *Content Blockchain*, the server also calculates its hash and stores it in the *Check Blockchain*. It is essential in reaching the consensus that validators check that the hash and the related content matches, to maintain consistency between the two blockchains. Admins are the only ones allowed to store content hashes and participating in the consensus algorithm, to limit clients overhead. Clients participate in this blockchain to have a local copy of the content hashes, and make quick and secure integrity checks. After the client receives an object, it can check its integrity by calculating its hash and comparing it with the one stored in their local copy of *Check Blockchain*. If hashes are equal, the object is intact. Servers use the same mechanism to check whether the content received from the *Content Blockchain* is the one uploaded by an Admin. Since storing the hash of the object requires the network's consensus, the hash is always correct, and the server cannot manipulate it.

Both *Content* and *Check* Blockchains' Admins are meant to be controlled by the single company managing the CDN, thus, they are naturally incentivized to follow the protocol. For further details, please see Sect. 5.

3.3 Typical Usage

Figure 1 shows how the presented system distributes the servers' content and permits the client to check integrity. First, an Admin wants to upload new content. After the system checks and authorizes them, a new upload request is sent among the *Content Blockchain*. When the validators approve the request, a copy of the object is distributed on each server (according to Blockchain technology),

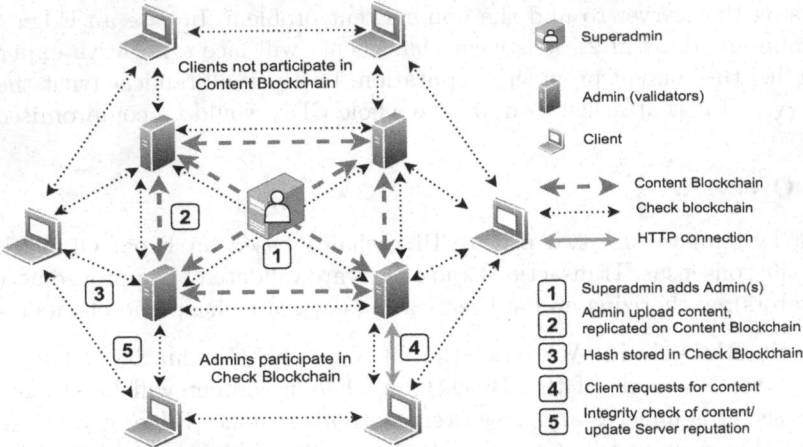

Fig. 1. Overview of the content delivery and integrity checking system.

and its hash is calculated and stored in the *Check Blockchain*. Servers can calculate and check the hash to verify an attacker did not modify the transmitted content. Clients can ask for that object at any time. When it is received, the client calculates its hash and compares it with the hash in their local copy of the *Check Blockchain*. If they are equal, the integrity is verified; otherwise, the client can reject the content and ask another server.

3.4   Benefits and Drawbacks

With our system, we can limit or solve the problems presented in Sect. 3.1. Using the *Check Blockchain*, Edge servers can check content integrity. If an attacker modifies the content during the transmission (scenario 1), the network would immediately notice it; otherwise, the Blockchain technology ensures the content on all the servers is always correct and updated. In fact, a single shared ledger among interested parties can reduce the complexity of managing the whole system, removing the verification, reconciliation, and clearance processes. The *Check Blockchain* also permits clients to easily verify the integrity of the received content (scenario 2). Finally, the single point of failure of the Origin server is removed (scenario 3). Since the replicas are now actively involved in the network (they are *Content Blockchain* participants and possibly validators), if a server is compromised and tries to upload malicious content, the consensus will not be reached. An attacker should at least compromise 50% + 1 servers to succeed.

In this system, we have some drawbacks as well. First, all the servers must have all the content the system can serve. However, if the *Content Blockchain* contains only the more requested resources or their URIs, management costs can be reduced. Second, clients need a tool (e.g., browser add-on, or integrated in the App) to check content integrity automatically. Last, keeping the Blockchain updated has some network costs, but the PoA consensus removes usual mining operations [9]. Precise tests should be executed to evaluate them.

4 Experiments

In this section, we present a prototype of our system, followed by its evaluation.

4.1 Implementation

We implemented a prototype of the presented system on Ethereum [17] private testnet. The network was composed of few nodes, one Admin and one Superadmin, and a single validator. For *Content* and *Check* Blockchains we developed different Smart Contracts. We present the main functionalities of the system.

Access Control System. The blockchain owner nominates trustworthy nodes (addresses) as Admins, to maintain the blockchain (as validators) and manage the content, and Superadmins to governate Admins. A Smart Contract is used to map a user's address with its privileges (Admin, Superadmin, not present). The contract allows to check user privileges and Superadmins to modify Admins.

Content Managing. The Content on the servers is stored in the *Content Blockchain*. An object is created or edited only by (Super)Admins and stored in a Smart Contract with the following attributes: owner (i.e., the uploader Admin), name, description, timestamp of upload, data, and data hash (calculated by the smart contract, and can be used for immediate checks by the servers). To find an object in the Blockchain, we used a map containing all the objects' addresses. When an object is created, its address is added to the Map. Objects are automatically organized in groups (of 4 in our case), and so are their hashes. Hashes are combined in Merkle Trees [11] to save space on the *Check Blockchain*. Only one hash is stored for each group (see Integrity Checking below). The contract allows (Super)Admins to create or edit an object and to manage the objects Map. An object cannot be deleted from the Blockchain since the technology does not permit it, but an Admin can remove its entry in the Map.

Request of an Object. A client can request an object of the Content ordinarily (e.g., HTTP request). The server searches in the objects Map the address of the requested item, and sends it to the client (e.g., download link).

Integrity Checking. To check the Content integrity and to save space, we used Merkle Trees in the *Check Blockchain*. A Merkle Tree is a tree in which every leaf node is labeled with the hash of a data block, and every non-leaf node is labeled with the cryptographic hash of the labels of its child nodes. Instead of storing one hash per object, using a Merkle Tree of N leaves, storing one hash for every N objects is possible. To check if an object is intact when the clients request that object, the server sends it with the related objects' hashes. Then, it is sufficient to calculate the root hash of a new Merkle Tree, composed by the calculated hash of the received object and the hashes of the related objects, in the right order, and compare the result with the root hash in the *Check Blockchain*. According to hash function properties, it is almost impossible for servers to change the object and send fake hashes to match the Blockchain's hash.

Reputation Management. When a client checks the hash of the requested object, the result can be positive or negative. If positive, then nothing happens, so the network is not uselessly stressed. If negative, the client automatically uses a Smart Contract to report the misbehaving server and the faulty object. A server score is updated based on negative feedback to be used by clients in deciding what server to request the object. A Superadmin can check what content is badly served from a server and reset the score.

4.2   Evaluation

To evaluate the system, we focused on client overhead. We identified as main sources of overhead the storage used for a local copy of the *Check Blockchain*, and the time to check content integrity, which might limit content fruition. Table 1 shows the required space to store object hashes. The space required to store the hashes (32 bytes each) of 30 million objects, using Merkle Trees of 32 leaves, is 30 Mb (negligible), and the number of leaves can be increased. Considering the time to check content integrity, the client has to retrieve the hash from the blockchain, calculate the new hash, make a comparison, and update the server's reputation. Retrieving the hash is immediate (a Map lookup is $O(1)$). Computing hashes is very fast; on our machine (i7-10th gen, 1.30 GHz * 8), a SHA3-256 of 1 GB file took 7 ns. A compare operation is fast, and servers' reputation can be updated asynchronously, without impacting content fruition.

Since this work provides a proof-of-concept, it is out of scope to carry out thorough evaluations (e.g., connection costs, time to create a block, resources to store content). We remind the readers that we used Ethereum to develop a system prototype and prove its feasibility. Still, ad-hoc private blockchain(s) should be built to efficiently support our proposal in terms of data-storage costs or an appropriate block-size. In our proposal, the *Content Blockchain* could either contain popular content or all the data in case of small files (e.g., documents, songs), without impacting much on the costs (similar to CDNs). In case of integrating big data and blockchains, scalable solutions have been reported in [6], (e.g., BigChainDB, HBaseChainDB) or proprietary solutions exist, like StorJ[1]. For data propagation time, the entrance costs of a new server depend on the content size, but they should not differ much from simply replicating a server as in a CDN. Moreover, once the servers are set and operative, the propagation time differ from a CDN by the speed of consensus and block generation, which are quick with PoA. To validate blocks, computations are mainly limited to hashes calculations, which are fast by design [15].

---

[1] https://storj.io/how-it-works.

Table 1. Example of required space on clients.

Number of objects	Simple map	Merkle Tree (4 leaves)	Merkle Tree (32 leaves)
100'000	3,05 Mb	0,76 Mb	0,095 Mb
1'000'000	30,52 Mb	7,63 Mb	0,95 Mb
30'000'000	915,52 Mb	228,88 Mb	28,61 Mb

5   Discussion

We want to emphasize our system helps to solve trust issues in a Server–Client architecture and is not meant to share content among peers, even if Blockchains are used. We expect the system to be used in real-world applications by content platforms with limited upload ratio, e.g., Netflix. The CDN to provide content is built upon the private *Content Blockchain* (participants are servers of the company), while the end-users rely on the *Check Blockchain* (also private) to verify content integrity. Despite being a p2p network, Admins and Superadmins are legit in our scenario. The company itself trusts Admins in charge of uploading new content (e.g., videos), and if compromised, the network notices it immediately. Our system only removes trust needs between Edge servers and between server and client. Similarly, the end-users must trust the *Check Blockchain* managed by the company itself, incentivized to maintain the blockchains to satisfy users.

The *Content Blockchain* scalability is a concern to consider. All modifications and versions of the content remain in the blockchain, growing in space. However, the content released for the public to view, e.g., songs or movies, is hardly modified. Furthermore, the company that manages both *Content* and *Check* Blockchains could ideally recreate the *Content Blockchain* periodically, preserving only the updated content, using the same Names and Hashes present in the *Check Blockchain*, to make the changes invisible to end-users. Finally, PoA enhances the scalability by not requiring costly operations related to mining.

Another concern is end-users' burden. New subscribers have to join the *Check Blockchain* and reconstruct its current state. Even if it seems extremely slow, in practice, this will not affect the users much. As shown in Sect. 4.2, storing 100'000 objects hashes requires around 0.1 Mb. Considering that Netflix US (biggest world movie platform[2]) has around 5800 titles[3], and *Check Blockchain* transactions are mainly new hashes storing and negative reviews (should not be frequent), the blockchain size would be of few Mb, downloadable in few seconds.

Finally, a blockchain can be attacked by owning at least 50% + 1 nodes of the network. While this is difficult on the *Content Blockchain* (many servers should be compromised simultaneously), it might happen in the *Check Blockchain*, by creating multiple user accounts. However, clients have no permission to modify content hashes, so an attack cannot impact other users. Fake negative reputation

---

[2] https://www.digitaltrends.com/movies/best-media-streaming-sites-services/.
[3] https://www.comparitech.com/blog/vpn-privacy/netflix-statistics-facts-figures/.

updates can be done on a server, causing a Denial of Service (DOS) attack if the server is disposed. Still, usually, users have to pay to join a platform, which reduces the creation multiple accounts. Also, we assume the company can verify servers' state and reliability of reputation updates by checking servers' logs.

6   Future Works and Conclusion

In the presented system, we found a solution for trust issues in a CDN. Blockchain technology and its security characteristics allow servers to securely distribute content among them and clients to check content integrity, removing the Origin server as a single point of failure. The prototype built on Ethereum demonstrates such a system's feasibility, but an ad-hoc Blockchain should be implemented to fit the requirements better. Among the improvements, the content data in the *Content Blockchain* could be replaced with a URI or similar for scalability purposes, and a solution should be found for sharing dynamic content too.

References

1. Adelsbach, A., Rohe, M., Sadeghi, A.R.: Towards multilateral secure digital rights distribution infrastructures. In: Proceedings of the 5th ACM Workshop on Digital Rights Management, pp. 45–54. ACM (2005)
2. Ak, E., Canberk, B.: BCDN: a proof of concept model for blockchain-aided CDN orchestration and routing. Comput. Netw. **161**, 162–171 (2019)
3. Bayardo, R.J., Sorensen, J.: Merkle tree authentication of http responses. In: Special Interest Tracks and Posters of the 14th International Conference on World Wide Web, pp. 1182–1183. ACM (2005)
4. Cloudflare: Cloudflare CDN. https://www.cloudflare.com/cdn/. Accessed 10 December
5. Costa, M., et al.: Vigilante: end-to-end containment of internet worms. In: ACM SIGOPS Operating Systems Review, vol. 39, pp. 133–147. ACM (2005)
6. Deepa, N., et al.: A survey on blockchain for big data: approaches, opportunities, and future directions. arXiv preprint arXiv:2009.00858 (2020)
7. Kishigami, J., Fujimura, S., Watanabe, H., Nakadaira, A., Akutsu, A.: The blockchain-based digital content distribution system. In: IEEE Fifth International Conference on Big Data and Cloud Computing (BDCloud). IEEE (2015)
8. Li, H., Wang, K., Miyazaki, T., Xu, C., Guo, S., Sun, Y.: Trust-enhanced content delivery in blockchain-based information-centric networking. IEEE Netw. **33**, 183–189 (2019)
9. Li, X., Jiang, P., Chen, T., Luo, X., Wen, Q.: A survey on the security of blockchain systems. Futur. Gener. Comput. Syst. **107**, 841–853 (2020)
10. Maniatis, P., Rosenthal, D.S., Roussopoulos, M., Baker, M., Giuli, T.J., Muliadi, Y.: Preserving peer replicas by rate-limited sampled voting. In: ACM SIGOPS Operating Systems Review, vol. 37, pp. 44–59. ACM (2003)
11. Merkle, R.C.: A digital signature based on a conventional encryption function. In: Pomerance, C. (ed.) CRYPTO 1987. LNCS, vol. 293, pp. 369–378. Springer, Heidelberg (1988). https://doi.org/10.1007/3-540-48184-2_32

12. Michalakis, N., Soulé, R., Grimm, R.: Ensuring content integrity for untrusted peer-to-peer content distribution networks. In: Proceedings of the 4th USENIX Conference on Networked Systems Design & Implementation (2007)
13. Qin, F., Tucek, J., Sundaresan, J., Zhou, Y.: Rx: treating bugs as allergies–a safe method to survive software failures. In: ACM SIGOPS Operating Systems Review, vol. 39, pp. 235–248. ACM (2005)
14. Seshadri, A., Luk, M., Shi, E., Perrig, A., van Doorn, L., Khosla, P.: Pioneer: verifying code integrity and enforcing untampered code execution on legacy systems. In: ACM SIGOPS Operating Systems Review, vol. 39, pp. 1–16. ACM (2005)
15. Tsudik, G.: Message authentication with one-way hash functions. In: INFOCOM 1992. Eleventh Annual Joint Conference of the IEEE Computer and Communications Societies, pp. 2055–2059. IEEE (1992)
16. Vu, T.X., Chatzinotas, S., Ottersten, B.: Blockchain-based content delivery networks: content transparency meets user privacy. In: 2019 IEEE Wireless Communications and Networking Conference (WCNC), pp. 1–6 (2019)
17. Wood, G.: Ethereum: a secure decentralised generalised transaction ledger. Ethereum Proj. Yellow Pap. 151, 1–32 (2014)

Lattice-Based Proof-of-Work
for Post-Quantum Blockchains

Rouzbeh Behnia[1]([✉]), Eamonn W. Postlethwaite[2], Muslum Ozgur Ozmen[3],
and Attila Altay Yavuz[1]

[1] University of South Florida, Tampa, FL, USA
{behnia,attilaayavuz}@usf.edu
[2] Information Security Group, Royal Holloway, University of London, Egham, UK
eamonn.postlethwaite.2016@live.rhul.ac.uk
[3] Purdue University, West Lafayette, IN, USA
mozmen@purdue.edu

Abstract. Proof of Work (PoW) protocols, originally proposed to circumvent DoS and email spam attacks, are now at the heart of the majority of recent cryptocurrencies. Current popular PoW protocols are based on hash puzzles. These puzzles are solved via a brute force search for a hash output with particular properties, such as a certain number of leading zeros. By considering the hash as a random function, and fixing *a priori* a sufficiently large search space, Grover's search algorithm gives an asymptotic quadratic advantage to quantum machines over classical machines. In this paper, as a step towards a fuller understanding of post quantum blockchains, we propose a PoW protocol for which quantum machines have a smaller asymptotic advantage. Specifically, for a lattice of rank n sampled from a particular class, our protocol provides as the PoW an instance of the Hermite Shortest Vector Problem (Hermite-SVP) in the Euclidean norm, with a small approximation factor. Asymptotically, the best known classical and quantum algorithms that directly solve SVP type problems are heuristic lattice sieves, which run in time $2^{0.292n+o(n)}$ and $2^{0.265n+o(n)}$ respectively. We discuss recent advances in SVP type problem solvers and give examples of where the impetus provided by a lattice based PoW would help explore often complex optimization spaces.

Keywords: Blockchains · Proof-of-work · Post-quantum
cryptography · Consensus protocols · Lattice-based cryptography

The work of Rouzbeh Behnia and Attila Yavuz is supported by the NSF CAREER Award CNS-1917627 and an unrestricted gift via Cisco Research Award.
Eamonn W. Postlethwaite is supported by the EPSRC and the UK government (grant EP/P009301/1).
Work done in part when Muslum Ozgur Ozmen was at the University of South Florida.

J. Garcia-Alfaro et al. (Eds.): DPM 2021/CBT 2021, LNCS 13140, pp. 310–318, 2022.
https://doi.org/10.1007/978-3-030-93944-1_21

1 Introduction

Consensus mechanisms are at the heart of the decentralized nature of blockchains. Proofs of Work (PoW), based on computational power, and Proofs of Stake (PoS), based on some notion of "stake" in the system, are amongst the most common types of consensus mechanisms. Cryptocurrencies like Bitcoin [24] rely on PoW based on brute force hash computations to ensure decentralized trust, at the cost of terawatts of energy.[1] The hash functions used in such cryptocurrencies achieve desirable security properties against quantum adversaries when modelled as a random oracle [28]. Despite this, Grover's search algorithm [17] gives an asymptotic advantage to quantum computers when solving hash based PoWs. While some advantage over classical computers may agree with the nature of PoW protocols (more expensive or powerful machines should perform better), we consider it a valuable research topic to reduce this advantage, e.g. because quantum computers may exist for some time before being available to the public.

Our Contributions. *The main goal of this paper is to address the research gap in the state-of-the-art by creating a novel consensus protocol (specifically, a PoW algorithm) that reduces the advantage of quantum computers over classical ones, has fast verification, and adjustable difficulty.* To achieve this goal, we propose a new PoW protocol called LPoW based on the Hermite-SVP problem. Given the current understanding of SVP type problems, LPoW satisfies the following properties [1, Section IV]:

- LPoW provides little quantum advantage; the asymptotic quantum advantage against SVP is less than the quadratic speed up of Grover's algorithm.
- LPoW is hard to solve but easy to verify. Finding a solution is equivalent to solving Hermite-SVP with a small approximation factor. Verification is equivalent to calculating a norm, an nth root, and some multiplications.
- The parameters of LPoW are easy to fine tune to adjust its difficulty. In particular increasing the dimension of the lattice has a well studied effect on the computational resources required to solve the PoW.

  A secondary goal of the this paper is to create a PoW protocol that encourages further experimentation with, and understanding of, practical algorithmic improvements for solving SVP type problems. In [18] the authors suggest harnessing both the energy spent on hash puzzles and the demand to mine cryptocurrencies to improve the state-of-the-art in discrete log cryptanalysis. Following [18], and given that the difficulty of SVP is fundamental to the security of lattice based submissions to NIST's post quantum standardization process,[2] an SVP based PoW can similarly leverage this energy and demand to aid in understanding the cryptanalysis of the SVP problem. In Sect. 3.1 we discuss several areas of SVP solving strategies which could benefit from increased attention.

---

[1] https://cbeci.org/.

[2] https://csrc.nist.gov/projects/post-quantum-cryptography.

Limitations. If we assume a given hash function is a random oracle, then Grover's algorithm gives the optimal speedup against PoW based on this hash function, and cannot be parallelized except in the trivial manner [29]. Effectively this means that the PoW parameters, e.g. the number of leading zeros required in the hash output, will only have to increase to account for increased computational strength, and not fundamentally new algorithmic techniques. This is not necessarily the case for the specific lattice problem we consider; we do not have any proofs of optimality for the algorithms currently used to solve it. In effect, this means that the PoW parameters, i.e. the lattice rank, may need to be increased to account for algorithmic improvements, as well as for increased computational strength. We note that the best known time complexity for solving the SVP puzzles we consider is $2^{\Theta(n)}$ for lattices of rank n, and that any change to even slightly subexponential in n would represent a huge moment in the theory of lattices. Therefore, we do not expect to have to increase the rank too much, even to account for any algorithmic improvements.

2 Preliminaries

For $n \in \mathbb{N}^+$ let $[n] = \{1, \ldots, n\}$. For a finite set S, let $x \leftarrow \mathcal{U}(S)$ denote a uniform sample. Let $m(n)$ represent the cost of multiplying two n bit numbers. Let $\| \cdot \|$ represent the Euclidean norm. Proof of work protocols enable a prover to prove to a verifier that it has executed a certain amount of work. We adopt the definition of such protocols from [5], which consists of algorithms that *generate* a challenge, *solve* such a challenge, thereby producing a proof of solution, and finally *verify* that this proof is correct. This triple of algorithms must satisfy the following.

Definition 1. *A $(t(n), \delta(n))$-Proof of Work (PoW) consists of three algorithms* (Gen, Solve, Verify) *that satisfy the following.*

- *Efficiency:*
  - Gen(1^n) *runs in time $\tilde{O}(n)$.*
  - *For any $c \leftarrow$ Gen(1^n), Solve(c) runs in time $\tilde{O}(t(n))$.*
  - *For any $c \leftarrow$ Gen(1^n), $\Pi \leftarrow$ Solve(c), Verify(c, Π) runs in time $\tilde{O}(n)$.*
- *Completeness: For any $c \leftarrow$ Gen(1^n) and any $\Pi \leftarrow$ Solve(c), we have* $\Pr[\text{Verify}(c, \Pi) = acc] = 1$.[3]
- *Hardness: For any polynomial l, any constant $\epsilon > 0$, and any algorithm* Solve$_l^*$ *running in time $l(n)t(n)^{1-\epsilon}$ when given as input $l(n)$ challenges $\{c_i \leftarrow \text{Gen}(1^n)\}_{i \in [l(n)]}$, over the randomness of* Gen, *we have* $\Pr[\text{Verify}(c_i, \Pi_i) = acc, \forall i \mid (\Pi_1, \ldots, \Pi_{l(n)}) \leftarrow \text{Solve}_l^*(c_1, \ldots, c_{l(n)})] < \delta(n)$.

Efficiency ensures that verification runs in (near) linear time. Efficiency and completeness together ensure that a prover that performs roughly $t(n)$ operations can prove to the verifier that it has done so. Hardness requires that the prover has, e.g. a negligible chance, for δ some negligible function of n, to convince the verifier without performing $l(n)t(n)$ operations. This remains true, even if the prover may compute on the $l(n)$ challenges together.

---

[3] Our Verify is deterministic, originally this probability is taken over its randomness.

2.1 Lattices and Lattice Problems

An n dimensional lattice Λ of rank $k \leq n$ is a discrete additive subgroup of $\mathbb{R}^n$. Given k linearly independent basis vectors $\{\vec{b}_1, \ldots, \vec{b}_k\} \subset \mathbb{R}^n$, the lattice generated by $\mathbf{B}$, i.e. their concatenation as column vectors, is denoted by $\Lambda(\mathbf{B}) = \{x_1 \cdot \vec{b}_1 + \cdots + x_k \cdot \vec{b}_k : x_i \in \mathbb{Z}\}$. The volume of Λ is defined as $\mathrm{vol}(\Lambda) = \sqrt{\det(\mathbf{B}^t \mathbf{B})}$ for any basis $\mathbf{B}$ of Λ (the volume is independent of the choice of basis). We will consider only full rank lattices, where $n = k$ and $\mathrm{vol}(\Lambda) = \det(\mathbf{B})$.

Definition 2. *The* minimum distance *of Λ is $\lambda_1(\Lambda) = \min\{\|\vec{v}\| : \vec{v} \in \Lambda \setminus \{0\}\}$. A solution to γ-approx-SVP for $\gamma \geq 1$ is a vector $\vec{v} \in \Lambda \setminus \{0\}$ such that $\|\vec{v}\| \leq \gamma \cdot \lambda_1(\Lambda)$.*

An immediate corolloary of Minkowski's theorem, in the Euclidean norm, proves that $\lambda_1(\Lambda) \leq \sqrt{n} \cdot \mathrm{vol}(\Lambda)^{1/n}$. The *Gaussian heuristic* estimates the number of lattice points of a lattice Λ contained in a measurable set S as $\mathrm{vol}(S)/\mathrm{vol}(\Lambda)$. When applied to a hypersphere it gives the following estimate for $\lambda_1(\Lambda)$.

Definition 3. *Let $gh(\Lambda)$ be the Gaussian heuristic estimate for $\lambda_1(\Lambda)$. Using the Gamma function, it is $gh(\Lambda) = \frac{\Gamma(n/2+1)^{1/n}}{\sqrt{\pi}} \cdot \mathrm{vol}(\Lambda)^{1/n}$.*

We note that the above is a heuristic for the length of the shortest non zero vectors in a lattice, and the existence of a vector slightly larger than this heuristic will be important for our construction. There are many asymptotic and experimental works that determine the usefulness of the Gaussian heuristic in different settings. For a theoretical introduction, see e.g. [9, Section 3.1.2], for experimental evidence that it is accurate for $n \geq 50$ see [9, Section 3.1.3], and for an asymptotic statement see e.g. [22, Thm 4]. More practically, Blichfeldt's inequality [7] tells us that any lattice Λ has $\lambda_1(\Lambda) \leq \sqrt{2} \cdot (1 + n/2)^{1/n} \cdot gh(\Lambda)$. For n which are reasonable for PoW purposes, $\sqrt{2} \cdot (1 + n/2)^{1/n}$ is essentially $\sqrt{2}$, and we shall consider it as such for ease of exposition.

Definition 4. *The α-Hermite-SVP, or α-HSVP problem is, given a lattice Λ, to find a vector $\vec{v} \in \Lambda \setminus \{0\}$ such that $\|\vec{v}\| \leq \alpha \cdot \mathrm{vol}(\Lambda)^{1/n}$.*

Instances of Hermite-SVP are given as a lattice basis, which much be somehow sampled. We generate Goldstein–Mayer lattices [16] as $\Lambda(\mathbf{B})$ for

$$\mathbf{B} = \begin{pmatrix} p & x_2 & \cdots & x_n \\ 0 & 1 & \cdots & 0 \\ \vdots & & \ddots & 0 \\ 0 & 0 & 0 & 1 \end{pmatrix} \tag{1}$$

where p is a large prime and $x_i \leftarrow \mathcal{U}(\{0\} \cup [p-1])$ are i.i.d. These lattices have $\mathrm{vol}(\Lambda) = p$ and provide a way to sample "uniformly" from all lattices of this volume [9, Section 2.3]. For example, the Darmstadt SVP Challenge[4] uses $\log_2 p \approx 10n$ and sets $\alpha = 1.05 \cdot \Gamma(n/2+1)^{1/n}/\sqrt{\pi}$. This α is such that a solution to α-HSVP has length at most $1.05 \cdot \mathrm{gh}(\Lambda)$, and is therefore a constant factor smaller than $\alpha' = \sqrt{2} \cdot \Gamma(n/2+1)^{1/n}/\sqrt{\pi}$ that guarantees a solution to α'-HSVP. However, we expect 1.05^n lattice vectors of length at most $1.05 \cdot \mathrm{gh}(\Lambda)$ for $n \gtrsim 50$ [9, Section 3.1], and the probability of such a short vector not existing to be negligible.

3   Proposed PoW Protocol, LPoW

Before we propose our new PoW protocol, we give a brief précis of how instances of Hermite-SVP problems are solved. One can solve SVP on Λ using a variety of families of algorithms. The family we consider is heuristic lattice sieves, which have the best known classical and quantum time complexity, standing at $2^{0.292n+o(n)}$ [6] and $2^{0.265n+o(n)}$ [20] respectively. However, it is not necessary to call lattice sieves in the full dimension of the lattice to solve SVP type problems [11]. Instead sieving in dimension $n - \Theta(n/\log n)$ suffices under certain heuristic assumptions. There also exist many further heuristic techniques that provide significant practical speedups [21,27]. Finally, a framework that collates, extends, and implements these techniques holds the record for the highest dimension SVP challenge solved [2,13]. The techniques mentioned above depend non trivially on the "quality" of the lattice basis being used, informally; how short and close to orthogonal its basis vectors are. Therefore lattice reduction algorithms such as BKZ are employed [10,26], which themselves require SVP oracles for lower dimensional projected sublattices. The constant suppressed in the $\Theta(n/\log n)$ above will depend on the methods used to improve the quality of the basis. Some experimental values may be found in [2, Fig. 3b].

The high level design of our PoW follows Definition 1. We set n as the dimension of the lattice and let α, p follow the Darmstadt SVP Challenges.

Definition 5. *Let* LPoW *be defined by the following triple* (Gen, Solve, Verify).

- Gen$(1^n; r)$, *for explicit randomness* r *derived from the previous block. First, sample a prime* p *of bitsize* $10n$, *then sample i.i.d.* $x_2, \ldots, x_n \leftarrow \mathcal{U}(\{0\} \cup [p-1])$, *to form a basis* $\mathbf{B}$ *as in* (1). *Let* $\alpha = 1.05 \cdot \Gamma(n/2+1)^{1/n}/\sqrt{\pi}$. *Return* $c = (\alpha, n, \mathbf{B}, p)$.
- Solve(c), *the miner parses* c *as* $(\alpha, n, \mathbf{B}, p)$ *and attempts to find a vector* $\vec{v} \in \Lambda(\mathbf{B}) \setminus \{0\}$ *such that* $\|\vec{v}\| \leq \alpha \cdot p^{1/n}$. *It outputs* $\Pi = (\vec{v}, \vec{\nu})$, *where* $\vec{v} = \mathbf{B} \cdot \vec{\nu}$ *and* $\vec{\nu} \in \mathbb{Z}^n$.
- Verify(c, Π), *parses* c *as* $(\alpha, n, \mathbf{B}, p)$ *and* Π *as* $(\vec{v}, \vec{\nu})$, *and outputs* $acc = \|\vec{v}\| \leq \alpha \cdot p^{1/n} \wedge \vec{v} = \mathbf{B} \cdot \vec{\nu} \wedge \vec{\nu} \in \mathbb{Z}^n$.

---

[4] https://www.latticechallenge.org/svp-challenge/.

We use an extendable output function, e.g. [14], to extract sufficient randomness from the previous block. We weaken ever so slightly the efficiency requirements of Gen and Verify. For Gen it is not known how to generate an n bit prime in $\tilde{O}(n)$. Indeed, the prime number theorem tells us that an n bit odd number is prime with probability approximately $1/n$ and no known primality test runs in polylog(n). Instead, by using the Miller–Rabin test [25] with $O(n)$ random bases on uniform odd n bit integers, we may generate a probable n bit prime in expected time $O(n^3 \cdot m(n))$ [15, Thm 12.2.2]. If required, in expected time $O(n^{5+o(1)})$ one can provable generate a prime [15, Sec. 12.1.3]. As Verify requires the multiplication of a matrix and a vector, it costs $O(n^2 \cdot m(n))$.

Theorem 1. *Let* $t_c(x) = 2^{0.292x+o(x)}$ *and* $t_q(x) = 2^{0.265x+o(x)}$, *and* $\delta(n)$ *be a negligible function of* n, *then, under current SVP solving techniques, there exists an* $x(n) \in n - \Theta(n/\log n)$ *such that* LPoW *is a* $(t_c(x(n)), \delta(n))$ *PoW against classical computers, and a* $(t_q(x(n)), \delta(n))$ *PoW against quantum computers.*

Proof. We may generate a probable $10n$ bit prime in expected time $O(n^3 \cdot m(n))$, and $n-1$ samples from $\mathcal{U}(\{0\} \cup [p-1])$ in time $O(n \log n)$, and hence a challenge c. The most efficient known algorithms Solve on input a challenge c call at least one, and at most poly(n), SVP oracles in dimension in $x(n) \in n - \Theta(n/\log n)$ [2, 11]. Therefore in the classical case $t(n) = t_c(x(n))$, and in the quantum case $t(n) = t_q(x(n))$, using the most efficient known classical and quantum SVP oracles. Note that $n - cn/\log n \in \Theta(n)$ for any constant c, and while we do not prove that the SVP oracle must be called in dimension $x(n) \in \Theta(n)$, any $x(n) \in o(n)$ would imply a subexponential time algorithm for our α-HSVP problem, and therefore for α^2-approx-SVP [23, p. 25]. As $\alpha^2 \in O(n)$, this would be a major breakthrough. Verifying a solution to a challenge can be performed in time $O(n^2 \cdot m(n))$. This concludes the discussion on efficiency.

We expect 1.05^n solutions for a challenge, for large n, and therefore the PoW is complete with all but negligible probability. To make it perfectly complete one may take instead $\alpha' = \sqrt{2} \cdot \Gamma(n/2 + 1)^{1/n} / \sqrt{\pi}$ and set n larger as appropriate to maintain a desired cost for Solve. Finally, it is not known how to use information from independent random lattices as advice for Hermite-SVP problems in other random lattices, and so we have $\delta(n) \in \text{negl}(n)$.

3.1   Discussion

We calculate a value of n that we expect to very roughly match the current cost of mining a Bitcoin, 21.45 terahashes.[5] Assuming SHA-256, on input 64 bytes, takes approximately 1500 cycles, this gives approximately 2^{55} cycles. The top few data points of [2, Table 2], which uses identically generated random lattices, have dimensions $151, 153, 155$ and approximate cycle counts $2^{56}, 2^{57}, 2^{57}$ respectively. Therefore we suggest $n \geq 150$, at least given when counting cycles. The recent work of [13] applies GPU cores to the same challenges up to $n = 180$, and [13, Table 1] gives another set of experimental values against which

---

[5] https://btc.com/stats/diff, retrieved 2021/03/06.

to parameterize the necessary difficulty. We list here topics that could benefit from the attention LPoW may bring to Hermite-SVP. As mentioned in Sect. 3, heuristic techniques for solving SVP, e.g. the amount of attainable "dimensions for free" $\Theta(n/\log n)$, depend on the quality of the lattice basis. Clearly, the hidden constant is important. In [2,11] some analyses of attainable dimensions for free are given. Given the public availability of G6K,[6] a more thorough survey of how the variants of BKZ, insertion scoring functions, sequences of instructions, and new filtering techniques such as [13, Sec. 6], affect these dimension saving techniques is possible. A downside of sieving is the exponential memory cost, which may lead to memory access delays that become a bottleneck. It has been suggested that this could be partially mitigated by hardware implementations of sieves [12,19]. Given the enormous resources put into developing ASICs for hash based PoWs, one may expect similar advances to be feasible in the case of LPoW, as well as advances beyond the parallelism offered by G6K [2, App B]. In particular, one may hope for advances upon previous work on distributed sieving [8] to larger or more general contexts.

Finally, recent works on concrete quantum circuits and the application of error correction estimate the speedups attainable in practice from quantum search when used in the context of hash functions [4] and lattice sieves [3]. While the cited works suggest that, under our current understanding of quantum computers, little to no advantage would be gained from the use of a quantum computer when solving PoW today, we are considering the case where e.g. improvements in classical computational power push the required hardness of PoW into ranges where a quantum computer would provide a meaningful advantage, or where more efficient error correction of quantum circuits is available. At worst, we have specified a new PoW based on well studied hard problems. This work ultimately derives from our desire to create a PoW that future proofs blockchains against giving a large advantage to quantum computers.

References

1. Aggarwal, D., Brennen, G.K., Lee, T., Santha, M., Tomamichel, M.: Quantum attacks on bitcoin, and how to protect against them. arXiv preprint arXiv:1710.10377 (2017)
2. Albrecht, M.R., Ducas, L., Herold, G., Kirshanova, E., Postlethwaite, E.W., Stevens, M.: The general sieve kernel and new records in lattice reduction. In: Ishai, Y., Rijmen, V. (eds.) EUROCRYPT 2019. LNCS, vol. 11477, pp. 717–746. Springer, Cham (2019). https://doi.org/10.1007/978-3-030-17656-3_25
3. Albrecht, M.R., Gheorghiu, V., Postlethwaite, E.W., Schanck, J.M.: Estimating quantum speedups for lattice sieves. In: Moriai, S., Wang, H. (eds.) ASIACRYPT 2020. LNCS, vol. 12492, pp. 583–613. Springer, Cham (2020). https://doi.org/10.1007/978-3-030-64834-3_20
4. Amy, M., Di Matteo, O., Gheorghiu, V., Mosca, M., Parent, A., Schanck, J.: Estimating the cost of generic quantum pre-image attacks on SHA-2 and SHA-3. In: Avanzi, R., Heys, H. (eds.) SAC 2016. LNCS, vol. 10532, pp. 317–337. Springer, Cham (2017). https://doi.org/10.1007/978-3-319-69453-5_18

---

[6] https://github.com/fplll/g6k.

5. Ball, M., Rosen, A., Sabin, M., Vasudevan, P.N.: Proofs of work from worst-case assumptions. In: Shacham, H., Boldyreva, Λ. (eds.) CRYPTO 2018. LNCS, vol. 10991, pp. 789–819. Springer, Cham (2018). https://doi.org/10.1007/978-3-319-96884-1_26
6. Becker, A., Ducas, L., Gama, N., Laarhoven, T.: New directions in nearest neighbor searching with applications to lattice sieving. In: Proceedings of the Twenty-Seventh Annual ACM-SIAM Symposium on Discrete Algorithms, SODA 2016, Philadelphia, PA, USA, pp. 10–24 (2016)
7. Blichfeldt, H.F.: The minimum value of quadratic forms, and the closest packing of spheres. Math. Ann. **101**(1), 605–608 (1929)
8. Bos, J.W., Naehrig, M., van de Pol, J.: Sieving for shortest vectors in ideal lattices: a practical perspective. Cryptology ePrint Archive, Report 2014/880 (2014)
9. Chen, Y.: Reduction de reseau et securite concrete du chiffrement completement homomorphe. Ph.D. thesis, Université Paris Diderot (2013)
10. Chen, Y., Nguyen, P.Q.: BKZ 2.0: better lattice security estimates. In: Lee, D.H., Wang, X. (eds.) ASIACRYPT 2011. LNCS, vol. 7073, pp. 1–20. Springer, Heidelberg (2011). https://doi.org/10.1007/978-3-642-25385-0_1
11. Ducas, L.: Shortest vector from lattice sieving: a few dimensions for free. In: Nielsen, J.B., Rijmen, V. (eds.) EUROCRYPT 2018. LNCS, vol. 10820, pp. 125–145. Springer, Cham (2018). https://doi.org/10.1007/978-3-319-78381-9_5
12. Ducas, L.: Shortest Vector from Lattice Sieving: A Few Dimensions for Free (talk), April 2018. https://eurocrypt.iacr.org/2018/Slides/Monday/TrackB/01-01.pdf
13. Ducas, L., Stevens, M., van Woerden, W.: Advanced lattice sieving on GPUs, with tensor cores. Cryptology ePrint Archive, Report 2021/141 (2021). https://eprint.iacr.org/2021/141
14. Dworkin, M.J.: FIPS PUB 202: SHA-3 Standard: Permutation-Based Hash and Extendable-Output Functions. Federal Inf. Process. Stds. (NIST FIPS) (2015). https://nvlpubs.nist.gov/nistpubs/FIPS/NIST.FIPS.202.pdf
15. Galbraith, S.D.: Mathematics of Public Key Cryptography. Cambridge University Press, Cambridge (2012)
16. Goldstein, D., Mayer, A.: On the equidistribution of Hecke points. Forum Mathematicum **15**(2), 165–189 (2003)
17. Grover, L.K.: A fast quantum mechanical algorithm for database search. In: Proceedings of the Twenty-Eighth Annual ACM Symposium on Theory of Computing, STOC 1996, pp. 212–219. Association for Computing Machinery, New York (1996)
18. Hastings, M., Heninger, N., Wustrow, E.: Short paper: the proof is in the pudding. In: Goldberg, I., Moore, T. (eds.) FC 2019. LNCS, vol. 11598, pp. 396–404. Springer, Cham (2019). https://doi.org/10.1007/978-3-030-32101-7_24
19. Kirchner, P.: Re: Sieving vs. enumeration, May 2016. https://groups.google.com/forum/#!msg/cryptanalytic-algorithms/BoSRL0uHIjM/wAkZQlwRAgAJ
20. Laarhoven, T.: Search problems in cryptography. Ph.D. thesis, Eindhoven University of Technology (2015)
21. Laarhoven, T., Mariano, A.: Progressive lattice sieving. In: Lange, T., Steinwandt, R. (eds.) PQCrypto 2018. LNCS, vol. 10786, pp. 292–311. Springer, Cham (2018). https://doi.org/10.1007/978-3-319-79063-3_14
22. Li, J., Nguyen, P.Q.: A complete analysis of the BKZ lattice reduction algorithm. Cryptology ePrint Archive, Report 2020/1237 (2020). https://eprint.iacr.org/2020/1237
23. Lovász, L.: An Algorithmic Theory of Numbers, Graphs and Convexity. Society for Industrial and Applied Mathematics (1986)

24. Nakamoto, S.: Bitcoin: a peer-to-peer electronic cash system (2008). https://bitcoin.org/bitcoin.pdf
25. Rabin, M.O.: Probabilistic algorithm for testing primality. J. Number Theory **12**(1), 128–138 (1980)
26. Schnorr, C., Euchner, M.: Lattice basis reduction: improved practical algorithms and solving subset sum problems. Math. Program. **66**, 181–199 (1994)
27. Teruya, T., Kashiwabara, K., Hanaoka, G.: Fast lattice basis reduction suitable for massive parallelization and its application to the shortest vector problem. In: Abdalla, M., Dahab, R. (eds.) PKC 2018. LNCS, vol. 10769, pp. 437–460. Springer, Cham (2018). https://doi.org/10.1007/978-3-319-76578-5_15
28. Unruh, D.: Computationally binding quantum commitments. In: Fischlin, M., Coron, J.-S. (eds.) EUROCRYPT 2016. LNCS, vol. 9666, pp. 497–527. Springer, Heidelberg (2016). https://doi.org/10.1007/978-3-662-49896-5_18
29. Zalka, C.: Grover's quantum searching algorithm is optimal. Phys. Rev. A **60**, 2746–2751 (1999)

Blockchain-Based Two-Factor Authentication for Credit Card Validation

Suat Mercan[1]([✉]), Mumin Cebe[2], Kemal Akkaya[1], and Julian Zuluaga[1]

[1] Florida International University, Miami, FL 33199, USA
{smercan,kakkaya,andrew}@fiu.edu
[2] Marquette Univesity, Milwaukee, WI 53233, USA
mumin.cebe@marquette.edu

Abstract. The widespread adoption of the e-commerce and web-based business has brought great increase in credit card utilization for online transactions which in turn resulted in sophisticated fraud attempts. Accurate fraud prevention and detection is a key concern in cashless economy. Multifactor authentication among others such as machine learning based behavioral analysis, data mining, black listing is one of the effective methods augmenting primary information checking. SMS messages are sent to registered phone in addition to credit card information as a second level protection. However, this information might be vulnerable to various attacks as some third party services are in the game. This paper proposes adoption of blockchain as a secure platform to store the second factor security information. User's mobile device signature attested by the bank is stored in a permissioned blockchain. This information is accessed by the merchant through user-friendly QR-code reading interface in order to verify that the user has the registered device. We present system design along with potential threats and security analysis.

Keywords: Blockchain · Two-factor authentication · Fraud detection

1 Introduction

Online credit card transaction is the base of e-commerce where anyone can purchase goods and services from merchants across the world. Unfortunately, payment cards are susceptible to fraud, and the majority of card fraud happens during online payments [6]. Deep consumer adoption of the technology has made credit card companies struggle improving and securing the technology against increasingly complex and evolving fraudster schemes. Credit card fraud has been a standing issue for financial institutions. Worldwide fraud loss is around 25 billion dollars and Card Not Present (CNP) accounts for more than 70% [1].

Current fraud reduction methods appear in various forms. Card verification value (CVV2) and Address verification Service (AVS) are the basic methods [6]. Fraudsters can easily obfuscate their data to defeat the conventional detection methods that rely on device and browser fingerprint information such as

© Springer Nature Switzerland AG 2022
J. Garcia-Alfaro et al. (Eds.): DPM 2021/CBT 2021, LNCS 13140, pp. 319–327, 2022.
https://doi.org/10.1007/978-3-030-93944-1_22

IP address, geolocation etc. In addition to this information, cardholder's spending behaviour is also analysed to determine the legitimacy using statistical and machine learning based methods [4] which is in fact a binary classification problem. Transactions are monitored based on certain parameters such as user's location, amount, purchase category etc. Despite the continuing efforts, current methods are still susceptible to false positive and false negative decisions. 97% of flagged transactions are actually legitimate which causes inconvenience and unsatisfactory shopping experience [2] and decreased shopping rate.

Such frauds especially put e-commerce merchants into a difficult situation. This is because, while card present (CP) losses are beared by the banks, merchants are still held accountable for CNP [10]. Because of this liability burden, e-commerce merchants have great incentive to prevent or reduce card fraud actively. In this respect, one of the solutions adopted by them is two-factor authentication (2FA). Most common 2FA method is sending one time password via an SMS message to a registered phone number. However, this technique is also vulnerable to various attacks such as man-in-the-middle (MitM) as the data goes through third party service provider.

To this end, in this paper, we propose a blockchain-based out-of-band verification scheme which relies on the cooperation of merchant and issuer bank. The proposed system is a second layer security feature that can be incorporated if desired by merchant with cooperation of banks. We consider e-commerce merchants to combat online transaction fraud effectively. The proposed system requires the bank storing a pre-approved signature of user device with its attestation in the blockchain. Then, the merchant is able to control the device signature on the blockchain to check if they match. After this first authentication, the merchant goes to second regular check via payment platform such as Visa. The proposed approach is evaluated by determining potential security threats and how they are addressed in the framework. In addition, we performed some tests on hyperledger to evaluate the feasibility.

The reminder of this paper is organized as follows: Sect. 2 presents preliminaries. In Sect. 3, we explain the proposed approach. Section 4 presents evaluation of the approach.

2   Related Work

Various fraud detection methods have been introduced including multifactor authentication, machine learning based methods [3]. CVV, 3 digit security number, and AVS are fundamental information required from user. Behavioral analytics and fingerprinting refers to monitoring suspicious activities and pattern for which supervised and unsupervised methods are utilized to model Some researchers label this problem as an outlier detection or anomaly detection problem [9]. Anomaly detection is looking into key factors, such as IP addresses, to detect anomalies in transactions. However, fingerprinting can be hidden by fraudsters. Supervised fraud detection methods rely on a set of previously known and labeled fraudulent transactions. Once similar transactions are identified by the model that have certain attributes, they are tagged and classified as fraud and the system can decide not to process it. These models can expand to learn fraud based on tagged transaction that are later classified by an administrator. Methods based on Bayesian Network, Decision tree, Support vector machine exist to tackle this problem. While the machine learning algorithms may give false positives and negatives which either may result in fraud or customer inconvenience. Two factor authentication [7] has also been adopted in order to increase the level of security. The general approach is sending one-time password to the user via registered phone. Transmitting a text message through a third party may be susceptible to man-in-the-middle (MitM) attack.

3 Preliminaries

3.1 Background

For every online credit card transaction there are essential parties involved: *client cardholder, merchant, issuing bank, acquiring bank, a payment processor, and a credit card network* as shown in Fig. 1 [8].

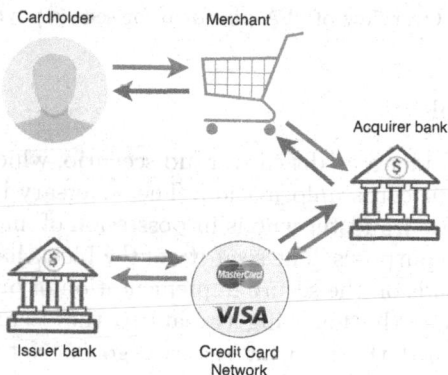

Fig. 1. Credit card payment system.

In an e-commerce CNP scenario, merchants need payment processors services in order for them to accept credit card transactions on their website. When a user decides to make a purchase online, the merchant will require a form to be filled out with pertinent details regarding the payment method. The payment processor will transfer the information to the acquiring bank, the bank will forward to the credit card network, who checks that the issuing bank's account has the funds available. The credit card network requests the payment authorization from the issuing bank including details from the card: credit card number, card expiration date, billing address for AVS, CVV, and payment amount [8]. The issuing bank receives the request from the network and validates that all the details are correct and that the funds are available. Then it will approve the transaction and send back an approval code through the credit card network.

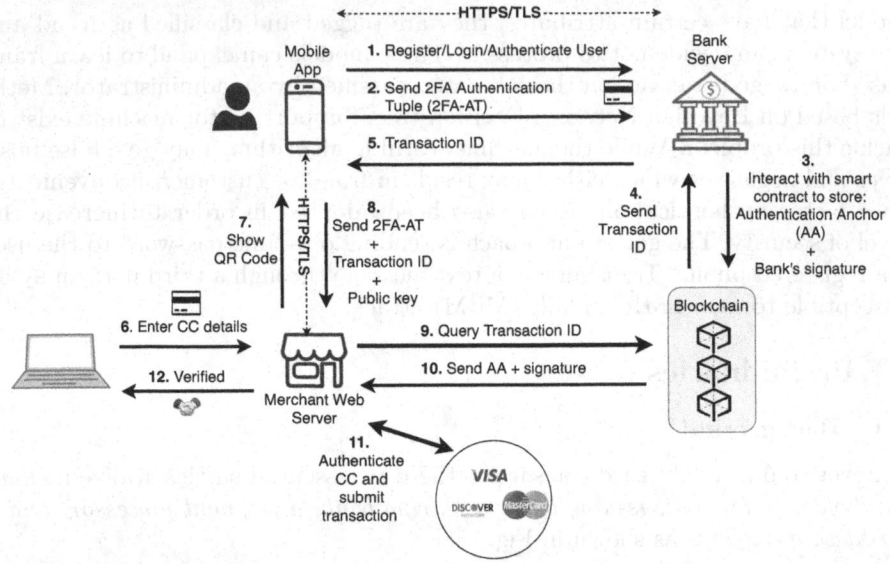

Fig. 2. Overview of 2FA platform for secure payments.

3.2   Attack Model

In this paper, we consider a credit card fraud scenario, which is very common in U.S using stolen credit cards' information. The adversary is determined to be a professional systematic fraudster who is in possession of many stolen credit card details with lucrative purposes. The security of the blockchain-based authentication framework depends on the secure implementation of proposed 2-FA system. Therefore, we consider the following threats to the security of the proposed approach and identified the relevant security goals. Note that in our attack model, we assume that the mobile device is tamper-proof through Hardware Security Modules (HSMs) that provide device-level controls to protect deployed keys. Therefore, mobile device infiltration is out of scope. In addition, our model assumes that merchant and bank are trusted parties.

Threat 1: In this attack, the attacker disguises itself as a mobile device user for pushing false authentication attestation into our multi-factor framework by obtaining the private keys that are used to sign the data.

Threat 2: In this attack scenario, the attacker attacks the mobile device communication layer and performs a man-in-the-middle (MitM) attack for altering the transactions.

Threat 3: In this attack scenario, the attacker can counterfeit data in the permissioned Blockchain.

4 Blokchain-Based 2-FA Framework for Transaction Authentication

4.1 Overview

The overall framework can be described as a blockchain-based 2FA approach consisting of smart contracts running on a permissioned blockchain along with some off-chain operations that bridge the end-users and banks as shown in Fig. 2. The permissioned blockchain will just run among banks as a result of a consortium agreement between them.

The first phase of the proposed framework is the registration that starts with generating the *2FA authentication tuple* (AT) by the end user's mobile device. The *2FA authentication tuple* is a bundle of device ID, a random challenge, and public-private key pair that acts as a unique, persistent authentication factor. The user sends the tuple to securely completing the registration of the mobile phone as a 2FA device. The bank combines the tuple and CC information to produce an *authentication anchor* (AA) by hashing the combination. Then, the bank submits produced anchor to blokchain by interacting with a smart contract on the blockchain.

When purchasing an item, the customer uses the merchant website and provides card-holder information such as card number, CVV, expiration date, etc. The merchant then verifies that who has provided the card information also has the mobile device associated with that card by interacting with blockchain and the mobile device. After this step, the merchant is now ready to initiate a transaction over the regular payment systems (e.g., Visa, Mastercard, etc.). With these steps, the merchant first ensures that the customer who provides CC information also carries the associated mobile device by interacting with the merchant and the card is still valid with a sufficient balance.

4.2 Registration Phase

The system first requires registration of the end user's device to the system. To do so, the end-user logins to the bank using its regular credentials over the bank application ❶. Then, s/he performs registration by sending the 2FA tuple, which is a bundle of the device ID (e.g., IMEI, Unique AppID, etc.) and a nonce. In addition to that, user device generates a public-private key pair for this device registration and sign the hash of the bundle. The 2FA tuple contains hash of the device ID, random challenge bundle and signature of the hash by using the freshly generated private and public key couple ❷. The bank then creates an *AA* by a combination of 2FA and hash of CC values with its signature. The bank triggers a smart contract called "Registration Contract" to cryptographically bind trusted bank identity and an off-chain 2FAtuple with CC information on the blockchain ❸. The Registration Contract acts as a logically centralized but physically decentralized lookup table mapping each bank, CC, and mobile device IDs. When the blockchain transaction is confirmed, the bank relays the transaction ID of the registration step to the mobile device, which will be used in the system again **4**, **5**. When the user wants to update the AA, it just creates another registration phase following the same process. But this time bank first burns the previous anchor of the user and stores the new one on the blockchain by triggering "Burn Contract" which basically re-signs the previous AA with a public address known as "eater address". This is viewable by all nodes and invalidates that AA. The status of these coins is published on the blockchain.

This framework allows the user to view the bank as a proxy while interacting with smart contracts and introduces a secure layer between the user's mobile device and the blockchain while transferring the AA. This structure also helps a convenient way to update the user's mobile device while maintaining a persistent AA. In cases where the user's mobile device was able to submit its AA to the blockchain directly, the user would lose control over the previous AA when the device that holds the previous AA was lost. However, with this arrangement, the bank works as a delegation point for the user to recover its 2FA anchor and connects it to a new device.

4.3 Second Factor Authentication Phase

The second-factor authentication defines how the end-user interacts with the merchant website to perform a secure transaction and ensures that only 2FA authenticated card information is used for purchases. This step's primary goal is to manage the end user's registered device information to perform the requested purchase. The main idea is that the merchant has to authenticate the CC information via interacting with the registered mobile device before issuing the purchase order. In addition, quality of user experience is one of the preeminent goals of this phase while interacting with merchants, blockchain, and end-device. Thus, the interaction between merchants and end-users is established through a *QR code* mechanism. This provides a usable environment for a user to submit the required AA to the merchant to confirm that the CC belongs to him. In fact, the AAs are technically *zero-knowledge proofs*, which means that the phone-owner can prove his signature without sharing his information.

When a user presents CC information to carry out a purchase **6**, the merchant performs a 2FA before forwarding the transaction to existing payment systems. In order to do that, the merchant generates a QR code with a fresh random challenge to prevent a replay attack. The QR code contains the challenge, provided CC, and Rest API URL Address to retrieve required proofs from the user-end device **7** using a challenge-response protocol. The user scans this code with the app and is presented a verification screen where s/he can verify the interaction using his/her fingerprint. Once the action is taken, the mobile app returns signed challenge data with the associated private key, signed 2FA tuple, transaction ID of blockchain, and corresponding public key **8**.

The merchant queries the blockchain via "Query Contract" by providing the transaction ID (e.g., retrieved from the mobile device) and fetches the stored AA to confirm CC and mobile device validity **9**, **10**. First, it checks whether the hash of CC equals to the first of AA, which contains the hash of CC information. Then, it checks whether it confirms the signature of 2FA tuple with the second part of AA by using the fetched public key from the mobile device. Finally, it also confirms the signature of challenge-response message using the same public key. These steps ensure that this CC and 2FA tuple are associated before in an immutable way. The user is able to confirm signatures of both stored AA on blockchain and fresh challenge-response.

After these steps, the merchant is now certain that the user who provided CC details also carries the registered device. Finally, it forwards the CC details to the payment system to confirm that it has enough balance and is still valid **11**. If the payment system confirms the transaction, the merchant and user successfully complete the process **12**.

5 Evaluation

In this section, we evaluate the proposed framework in terms of its security features and performance via implementation.

5.1 Security Analysis

In this section, we consider all the attacks mentioned in our Threat Model in Sect. 3 and analyze how our proposed framework addresses these attacks.

Threat 1: In this scenario, the attacker tries to masquerade a mobile device for submitting bogus AA into the blockchain system. To do so, the attacker needs to derive the private keys of the mobile device to prepare that attestation. We argue that even if the attacker may access to a mobile device by leveraging a vulnerability, the attack will be thwarted due to secure integrated chips (e.g., Titan-M and TrustZone) in modern mobile devices.

Threat 2: In this attack scenario, the attacker may perform a MitM attack on communication channels between the mobile device and the bank, the bank and the blockchain peers, the merchant and the mobile device, the merchant and the blockchain peers. As described in Sect. 4, these communication channels are protected by public-private key pairs of parties by creating a secure tunnel and thus prevents any modification attempts. It is also important to note that our system addresses the threats coming from mobile operator in regular SMS-based 2FA systems. Since our system eliminates mobile operator, thus removes the risk emerging from this point.

Threat 3: In our framework, blockchain acts as an unbreakable seal to provide the integrity of the submitted AA. This is due the fact that, permissioned blockchain is a network that contains many parties. This makes our platform very secure against any single point of failure attacks since the validation of an AA depends on many validators. Thus, modifying a transaction requires fooling all parties to confirm that update, which is not possible.

5.2 Hyperledger Performance

We also implemented a Proof-of-Concept adapting Hyperledger Fabric [5] to test the feasibility of our framework in terms of latency and throughput. Hyperledger is a permissioned blockchain platform where access is restricted to stakeholders unlike the public blockchain where anyone can access the produced blocks. The blockchain consortium is expected to include participating banks where each entity should run a node. The main reason using a hyperledger like permissioned blockchain is that only participating banks should have access to the platform.

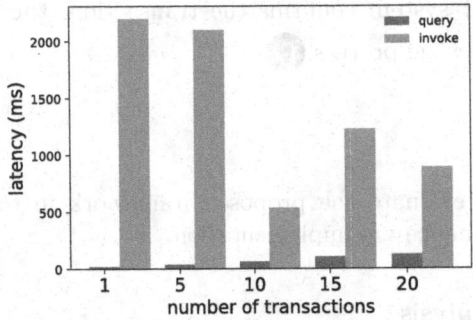

Fig. 3. Blockchain transaction times.

Since the time is crucial for customer satisfaction and transaction delay is the dominant factor in our system, we looked in to transaction latency for write (invoke) and read (query) operations. A bunch of transactions, from 1 to 20, is submitted to Hyperledger concurrently in order to test the performance. The results are shown in Fig. 3. As seen, the query latency increases from 20 ms to 100 ms with increasing number of transactions, which still can be considered fast. Average time of invoke operation, on the other hand, depends on the number of transactions submitted together and the blocksize. For a single transaction, it takes around 2 s because it waits for block timeout to submit the block for validation. When we look at 10 transactions, the average latency is much lower because the block is submitted immediately. This pattern will continue up to a saturation point which is generally measured as 140 tps, then it will start increasing.

6 Conclusion

In this paper, we proposed a CC fraud prevention system that preauthorizes online transactions using an out-of-bound authentication method, ultimately as an effort to protect merchants from fraud. The system utilizes a permissioned blockchain framework to store user information attested by the bank. The merchant is able to ask the purchaser to prove this transaction as authorized by scanning a unique QR code with the mobile app. The merchant can verify the user by checking the blockchain. We provided the security analysis and performance evaluation to demonstrate our framework's security and feasibility.

References

1. Us payments forum. Card-not-present fraud around the world. https://www. uspaymentsforum.org/wp-content/uploads/2017/03/CNP-Fraud-Around-the-World-WP-FINAL-Mar-2017.pdf
2. Verifi inc. what every card not present merchant should know. https://www.verifi. com/wp-content/uploads/2014/05/Verifi_eBook_web_noCNP.pdf
3. Adepoju, O., Wosowei, J., Jaiman, H., et al.: Comparative evaluation of credit card fraud detection using machine learning techniques. In: 2019 Global Conference for Advancement in Technology (GCAT), pp. 1–6. IEEE (2019)
4. Awoyemi, J.O., Adetunmbi, A.O., Oluwadare, S.A.: Credit card fraud detection using machine learning techniques: a comparative analysis. In: 2017 International Conference on Computing Networking and Informatics (ICCNI), pp. 1–9. IEEE (2017)
5. Cachin, C., et al.: Architecture of the hyperledger blockchain fabric. In: Workshop on Distributed Cryptocurrencies and Consensus Ledgers, vol. 310, p. 4 (2016)
6. Conroy, J.: Card not present (CNP) fraud in a post-EMV environment. Aite Group, June 2014
7. Deshe, W., Chen, B., Chen, J.: Credit card fraud detection strategies with consumer incentives (2018)
8. Papadimitriou, O.: How credit card transaction processing works: steps, fees & participants. Wallethub, Abril (2009)
9. Porwal, U., Mukund, S.: Credit card fraud detection in e-commerce: an outlier detection approach. arXiv preprint arXiv:1811.02196 (2018)
10. Roggio, A.: 3 reminders about online payment fraud (2018)

Homomorphic Decryption in Blockchains via Compressed Discrete-Log Lookup Tables

Panagiotis Chatzigiannis[1]($\boxtimes$), Konstantinos Chalkias[2], and Valeria Nikolaenko[2]

[1] Novi/Facebook/George Mason University, Fairfax, USA
pchatzig@gmu.edu
[2] Novi/Facebook, Fairfax, USA
{kostascrypto,valerini}@fb.com

Abstract. Many privacy preserving blockchain and e-voting systems are based on the modified ElGamal scheme that supports homomorphic addition of encrypted values. For practicality reasons though, decryption requires the use of precomputed discrete-log (*dlog*) lookup tables along with algorithms like Shanks's *baby-step giant-step* and Pollard's *kangaroo*. We extend the Shanks approach as it is the most commonly used method in practice due to its determinism and simplicity, by proposing a truncated lookup table strategy to speed up decryption and reduce memory requirements. While there is significant overhead at the precomputation phase, these costs can be parallelized and only paid once and for all. As a starting point, we evaluated our solution against the widely-used *secp* family of elliptic curves and show that we can achieve storage reduction by 7x–14x, depending on the group size. Our algorithm can be immediately imported to existing works, especially when the range of encrypted values is known, such as in Zether, PGC and Solidus protocols.

Keywords: Discrete log · ElGamal · Homomorphic encryption · Precomputation

1 Introduction

Over the last few years, we have witnessed an increasing number of decentralized payment systems that use the additively homomorphic ElGamal scheme to offer non-interactive confidential amounts [2,6,8,10,11]. However, for efficiency purposes, this ElGamal variant requires a precomputed discrete-log lookup table. The latter is because the ciphertext carries the message in the exponent of the group's base point, and without caching, it's only decryptable via bruteforcing.

Typically, for most financial applications, the max transaction amount ranges from 2^{32} to 2^{64}, as this is usually enough to encode even the largest reasonable balance. Generating and loading a table for billions and trillions of elements is impractical though, especially for constrained devices such as mobile phones, IoT devices and light clients in general. For instance, when using the 256-bit

© Springer Nature Switzerland AG 2022
J. Garcia-Alfaro et al. (Eds.): DPM 2021/CBT 2021, LNCS 13140, pp. 328–339, 2022.
https://doi.org/10.1007/978-3-030-93944-1_23

secp256k1 elliptic curve where a group point is serialized in 33 bytes (in compressed form), 132 GB are required to store 2^{32} elements in binary format.

While solutions exist that trade storage space for less computations, they increase the overall storage costs by several orders of magnitude or they are not deterministic. In this paper we propose an extra layer of compression that is compatible with Shanks algorithm (also known as *baby-step giant-step*), that reduces the lookup table size by a constant factor *without* any additional decryption cost. Our methods only require a precomputation phase and produce collision-free tables[1] with size independent of the elliptic curve field size; the larger the size, the better the compression rate. We also leverage the fact that some blockchain systems' encrypted content (e.g., Zether [6]) is accompanied by range proofs, and we use this information to slightly speed up decryption.

In the implementation section, we present a few strategies for precomputations and actually provide complete compressed lookup tables for NIST's secp256r1 curve as a starting point. Protocol designers can follow our recommendations to also create tables for curves of their choice, which will eventually result in a template repository for the most popular curves that will help the adoption and efficiency of additively homomorphic encryption schemes in general.

2   Background

Here we provide background on small *dlog* lookups. We first describe how modified ElGamal encryption works as a common use-case, then review related works in improving lookup table efficiency for recent blockchain-based systems requiring such tables, which can benefit from our work.

2.1   Additively Homomorphic ElGamal Encryption

Modified ElGamal encryption [19] consists of the following algorithms:

- pp ← Setup(1^λ): On input of security parameter λ, outputs public parameters pp = $(\mathbb{G}, g, p)$ where g is generator of cyclic group $\mathbb{G}$ of prime order p. We consider these parameters as a default input to all following algorithms and we omit them for simplicity.
- (pk, sk) ← Gen(): Outputs a secret-public key pair as sk ← $\mathbb{Z}_p$, pk = g^{sk}.
- (c_1, c_2) ← Enc(pk, x): Samples r ← $\mathbb{Z}_p$, computes $c_1 = g^r, c_2 = g^x \cdot pk^r$ and outputs ciphertext $C = (c_1, c_2)$.
- x ← Dec(sk, (c_1, c_2)): Compute $g^x = c_2/c_1^{sk}$. While x cannot be directly computed from g^x, it can be recovered through a pre-computed lookup table, assuming that the message space is relatively small, i.e., up to 2^{32}.

The scheme is additively homomorphic because it holds that $\mathsf{Enc}_A(pk, x_1) \cdot \mathsf{Enc}_B(pk, x_2) = (c_{1_A} \cdot c_{1_B}, c_{2_A} \cdot c_{2_B}) = \mathsf{Enc}(pk, x_1 + x_2)$.

---

[1] Similar compression techniques are also discussed in [3], but our work focuses on collision-free tables per group to completely avoid false positives.

Also, note that the message space is in $\mathbb{Z}_p$, and thus 0 is not included. There are various methods to support encryption of 0, for instance by mapping the message space $\{0, ..., p-2\}$ to $\{1, ..., p-1\}$ at the application layer.

2.2   Improving Efficiency of Discrete Log Lookup Operations

A naive approach for lookup tables would require precomputing all (x, g^x) tuples up to a maximum value and storing them in a file, where $x \in [1, N]$; N is usually a power of 2, thus $N = 2^n$. Typically, generating this file requires resource-intensive bruteforcing and $O(N)$ storage, but the lookup cost is amortized to $O(1)$.

Shanks algorithm [18] enables a space-time tradeoff for the naive solution. It defines a baby-step with stores (x, g^x) for all $x \in [1, 2^\alpha]$ in a lookup table M, and up to 2^β giant-steps, with $\alpha + \beta = n$. To recover the discrete log of $c = g^x$, it computes the giant step as g^{2^α}, initializes counter $i \to 0$, and checks if c/g^{i2^α} exists in M. If the lookup is successful: return $x + i \cdot 2^\alpha$, else increment i and repeat lookup. This algorithm has $O(2^\alpha)$ storage and requires 2^β multiplications (elliptic curve point additions) in the worst case, which can be amortized per application. There are also followup works that improve on the average expected computation costs by a constant factor [4,17].

Existing practical approaches for finding *dlog* in a small interval build on top of Pollard's rho and kangaroo methods [1,3,12,13,16], mainly focusing on improving the average-case complexity. In contrast, we mainly focus on Shanks method, because its practical average-case complexity is within a constant factor of its worst-case complexity, thus giving an algorithm that will perform well in practice for all instances (even for adversarially chosen ones).

2.3   Related Blockchain Works that Require Precomputed Tables

Solidus [8] is a permissioned, distributed payment system that associates user accounts with Banks, which in turn maintain a private data structure containing their user account public keys and the respective balances. Solidus utilizes modified ElGamal encryption to achieve its needed additive homomorphism, with balances represented in the exponent. The authors apply Shanks algorithm in their implementation to represent up to 2^{32} values.

Zether [6] is a distributed confidential payment system implemented on top of an Ethereum smart contract by converting Ethereum coins to native Zether tokens. These tokens are represented in encrypted form within the contract internal state using the additively homomorphic version of ElGamal encryption scheme, and are accompanied by range proofs. Original Zether's implementation considers a range of 2^{32}, but supporting 64 bits is possible by splitting into 2 amounts of 32 bits each (most and least significant bits, respectively); then encrypt each one of them separately. Interestingly, the authors refer to decryption via bruteforcing without references to optimized solutions or precomputed tables. As they claim, this is not considered an issue because a) decryption is happening off-chain b) bruteforcing would occur only rarely, i.e., when the amount is unknown.

PGC [10] is another distributed, confidential payment system, which uses a customized ElGamal encryption variant with an extra generator h in its public parameters that enables proving relations between ciphertexts encrypted under different public keys. PGC is one of the few works that recognizes the problem of efficient small *dlog* lookup tables, and while it highlights the greater efficiency of heuristic approaches like *kangaroo*, it still opts for Shanks to enable easy amortization for the time-space tradeoff and parallelization. In their proof of concept implementation [2], the authors assume up to 2^{32} values and utilize a 264 MB lookup table by precomputing 2^{23} 33-byte secp256k1 elements; then requiring at most $2^9 = 512$ giant Shanks steps during decryption.

Quisquis cryptocurrency [11] has a unique account balance representation, combining public keys and additively homomorphic commitment scheme tuples with balances represented in an exponent within the commitment. The system considers ranges up to 2^{32} without specifying any time-space tradeoff algorithm.

Although blockchains is our primary focus, other areas that use homomorphic encryption would also benefit from our construction, e.g. e-voting schemes [15].

3   Methodology

Our goal is to compute a lookup table for $g^x \ \forall x \in [1, 2^n]$. Assuming an elliptic curve (EC) over a finite field $\mathbb{F}_q$ for a security parameter λ, the uncompressed serialized representation of an EC point is $2\log q$ bits. Typically however, a compressed format of $q' = \log q + 1$ bits is selected, where only one coordinate and additional sign bit are enough to reconstruct the EC point. We define our initial table construction algorithm ComputeTable() with output to file f: Pick some $\tau < q'$, append $g^x = b_1 b_2 \ldots b_\tau$ to f where $b_i \in (0, 1)$.

Then our second important optimization relies on picking a "truncation" parameter τ. As it involves the birthday paradox, τ needs to be carefully considered. Picking a τ too small (meaning that the "chopped" portion of g^x is large), many collisions among the whole table will occur, which might result in ambiguities during lookup operations (e.g. on ElGamal decryption).

Therefore at this stage we elect a conservative approach similarly to [14]. Note that an approximation of collision probability[2] via Taylor series expansion is $\Pr[n, \tau] \approx 1 - 1/e^{2^{(2n-\tau-1)}}$. One can safely pick $\tau = 80$ for a table with 2^{32} elements, because $\Pr[\exists \text{ collision}] \approx 1/132{,}000$. ComputeTable() provides an immediate benefit for memory and computation requirements, bringing down storage from $q'2^n$ to $\tau 2^n$.

3.1   Ideal Truncation

The first precomputation phase ComputeTable() was a warm-up and required to minimize memory and storage requirements; essentially all our methods for compressing lookup tables rely on truncating (or omitting) redundant information from small *dlog* lookup tables. We describe our generic approach as follows:

---

[2] While we assume the binary representation of g^x is random, we can employ a hash function if g has some special property.

Given the precomputed table in f (which is already less than half the size of the naively-precomputed full table), there exists an *ideal* encoding where each value can be *uniquely* represented with n bits of information, thus bringing the total size of the table to $n2^n$ bits. We denote this ideal encoding as $F_{ideal}(g^x) \rightarrow \tilde{g}^x$ where $|\tilde{g}^x| = n$. Note that this ideal encoding does not depend on q'. For decrypting g^x, we would need to sequentially parse the table until its encoding $\tilde{g}^x$ is found, and return its position in the file as x. Essentially, this ideal encoding F_{ideal} is a compression technique that provides great savings in storage; in particular, the end compression ratio is $\frac{q'}{n}$ and the space cost savings are significant in typical implementation scenarios where $n << q'$. Note that after the compressed table has been computed, there are no additional computation costs during decryption, as the lookup costs remain amortized $O(1)$.

The above technique is compatible with existing algorithms with time-space tradeoffs, as discussed in Sect. 2.2. For instance, one could implement Shanks algorithm with an even smaller baby-step lookup table. In this case however, uniqueness must still be ensured not just for the values in the baby-step lookup table, but for all possible values generated by the giant steps, else any ambiguity would still make a ciphertext decryption possible into different values. Therefore, the baby-step lookup table would be $n2^\alpha$ bits in size using the ideal encoding F_{ideal}. As an example, Zether with the NIST-P256 curve, $2^{32} - 1$ max value and Shanks parameters $\alpha = 24, \beta = 8$, would normally have a lookup table of size $264 \cdot 2^{24}$ bits or about 528 MB. Using an ideal encoding F_{ideal}, its size would only be $32 \cdot 2^{24}$ bits or about 64 MB (decreased by a factor of 8.25), which is the best possible compression that can be achieved while ensuring unique representation of all elements.

3.2   Variable-Length Truncation

In the previous paragraph we described an ideal encoding function F_{ideal} which maps values g^x of length q' to short, unique bit strings a of length n. However, assuming all g^x values have a uniform distribution, constructing such an ideal function that ensures uniqueness among all strings is challenging and potentially impractical to find. Therefore to approximate this ideal encoding as much as possible, we define VarTruncate(), shown in Algorithm 1.

In a nutshell, this algorithm works as follows. Similarly to Shanks scheme, we pick the baby-step giant-step parameters α and β respectively. We also choose truncation parameters τ_{start} and τ_{stop} (where $\tau_{start} > \tau_{stop}$), which respectively direct the algorithm on how many bits should start the binary representation for each element with, and how many bits should try to represent the elements in an unambiguous way. The algorithm also needs as input data a set of uncompressed precomputed tables $A_1, ..., A_p$, which are partitioned to lower RAM requirements. Then the algorithm, after initializing a variable truncation index table C, it starts from the "conservative" truncation parameter τ_{start} and checks uniqueness of truncated elements for a baby-step table A2 against all truncated elements of a (precomputed) full table A1. If a collision is found, we update the respective index in C with the previous collision-free truncation parameter τ.

Input   : Generator g, Shanks parameters α, β, truncation start-stop
　　　　　$\tau_{start}, \tau_{stop}$, $p = \#$ of partitions
Data   : Precomputed tables for $[1, 2^{\alpha+\beta}]$: $A_1, ..., A_p$
Output : List C that stores where collisions found per index
$B \leftarrow [\ ]$, $C \leftarrow [0]^{2^{\alpha}}$;
for $i = 1, i = 2^{\alpha}, i + +$ **do**
　| $B.\text{append}(g^i)$
end

\\ Check for collisions between elements of B and those from $2^{\alpha} + 1$ to $g^{2^{\alpha+\beta}}$
for $\tau = \tau_{start}$; $\tau \geq \tau_{stop}$; τ- - **do**
　| **for** $i = 1, i \leq p, i + +$ **do**
　|　| $A^{\tau} \leftarrow \text{set}()$;
　|　| **for** $elem$ in A_i **do**
　|　|　| \\ we skip the first 2^a elements in A_1 only
　|　|　| **if** $i \neq 1 \vee elem.index > 2^{\alpha}$ **then**
　|　|　|　| \\ $elem_{[\tau]}$ = truncated-$elem$ to τ
　|　|　|　| $A^{\tau}.\text{add}(elem_{[\tau]})$
　|　|　| **end**
　|　| **end**
　|　| **for** $elem$ in B **do**
　|　|　| **if** $C[elem.index] == 0$ **then**
　|　|　|　| **if** $elem_{[\tau]} \in A^{\tau}$ **then**
　|　|　|　|　| $C[elem.index] = \tau$
　|　|　|　| **end**
　|　|　| **end**
　|　| **end**
　| **end**
end
\\ Check for "self"-collisions among elements of B
for $\tau = \tau_{start}$; $\tau \geq \tau_{stop}$; τ- - **do**
　| $B^{\tau} \leftarrow \text{map}(key : elem_{[\tau]}, value : boolean)$; \\ stores (key, value) pairs
　| \\ 1st pass to track collisions
　| **for** $elem$ in B **do**
　|　| **if** $elem_{[\tau]} \notin B^{\tau}$ **then**
　|　|　| $B^{\tau}.add(elem_{[\tau]}, false)$
　|　| **end**
　|　| **else**
　|　|　| $B^{\tau}.set(elem_{[\tau]}, true)$
　|　| **end**
　| **end**
　| \\ 2nd pass to update C
　| **for** $elem$ in B **do**
　|　| **if** $B^{\tau}.getValue(elem_{[\tau]}) == true \wedge C[elem.index] < \tau$ **then**
　|　|　| $C[elem.index] = \tau$
　|　| **end**
　| **end**
end

Algorithm 1: Variable truncation algorithm VarTruncate()

This process is repeated by decrementing that parameter (i.e. truncating more bits). Note this process is done in two separate phases, one for checking for collisions of baby-step elements against all values in range $(2^\alpha, 2^{\alpha+\beta}]$ (to ensure that no collisions occur even when doing giant steps) and then for self-collisions between baby step elements.

Therefore from C we can serialize the respective table for 2^α elements by interleaving ($\lceil \log(\tau_{start} - \tau_{stop}) \rceil$) bits per element. These bits encode the variable length and is necessary to make serialized parsing possible. Alternatively, we can reduce the number of those encoding bits by assigning them into k groups $G_1, G_2, .., G_k$, therefore needing $\lceil \log k \rceil$ bits per element. For instance, we can decrement τ by 2 bits each time instead of 1, and group G_1 would represent lengths of τ_{start} and $\tau_{start} - 1$ bits, group G_2 would represent lengths of $\tau_{start} - 2$ and $\tau_{start} - 3$ bits etc. Also, depending on the results, we might have these groups contain an uneven number of bit representations. For example, truncating with τ_{start} usually turns out to contain relatively very few elements, and therefore devoting a group for a very small population won't be efficient overall. Still each group G must encode the maximum τ that is included in that group, denoted by $\max \tau_G$. The total size of the serialized lookup table will then be

$$\sum_{i=1}^{k} (\max \tau_{G_i} \cdot |G_i|) + \lceil \log k \rceil \cdot 2^\alpha$$

where $\sum_{i=1}^{k} |G_i| = 2^\alpha$ and $\max \tau_{G_k} = \tau_{start}$. Note that even though the "grouping" approach reduces the factor $\lceil \log k \rceil \cdot 2^\alpha$, the granularity of the algorithm is also reduced, which overall increases the total size. On the other hand, more fine-grained groups will decrease the overall needed storage of the serialized lookup table, but will result in slightly increased computation cost in hashmap lookups[3].

As a special case of VarTruncate(), we can define FixedTruncate() (equivalently to [14]) where the algorithm stops when at least one collision is found. This essentially implies having a single group G_1 for all bit truncations we consider. In this case, no length encoding bits are needed, however the overall space savings are not optimal.

3.3   Optimizations

Although FixedTruncate() is a great step for decreasing lookup table costs, there is still room for further compression. In a concrete example with $n = 32$, the probability of no-collision for $\tau = 62$ is about 13% so attempting to truncate to a set with non-colliding elements might not be easy. However we can pick τ random bit positions instead and make non-collision tests, and keep testing combinations of those positions until we successfully get a non-colliding set. Then, the resulting

---

[3] Note that the cost of a hashmap lookup is insignificant compared to elliptic curve (EC) point addition (about 40 times in our implementation), while a scalar to EC point multiplication is around 32 times more expensive than EC point addition using the *double-and-add* method for small 32-bit scalars.

Input : Generator g, truncation paramenters $\tau_{start}, \tau_{stop}$ and encryption c
Data   : Hashmap M for variable-length truncated elements in the range
$[1, 2^\alpha]$
Output : Value x where $g^x = c$
$s \leftarrow g^{2^\alpha}$;
for $i \leftarrow 0; i < 2^\beta; i++$ do
$\quad$ for $\ell = \tau_{stop}, \ell = \tau_{start}, \ell++$ do
$\quad\quad$ if $c_{[\ell]} \in M$ then
$\quad\quad\quad$ | return $M.idx(c_{[\ell]}) + i2^\alpha$
$\quad\quad$ end
$\quad$ end
$\quad c \leftarrow c/s$;
end
return "Not found"

Algorithm 2: Lookup decryption algorithm

truncated table needs to be accompanied by the subset of those indices that it corresponds to, and only these indices would need to be looked up on receipt of g^x. We refer to these bits as the *subset*. Note that in the above example, for $\tau = 60$ the probability of success becomes very small and given the computationally intensive process of finding a non-colliding *subset* makes further compression using this method practically infeasible. As an alternative and more practical approach, one can try hashing all points with some salt/counter, then truncate and check for collisions, instead of looking for optimized subsets [3].

3.4 Relaxed Collisions and Template Distribution

In the algorithms previously discussed, we require zero collisions among truncated elements. However we could tolerate a *few* collisions among those elements (say κ collisions), which would reduce the table size even more as discussed in [3]. In case of ambiguity due to collisions in the lookup operations, up to κ exponentiations will be needed (worst case) to resolve this. As that these collisions imply additional exponentiations during lookup, this approach is essentially a space-computation tradeoff. For instance, in VarTruncate() group G_k (or even group G_{k-1}) typically contain relatively few elements, so one could discard these groups entirely to save 1 bit per element of encoding overhead, and provide those elements in a separate list L; then, one exponentiation would be needed in those (rare) cases.

Note that in some environments (e.g. limited connectivity, expensive cellular data etc.), downloading lookup tables, even if compressed, might still be prohibitive. However, one could construct a *template* using the output C from VarTruncate() or even simply τ from FixedTruncate(), and distribute these values only, which can be used as "advice" for the decrypting party to run the respective sub-algorithms directly with much less heavy computations.

4   Implementation

As discussed, the precomputation phase for compressing lookup tables is the most computationally-intensive process. The lookup table would need to be pre-computed first using ComputeTable(), then further compress it by VarTruncate() or FixedTruncate(). However as shown from the existing applications in Sect. 2.3, a typical table decrypts up to 2^{32} values, and further optimizations are required to perform this step in a reasonable time with consumer-grade hardware. First, given that exponentiations are more expensive computationally, instead of computing g^x for all $x \in [1, n]$ separately, we can iteratively compute each $g^x = g^{x-1} \cdot g$ as multiplications are cheaper operations. Also, naively loading a huge table in memory and checking for collisions might be prohibitive in terms of computation and RAM. Therefore, we divide the table into parts (similar to our approach in Algorithm 1), then cross-check for collisions among all of them.

Note that the precomputation phase can be further improved by parallelization, e.g. assign threads to different truncation factors and merge the computed results after. Also, although a hashmap is usually preferred, for variable-length encoding, a trie structure might also be used for storing the needed compressed elements in memory, otherwise a few truncate-retries in the hashmap might be required. Again we stress that this computationally-intensive phase only needs to be performed once per curve and parameter set.

4.1   Truncation Algorithm Evaluation

We first implement FixedTruncate() for the secp256r1 and secp256k1 curves. We truncated from the MSB side by omitting the sign bit and we derived tables of unique size for 2^{32} with 64 bits per value, which results from 141 GB to a compressed 34 GB table in binary format, providing a compression factor over 1:4.

As discussed, the compression factor increases with the security parameter, e.g. for the secp521r1 curve it would be 1:8.35. As a starting point, we provide a precomputed table for the secp256r1 curve and 2^{28} values [9] of 2 GB size. This table can be safely used in conjunction with Shanks up to 2^{32} values, as it is part of a 2^{32} truncated table where we ensure that no collisions exist. Normally, a final exponentiation would be needed to ensure that no value outside this range (or even a "garbage" value) has been encrypted with same prefix (or suffix), but we leverage existing range proofs in many blockchain systems to ensure this is not a possibility. However, if no indication about the max value exists, the final exponentiation can

Table 1. Variable length truncation for the secp256k1 curve with $n = 32$, $\alpha = 20$, $\beta = 12$, $k = 4$.

Bits	Bits +encoding	# elements	Total size
32	35	385479	13491765
36	39	599610	23384790
40	43	59450	2556350
44	47	3786	177942
48	51	238	12138
52	55	12	660
56	59	1	59
Size: 4.72 MB		Compress: 1:6.98	

be performed by utilizing the faster "windowed" methods, such as w-ary non-adjacent form (wNAF), which require small cache tables to speed up the exponentiation cost by a large degree [5].

For VarTruncate(), we evaluate our compression factor with the secp256k1 curve for $n = 32$, $\alpha = 20$, $\beta = 12$ and $k = 7$. These parameters are consistent with existing implementations in the blockchain domain as we discussed in Sect. 2.3, and our results are shown in Table 1. Note this requires $\lceil \log k \rceil = 3$ bits of length encoding per element, which overall results in about 393 KB encoding overhead. We also performed tests for $n = 20$, $\alpha = 20$, $\beta = 0$ and $k = 7$ for the secp256k1 and secp521r1 curves, where we achieved a compression factor of 1:10 and 1:20 respectively. For $k = 4$ in the secp256k1 curve shown in Table 1, the compression factor slightly reduces to 1:6.85.

4.2   Complexity Analysis and Comparison

For generating a compressed lookup table g^x for $x \in [1, 2^n]$, our algorithm VarTruncate() includes a computationally intensive overhead in addition to just generating the table, similar to [14]. Specifically, [14] has an $O(2^n)$ computational overhead, while our algorithm has $O(k2^n)$ complexity. However this additional cost is paid only once for a specific set of parameters, while our algorithm achieves a) a significant improvement in compression factor and b) collision free encoding which simplifies used data structures.

For recovering the discrete log of g^x, the probabilistic [3] has $O(c2^{n/3})$ computation and storage complexity on average (for a very small $c < 2$), while our decryption computational cost involves $O(2^\beta)$ multiplications and $O(k2^\beta)$ map lookups in the worst case, where k is the number of utilized truncation groups. Note that regular Shanks has a lookup multiplication complexity of $O(2^{\beta_2})$, for $\beta_2 > \beta$ (typically, for 256-bit curves $\beta_2 \approx \beta + 3$), when using the same precomputed table size with our scheme.

5   Conclusion

We presented and implemented several methods for $dlog$ table compression by wisely truncating the serialized bytes of elliptic curve points, while guaranteeing no collisions. The proposed deterministic algorithm results in faster table lookups in addition to reduced storage and memory requirements. Although our technique relies on a potentially expensive precomputation phase, it is performed once per curve group and desired table size. Concretely, we show how we compress such tables for small ranges by up to a factor of 7 to 14 for 256 and 521-bit curves, respectively. For instance, the PGC [10] protocol currently implements a precomputed table of 264 MB table size (using $\alpha = 23$ and $\beta = 9$) for a 256-bit curve and 2^{32} max amount range [2]. With our algorithm, that could be improved by requiring a variable-length table of roughly 38 MB, which would make it applicable to mobile wallets and blockchain IoT devices.

Our work has additional advantages when encrypted content is accompanied by range proofs [7] or when faster windowed exponentiations are applied [5]. We also pave the way for the cryptography and blockchain community to create publicly-available compressed tables for commonly-used elliptic curves, by providing the first compressed 2^{32} lookup table for the secp256r1 curve [9]. Finally, we introduce the concept of optimized compression *templates* per curve, which will help developers and apps to recompute and verify such tables faster, especially when downloading is expensive or if bigger ranges (i.e. up to 2^{40}) are required.

References

1. Cube-root discrete-logarithm algorithms for secure groups. http://cr.yp.to/dlog/cuberoot.html
2. libpgc: a c++ library for pretty good confidential transaction system. https://github.com/yuchen1024/libPGC/tree/master/PGC_openssl/PGC
3. Bernstein, D.J., Lange, T.: Computing small discrete logarithms faster. In: Galbraith, S., Nandi, M. (eds.) INDOCRYPT 2012. LNCS, vol. 7668, pp. 317–338. Springer, Heidelberg (2012). https://doi.org/10.1007/978-3-642-34931-7_19
4. Bernstein, D.J., Lange, T.: Two grumpy giants and a baby. Cryptology ePrint Archive, Report 2012/294 (2012). http://eprint.iacr.org/2012/294
5. Blake, I.F., Murty, V.K., Xu, G.: A note on window τ-naf algorithm. Inf. Process. Lett. **95**(5), 496–502 (2005)
6. Bünz, B., Agrawal, S., Zamani, M., Boneh, D.: Zether: towards privacy in a smart contract world. In: Bonneau, J., Heninger, N. (eds.) FC 2020. LNCS, vol. 12059, pp. 423–443. Springer, Cham (2020). https://doi.org/10.1007/978-3-030-51280-4_23
7. Bünz, B., Bootle, J., Boneh, D., Poelstra, A., Wuille, P., Maxwell, G.: Bulletproofs: short proofs for confidential transactions and more. In: IEEE S&P (2018)
8. Cecchetti, E., Zhang, F., Ji, Y., Kosba, A.E., Juels, A., Shi, E.: Solidus: confidential distributed ledger transactions via PVORM. In: ACM CCS 2017 (2017)
9. Chatzigiannis, P.: Compressed small discrete-log table python code and secp256r1 precomputed table. https://github.com/PanosChtz/Homomorphic-DLog-lookup-tables
10. Chen, Yu., Ma, X., Tang, C., Au, M.H.: PGC: decentralized confidential payment system with auditability. In: Chen, L., Li, N., Liang, K., Schneider, S. (eds.) ESORICS 2020. LNCS, vol. 12308, pp. 591–610. Springer, Cham (2020). https://doi.org/10.1007/978-3-030-58951-6_29
11. Fauzi, P., Meiklejohn, S., Mercer, R., Orlandi, C.: Quisquis: a new design for anonymous cryptocurrencies. In: Galbraith, S.D., Moriai, S. (eds.) ASIACRYPT 2019. LNCS, vol. 11921, pp. 649–678. Springer, Cham (2019). https://doi.org/10.1007/978-3-030-34578-5_23
12. Galbraith, S.D., Gaudry, P.: Recent progress on the elliptic curve discrete logarithm problem. Des. Codes Cryptogr. **78**(1), 51–72 (2015). https://doi.org/10.1007/s10623-015-0146-7
13. Galbraith, S.D., Wang, P., Zhang, F.: Computing elliptic curve discrete logarithms with improved baby-step giant-step algorithm. Cryptology ePrint Archive, Report 2015/605 (2015). http://eprint.iacr.org/2015/605
14. Mavroudis, V.: Computing small discrete logarithms using optimized lookup tables (2015). USCB, Koç Lab

15. Peng, K., Aditya, R., Boyd, C., Dawson, E., Lee, B.: Multiplicative homomorphic e-voting. In: Canteaut, A., Viswanathan, K. (eds.) INDOCRYPT 2004. LNCS, vol. 3348, pp. 61–72. Springer, Heidelberg (2004). https://doi.org/10.1007/978-3-540-30556-9_6
16. Pollard, J.M.: Monte Carlo methods for index computation mod p. Math. Comput. **32**, 918–924 (1978)
17. Pollard, J.M.: Kangaroos, monopoly and discrete logarithms. J. Cryptol. **13**(4), 437–447 (2000). https://doi.org/10.1007/s001450010010
18. Shanks, D.: Five number-theoretic algorithms (1973)
19. Ugus, O., Hessler, A., Westhoff, D.: Performance of additive homomorphic ecelgamal encryption for tinypeds. 6. Fachgespräch Sensornetzwerke (2007)

Author Index

Printed in the United States
by Baker & Taylor Publisher Services